PRAISE FOR
THE UPSIDE OF

G000042180

"By turns loving and cruel, heated and chilling, adventurous and terrifying, Adam's tale captures the imagination and fills the mind with stories that linger on long after the last page has been turned. An indelible read."

KATHY HEFFERNAN, Advance Readers Association, Canada

"A vivid retelling of the events of one man's life, the sum of which amounts to an extraordinary tale. The writer has crafted the story with striking attention to detail. Fans of historical fiction, particularly regarding the WWII era, will especially appreciate this superb debut novel."

KIRSTEN BELITZKY, Creator of Flashlights on the Beach: A Path to Happiness

"Adam Baumann is a 20th Century hero—a mixture of the ambition and independence of an Ayn Rand hero with the tender heart and family devotion of an ordinary man. Roxi Harms does a magnificent job of capturing the complexities of Baumann's character, both the extraordinary and the ordinary. With skill and detail, she brings to life the story of a man who triumphed over the limitations of history to become his greatest self."

GINGER MORAN, Author of The Algebra of Snow

"Based on real events crafted into a beautiful narrative, The Upside of Hunger reveals the story of Adam, his incredible life, and the fascinating history of his family... readers will become invested in the Baumann family and their story, unable to put it down until the very last page."

MELISSA KOONS, Author of Orion's Honor

"Harms takes history and puts a human face to it."

ROXAS JAMES, Author of Unexpected and Reflections of Yellow Brick

THE
UPSIDE
OF HUNGER

a true tale

ISBN 978-0-9975670-8-3

Book design by Heidi Miller
Cover design by Heidi Miller and John H. Matthews

THE UPSIDE OF HUNGER

a true tale

ROXI HARMS

AUTHOR'S NOTE

The Upside of Hunger is based on a true life story which was shared with the author over the course of more than 400 recorded interviews. All events and characters are real. Much effort has been put into ensuring the accuracy of dates and locations. In some cases, where the passage of time has faded the details of memory, or for ease of reading, fictional names have been created and dates have been estimated. Dialog between characters and characters' inner thoughts have been developed by the author to bring to life the stories told in the interviews. Where historical speeches are quoted, excerpts, rather than entire speeches, are used for brevity. And although much research was completed in the pursuit of historical and cultural accuracy, this book is a novel and is not intended as a history text or a biography.

FOR MY MOM,
*the bravest and most resilient
person I know*

TABLE OF CONTENTS

PART ONE
Hungary

"We grow great by dreams. All big men are dreamers. They see things in the soft haze of a spring day or in the red fire of a long winter's evening. Some of us let these dreams die, but others nourish and protect them; nurse them through bad days till they bring them to the sunshine and light which comes always to those who sincerely hope that their dreams will come true."

WOODROW WILSON

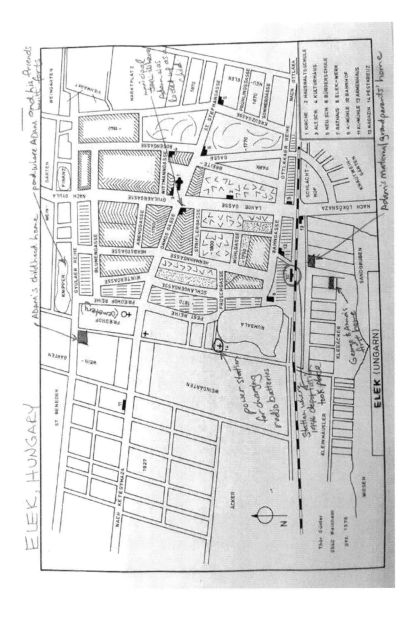

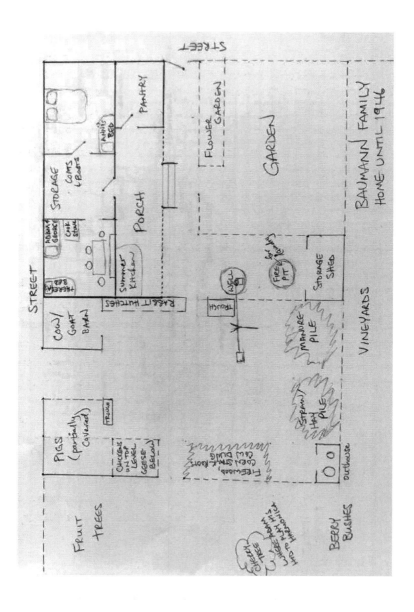

CHAPTER ONE

Western Hungary, December 1941

"I'm sorry to bother you so late." The voice at the front door could be heard clearly in the dining room.

Adam froze, a forkful of tender boar and rich, savoury gravy half-way to his mouth. *He'd been found.* For an instant, he was flooded with fear. Then the fear turned to anger. *I'm not going back to pruning grapevines and shovelling shit,* he thought. Suddenly, he thought of his mom and his sisters, and was filled with an urgent longing for home. God, he missed them.

"My name is George Baumann," the voice at the door continued, "and I'm looking for my 12-year-old son. I understand from the people in the village that you have a young boy staying here."

"Please come in, Mr. Baumann," came the Count's voice. The creak of the big iron hinges reached their ears, telling them the door had been opened wide. The Countess, seated at the end of the heavy wooden dining table, fixed her gaze on Adam. The hinges creaked again as the thick wooden door swung shut. "It's true that we have had an orphan boy staying here for a few months. We were just having some supper. Come this way to the dining room and I'll introduce you."

First the Count, and then the visitor appeared in the doorway, bringing with them a draft of crisp winter air. The room went unnaturally quiet. But not an empty quiet.

Then the newcomer spoke. "Adam. Thank God."

His dad stood there, eyes locked on him. Now what? What kind of licking would be judged suitable? But strangely, his dad didn't look angry. His eyes were glistening. Adam wasn't sure what to do. He swallowed past the sudden lump in his throat.

"Hi, Dad," he said in a choked voice. "What are you doing here?"

"What am *I* doing here?" Adam's father exclaimed, then rushed on. "Your mother has been crying non-stop. It's been damn near four months.

We'd almost given up when we got your letter. I took it to the train station and they knew the town on the postmark. I would have been here last night if we hadn't been sidelined for the afternoon to let military supply trains through to Hitler's operations in the east. When I finally got to the village, the first person I asked knew about you. Seems like everybody around here knows about the *orphan* living with the Count."

His dad stopped and looked around as if he'd just remembered there were others in the room. Adam watched as he gazed at the Count and Countess and the little girl who stared up at him from her seat across the table from Adam. His eyes continued around the sumptuous, candle-lit room, taking in the stag's head on the end wall, and the ornately framed painting of a large man, draped in jewels and furs, sitting in a throne-like chair.

"We are most pleased to see you, Mr. Baumann," said the Count. "Adam's memory has been failing him, and I'm afraid he hasn't been able to remember where he's from. Your finding us is most fortunate indeed." He spoke calmly.

"Won't you sit down?" said the Countess who had risen to stand beside her husband. "You must be hungry after travelling all day. May I fix you a plate?"

After a moment, Adam's dad answered hesitantly. "Well, yes. Please forgive my manners ma'am. It's a pleasure to meet you."

"It's a pleasure to meet *you*," she replied with a warm smile. "My name is Marika. And this is our daughter, Irena. Please, sit," she said, gesturing to the chair her husband had pulled out beside the little girl.

After staring for a moment at the brightly painted hearts and flowers adorning the tall wooden chair back, and the rich brocade on the seat, he seemed to make up his mind and sat down. He shifted uncomfortably as his eyes flitted around the room again, from the candlelight dancing on the embroidered draperies to the silver serving dishes in the centre of the table where the Countess was filling a plate.

The modernization that was occurring in much of the world had not yet reached rural Hungary, and the daily lives and trappings of the nobility remained much as they had been for generations. Not much had changed for the Baumanns in generations either, but that was the extent of what the guests had in common with their hosts. As Adam followed his dad's gaze around the room, seeing the things that had become familiar to him in the past months, the contrast between the shabbiness of his father and everything else in the room startled him a bit.

"Where have you travelled from exactly?" the Countess asked, placing a heaping plate of food in front of their new guest. The potatoes, mixed smooth with milk and butter, had become a favourite of Adam's. The rich gravy the Countess had poured over the pile of sliced boar threatened to flow over the side of the plate. His dad would love it.

"Elek, clear across Hungary on the eastern border with Romania," his dad answered, looking down at the food. The Count reached over Adam's dad's shoulder to pour wine into the pewter goblet he had placed there.

"Please eat, everyone, before it gets cold," said the Countess, looking around the table.

Adam stared down at his plate. He'd just been so tired of the yelling and the spankings. And all the sameness. Nothing ever changed in Elek. Chores, school, lickings, more chores. That last fight he'd had with his dad was the same as countless others. But then he'd made the spur-of-the-moment decision to leave, and everything had changed. Walking mile after mile, hitching rides when he could, every day had been filled with new sights. Every turn had held more excitement than he'd ever felt before in his life. And then being invited to live with the Count and his family. Life had never been so good. But he missed his mom and although he'd tried his best not to think about it, the thought of the worry he'd caused her hovered constantly in the back of his mind like a bad dream that wouldn't fade. She'd be waiting at home for him to return with his dad. And his dad, who had a strange, mildly puzzled expression on his face when Adam dared to look over, well, his dad had come a long way to find him.

CHAPTER TWO

Elek, Eastern Hungary

Like most people in the village of Elek, the Baumanns were descended from German settlers who had arrived some 200 years ago. Conditions back in Germany in the early 1700s had been harsh, unless you were a land baron or a member of the clergy, and the Baumanns were neither. Along with millions of other peasants, hunger was the only thing they had plenty of. When a nobleman named Harrucher arrived to solicit Catholic families to settle vast stretches of land in the recently conquered Kingdom of Hungary, granted to him by the Habsburg Monarchy, Gottfried and Ursula Baumann had bravely raised their hands. They were hungry for change. Perhaps that was where Adam got it from.

A procession of horse-drawn wagons loaded with the meagre belongings of the immigrants laboured eastward across Germany, covering several hundred kilometres before loading onto crude barges and floating down the mighty Danube through Austria, part of present day Slovakia, and into Hungary. Near Budapest they disembarked and continued east. By the time they reached the promised land, they'd covered over 1,100 kilometres.

The Kingdom of Hungary had been decimated by 150 years of Turkish occupation. Forests had been chopped down or burned, farms pillaged and left dormant, their inhabitants dead in their burned-out homes. Without the rich vegetation holding the land in place and absorbing the crisp, sweet water of the rivers, the vast plains had flooded. As the decades passed, riverbeds, fields, and roads blended together and vast swamps had appeared, covered in dense brush and emitting noxious vapours. Mosquitoes flourished, while water fit for human consumption became difficult to find. A permanent change in the ecosystem had occurred in those dark times, and now the task of the German settlers was to make the land productive again.

Alongside several other families, the Baumanns were assigned to settle in Elek, an ancient townsite near the Romanian border that had flourished in the middle ages. Despite the conditions, or perhaps because of them, the new settlers toiled tirelessly, defeating the ravages of hunger, fending off raids by tribes from the east, defending themselves from the elements, and nursing their sick through the endless waves of typhoid, malaria, and dysentery. Slowly, their persistence began to pay off and a functioning community took shape.

As time passed, dams were built and dikes constructed to better control the river system across the plains. Flooding became a less constant threat. Bit by bit, the growing system of drainage ditches in and around Elek rendered more land dry enough to plant and yields gradually grew. With the passing of time, residents came to understand their new land, passing that knowledge down to each new generation of Germans born there in Hungary.

These years were filled with challenges we can barely fathom, but the Baumanns were also blessed, for the three sons born to Ursula thrived, becoming the genesis of a long line of Germanic Hungarian Baumanns.

By the early 1800s, Elek included a smattering of Hungarians and Romanians, and a community of Gypsies had sprung up on the south edge of town beside the sand pit, where they scratched out a living using their wagons to haul sand to building sites as the town grew. By the dawn of the 1900s, the village was home to over 5,000 residents. No longer living under the oppression of serfdom, people prospered or struggled according to their individual nature, and over the generations, the population became comprised of landowners in their own right, whose families had worked diligently to purchase land and make it productive, tradesmen who had developed successful businesses, subsistence farmers, and variations in between. Churches and schools had been built and municipal order had been established. The grassy banks of the wide, acacia-lined roadways made tasty feeding grounds for small livestock, and a shared pasture had been staked out for communal cattle grazing.

The high water table in the area fed the wells that were dug as each new home was staked out and built. But drinking water remained a problem. The area had never recovered from the layers of rotting sediment left by the Turks, giving the water a most unpleasant taste and smell, which the people suspected contributed to long-term illness. The snow and rain they captured for fresh water was never adequate, and year after year, residents attempted to dig deep enough to find a clean source. Finally, in 1894, they succeeded, striking an artesian water supply that was pure and fresh. A large, central well was established, equipped with a system of pulleys and buckets. The town well became a new meeting place, where women and children came regularly to lower their buckets down and hoist up clean water to carry home to their families.

Since that courageous journey halfway across Europe to an unknown land nearly two centuries earlier, the people of Elek hadn't ventured far. It was as if that great trek had created in them an innate need to stay close to home so as to never feel that detached again. Of course, long distance travel and communication remained limited the world over in those years, but in Elek and neighbouring villages, interest in the world beyond was exceedingly minimal, and a few kilometres between farms was as far as most had ever ventured. Nostalgia for the German motherland remained strong, and people held fast to the ways of life that linked them with their heritage, taking comfort in the small, static world they'd created.

In the late 1860s, Adam's great-grandmother, unwed at the time, gave birth to a son. The young mother called her baby son Florian and gave him the Baumann family name to pass down to his sons and grandsons. From a young age, Florian had an uncommonly adventurous spirit and a talent for music, traits he was to pass down to his grandson, Adam, decades later.

Florian's musical abilities earned him an invitation to participate along with a group of some thirty-odd other young teens from Elek in an unprecedented trip to the United States in 1882, organized by the charming and somewhat mysterious leader of the youth brass band at the time. Florian was amazed at the things he saw in the world beyond Elek. After his return, he tried to explain what he'd seen. Farmers in other parts of Europe and in America had wheeled devices that they filled with corn seed and as they pulled them across the field with a horse, seeds were dropped at perfect intervals. They had machines they could drag behind a team of donkeys and cut a swathe almost two fathoms wide. Some of the boarding houses the band had stayed in had water piped into a water closet on each floor for washing, and indoor privies. But no one was particularly interested in Florian's fantastic tales. The people of Elek were proud of what they'd accomplished in their colony and so they continued with their traditional ways, hoeing the land in the spring and harvesting with scythes each autumn.

After his return from abroad, Florian Baumann apprenticed as a carpenter and after a time, he started a family. Although he was a good provider, life never seemed to meet the expectations of his wife Veronica, whose disposition became increasingly bitter as she raised her children, and they in turn raised theirs. Florian, on the other hand, had a ready smile and a twinkle in his eye as their eleven children, including his first son, whom they named Florian for his father, and his second son, who was called George, grew up in their little three-room home at the edge of the town's vineyards.

Adam's maternal grandfather, Johann Bambach, was born in 1887. Like the Baumanns, the Bambachs had immigrated from Germany many generations earlier. Around the age of twenty, Johann and his bride Maria settled into a little tenants' hut on one of the big farms outside of Elek, tending the animals and crops while the landlord lived in a fancy house in town with his family. As each of their two sons and three daughters grew big enough to lift and carry, Johann hired them out as farm hands and housemaids, as his father had done before him. But for as young as he'd started working, Johann had never developed a taste for it, and when his children's meagre pay became adequate to support the family, he moved them into a little house in the poor end of Elek, near the Gypsy settlement, and took on the less demanding job of town cow herder. Each morning during the summer months he slowly herded the cows of the townspeople to the communal pasture, kept an eye on them through the day as they grazed, and then followed them back through the streets as they headed home for milking. Meanwhile, in the kitchens, laundry sheds, and barnyards of various Elek residents, his eldest daughter Anna was growing into a hardworking, capable young woman.

CHAPTER THREE

On a crisp, spring afternoon in 1925, three decades after the citizens of Elek struck clean drinking water, Anna Bambach lowered her buckets down the shaft of the town well one at a time, filling them with cool, sweet water. George Baumann, 21 at the time, spied the pretty 16-year-old as he strolled home from the fields enjoying the spring sun on his tired shoulders. Much to his mother's disappointment, it wasn't long until George decided Anna was the one for him. The family of the girl that Veronica Baumann had lined up to marry her son, had a cow, and thus, the girl would bring a calf to the marriage. Anna's father on the other hand, was a lazy man, and Anna brought nothing. But George was determined.

After the wedding, George and Anna moved an extra bed into the kitchen at Anna's parents' house. Her mom appreciated Anna's help in the house and garden, and the prospect of another man to provide for his family suited Johann as well.

George landed a job for the village, driving the team of horses that pulled the mayor's carriage. The mayor's travel needs weren't great though, and most days, George stood in front of the church at dawn with all the other men and boys, each hoping the land-owning farmers would pick him when they came with their wagons looking for workers to bust their backs in the fields for the day. Each time George was picked, it put a pengoe or two in his pocket and every bit helped.

A year later, George and Anna's first child, little Theresa, was born. It wasn't long after that George heard about a landowner who was looking for a tenant to work his farm so he could move his own family into town where his children could attend school. With a roof over their heads and permission to raise a few of their own animals alongside the livestock they tended for the landlord, the young couple was set.

Relieved to be out of his in-laws' home, George worked hard. But it wasn't long before he began to resent being beholden to the rich farmer who owned the land. With dogged determination, he focused on ways to buy and fatten up one animal after another, envisioning the day he could move his little family into a house of their own.

CHAPTER FOUR

Elek, Hungary February 1929

If you were to look into the newspaper archives for Europe in the winter of 1929, you would find that February 10th of that year was the coldest night that had been recorded in Hungary in sixty years. The ground had frozen so hard that gaping cracks appeared, and Johann Bambach, being a miserly man, cursed angrily as his pocketknife fell from his frozen fingers and bounced into one of these cracks, never to be retrieved.

Inside Johann's little house, the midwife was preparing his 19-year-old daughter, Anna, for the arrival of her second child. Firewood had run out, and the meagre pile scrounged from the roadside and snapped from the frozen trees in the orchards under the cover of darkness, was the last resort to keep the little hut warm enough for Anna and the baby she was labouring to bring into the world. As the heat from the stove met the icy cold of the mud walls and ceiling, droplets formed. A blanket was draped awkwardly above the bed to catch the drops before they could land on the straining young woman.

"Thank you, Mama," Anna murmured as Maria Bambach tucked warm bricks into the bed so her daughter wouldn't catch a chill between contractions.

"Not long now, sweetheart. Stay strong," her mother replied to Anna with a kiss on her forehead. The night wore on and as the cold outside reached its sixty-year low, the pains came closer together, each worse than the last. As this child would prove time and time again throughout his life, he was not going to let the weather, or any other adverse conditions get in his way.

The cold snap began to ease the following morning. As the first weak rays of winter sun lit up the frosty windows, the midwife laid Anna's new son in her arms, just as she had done with little Theresa two years earlier in the same room. The connection between Anna and her baby boy began easily as he latched onto his mother and suckled hungrily.

By mid-week, with temperatures back to mid-winter norms, it was safe to remove the rolled-up towels from around doors and windows, and for George Baumann to collect his young wife, newborn son, and toddler daughter and take them back home to the little tenants' hut out on the farm.

Their son was baptized a few days later, on the first day of the Catholic Church Carnival, appropriate for such a happy occasion. The families of the young parents met at the church and looked on happily as the godparents strode up the aisle with the baby and placed him beside the tub of holy water. Solemnly, the priest performed the sacramental rite, giving grace to the soul of the baby boy, whose name was Adam.

CHAPTER FIVE

A son brought a sense of contentment to the little Baumann household. In six or seven years, Adam would be big enough to help around the farm, and George could begin passing on all of the things he'd learned about raising crops and livestock and providing for a family.

Little Adam's first challenge in life came at just a couple of months of age, when Anna weaned him. Planting season was coming and suckling a babe throughout the day would hinder her work. At first, she thought he just needed a day or two to adjust to cow's milk. But three days later, baby Adam was spitting up every time she fed him and he seemed to be losing weight. He even spit up the goat's milk they tried. Her own milk had dried up quickly, and Anna began to panic.

By the time a neighbour suggested sheep's milk, little Adam was gaunt. His non-stop crying had diminished to a feeble mewing sound. George raced to fetch some sheep's milk, and for the first time since drinking his own mother's milk, their baby son drank a couple of ounces and settled into a deep sleep. Within a couple of days, the colour returned to Adam's little cheeks. And so it happened that George headed off to the market to find and barter for a female sheep in its milking season.

A few short months after recovering from near starvation, Adam narrowly eluded death once more. Oblivious, he lay where Anna had placed him in the shade on the roadside while she foraged nearby, as a team of horses, spooked by the same ewe who had saved his life, careened by, the wheels of their wagon ripping across his blanket inches from his tiny body.

At two, he tumbled from the wagon bed onto the soft, freshly turned field as his unsuspecting parents continued on to the farmhouse, only to be found an hour or more later, toddling along in the right general direction.

Just as winter began to loosen her icy grip on Elek the next winter, three-year-old Adam fell ill with what the doctor called darm-katarrh. Healthy adults normally survived, the doctor explained, but with a toddler, they should be prepared for the worst. In those times, a case of gas-troenteritis in rural Hungary was often a death sentence for young children and the elderly. Adam spent a week or more slipping in and out of consciousness, unable to eat or keep liquids down. Then, slowly, while his mother fed him tiny morsels of preserved fruit she'd walked miles from farm to farm to find so late in the season, he recovered.

Adam's life would be plagued by challenges much greater than those that dotted his earliest years. Some challenges he created, others history created for him.

But that first summer, they were happy, and as George and Anna toiled through the harvest, putting food by for the winter, they had no way of knowing, nor would they have cared that the great stock market of America had crashed. In Elek, things continued as usual. To the west, however, in the motherland, the economic crash brought crisis and created fertile ground for the radical ideas of a calculating man named Adolf Hitler. Just a few short years later, having saved enough for a tiny home of their own near the Gypsy neighbourhood in town, the family welcomed a second son whom they named George, unaware that Hitler, by then head of Germany's newly elected Nazi government, had just passed the Enabling Act, giving himself the powers of a dictator and in so doing, changing the course of their lives forever.

CHAPTER SIX

Christmas 1933

Adam could smell onions on his mom's hands as she leaned down and fastened the top button of his coat under his chin.

"Don't stand at the window so long this time," she said patiently. It was December and the owners of the general store had been constructing a life-sized Christmas scene in the front window that had the children of Elek mesmerized. "When you start to feel cold, you tell Joe it's time to come home. You're almost five, and Joe's littler than you, so you need to take care of him."

The dirt floor and thick mud walls of the little kitchen held the chill of the winter air. They'd had a quick fire to warm their breakfast, but the dwindling pile of firewood on the porch together with the remaining sacks of husks and corn stalk roots they'd gathered in the fall had to last through the winter, and the stove wouldn't be stoked again until it was time to cook dinner. His dad was out shovelling snow for anyone who would pay. The best days were when someone paid with wood or a few lumps of coal.

Adam reached up impatiently and pushed at his woollen hat, which kept slipping down over his eyebrows. With a thumb sticking out of a hole in his mitten, he scratched at his itchy forehead. The hat and mittens were hand-me-downs from his cousin Uchie. His mom said he'd grow into them.

"Yes, Mama, I promise I'll bring Joe and come home," said Adam. A few days ago, they had stood in front of the display until one of the neighbours saw them and brought them home. Joe had cried when his fingers and nose warmed up enough to ache. Shoving his hat up again, Adam looked towards the door. Joe would be waiting outside. He'd make sure his friend didn't freeze this time.

"Okay, go." Anna smiled gently and stood up.

Flashing his mom a smile in return, Adam flew out the door into the sparkling winter air and leapt from the porch, landing solidly in the fresh powder. Sure enough, Joe was waiting in the snowy street, shuffling his feet. His face lit up like it always did when he saw Adam.

"C'mon!" Adam said excitedly, as Joe fell into step beside him.

The two little boys trekked hurriedly towards the train tracks, bundled in their winter layers. Across the tracks, Adam grabbed Joe's hand and led him toward the main street. Turning left, they stopped to wait as a horse drawn wagon rolled past, the rattle of the wheels muffled in the snow.

"Hurry Joe," Adam said as the sign above the door of the general store came into view. They picked up their pace. Last time, the old man who owned the store had been on his ladder inside the window case, adding to the display, and Adam couldn't wait to see it.

In front of the huge window, they stood motionless, gazing up.

"Look at the star, Adam," breathed Joe, his eyes as big as saucers.

Adam looked at the big sparkly star hanging in the pretend sky over the manger, then to the left and the right. Jesus' mom and dad were there with their donkey and the baby lying in the hay. The family's sheep were lying around them in the hay too. The best part was the three rich guys with their fancy dresses and shiny crowns full of jewels. Every time someone opened the front door of the store, the big star blew gently in the breeze. St. Nicholas stood over at one side with a sack over his shoulder. He hadn't been there last week. His coat and pants were better looking than what the real St. Nicholas had been wearing when Adam saw him at the church the other day. His real coat didn't have those nice buttons down the front, and his beard was a lot shorter in real life. Adam liked the one in the window better, with his big smile and shiny boots.

Theresa had said that St. Nicholas would bring them treats, and Adam had been excited. But when St. Nicholas came into the church, he wasn't smiling.

"Ho, Ho, Ho! Have you been good all year?" he'd demanded of Adam, then looked expectantly at Adam's mom and dad.

His mom had said yes, but his dad hadn't answered.

"You must listen to your parents and never ever disobey or deceive them. I want you to say a prayer to the Holy Father and promise that you'll be a good boy next year. Do you think you can be a good boy?"

Adam had nodded silently, not taking his eyes off the old man. Then he knelt and prayed his very best, promising God and St. Nicholas that he would be good. He'd done what they all expected apparently, since St. Nicholas didn't talk to him any further. And the little bag of nuts and dried fruit had tasted delicious.

Adam realized with a start that he was cold and looked anxiously down at Joe. His little friend was staring happily into the display, big eyes filled with wonder. His nose was running and smeared across his pudgy cheek where he'd wiped it with his sleeve.

"Come on Joe, we have to go home and warm up," he said with authority, grabbing Joe firmly by the hand.

"Okay, Adam," came Joe's ready response, as he gazed trustingly up at Adam. Adam smiled happily as they began the trek home.

He might not have quite grasped it yet, being only four years old, but Joe's trust stirred something in Adam. When Joe's mom came over to talk to him late the following summer and asked him to look after Joe on the walk to and from kindergarten, he was only too happy to help. From that point on, Adam understood that some people need a little help in life and it's the responsibility of the ones who don't, to give it.

CHAPTER SEVEN

Early Summer 1935

Kindergarten was almost finished, and the streets of Elek were muddy with the spring melt. Adam and Joe laughed as they raced across the tracks and headed into their street.

"Hey, Joe!" Adam yelled as he jumped and landed in a puddle as hard as he could.

"Oh yeah?" laughed Joe as he hopped into the puddle beside Adam, soaking them both a little bit more. Giggling, Joe ran ahead towards his gate, narrowly escaping the next splash.

"See you tomorrow," said Adam as Joe opened his gate and Adam turned to head into his own yard.

Mr. Fuchs' bicycle was leaning against the porch. Adam raced to the porch and leapt up the steps, then slammed open the door and wheeled around the corner into the kitchen.

"Is Resi home?" he demanded, using his sister Theresa's nickname. He looked around excitedly.

His dad was sitting at the kitchen table, while his mom stood at the stove stirring a pan. The air smelled like onions and bacon. Both his parents turned as he burst into the room.

"No, Adam," his mom responded quickly. "Dad had to leave her at the eye hospital for a while longer. Your dad's tired after riding all that way. Why don't you take George and go out and play in the yard?"

Poor Resi! The sickness in her eyes that had started last year had gotten worse. It stopped her from going to school and from doing anything fun, and now she couldn't even come home most of the time. She'd hardly been home at all since Christmas and Adam missed her dreadfully. Dad was always working extra for Mr. Fuchs so he could borrow the bicycle to pedal to the hospital to visit her and talk to the doctors, and every time they hoped he'd bring her home. Adam had asked a couple of times if he could go along, but his mom and dad said it was 80 kilometres, too far for his dad to double him on the bike.

Heavy with disappointment, Adam turned to where George was sitting on the floor with his little fist in his mouth, spittle running down his chin and chest.

Just as he was about to pick up his little brother, Adam's dad turned and took a good look at him. "What the hell happened to you?" he demanded. "Look at you. Now your mother will have to scrub the mud from those trousers. Don't you think she has enough work? Did you crawl home or just roll in every puddle?"

Standing and striding to where Adam had stopped in his tracks, his dad reached down and grabbed him by the back of his pants and lifted him off the floor. "It's about time you learned a lesson. I'll teach you to fool around and make a goddam mess when you should be coming straight home," he sputtered as he headed out the front door and down the steps towards the wood pile, Adam swinging along in midair at his side.

Suddenly there was a loud ripping sound and Adam tumbled to the ground. He looked up at the tatters of his worn pants in his father's big hand.

"What the hell?" his dad yelled. A string of Romanian cuss words followed. Adam cowered. He'd felt the sting of his dad's temper the first time when he was three, after he'd eaten the Christmas candies and rehung the empty wrappers from the branches. But this time his dad started to laugh.

"Anna, come out here and look at this. He's fallen right out of his britches. He gets them full of mud, and then he falls right out of them. Now we gotta get this goddam kid some new trousers on top of everything else."

That night in bed, Adam was still thinking about his sister. He wondered for the millionth time if she was lonely at the hospital all by herself. Dad had said there were other kids there, even some as little as George, getting their eyes fixed. So maybe she wasn't lonely. He rolled over again. He didn't want to go to sleep yet. It was boring lying there. After staring around for a few more minutes, Adam slipped out from under the blanket and tiptoed into the kitchen where his mom and dad sat at the table talking quietly. His dad's back was towards him.

"I'm still thirsty," he said quietly.

"Adam, what did I tell you?" his dad's voice was menacing as he turned around and stood up. "You already had a drink." Before Adam could move, his dad had crossed the floor and swatted him across the head. "Now get back to bed and stay there!"

Back in bed, Adam rubbed his cheek. He was just thirsty. Nothing to get so mad about. After a few more tosses and turns he drifted to sleep.

CHAPTER EIGHT

The summer after kindergarten, the warden who guarded the vineyards that grew on town property died suddenly. The job came with a house. George Baumann quickly recognized the opportunity and applied for the job. A house meant they could rent out their little house and bring in a little extra money.

Adam had been a bit sad to be leaving little Joe. But Joe's mom said Joe knew the way to school well enough now, and Mama said there would be other kids to play with in the new neighbourhood. And best of all, the old warden's dog, Kave, came with the new house!

Mama was right. The family across the street from the new house had two boys, Michel and Tony Pender, and soon the three were fast friends, spending long summer days exploring the nooks and crannies of the neighbourhood.

"Look at those birds flying in under that roof," said Tony, pointing. "Nobody lives in that place. I bet there are nests under there."

They peered up under the eve of the deserted house and sure enough, a row of mud and wattle nests lined the top of the wall. A chorus of tiny chirps was audible.

"Baby birds! I wonder if they've got feathers yet. They're really funny looking before they get feathers," said Michel, then looked at his older brother. "Tony, climb up there and get one. Let's see if they can fly yet," he continued excitedly.

Tony looked at the wall. Like many houses in Elek, this one was built a few feet off the ground in case of flooding. The nests were a long way up. There was a barbed wire fence running alongside the house with one post leaning against the wall.

"I'm not climbing up there. That wire won't hold me. You climb up," Tony said.

"No way, there's nothing to hang on to," replied Michel.

The three boys stood staring up at the nests, listening to the baby birds. Mother birds circled against the blue sky above, swooping down every lap or two, trying to scare the boys away.

"I'll do it," said Adam. "I bet I can reach the nests if I stand on that post."

He was tall for six, almost as tall as Tony, three years his senior. Carefully, holding first onto the post and then leaning his hands against the wall of the house as he got higher, Adam climbed carefully, lifting each bare foot from one wire up to the next, until he stepped gingerly onto the top of the post. He stood still for a minute to get his balance, both hands pressed flat against the wall, feet gripping the top of the post like a bird on a perch. Glancing down, he saw Tony and Michel watching intently. Slowly, he stretched out a hand and reached into the nearest nest until he sensed the quivering warmth of a baby bird under his fingers.

Suddenly, the post shifted slightly. Adam's arms flailed for something to grab onto but found only empty air as he slipped from the post and landed with a thud on the packed earth between the grapevines. Dazed, he lay with his eyes closed for a moment. When he opened them, Michel and Tony were staring down at him.

"Are you okay?" Tony sounded scared. "Look at your leg!"

Adam lifted his head and looked down to where pain was burning through his lower leg. Blood was running from a long gash down the length of his calf. As he stared at it, tears sprung to his eyes.

"We better go get your dad," said Tony, and before Adam could respond, Tony and Michel took off at a run.

Adam lay staring at the sky for a minute, then turned his head and looked at the fence. His eyes focused on the red bits hanging from some of the barbs. It was flesh torn from his leg!

"Christ, Adam, what have you done now?" said his dad as he came running down the row of vines to where Adam lay.

"I was trying to see the baby birds up there," Adam pointed weakly to the nests, then wiped at his tears with his arm. "Michel and Tony were too scared to climb up."

His dad gathered him carefully into his big arms, and Adam winced as his leg jostled.

"You're lucky you didn't land on a stake," his dad said as he walked towards their house.

As his dad set him down on the bed at the back of the kitchen, he explained to Adam's mom, "He was climbing on the barbed wire fence, trying to reach a goddam birds nest with those Pender boys, then fell and landed squarely between two rows of stakes. A few inches either way and he'd have a hole in his head too."

"It's bleeding a lot," said his mom as she sat down on the edge of the bed beside him and wiped at his leg with a cloth, trying to see the wound. "It's deep and long. I think you'd better get the doctor."

"Goddammit," said his dad as he went back out the front door.

An hour later, Adam shrieked again as the doctor pushed the needle in for the last stitch. Little George sat on the floor nearby, wailing along with his brother, his pudgy tear-streaked cheeks red from the effort. Their mom and dad were holding Adam as still as they could.

"Okay, that should be enough," the doctor said, sounding relieved.

Adam's screams subsided to loud sobs. His whole leg was throbbing unbearably from the stitching as the doctor bandaged it up tightly and moved away to pack his equipment back into his bag. Adam's mom rocked him and wiped his tears while his dad walked with the doctor out onto the porch. As Adam quietened down, little George's cries faded to a whimper. There was a murmur of conversation out in the yard, and then his dad strode back into the kitchen.

"He says it will heal fine. We just have to keep it clean so it doesn't fester, and he'll have to stay in bed for a couple of days." His dad sounded relieved, but then his tone changed. "A doctor costs a lot of goddam money, Adam. Climbing that fence was stupid. Next time think a little bit." Adam stopped crying as his dad lectured him. Then his dad turned on his heel. "I gotta get back to work," he said, disappearing through the door.

CHAPTER NINE

The wound healed well enough, although the scar on Adam's left calf would be a permanent reminder of that carefree summer between kindergarten and grade one. Soon after, his father decided Adam was old enough to help with the chores. He showed Adam how to take the brood hen out of her pen, knot a string around her leg, and find a spot along the roadside with lots of chickweed where he could tie her for the day. The chicks would stay near their mother, practicing their scratching and pecking. Then the goat had to be taken out and tethered where there was lots of grass or a green tree to munch on. It was important to tie the rope tightly so the goat didn't get away. After school, he was to come straight home and get the chickens and the goat back into their pens in the yard and fill their water troughs. Weekends he mucked out the pens and whatever else his dad said needed doing.

At first it was kind of fun having some grown-up jobs.

In the springtime of second grade, Adam's grandma on his dad's side, Veronica Baumann, died. He wasn't sad. She'd always been so crabby. He did miss Grandpa Florian, who had been gone a couple of years already. He missed climbing into his grandpa's big lap and smelling the wood smell that clung to him. His grandpa told Adam about the things he built for people while Adam picked out the sawdust stuck in his beard. He especially loved lighting his grandpa's pipe. His grandpa needed help to light it because it was so long. He showed Adam how to strike the match and hold it so the flame wouldn't go out, and then hold it in the end of the pipe where the tobacco was. It would glow red when Adam held the match there and Grandpa sucked on the other end. Yes, he missed his grandpa.

Tradition said that the eldest son had first rights to the family home, but Adam's Uncle Florian, his dad's eldest brother and namesake to their father, was settled in nearby Gyula with his family and uninterested in the little house in Elek. Adam's dad jumped at the chance to take over the family home, puffing out his chest like a peacock when he told his friends he would be raising his family in the home where he was born and his father before him was born. Soon they had the old home looking new again, with whitewash covering the mud walls on the outside, and the dirt floors inside hardened with a thick slurry of blue clay from the Gypsies mixed with fresh cow dung to give it a good shine when it dried.

The house was across from the cemetery, on a corner lot with vine-yards and orchard on two sides. With three rooms, it was bigger than the other houses they'd lived in. The room in the middle where the front door entered was for storage. To the right was the bedroom where Adam's parents would sleep in the double bed and he would share the single bed against the wall with his dad's youngest sister, Aunt Louise, who was seventeen and unmarried. The kitchen, to the left when you came in the front door, had a table big enough for the family to sit for meals, a cook stove, and two little cots for Theresa and George. The pantry and the summer kitchen were on the porch, for the months when it was too hot to prepare and eat meals inside.

A big garden for summer vegetables filled most of the front yard, except the spot where the copper laundry pot hung over the firepit at one end. The back yard was for animals. A little shelter for the cow and goat was tucked against the end wall of the house. Opposite were the pig pen and the chicken coop. A low roof covered part of the pig pen, giving shelter for the pigs and a place for the chickens to roost. When the animal pens were mucked out, the manure was piled beside the outhouse, waiting to be spread on the gardens each year.

Winter vegetables like potatoes, beans, and cabbage, the types of vegetables which could be grown in the fall and kept well over the winter, would be planted in the garden space out back in the orchard. Stacked against the end of the porch were the rabbit hutches. From the day they moved in, Adam was responsible for the rabbits, filling their cages with fresh grass morning and night, and learning from his dad how to tell males from females and when to put them in a cage together so they would make baby rabbits.

CHAPTER TEN

His dad's temper worsened as time passed. Or maybe it was Adam's behaviour that worsened. At eight, he had come to think of after-school fun as a gamble. If he could participate in whatever the kids got up to that afternoon, then hightail it home and get his chores done before his dad got there, he won. Otherwise, he lost. And the penalty for losing was a spanking.

"I gotta get home," Adam said to his new friend Franz Wittman. Even though Franz was in grade four, a year ahead of Adam, the two had become close, walking to and from school together and playing on week-ends if Adam finished his chores.

Adam knew he shouldn't have stayed late again, but the kids had started a game of soccer using a new ball that one kid's dad, a shoemaker, had fashioned from scraps of leather stitched together around an inflated pig bladder. It was brilliant!

Adam's mom and grandma were sitting in the summer kitchen on the porch when he got there, chatting quietly over the steady rhythm of pea shells being cracked open and peas dropping into the bowls on their laps.

"Hello, Adam," his grandma said with a big smile as he walked up onto the porch. His grandma on his mom's side was gentle, just like his mom. "Why are you limping again?"

"Me and Franz were racing and I stepped on a thorn." It was still warm enough and the ground was dry, so he hadn't started wearing his shoes yet, except to school.

"You need to be more careful," she chided gently. "Here you go, I brought you a little treat."

Yum! She must have sneaked the cookie out of the house, Adam thought as he took it from her. Grandpa Johann got mad when she gave them treats. He said they needed their food for themselves.

"Thank you, Grandma!" Adam headed into the house, savouring the cookie as his grandma picked up where she'd left off the conversation.

"Anyway, Anna, if those medicine drops aren't helping her eyes, why not try it? I heard from my cousin in Gyula that the warm urine helped the son of one of her neighbours."

Ewwwwww, warm pee in Resi's eyes? thought Adam as he put his books on the table. Just then he heard the front gate open.

"Adam!" his dad bellowed from the yard.

The women stopped talking. Adam shoved the rest of the treat into his mouth and chewed fast, then walked out the front door onto the porch. His mom and his grandma sat very still.

"Why is that damned goat still out? I've told you a hundred times to come straight home from school and do your chores. Who do you think you are?"

His dad's face was red. He strode up the steps, shoved Adam out of the way, and disappeared into the house. A couple of seconds later he was back with his leather razor strap in his hand.

Shucks! The strap hurt more than a stick of kindling.

"Get over here," his dad barked as he sat down heavily on the bench that ran the length of the summer table.

Adam walked over dutifully, undid his pants, and leaned over his dad's knee.

"Owwww! Owwwww! Owwwwww!" he yelled each time the strap hit his rear end.

"Next time, you come straight home and look after those animals, do you hear me?" his dad asked when he stopped swinging, his voice still raised.

"Yes, Dad," Adam said quietly as he stood and pulled up his pants.

"I gotta get over to the Mahlers' and mix the cattle mash. Hang this back up," he ordered, thrusting the strap at Adam. It was kept on a nail in the kitchen door frame where his dad could grab it to sharpen his razor in the morning.

When Adam came back out from replacing the strap on the nail in the kitchen, his dad was gone.

"Come here Adam," said his grandma holding out her arms. "Are you okay?" she asked, pulling him down onto her lap into a warm, soft hug.

"I'm okay, Grandma," Adam replied, his voice muffled, as she held his face against her neck and rocked side to side.

"That man and his temper," she muttered, and rocked a few more times. "Now go and do your chores like a good boy."

Getting up from his grandma's lap, Adam leapt down the steps and jogged out the front gate and down the street to where he'd tied the goat this morning. As he untied the knot, he started to whistle. Would they really put pee in Resi's eyes, he wondered, whistling absentmindedly as he headed back towards the house with the goat.

CHAPTER ELEVEN

1938

Not long after their first Christmas in the family home, a new baby appeared. Adam, Theresa, and little George had been visiting at their grandparents' house overnight, and when they got home, there she was, with big blue eyes and a bit of soft white hair. They called her Anni.

By the time Anni was walking, her blue eyes, blonde curls, and sunny personality had captured the hearts of relatives and neighbours alike. Even Adam slowed down long enough to pick his little sister up and carry her around the yard or tickle her until she giggled.

"Ad-am," said little Anni, arms outstretched, when Adam got home from running an errand for his mom one afternoon. He tossed the empty egg basket and the box of matches he'd gotten in trade for the eggs at the general store, onto the counter. Adam could hardly remember what it was like before they had Anni. He walked over to where his baby sister, a year and a half now, sat on the bed he shared with George.

When Anni was born, his dad had put a cot in the bedroom for her and moved Adam's bed out into the kitchen. Aunt Louise had saved her earnings from doing laundry and mending for the rich farmers and used it for a ship crossing, so George shared the bed with Adam now, leaving Theresa with a bed to herself on the opposite wall of the kitchen. Theresa didn't have to go to the eye hospital anymore. The doctors said there was nothing they could do. Although Adam knew it was hard for her sometimes, not being able to see very well, and being stuck at home all the time, he was glad to have his big sister back.

"Anni up, Ad-am. Peees." She reached her arms up again, and Adam reached down to pick up his little sister.

"What did you do today?" Adam said, carrying Anni out onto the porch where their mom was chopping vegetables in the heat of the summer kitchen. Adam pointed towards the yard. "Look, there's Resi. What's she doing?"

Mimicking her big brother, Anni pointed to where Theresa was kneeling in the dirt, pulling weeds. "Gaw-den," replied the toddler.

"Adam, can you please fetch the wagon from the shed and go get the batteries?" asked Adam's mom.

"Sure," said Adam, setting Anni down and heading into the back yard to retrieve the wagon.

A couple of years earlier, people from Elek had started leaving to work in Germany, bringing a lot of interesting stuff back to sell when they came home for visits. The economy in the motherland was booming thanks to the brilliant Führer. Adolf Hitler had led Germany out of the Great Depression faster than any other country in Europe, Adam's dad and his friends bragged to each other regularly. If only they had a good German leader like Hitler here in Hungary, they said. In Germany, new factories were opening, autobahns were being built, and workers were in demand everywhere.

Although George Baumann hadn't gone to work in Germany, his hard work and determination to get ahead had been paying off at home in Elek. With the earnings from selling their first little house, and his growing list of vineyard maintenance contracts, he no longer had to worry so much each day about feeding his family and keeping them warm. Still, he didn't spend money lightly. But when he'd heard about the radios people were bringing back from Germany, he'd counted out enough pengoes to buy one and the batteries to operate it. That radio had become George's most prized possession. A couple of nights a week, the men from the neighbourhood would come over after supper to listen to the news, and then they'd usually leave the radio on, playing music for a while. Adam listened intently to it all. The German broadcasters sounded a bit strange. Some of the words were different from how they talked in Elek, but he got used to it. After the news about Germany, they had news about other countries, sometimes even about America. When the music came on, Adam sat tapping his foot until everyone had gone home and his dad turned off the radio and put it away.

As Adam pulled the little wagon into the yard at the power plant, he waved at the attendant, then carefully unhooked the batteries where he'd put them on the platform to charge that morning before school. Bending his knees a little, and heaving with all his might, he lifted the box of batteries from the platform onto the wagon. Slowly, he made his way home, careful not to pull the wagon through any big holes. If any of the connections between the four batteries in the box came loose, Dad would fly off the handle.

As soon as he finished his supper, Adam's dad pushed back his chair and stood up. A moment later he reappeared in the doorway, leaning to one side to offset the weight of the battery box in his other hand. Carefully, he set the box down in front of the radio, and gently connected the wires, one by one. When he had them all adjusted so that they all stuck out of the box at the same angle, he reached up and turned the knob on the radio. After a minute, music began to emerge from the static. Just as his mom finished clearing the table, Adam heard the front gate open.

A few minutes later they were all seated around the radio, eager to hear the day's news.

"The Führer this week approved two new laws. The Decree on the Confiscation of Jewish Property, which regulates the transfer of assets from Jews to non-Jewish Germans, shall be effective immediately. All Jews are required to report to their town hall to proceed with the transfer of assets. Any Jews not transferring their assets within one week will be arrested. The second new law was announced by the Reich Interior Ministry, revoking all German passports held by Jews. All Jews are required to surrender their passports, which will be replaced by new passports stamped with the letter 'J'. Further, the Führer has announced his intention to pass a Decree on the Exclusion of Jews from German Economic Life. This Decree is expected to come into effect next month. All Jews operating a business which they own are advised to begin preparations for winding up the business and closing it within the month.

In international news. . . "

"They're getting pretty tough on the Jews," one of the men said, when the news was over.

"I wonder if the Wilde will shut down," one of the other men said. The Wilde was a big store in Elek run by a Jewish family, where Adam's mom bought wool and fabric and everything else she needed to make their clothes.

"Do you think they'll pass the same laws here? Can Hitler tell Hungary what to do?" someone wondered out loud.

Neither the people around the radio that evening, nor anyone around the world had any idea yet about the power Hitler would wield in the years to come.

CHAPTER TWELVE

It rained hard that night, a cold rain. Not cold enough to be snow, but it wouldn't be long. The next morning, the ground was muddy and the wet grass froze Adam's hands as he filled the sack with grass for the rabbits.

Franz was waiting on the road outside his house when Adam got there. Franz's family was pretty rich. They lived in a fancy house in town and they also had a big farm outside of town. Still, he was a good guy.

"Look at him." Adam pointed to a kid walking ahead of them. "That fancy white suit would look better with a little mud on it, don'tcha think?" The kid was in grade three like Adam. His house was even bigger and fancier than Franz's house, and it annoyed Adam how he strutted around at school like a peacock in his fancy clothes with that smug look on his face.

Franz grinned at Adam and raised his eyebrows.

"I'll run ahead and find a puddle he'd look good in," Adam said quietly out of the side of his mouth. "You talk to him and tell him a good story about something so he doesn't notice me."

Franz grinned wider. "Good plan!"

As Adam ducked behind the next house to make his way ahead of the boy, he looked back and saw Franz speed up as he called to the boy, "Heinz, wait up!"

When he'd found a mud puddle with a big tree next to it, Adam ducked down behind the tree and watched for them. He didn't have to wait long. Franz was striding along, waving his arms around telling a story and Heinz was listening intently. When they reached the edge of the mud puddle, Adam stuck his foot out from behind the tree.

"Ahhhh!" yelled Heinz as he landed in the mud.

"Nice brown suit!" yelled Adam over his shoulder as he and Franz darted away, hooting with laughter. Heinz didn't look so smug now.

"Does anyone know which river is longer, the Rhine or the Danube?" Mr. Tihanyi asked after the bell rang and everyone had quietened down. Geography was Adam's favourite subject.

When no one answered, Mr. Tihanyi continued. "The Danube is actually twice as long as the Rhine, starting in Bavaria and flowing all the way to the Black Sea. The Romans used the Danube very strategically, for transporting cargo on large ships during times of peace, and in wartime, the ancient Roman navy used very small rowboats for carrying special messages and other secret activities. These little spy boats were called 'musculi,' which means 'little mice.'"

Adam's mind wandered as Mr. Tihanyi went on to talk about other things. Imagine sailing a boat on the Danube, or on the Rhine, or rowing one of those little boats carrying secret messages. All the things you would see...

'Smack!'

"Owwwww!" said Adam as Mr. Tihanyi glared down at him, tapping the wooden ruler that he had just smacked Adam across the head with against his palm.

"Maybe that will help you pay attention," he said as Adam rubbed his ear. Just then the door opened and the priest walked in. "Time for Catechism," said Mr. Tihanyi as he walked over to his desk to pick up his satchel before leaving the classroom.

Every week the priest came in and droned on for an hour about Jesus being dunked in the River Jordan, getting nailed to the cross, rising from the dead, and on and on. Jesus this and Jesus that. They'd heard it all before.

Adam's mind wandered back to what he'd heard on the radio the night before, as he rubbed his stinging ear. Suddenly a thought came to him.

"Father!" he interrupted, putting his hand high in the air.

The priest looked annoyed.

"Yes Adam?" he asked in a clipped tone.

"Wasn't Jesus a Jew?"

The priest's face turned stony as he stood up and slowly answered. "You are a smart mouthed boy and you need to learn some respect."

"But wasn't he descended from Judah so he's a Jew?" Adam remembered learning this in some of their earliest lessons at church.

At this, the priest turned and strode over to the can of bamboo sticks in the corner of the room, selected the biggest one, and then strode to Adam's desk. He towered over Adam in his black robe and glared down. "Fingertips!"

Seeing no way out of it, Adam slowly raised his hands, palms up and then bent his fingers so his fingertips were sticking up.

Whack! Whack! Whack!

Adam winced. Fingertip caning really hurt and the priest knew it, but Adam wasn't going to give him the satisfaction of crying out.

The priest strode back to the can and reinserted the bamboo rod as Adam looked down at his smarting fingertips. He looked back up as the priest marched back towards him.

"Owww!" Adam yelled in surprise, as the priest pulled him to his feet by the same ear that Mr. Tihanyi had hit with his ruler.

The priest led Adam roughly from the room and down the hall to the principal's office where they entered without knocking.

"This boy is unruly and needs to be severely punished!" he shouted at the principal.

Adam looked at the principal innocently and blinked.

"And what has he done this time, Father?" the principal asked calmly.

"He interrupted the catechism lesson and he called Jesus a dirty Jew!"

Looking first at Adam, whose head was tilted to the side by the priest's hold on his ear, then at the priest, the principal's face remained expressionless. The priest waited for the import of what he'd said to sink in.

"Adam, what do you have to say for yourself?" the principal finally asked.

"Well, I remember that Jesus was descended from Judah, and I thought that made him a Jew, so I asked."

The principal hesitated a moment. "I'm very sorry, Father, but that's the way I remember it too. I'm quite sure I was also taught that Jesus was a Jew."

Adam stumbled slightly as the priest released his ear with an exasperated little shove.

"Well, it's not what he said exactly, it's the way he said it! This boy is full of disrespect. He needs discipline!" And with that, the priest spun around and, robes flaring out around him, strode from the office.

Adam thought he saw a hint of a smile flit briefly across the principal's face before he spoke. "Adam, why do you insist on annoying your teacher and the good Father?"

Adam looked down at his feet and then back up at the principal.

"I wasn't trying to annoy him, I just remembered hearing on the radio about Jews last night and I wondered about Jesus."

The principal was quiet for a moment. "Go back to class, pay attention to your lessons, and behave yourself."

"Yes sir," Adam said. He was right about Jesus being a Jew, he thought as he headed back to class, and the principal wasn't really angry with him.

At nine, Adam had begun to trust his own instincts, even in the face of contradictory information from those more learned than he. This trait, the same as that which marks the great world changers, would pay off time and time again throughout his life.

CHAPTER THIRTEEN

One afternoon not long after, when he'd finished the rest of his chores, Adam opened the door of the cage where he kept the rabbits that were ready to eat. Pulling one out by its ears, he shut the door, and grabbed the stick from where it was tucked in between the end cage and the barn door. *WHACK!* The rabbit went limp. He had to hit quick and hard on the back of the head just below the base of the ears, so that it was fast and didn't hurt. He didn't like to think he was hurting them. When he'd finished skinning and cleaning the first one, he selected another one and started again. Just like his dad had taught him. Kill, bleed, hang from the wire in the barn doorway so he could slice the fur down the back legs and pull it off, then cut the skinned rabbit open and get rid of the guts and head, but always keep the heart and liver for his mom to use. They ate a lot of rabbit over the summer and fall while the pigs were growing, so it was pretty routine, and Adam's mind started to wander.

It was about a week since he'd seen the neighbour's rabbits. The goat had been pacing up and down along her little fence, bleating non-stop. *'Take that goat over to old man Haas' billy-goat, Adam, she's ready to breed,'* his dad had said.

When Adam followed Herr Haas through his barn a little later, leading the nanny goat, he couldn't help but stare at the rabbits in the stacks of cages just inside the door. They were something else! Especially the big buck in the first cage. He was a beautiful, soft grey colour and his ears were huge and floppy. His own rabbits were nowhere near that good looking. Or that big. He had a nice black from a trade with Franz, but this grey was way nicer. And those ears!

He'd been thinking about that buck all week. Everyone knew Herr Haas hated kids. He wouldn't be interested in trading for any of Adam's rabbits. How could he convince Haas to let him borrow the buck?

Mulling over what he would say to the old curmudgeon, Adam picked the two skinned rabbits up by their back legs and held them in one hand, their tiny organs in the other, and took them to where his mom and Theresa were working on the porch in the summer kitchen. Mom was chopping vegetables and Theresa was stoking the cooking fire. Little George was nowhere to be seen. Anni was sitting in the corner banging a dried corn cob on the floor and babbling away in baby talk. She smiled up at Adam and bobbed her curly blonde head at him.

"Ad-am, up?" she raised her little arms and smiled disarmingly.

"Here you go, Mom," he said, swinging the rabbits up onto the counter where she was working. He placed the hearts and livers beside the two carcasses.

"Thank you, Adam," she gave him a warm smile and continued chopping.

"Not right now, Anni. Bye, bye," he said, exaggerating a wave to her.

She rewarded him by waving back with her pudgy arm. "Bye, bye, bye."

Adam jumped from the porch, his bare feet making a little cloud of dust as he landed on the dry ground. Rinsing his hands quickly in the water trough, he ran out onto the street. He'd decided what he would say to Herr Haas, and if he hurried, maybe he could even borrow the buck and breed a couple of his females before supper!

Herr Haas and his wife lived two doors away, and as Adam came to their front gate, he stopped and stood up straight, then opened the gate and went through, careful to latch it behind him. Adam could hear the sound of sweeping coming from the back yard. Walking softly past the porch steps, he looked around the corner of the house. Sure enough, there was Herr Haas, scowling as he swept the early autumn leaves into a pile. His old dog was lying nearby in the shade. That dog never left the old man's side. Adam paused and took a deep breath to speak, just as Herr Haas noticed him standing there.

"What do you want?" barked the old man.

Adam almost turned on his heel, but then he'd never have rabbits like those. Looking straight at Haas, he opened his mouth and forced himself to start talking. "Herr Haas, your rabbits are very good looking, much better looking than mine, you must be good at taking care of them, they're bigger and a beautiful colour and their ears are so big and floppy, and I wonder if you would consider letting me borrow one of your males,

that big grey one, for an hour or so to breed him with a couple of my females, I'll bring him right back and it won't take long, I promise." Adam's
words spilled out, tumbling over each other in their rush to be said. There,
it was done. He held his breath, clenching and unclenching his little fists
nervously as the old man's expression changed from shock to anger.

"The nerve of you! Those are my rabbits! No respect! Get outta my
yard, you rotten kid, before I make you sorry!" he sputtered as he started
towards Adam, waving the broom menacingly.

Ducking, Adam turned and fumbled with the gate latch, then took
off down the street. He stopped in front of his own gate and looked back.
The street was empty. Grumpy old jerk! It wouldn't cost him anything,
Adam fumed silently as he stomped into his yard.

For the next hour, Adam moped around the back yard, absentmindedly kicking at the splinters of wood around the chopping block and digging holes in the dirt with his toes. He'd asked so politely, much more
politely than the old grump ever was to anyone! The more he thought
about it, the madder he got. He wanted that big grey male, and it wasn't
fair of Haas to keep it to himself!

Suddenly, he smiled. Herr Haas didn't even need to know about it.

The next morning dragged by. His dad had left for the vineyards
long ago. Anni was at the table on the porch, pushing a bread crust around
in her cup of milk with a pudgy finger, chattering happily. In the yard,
Theresa was adding wood to the fire under the big copper pot, getting
ready to wash clothes. He watched from the steps as his mom cut a piece
from the block of soap she'd made a few days earlier, dropped it into the
steaming water, and stirred it in with the long-handled laundry paddle.
In the back yard, little George was wandering around, holding a stick between his short little legs, talking quietly to his "horse."

Adam reviewed his plan. The best time would be after the midday
meal, when Dad had gone back to the vineyards for the afternoon. Hopefully Herr Haas wouldn't have any chores to do in his back yard in the
afternoon. Adam headed back to muck out the pig pen while he waited.

An hour later, he leaned against the gatepost drawing in the dirt
with a stick. Finally, his mom announced that the clothes had boiled long

enough and began to pull them out to cool so that he and Theresa could wring the water out of them and hang them on the line.

His dad got home for lunch as they hung the last of the laundry, and while he washed up, Adam's mom ladled rabbit stew from the pot that had been bubbling away all morning. Everyone was moving so slowly today!

Sitting at the table, Adam swung his legs impatiently and swatted at mosquitoes, watching as his dad finally mopped up the last of his gravy with his last bite of bread, and stood up to go back to work.

Back in front of the rabbit cages, Adam moved rabbits around to empty out cages for the two females he'd selected. Everything needed to be ready so that he kept the buck for as short a time as possible. Next, he dashed inside to grab his sweater. He would need something to cover the buck with. In the kitchen, Theresa was setting up the sewing machine and his mom was measuring George's legs. Adam did his best to walk calmly out of the house and down the steps, then dashed through the back gate into the orchard. With any luck, things would be equally quiet in the Haas yard.

Herr Haas's barn came into view. The coast was clear. He quickly slid through the fence and dashed to the barn door. It was open a crack. Peering inside, Adam could just make out the rabbit cages. Everything was still, inside and out. Easing the door open a few more inches, he slipped inside and stopped for a moment to let his eyes adjust. The air in the barn was hot and stuffy. There he was! Adam reached out and opened the latch on the cage, then stuck his arm in and got a good grip on the buck's ears. Slowly, he pulled the big rabbit out of the cage.

"Hello," he whispered, holding the rabbit up to eye level, before wrapping the sweater around him and tiptoeing back to the door. Heart pounding, Adam peeked out through the crack. Still no movement in the yard. Cradling his precious bundle, he dashed to the fence and crawled through, then looked back. He was pretty sure he hadn't been seen.

Putting his bundle on the ground in front of the rabbit cages, Adam unfolded the sweater and grabbed the buck's big floppy ears.

"In you go!" he whispered, opening the first cage and pushing the male in.

The male and female sniffed each other briefly, and then the male jumped on top! Yahoo! It was working! As soon as they stopped, Adam moved the buck into the second cage, glancing over his shoulder around the yard to make sure no one was around. The sniffing began again. But this time it went on longer and then nothing. Come on! They were just sitting there. Adam waited a few minutes and weighed the options. Maybe he should take the buck back. At least he knew he had one female bred. Or he could risk keeping him a bit longer and try for two. He had a much better chance of getting the look of those grey rabbits into his herd if he had two litters to work with.

"Adam!" His mom's face appeared around the corner of the porch, startling him. "There you are. The scrap bucket is full. Can you come and get it and take it out to the chickens please?"

"Okay," he said, looking up nervously at his mom. But she hadn't noticed anything.

Obediently, he headed into the house and brought out the bucket of scraps. As quickly as he could, he dumped it in the chicken pen and spread it around a bit, then put it on the porch and raced back to the rabbit cage. They were still just sitting there! Had they moved? He couldn't tell, but he couldn't risk waiting any longer.

Re-wrapping the buck in his sweater, he retraced his steps to the fence behind the old man's barn and climbed through. Everything was quiet. The only sound he could hear was the buzzing of the bees in Herr Haas's garden. He started towards the barn, congratulating himself as he went. It was going to work. Even one grey litter would be a good start. He could work with it.

Suddenly, he heard the front door of the house open and the Haas' dog bounded around the corner into the back yard, barking at the sight of him.

"Shhhhhhh," Adam urged. But Herr Haas was already alerted, and as he came around the corner of the house, Adam froze, halfway between the fence and the barn.

"What the hell are you doing here?!" yelled Haas.

"Nothing," was all Adam could think to say, the bundle heavy in his arms.

"What's that you've got?!"

"Nothing," Adam repeated, heart in his throat.

"Show me what you've got!" demanded the old man.

Trapped!

Frozen to the spot, Adam unfolded the edge of the sweater covering the rabbit. The grey buck blinked limpid black eyes in the sunlight. Herr Haas strode towards them, his eyes bulging as he recognized what Adam was carrying. Reaching them, Haas reached out and wrenched the bundle from Adam's arms.

"Why, you little thief! You're stealing my buck!"

"I borrowed him! I was bringing him . . ." Adam tried to explain as he backed away, looking up into Herr Haas's enraged face, but the old man was too livid to hear him. As he continued to rage over top of Adam's explanation, Adam turned and ran.

"Stealing right under my nose! You rotten little no good thief! Come back here!" Herr Haas sputtered as he made a half-hearted attempt at pursuit. But Adam had already slipped through the fence and was almost out of sight.

"You're going to pay for this! I'll go to the police and report you, you little thief!" Adam heard behind him as passed the yard in between theirs and the Haas'. Slipping through the fence into his own yard, Adam stopped and leaned against the wall of the wood shed, panting, then looked around. Old man Haas wasn't behind him, and everything was still quiet here. No one had noticed the ruckus. What now? Heart still pounding, Adam digested what Haas had said. This was the biggest trouble he'd been in yet. What would Dad do when he found out? Leaning his head back against the wall, Adam closed his eyes and swallowed hard.

A couple of hours passed, and nothing happened. His dad came in from work, whistling, and washed up as usual. Maybe Haas had cooled off. Adam started to breathe a little easier as he and Theresa headed to the well to haul drinking water.

When they returned with the full buckets, everything had changed. Adam's heart pounded as his dad and Tony Stumpf Sr. stood up from where they'd been sitting on the porch. Tony sometimes came over and played cards with his dad, and Tony Junior had become a constant companion to Adam and Franz. But that afternoon Herr Stumpf was dressed in his policeman's uniform. Clearly, he was there on official business.

"Adam, what the hell is wrong with you?" Adam's dad yelled. His mom was standing behind his dad in the doorway of the house. Was she crying?

"Why?" asked Adam feebly.

"Stealing! I can't believe it. You're in big trouble this time," his dad paused and turned to the policeman. "I guess you better handle this, Tony."

The policeman stepped forward and spoke. "Adam, stealing is a very serious crime, and I've informed your father that it is my duty to lock you up in jail."

Looking at the three adults on the porch, Adam swallowed quickly and began to talk. "Hello, Herr Stumpf. Dad, I wasn't stealing the rabbit. I borrowed it to breed with two of my females because his rabbits are a very nice colour and a lot bigger than mine, but I was taking it back when he saw me. I wasn't stealing, I swear . . ." his voice trailed off. Adam looked from one man to the other, trying to read their faces.

His dad spoke in a low, angry voice. "You should be ashamed of yourself, Adam. And just wait until they let you go and you come home so I can deal with you. Now go with Tony and god-damn-well do what he says."

Adam could feel the stares of the neighbours as he balanced on the cross-bar of the policeman's bicycle. "I wasn't stealing it!" he wanted to yell. They rode without speaking, Herr Stumpf's arms bracing Adam on either side as he steered the bicycle.

A few minutes later, the black metal gates of the little jail yard adjacent to the town hall loomed in front of them, standing open, waiting. Tony steered the bicycle inside, past the police wagon and horse team, and pulled to a stop beside a dark jail cell.

The lock of the cell door sliding into place made a loud metallic 'clunk,' and the policeman strode out of sight, keys dangling from his hand. Adam stood just inside the door and looked around curiously. The air felt damp, and the dirt floor was cool on his feet. Sitting on the bench against the inner wall of the cell swinging his legs, he continued to inspect the jail cell. The bars were thick, and too close together for him to fit through. The concrete wall at the back was cool and damp to the touch. All the other cells were empty, as far as he could tell. He held still and listened but couldn't hear anything at all. It was really quiet in jail. Growing bored, he jumped up and walked the perimeter of the cell, testing the bars every few feet. It was wrong for him to be locked up. He wasn't a thief.

It was starting to get dark when Adam heard his dad's voice somewhere out in the direction of the street.

"That's probably long enough, hey, Tony?"

"Sure, George. I hope this taught him a lesson like you wanted. But he didn't cry or anything. Didn't even seem scared. Pretty brave for nine."

"He's the most stubborn kid I've ever seen," his dad replied, as their footsteps and voices got closer and the two men came into sight.

That night in bed, Adam thought about how they'd made him put his hand on the Bible and promise never to steal again. His dad just shook his head when Adam said, " I promise never to steal. And I swear I wasn't stealing the grey buck, just borrowing him and I was returning him when Herr Haas saw me. "

CHAPTER FOURTEEN

It was over six weeks since Adam's afternoon in jail, and his dad was still mad at him. But both of the females had had litters a couple of weeks ago, and after having a good look at the babies yesterday, he knew he had proof. He was planning to show them to his dad that afternoon. If they ever finished burying the grape vines. His dad was teaching him to prepare the vines to survive through the winter.

"Okay, now do this one. Gently! Okay, now cover it. You gotta learn this stuff, Adam. Knowing how to look after the grapevines will mean you can put food on the table for your own family someday. Unless you'd rather sit around the churchyard every morning hoping to be picked up for day labour and bust your back for a pengo or two. Look at me. I'm looking after grapes for almost every goddam farmer in Elek now. Because I do a good job," he paused as they finished and moved to the next vine.

"And that's why they give the work to your ol' man," the tirade continued. "And it's not just the grapes. You gotta know how to harvest the wheat. You're getting pretty good at tying the bales, but you gotta learn to do the scything too. If Geisler didn't trust me to do his wheat faster than any of the other guys in town and waste less, nobody would be dropping off those bags of wheat at the gate. Those are payment for doing a good job of the wheat harvest and that's the only reason we got enough flour all year long. And then you gotta know how to harvest corn properly, so you can get jobs doing that and get them bags of cobs for the stove." Another pause as they moved to the next vine.

"If those lazy farmers knew how to do any of the goddam work themselves, there wouldn't be any work for the rest of us. They got all the land, make all the money, and we do all the work. All the work that makes them all the money they spend on their fancy teams of horses and their fancy houses. And all they pay us is a few pengoes."

As they finished the last vine in the row, his dad finally stopped talking, standing up straight to stretch his back.

"Okay, I'll finish up this section. Faster on my own anyway. You go round up those geese and take them home. But take 'em over to the pond for a swim first."

Hooray! thought Adam.

"Quack, quack," he said in his best goose imitation a few minutes later as he approached the flock in the nearby field where they were feeding happily on wheat that had fallen during the harvest over the past few weeks. "Quack, quack, quack, quack," he continued. A few geese looked up at him. He started to back away, continuing to call them. Slowly he led the flock into town to the pond. From the bank he watched them splash around and preen themselves, a piece of dry grass sticking out of his mouth. Another month and they'd be stuck in their pens, hardly able to move, and he'd be shoving food down their necks with his fingers and tying their throats shut with a piece of corn husk to fatten them up for Christmas.

"Adam wants to show you something in the back yard before we sit down to eat," he heard his mom say from the porch an hour later.

He was standing in front of the rabbit cages when his dad came into the back yard with his mom trailing behind. The two mother rabbits sat quietly munching the grass he'd stuffed in with them in the other cage where he'd moved them temporarily so that his dad would have a clear view of the babies.

"Look," he said, pointing into the cage where the babies lay crowded together. "Look at how many grey babies there are. I've never had any grey babies before. And look at their ears." He couldn't help grinning as he waited for his dad to see that he'd been telling the truth.

His dad peered silently into the cage for a long moment, then turned and walked through to the front yard. Adam and his mom looked at each other, confused. Adam hastily closed and latched the cage, then rushed after his dad. As he stood at the front gate and watched, his dad turned into the Haas yard. A moment later, Adam heard his father's booming voice.

"Haas!"

George Baumann was a man firmly entrenched in a world where the man of the house reigned supreme and children obeyed without question.

Thus, Adam's mischievous nature was difficult for him. Perhaps that was why he had believed Haas over his son six weeks earlier. But the unshakeable belief in justice and truth with which Adam had been born had led him to stand his ground those six weeks, and that afternoon it had paid off. His dad had defended him to Haas, and all was right with the world.

CHAPTER FIFTEEN

Summer 1939

When he squinted a little bit, he could see them. He was sure of it. A thin line there on the horizon.

Adam was sitting on the front steps. His dad was already gone to the vineyards, and his mom was working quietly in the garden. Everyone else was still sleeping. The sun hadn't been up long enough to burn off the morning freshness.

They'd learned about the Carpathian Mountains towards the end of grade four, and he was sure he could see them in the distance on clear days like today. He sat a little longer, enjoying the sun on his face.

"You should probably get to your chores," his mom called out quietly from where she was kneeling between the rows of peas.

"Ya, I know," he replied, slowly getting to his feet. What he dreaded more than the chores was having to go to the church after breakfast for altar boy rehearsal.

Right from the start, Adam had told the priest that he really didn't want to be an altar boy. He'd explained it to his mom and dad too. He didn't want to wear that white dress and look like a girl, and he didn't want to ring the stupid bell or do any of the other stupid things the Father was trying to get him to do. There were plenty of boys who did want to do it and he wasn't one of them. Ever since his First Communion last year, he'd been trying to get out of being an altar boy. And here it was, Saturday, and he had had to spend half the day at it, practicing the special mass for the annual Church Festival the following weekend.

He wished he'd never done that stupid First Communion. The priest had talked to his parents after the ceremony and said how nice it would be to have a tall altar boy like Adam and they'd agreed.

But, then, if he hadn't done his First Communion, he wouldn't have his gold watch. He'd thought a lot about who to ask to be his sponsor. He'd known Martin a long time and the Mahlers were rich, which meant he'd probably get Adam a really good First Communion gift. And his mom had said that Martin would be really proud to be asked. It had turned out perfectly. Martin was proud. And Adam had received a beautiful gold watch. He kept it on a shelf by his bed, wrapped in the soft cloth and case that it had come in. Each night before bed, he wound it gingerly, then carefully rewrapped it and placed it back on the shelf. Someday he'd wear it in his pocket and pull it out to have a look any time he wanted.

The priest made them go through the mass three times that day to make sure they knew when to ring the stupid bells and when to say "Amen" and all that Latin stuff. They were finally done, and the other boys had gone. It was Adam's turn to put the robes away. As he carried the pile into the side room where they had to be folded up and put into the drawers, Adam's eyes lit on a jug of wine sitting on a little table near the door. He'd been repeating all that Latin nonsense for hours and he was thirsty. He glanced around. The priest was nowhere to be seen. Wait until the guys heard about this! Dropping the armful of robes on the floor, Adam went over to the jug and pulled out the big cork. Grabbing the wicker handles, he lifted the heavy bottle to his lips. Just as he felt the cool, sweet wine pouring down his dry throat, Adam heard a gasp.

"How dare you?" demanded the priest from a small doorway on the opposite side of the room.

Startled, Adam dropped the bottle back onto the table with a thud. The priest was charging towards him, his eyes bulging in rage.

"That is the blood of Christ!" the priest yelled as Adam fled out the door he'd come in through. Adam glanced over his shoulder as he leapt down the steps at the front of the stage. The priest was right behind him! He felt his heel catch on the bottom step, and with a crash he was on the floor in front of the first pew. Scrambling, he tried desperately to get away, but in an instant, the priest was on him, pinning him to the floor.

"An outrage! You have sullied the sacramental wine!" The priest twisted around to reach for something as he kneeled on Adam with his full weight. The next thing Adam saw out of the corner of his eye was the priest's arm raised in the air, a shoe clenched in his hand.

Whack! Adam felt the sting of the shoe on his backside. *Whack! Whack! Whack!*

The priest was stronger than he looked, that was for sure. Adam couldn't move, and as he struggled to get his breath, the beating continued.

"I will beat you within an inch of your life! And that is nothing compared to the punishment you will receive from God," the priest sputtered, out of breath from the exertion.

Whack! Whack! The blows continued to rain down. Finally, the priest gave one last W*hack!* with his shoe and pushed himself off of Adam, stumbling to his feet, winded.

"Get out of my church and do not come back until you are ready to confess. You are not fit to be an altar boy and I am sick of trying to train you. You are a disgrace."

Adam got up clumsily and limped to the side door as fast as he could, not looking back. Disregarding the stinging of his backside and legs, he ran awkwardly across the church yard, and down the street to the corner. Only when he was out of sight of the church did he stop and lean on a tree to catch his breath. Reaching back tentatively, he touched his backside. Owwww!

Slowly, as Adam caught his breath, the stinging dulled to an ache. The priest had said he wasn't fit to be an altar boy! Hooray! Adam stood up straight and grinned. That was worth several beatings. And he wouldn't have to be in the special mass next weekend. Adam began to whistle as he headed for home, limping only slightly.

CHAPTER SIXTEEN

September 2, 1939

Summers were always the busiest time in the fields but being excused from being an altar boy gave Adam a little extra time. He spent it practicing the harmonica his Uncle Florian had brought for him a few months back. He'd loved the little mouth organ immediately. By the end of the first day he'd been able to play the simple tune his uncle had shown him. Uncle Florian had cheered. Little Anni had clapped hard and squealed for more. His dad hadn't been impressed, though. Said Adam needed to spend that much effort learning more important things. Since that day Adam had learned many songs, practicing quietly, hidden high up in the cherry tree out back where no one could find him.

That afternoon he'd come down from the tree early. He had to fetch the radio batteries before supper, and he wanted to pick a bag of mulberry leaves first. Herr Schmidt had hatched a large batch of silkworms and he would pay for the leaves to feed to them. The school year was starting soon and pencils and books cost money, even more this year with little George starting first grade. His mom would be grateful for a few extra coins.

That evening, a hush fell over the room as it always did when Hitler came on the air. The men inched closer to the radio, listening to the impassioned words.

"For months, a problem has tormented all of us. Long ago the Diktat of Versailles bestowed this problem on us. In its depravity and degeneracy it has now become insufferable. Danzig was a German city and is a German city! The Corridor was German and is German! These regions owe their cultural development exclusively to the German Volk. Without this Volk, these eastern regions would still be plunged in the depths of barbarism.

"Danzig was torn from us! Poland annexed the Corridor! The German minorities living there are being persecuted in the vilest manner imaginable."

"Polish bastards," Adam's dad said over the radio. The other men murmured their agreement and then quietened back down to listen.

"I am wrongly judged if my love for peace and my patience are mistaken for weakness or even cowardice! Last night I informed the British Government that, under the circumstances, I no longer see any willingness by the Polish Government to enter into serious negotiations with us. And thus all attempts at mediation must be considered to have failed. For we had indeed received a response to our proposals which consisted of: 1. general mobilization in Poland and 2. renewed, heinous atrocities. I have therefore resolved to speak to Poland in the same language that Poland has employed towards us in the months past.

"I have solemnly assured the Western states, and I repeat this here, that we desire nothing of them. We shall never demand anything of them. I have assured them that the border separating France and Germany is a final one. Time and time again I have offered friendship, and if necessary close cooperation, to England. But love cannot remain a one-sided affair. It must be met by the other side.

"Germany is not pursuing any interests in the West. The West Wall delineates the Reich's border for all time. Our ambitions for the future are no different. And nothing shall ever change the Reich's standpoint in this matter."

Adam's dad got up and filled his glass from the wine jug on the table and passed the jug to the guy beside him.

"I am happy to be able to inform you of a special development at this point. You know that two different doctrines govern Russia and Germany. There remained but one question to be resolved: as Germany has no intent of exporting its doctrine, and at the moment, that Soviet Russia no longer contemplates exporting its doctrine to Germany, I no longer see any compelling reason why we should continue to take opposing stances. Both of us are aware that any struggle between our two peoples would merely benefit third parties. Hence, we have determined to enter into a pact which shall preclude the application of force between us for all time.

"And of one thing I would like to assure all of you here today: this decision signals a fundamental change for the future and is a final one! I believe the entire German Volk welcomes this political resolve. Russia and Germany fought each other in the World War only to suffer its consequences equally in the end. This shall not happen a second time! Yesterday in Moscow and Berlin, the Non-Aggression and Mutual Assistance Pact-which had originally entered into force upon signature-was accorded final ratification. In Moscow this pact was as warmly welcomed as you welcomed it here. I second every word of the Russian Foreign Commissar Molotov's speech."

Adam watched as this news was met with raised eyebrows and murmurs of surprise.

"Smart move. Too many goddam Russians to fight anyway. Leave 'em to freeze, I say," his dad said to the general agreement from his friends.

"Meanwhile I am equally determined to wage this war until the present Polish Government judges it opportune to assent to these changes, or another Polish Government shall be willing to do so.

"I will cleanse Germany's borders of this element of insecurity, this civil-war-like circumstance. I will take care that our border in the East enjoys the same peace as along any other of our borders.

"This night, for the first time, Polish regular soldiers fired on our own territory. We have now been returning the fire since 5:45 a.m.! Henceforth, bomb will be met with bomb."

"Give 'em what they deserve!" Adam heard one of the men say, from where he stood in the kitchen doorway listening to the broadcast.

"For over six years I have worked on the rearmament of the German defence force. I have spent over 90 billion on rearmament. Today our military is among the best-equipped in the entire world. It completely defies comparison to that of 1914! My confidence in it is unshakeable!"

"Germany is great again!" one of the men called out, to the cheers of the others.

"When I call on this defence force, and when I now demand sacrifice from the German Volk, even the ultimate sacrifice should there be need, then it is because I have a right to do this, because today I am as willing as I was before to make any personal sacrifice. I am asking of no German man more than I myself was ready to do through four years! Germans should not be asked to make any sacrifices I myself would not make without an instant's hesitation! I now wish to be nothing other than the first soldier of the German Reich.

"I expect of all of you as the Reich's emissaries henceforth that you shall do your duty wherever you may be assigned! You must carry the banner of resistance forth regardless of the cost.

"I expect every German woman to integrate herself into the great community-in-struggle in an exemplary fashion and with iron discipline! It goes without saying that the German youth will fulfill, with a radiant heart, the tasks the nation, the National Socialist state, expects and demands of it. Provided all of us form part of this community, sworn together, determined never to capitulate, then our will shall master all need."

The speech wrapped up a few minutes later, and the sound of trumpets filled the kitchen as a marching song came on the air. Adam moved in a little closer to hear the music as the men discussed what they'd heard. As he listened, he mulled over the speech. He could almost picture the soldiers in their fancy uniforms, marching to the drumbeat with their guns on their shoulders. Imagine climbing the Carpathians and marching all the way to Poland!

CHAPTER SEVENTEEN

Adam sat on the school steps with Franz and Stumpf a couple of weeks later, munching his lunch. "Let's get the fort finished tomorrow. Can you guys make it in the afternoon?"

"Where are you going? Can I come, Adam?" little Johann Zeidler said from where he'd been standing by himself watching the groups of kids playing in the yard. Johann had moved into Elek last year and even though he looked younger because of his size, he was in the grade five class with Adam and Stumpf.

Adam looked at Franz and Tony. They shrugged.

"I guess so. BUT... " Adam lowered his voice, "you can't tell a soul. I'm serious. No one but us three know about this, and you'll be the fourth and the only other one we'll let in. You got that?"

"You bet!" Johann beamed at the three taller boys and moved in closer.

"Okay, here's the plan," Adam continued in his hushed voice and the four closely shaven heads drew closer together in a circle. "Let's meet around two to work on the fort. Then we should have a little party to celebrate. I'll bring some bread. What can everyone bring?"

The hushed conversation continued until the bell signalled that it was time to go back to class.

"Hi, guys," Adam greeted his friends the next afternoon at the edge of the pond. Inside his shirt he held the end of the loaf that was left over from last week, and a little round loaf. It was still warm. Every Saturday when she baked bread, his mom made a miniature round loaf for each of the kids, for their lunch. "You didn't tell anyone where you were going, did you, Johann?"

"Nope, and I got us a smoke!" Johann announced with a proud smile, pulling his hand out of his pocket and opening it to reveal a hand-rolled cigarette and a couple of wooden matches.

"Good work!" Adam congratulated Johann with a slap on the

smaller boy's back, as Franz grinned and held open the bag he was carrying. Adam stuck his head in over top of the other boys. It contained a big pile of cherries that his friend must have stolen from the orchard beside his house, and the bottle of wine they'd siphoned out of Franz's dad's wine barrels yesterday after school.

"How about you, Stumpf? Any loot?" Adam interrupted amiably as the other two exclaimed over the wine stashed in the bag of cherries.

Tony produced a chunk of salami from inside his shirt and grinned.

"I hope your dad didn't see you take that. He might throw us all in jail." Adam grinned, and then turned his attention to more serious matters. "Okay, let's go. Quickly while there's no one in the road."

Adam glanced around, then knelt down and crawled gingerly between the tall reeds. "Careful," he cautioned the others over his shoulder. "Don't break any reeds. We don't want to leave a trail. The entrance has to be invisible!"

This end of the pond was the shallowest and always dried up late in the summer. The reeds were perfect for a fort, almost twice as tall as the boys. Last weekend they'd cleared out a nice big patch near the back of the pond, away from the street, and stacked the cut reeds in a pile in the clearing.

"Let's weave the biggest reeds together with some of the smaller ones like this for a roof," Adam began laying out tall reeds and demonstrated what he had in mind. "And we can make some little mats to sit on . . . "

The boys set their party supplies aside and got to work.

"Pretty nice!" said Franz a couple of hours later, surveying their work from where he was sitting. Sheltered under their new roof, the boys had arranged their goodies on a square mat made from reeds in the middle of the clearing, and were sitting around it on their new seats, munching dry bread and salami.

Adam pulled his mouth organ out of his pocket. "A song to officially open the fort!" he announced and began quietly playing the latest tune he'd been practicing. As he finished, his friends rewarded him with a round of applause and he stood to take a bow.

"And now, how about some wine and a smoke?" Adam's suggestion was met with enthusiasm. As Franz passed the wine and each boy took a swig, Johann handed Adam the cigarette.

"Here, Adam, you light it."

"Sure," said Adam and stuck the cigarette into his mouth as casually as he could while Johann flicked the end of a match with his fingernail a few times until it lit. Reaching his head forward to stick the cigarette into the flame, Adam sucked in and started to cough as he held the burning cigarette out to Franz. Soon all four boys were coughing and laughing at each other.

"My brother says he's going to join the German Army next year after his birthday," Franz said between coughing fits. "He wants to help Germany conquer Poland."

"Really? Wow," said Adam. "I'd love to march in the army. Oom, pah, pah, oom, pah, pah," he stood up and pretended to march, swinging his arms and legs as he made trumpet sounds. "And get to see mountains and rivers and other countries."

"Ya, but we have to go to grade eight now instead of grade six, so we can't go for a long time yet," said Johann as he passed the wine jug to Tony.

"We won't be old enough until way after grade eight, you dummy!" Adam laughed, punching Johann in the shoulder.

"I know that! I meant . . . never mind, just give me that smoke," Johann said, holding out his hand to Adam, who had taken another drag and started coughing again.

Adam's dad hadn't been happy when it was announced last year that mandatory school was increased to Grade 8. He only had a few grades of schooling himself and thought that more than six years was a waste of time.

"My dad told me we're learning proper German now because Hitler wants all of the Germans to be one country again and be the most powerful country in the world," said Franz. On the first day of school, the new teacher, Mr. Post, had explained that they would be studying German for an hour every day, learning to speak properly like they did in Germany, and learning to write in German.

"What do you guys think of Post?" Adam asked when his coughing subsided. They'd been in school for a few weeks already, and Mr. Post hadn't caned Adam yet or sent him to the principal.

"He's way better than Tihanyi, that's for sure!" said Stumpf.

"Yep, he's a lot smarter than Tihanyi," agreed Adam.

"Who isn't?" said Franz, and the boys laughed.

Soon, food, wine, and smoke all gone, it was time to head home for chores. Carefully, the boys exited the way they'd come, covering the entrance with fresh reeds before going their separate ways.

CHAPTER EIGHTEEN

October 6, 1939

"It was a fateful hour, on the first of September of this year, when you met here as representatives of the German people. I had to inform you then of serious decisions which had been forced upon us as a result of the intransigent and provocative action of a certain State."

They'd spent the day helping the Kellers butcher their pigs, and now the adults were sitting around the radio in the Kellers' kitchen. Adam and the other kids were listening quietly from the doorway.

"Since then five weeks have gone by. I have asked you to come here today in order to give you an account of what has passed, the necessary insight into what is happening at present and, so far as that is possible, into the future as well.

"For the last two days, our towns and villages have been decorated with flags and symbols of the new Reich. Bells are ringing to celebrate a great victory, which, of its kind, is unique in history. A State of no less than 36,000,000 inhabitants, with an army of almost 50 infantry and cavalry divisions, took up arms against us. Their arms were far-reaching, their confidence in their ability to crush Germany knew no bounds.

"After one week of fighting there could no longer be any doubt as to the outcome. Whenever Polish troops met German units, they were driven back or dispersed. Poland's ambitious strategy for a great offensive against the territory of the Reich collapsed within the first 48 hours of the campaign. Death-defying in attack, advancing at an unconquerable rate of progress, infantry, armoured detachments, air force and units of the navy were soon dictating the course of events.

"They were masters of the situation throughout the campaign. In a fortnight's time the major part of the Polish Army was either scattered, captured, or surrounded. In the meantime, however, the German Army had covered distances and occupied regions which twenty-five years ago would have taken over fourteen months to conquer."

Cheers broke out and people shushed each other as Hitler continued speaking.

"Even though a number of peculiarly gifted newspaper strategists in other parts of the world attempted to describe the pace at which this campaign progressed as not coming up to Germany's expectations, we ourselves all know that in all history there has scarcely been a comparable military achievement."

Adam's mom looked over to where little Anni had fallen asleep in the corner of the room and rose quietly to pick her up. After murmuring something to his dad and saying a quiet goodnight to Mrs. Keller, she motioned for Adam, Theresa, and George to follow her out the front door.

A couple of hours later, Adam's mom peered into the darkness towards the street from her seat on the porch. "What's that ruckus?" she asked no one in particular. Anni was tucked in her cot sleeping peacefully, and Theresa and George had gone to bed as well. The days were getting short and it was too dark to do any more mending, but his mom was waiting up for his dad who had stayed behind to listen to the rest of the radio broadcast. Adam was sitting on the steps with his arm around Kave, enjoying the quiet time with his mom and his dog. As they listened, laughter mixed with Romanian curse words, drifted from the street. Adam could make out two or three jovial male voices. A moment later they came into view.

"Open the gate, Anna! We've got a package for you," Herr Keller called out in a slurred voice and then burst into laughter along with Herr Hoffman who was stumbling along beside him. Herr Keller was straining slightly with the weight of the heavy wheelbarrow he was navigating towards their gate, and Adam's mom jumped up to pull the gate open and let the men through with their load.

"What's going on?" his mom exclaimed as she peered at the contents of the wheelbarrow. "George, what's wrong?"

With a sudden heave, Herr Keller dumped the wheelbarrow into the dirt at the bottom of the steps.

"Umph. Goddammit, Keller," his dad slurred as he struggled to sit up from where he'd been dumped.

"Here's the sausage master," Herr Keller chortled. "Home, safe and sound."

The three men laughed.

Adam felt the blood rise in his ears. How dare they treat his dad like that? He was tougher than both of them! Adam's mom stooped down beside her husband.

"Are you okay, George?" she asked as the two standing men continued to laugh down at their dusty friend on the ground.

"We're winning the war, Anna," his father mumbled up at his mom with a silly grin.

Herr Hoffman reached out a foot and nudged his drunken friend. It was too much for Adam. This was wrong! He flew down the steps and struck Herr Hoffman in the chest. The inebriated man stumbled backwards a couple of steps with a look of surprised amusement on his face.

"Stop it right now!" Adam yelled as he pummelled his dad's friend with his small fists. "You too!" Adam turned and struck out at Herr Keller, who was still holding the wheelbarrow.

Kave started barking at Adam's side.

"Now, son," Herr Keller dropped the wheelbarrow handles and tried in vain to grab Adam's flailing fists.

"You should respect my dad! You can't treat him like that!" Adam yelled over Kave's barking, an angry sob catching in his throat as he continued to throw punches at the two men.

"Adam, that's enough. Stop now," his mom's voice broke through his anger and he dropped his arms to his side, glowering at the men.

"Thas m'boy Adam," his dad slurred from the ground. "You should hear 'im play mouth organ. Learned in a day."

What? thought Adam, as he stood there catching his breath, still scowling at the two men. *He'd never heard his dad sound proud of his harmonica playing before.*

"I think you two had best go home," his mom said firmly to the two men.

Herr Keller grabbed the wheelbarrow handles and pulled it awkwardly back through the gate and onto the street, stumbling after his friend.

"Adam, grab his other arm. Let's get him in the house."

As the two of them strained with the weight of his dad, the merriment resumed out in the street, and then faded as the two happy drunks staggered away.

"Can you stand up, Dad?" Adam asked, his voice filled with concern.

As Adam and his mom lifted with all their strength, his dad grunted and lurched to his feet, leaning heavily on them. Slowly the threesome made their way up the front steps and into the house, where Theresa and little George had been watching in wide-eyed silence from the front door. Now they scurried backwards, out of the way.

"Let's lay him on the bed," panted Adam's mom. "Quietly, so Anni doesn't wake."

As they reached the edge of the bed, his dad sat down heavily and fell sideways. He grinned up at Adam and tried to focus as his wife lifted his legs on the bed so he could lie down properly.

"Thanks for looking after your ol' man, Adam. You showed 'em. You're a good boy," his voice trailed off as his eyes closed.

Adam and his mom left him there and went into the kitchen where Theresa and little George were sitting quietly with Kave.

"It's okay, kids. Your father just had too much schnapps. Some men do that all the time. We're lucky your dad isn't one of those. Time for bed now."

The next morning, his dad had already left for the vineyards when Adam got up. Adam noticed that he wasn't as short tempered as usual the next evening when he spoke to Adam, and that he went to bed earlier than normal. Other than that, life went on as usual, for the time being.

CHAPTER NINETEEN

As Hitler's war progressed through its first full year and into a second, Adam's parents and their friends continued to gather around the radio, listening to the Führer's impassioned speeches that detailed his heroic successes at defending Germany from the injustices being dealt from all sides. Hungary was joining what was being called the Axis, bringing the war close to home. Elek and the other German towns in the area had always felt isolated from the rest of the world, but with Germany sending regular envoys to make speeches in the town square every month or two, their emotional ties with the motherland felt stronger than ever. Passion and enthusiasm for the cause continued to grow. A local chapter of the Hitler Youth had even started up in Elek, and Adam had his very own brown shirt, almost like a soldier's uniform, to wear to the meetings.

When the war had been raging for almost two years, longer than anyone had expected, Hitler announced that the alliance with the Soviet Union was dead, and that German troops were poised for attack from East Prussia to the Carpathians, up and down the banks of the Pruth River, and from the lower Danube to the Black Sea. The kitchens of Elek were filled with animated discussions about the strategy and tactics. Then Hitler ordered Hungary to participate in the invasion. The numbers of Elek boys leaving to fight swelled. Adam and his friends watched in fascination when soldiers arrived home on furlough, fantasizing what it would be like going away, seeing the Russians up close, wearing a smart uniform and owning a gun and a pair of shiny boots.

With several teachers among those who had gone away to war, the school was feeling the impact too. The teachers who hadn't gone circulated between classes, teaching several grades at once. Adam had a good relationship with the new teacher, Mr. Post. In their interactions, he felt a mutual respect he hadn't experienced with other adults, and certainly not at school. His grades had been improving steadily, until he was at or near the top of the class in every subject. After a time, Mr. Post assigned Adam, together with the top girl in the class, to be his monitors, watching over their classmates while he juggled the heavy workload. Adam's new-found authority suited him well.

Grade six would be finished in a couple of weeks. Adam had taken up his usual post at the top of the school steps, where he could look down into the schoolyard and keep an eye on things over the recess break. He was watching some boys play tag in the warm sunshine, thinking about how much he wasn't looking forward to being out in the fields with his dad all summer, when a small group in the corner of the yard caught his eye. Two of the bigger boys in the class were following Otto Metzla around, poking him and mimicking his limp. Adam's eyes narrowed in anger. Metzla had been born with one leg shorter than the other. He already had it harder than the rest of them. They should all be looking out for him, not bullying him.

"Hey, Joe!" Adam called out.

His friend, Joe, was still shorter than him, and still stocky like when they were in kindergarten, but now he was strong. When Mr. Post had put Adam in charge, he had explained to Joe that he might need some help now and then, keeping the kids in line.

Joe turned from where he'd been talking to another kid and trotted over to Adam.

"There's two guys by the fence over there, following Metzla around. I want you to go and give them each a smack and tell them to mind their own business, okay?"

Without a moment's hesitation Joe agreed, turning in the direction Adam had pointed.

Adam watched as Joe approached the trio, and dutifully smacked each of the bullies across the side of the head. As Joe returned to what he'd been doing, the two bullies threw a scowl in Adam's direction and then turned and walked away from Otto. Otto headed over to Adam.

"Thanks, Adam," Otto said with a big smile.

Adam returned the boy's smile. "No problem, Metzla. Don't mention it."

CHAPTER TWENTY

Summer 1941

Kneeling between the rows of grapevines beside his father, Adam slapped at a mosquito, and wiped the sweat from his forehead. Summer was almost over, and as usual, it had been wasted. Too much time in the vineyards, missing out on whatever fun Franz and Stumpf were getting up to.

"I don't know why you need another two goddam years of schooling," his dad cussed for the hundredth time, as he carefully snipped a small green shoot off of the vine he was holding.

Each kid had to choose between the academic school or the trade school for grade seven and eight. His dad had decided Adam would go to the trade school. If his kids had to spend another two years in school, they might as well learn some practical stuff. Even so, Adam was relieved to have two more years at school.

As they sweated in the afternoon sun, his dad was explaining how to prune the grapes *again*. They'd been out here since the cool of the early morning, snipping off dead bits and suckers, and cutting back the vines where they needed to be cut back to get the most growth next season. He'd heard all this so many times. This was one of the bigger vineyards in Elek. They'd already covered a lot of ground this morning, and he'd be expected to stay out here until supper, that day and every day until school restarted. Adam looked up at the sun, directly overhead. Stumpf and Franz were probably cooling off in the pond.

"Now watch," his dad said as he pulled the carefully sharpened cutter from its slot in his tool box. Every once in a while, he told Adam to try it, and then criticized him. Mostly Adam moved the basket and tools along and picked up the bits that his dad cut off and dropped as he went.

"You see this? This is a sucker. You need to cut it off or it's going to take too much of the vine's energy and there won't be as many grapes next year," his dad droned on while he demonstrated for the millionth time.

Adam's mind drifted to the fort. They'd built it on the same spot again this year. No one knew about it other than him, Franz, and Stumpf, since Johann had moved away. A lot of the lickings he'd had over the summer were for getting home late. It was easy to lose track of time at the fort once he finally escaped his dad for the day, discussing the latest they'd heard on the radio about the war, or from their parents.

"Adam, are you even watching? Concentrate!" his dad bellowed, jerking Adam's thoughts back to the neat rows of vines.

"Yes, Dad. You look for a small shoot coming out of where the branch splits, and trim it off carefully and make sure you don't nick the main vine, and . . . ," Adam parroted, unable to suppress the boredom in his tone, though he knew full well it would anger his dad even more.

"Okay, smart ass, you do this row then, and show me what you've learned. And move fast 'cause you got another ten rows to do before we quit!" his father demanded, thrusting the cutter at his son.

Adam moved sullenly to the next vine and began examining it. *Who cares how to cut back the stupid grapes?* he thought again.

"You gotta learn how to do this work properly. There's a lot of vineyards left to do between now and when the snow flies. How the hell are you going to be any help to me if you can't do it right? You think it's okay to do a half-assed job? You're already 12, 13 after Christmas. You'll be the man of this family someday. How are you going to take over these vineyards? You have to show the owners that you can do good work. You have to prove that they can trust you to do it better than the other guys, like they trust me! How do you think I got all of these jobs?"

His dad stopped ranting and came over to peer over Adam's shoulder as he prepared to snip. Maybe he'd get it right and his dad would be pleased with him for a change. He should have watched more closely when his dad showed him.

"NOT THAT ONE! That's the best new shoot for next year, you idiot! You weren't watching! You're never going to learn to do it right because you think you're too good! Damn it all, get the hell outta here! I'll do it myself. Go home and finish digging the potatoes. It better be done by the time I get there and if I find one potato left in that garden, so help me!"

Throwing the cutter angrily to the ground, Adam turned to go and stumbled as his father's boot connected with his backside. Regaining his balance, he held his head up and strode away as his father turned his attention back to the vine, muttering angrily.

Reaching the end of the row, Adam burst into an angry run towards home, thoughts racing through his mind like a broken record as he ran down the dusty street, getting as far away from his dad as he could. He was never going to take over the stupid vineyard work. And he was never going to please his father even if he did, because he'd never do it just right. And who cared anyway?! He wasn't planning on spending his life in this boring little place working for the rich farmers, even if his father thought it was such a great achievement!

Adam turned into their front yard and stopped, panting as he bent over to catch his breath, hands resting on his knees.

What's the point? I'll dig the potatoes and that won't be done right either. And when he gets home, everybody will have to listen to the tirade about everything Adam does wrong. I'll get a lickin', and if Mom speaks up, she'll get a cuff.

Adam sat on the front step stewing, stabbing at the ground with a stick. A few minutes later he snapped the stick in half and stood up.

I'm going. I'm getting out of here. I don't need him and I don't need the stupid grape vines and I don't need a job working for the stupid rich farmers.

He would get as far away from Elek as he could. He could live on his own. He could make his own rules and do what he wanted. Suddenly, he was filled with elation like he'd never felt before. His thoughts swirled as he rummaged in the kitchen. It was laundry day at the Mahlers'. His mom would have Theresa and Anni with her there. He wondered fleetingly where George was. It didn't matter as long as he didn't show up in the next five minutes. Adam hastily arranged the food he'd gathered in the centre of a cloth and tied it up. He felt his pockets for his pocketknife and his harmonica, then turned and darted out the front door and down the steps. As he turned right into the street, he began to run, his bare feet pounding the dirt, his heart soaring. Right again at the corner and he was headed towards the train station in Kétegyháza, and freedom.

As he tired, Adam slowed to a walk, his lunch sack swinging from his hand. He spotted a good stick on the side of the road and picked it up. With his lunch sack tied to the end of it, he slung the stick over his shoulder and began whistling a tune as he walked. He'd be at the train station in less than an hour. He'd go west and see the mountains. Or maybe he'd live in Budapest. Adam started to whistle, thinking through all the possibilities.

As he approached the train station, he slowed down. He definitely wanted to go west. They'd read about the Alps in school, and Mr. Post had told them about when he'd travelled through the mountains. The land around Elek was so flat and boring. The Carpathians were to the east, but then he'd be in Romania. No, he should definitely go west. He scanned the station. A passenger train was just pulling out. It was going west, but it was already moving too fast to jump on. Turning, he strolled casually over to the area where the livestock trains came and went. There were a couple of trains sitting on the tracks. One of them was facing west. Adam scanned the length of it, his eyes stopping on a car near the back. Its door was part way open!

Looking over his shoulder, he picked his way across the tracks to the open car. Sticking his head into the gap, he glanced quickly from side to side and then tossed his stick inside onto the straw. Heaving himself up, he eased through the opening, then turned and looked back out, his heart pounding. The platform and rail yard were quiet. No one had seen him. Crawling through the straw, he sat against the back wall of the empty car and didn't move for a few minutes. The straw was clean and sweet smelling. A fly buzzed in through the door opening and back out again. It was warm in the box car. The late afternoon sun was shining directly into the partway open door, adding to the heat.

Opening his sack, Adam surveyed his supplies. He was hungry from the walk. A heel of bread, two sausages, a chunk of salami, a tomato, and an onion. He pulled out his pocketknife and made himself a sandwich. Just as he started to eat, he heard the train's engine let out a belch of steam and the car jolted forward. He was on his way! Getting to his feet, Adam walked over to the opening, staggering a bit with the movement of the train and sat down heavily where he could watch out the gap. The chuffing of the engine picked up speed as the wheels clattered against the tracks underneath him. His first train ride! As they rolled along, he munched his sandwich, watching as the houses turned to fields. A refreshing breeze blew in through the opening.

The train rolled along for the rest of the evening, slowing when they passed through populated areas, then resuming its steady pace. Adam's gaze stayed fixed on the scenery rolling by. He'd never been this far from Elek. As the light began to fade, the loud clackety-clack of the wheels slowed and the locomotive came to a stop. Adam peered out the door. They seemed to be on the edge of a small village. They'd definitely been heading west, towards the sunset, but he had no idea how far they'd come. After eating another sandwich, he curled up in a corner at the back of the boxcar and stared for a long while at the strip of pale moonlight coming in the boxcar door until finally, sleep came.

A jolt awakened him. The train had inched forward. A faint light was filtering into the opening of the box car door. As he sat up, the train began to move to the accompaniment of the now familiar engine sounds and the rhythm of the wheels against the tracks. He was thirsty. He looked around the car in vain. Out the doorway, he could see the yellow light of sunrise illuminating the fields and the farmhouses they were passing. As he untied his food bundle, he looked at what was left. Just enough for breakfast. While he chewed, the scenery changed. A lot of houses, and big buildings too. Lots of big buildings. This must be Budapest. He wondered if he should get off.

The station where they stopped was noisy. Peeking out, Adam could see people everywhere. Travellers sat on benches waiting, many with suitcases on the ground beside them. Others strode in both directions along the platform and up and down the stairs at the end. A man in a uniform stood gazing around watchfully, his hands clasped behind his back. The huge clock on the wall of the building said a few minutes after eight. Adam really wished he had something to drink. But if he got off here, he'd be seen for sure, and that guy in the uniform wouldn't let him get back on. As he wondered what he should do, the train began to move again.

Mid-morning, the locomotive stopped again, this time at a tiny station. He needed to find a drink and more food. After checking that the coast was clear, he jumped off and dashed over to the road that ran parallel to the tracks. Turning in the direction the train had been travelling, he started to walk.

The first farmhouse wasn't far. Crouching down behind a sprawling tree on the roadside, Adam surveyed the yard. There was no one around. Just as he was about to make a dash for the water barrel at the edge of the garden, the front door opened. Squatting back down, he watched as a woman came out of the house and strode purposefully into the rows of vegetables. Bending over, she held aside the green tops with her hand and studied the vegetables growing under them for a moment before pulling a handful of carrots. Next, she turned and picked a couple of onions from another row, then straightened and strode back into the house. Adam remained motionless for a few more minutes, waiting. There was no further sign of activity in the yard. Counting to three under his breath, he ran into the yard. Sticking his face into the water barrel, he took three big gulps, then grabbed a fistful of carrots and an onion before dashing back to the tree. Shaking, he looked back. No movement in the yard. Quickly he wrapped his cloth around the vegetables and tied it to the stick. Standing up, he stepped back into the road and casually strolled past the house. When the house was out of sight, he pulled a carrot out of the sack, rubbed the dirt off, and bit into it.

He'd finished all of the carrots and the onion when he heard a wagon approaching from behind. Keeping his eyes facing forward, he kept walking. Would they be looking for him this far from home? The man driving the wagon didn't show any interest in him. Nothing to worry about. The sun was hot. He was still thirsty. There was no water in the ditch this late in the summer. He needed to find another farmyard.

A little while later, Adam heard the rattle of another wagon behind him. Turning, he waved and the driver slowed down beside him.

"Hello," said the driver.

"Good afternoon, sir, do you think I could jump on and catch a ride?"

"Where you going?"

Adam hesitated, then said the first thing that came to mind. "To my aunt and uncle's farm west of here to help out with the wheat harvest."

"Sure, climb on," said the farmer with a friendly grin, motioning behind him at the mostly empty wagon. He slowed the horses to a stop while Adam climbed onto the wagon and settled down with his back against the side.

"Thanks," Adam called out to the farmer an hour later as he jumped off the back of the wagon and resumed his westward march.

As the sun headed for the horizon in front of him, he pulled out his harmonica and began to play. A few songs in, he was interrupted by a steady noise coming from around the bend up ahead. He stopped dead, then ducked off the road into the trees as a huge machine came around the corner. Behind it there was a second one. They had swastikas on the side. They must be army tanks! Wow, so that was what Hitler's tanks look like, he thought to himself as he started walking again. Amazing inventions those tanks. They'd heard all about them on the radio. No other armies had them, or not very good ones anyway. He wondered how many soldiers were inside each of them. And where were they headed? Maybe they were coming from Yugoslavia where the Germans and Hungarians had won that big battle. But that was months ago. No, they were most likely heading for Russia.

The sun had almost finished setting when he came to the next farm. After quenching his thirst in the horse trough, he climbed into the loft of the barn and settled down in the soft straw, out of sight of anyone who might come out to check the animals before bed. He'd walked far enough for one day, he thought, as the first star of the night appeared in the patch of sky visible through the opening at the end of the loft.

For days, Adam walked and hitched the occasional ride, slept in barns, and raided gardens. When he couldn't stand any more raw vegetables, he knocked on doors and offered to do chores in exchange for a meal. People were quick to take pity on him when they heard that his dad had died, leaving him and his mom and baby sisters to fend for themselves and that his uncle had promised them wheat for the winter if he helped with the harvest. He mumbled when he told his story, keeping his eyes downcast.

Finally, he reached the mountains.

Adam gazed around at the little village where his last ride had dropped him off. It was nestled on a plateau with tall mountains soaring skyward to the west. To the east, back the way he'd just come, the land fell away to the plains he could see in the distance.

His mouth watered as the smell of frying onions reached him. The sun was directly overhead, the early morning hint of autumn long since burned off. He hadn't had anything since a slice of bread and jam just after sunrise. He looked around. The smell must be coming from the tavern across the street. Adam walked over and stood in front of it, hesitating a moment, then pushed open the door and walked into the dim interior. He'd never been inside a tavern before. He could smell stale beer and wine mingled with the smell of food cooking.

"What do you want, kid?" Adam jumped and squinted towards where a voice barked out from behind the counter.

"Um. . . I was wondering if maybe I could do some work around here, in exchange for a meal?" Adam could see the man now, his belly protruding under a dirty apron.

"Where do you come from?" the man asked.

Adam thought for a second.

"Outside of Budapest. My parents are dead. I'm looking for a job."

The tavern keeper was quiet.

"Okay," he said a minute later. "You sweep and mop the floors and you can have lunch before the place gets busy."

Adam grinned. "Yes, sir!"

CHAPTER TWENTY-ONE

Western Hungary, Autumn 1941

As Adam sat savouring the last few bites of his pork cutlet and fried potatoes, watching the people walking by on the street outside the window, a pair of perfectly matched, fawn-coloured horses strutted into sight pulling a carriage. Their harnesses were brightly polished and their blond manes and tails were combed out and flowing. As they drew up in front of the tavern, Adam's eyes shifted to the driver climbing down from the front seat of the carriage and watched in awe as he came into the empty tavern, ducking his head to allow the feather adorning his hat to fit through.

"Good day," the man greeted the tavern keeper with a big smile as he settled onto one of the rough wooden stools at the bar, casually flicking his long red coat out behind him so as to not crush the gold embroidery. With his other hand, he removed his hat and set it on another stool, where it sat like a peacock perched next to him.

The two began to chat, but Adam couldn't make out their words. The tavern keeper poured a mug of beer from the tap on the bar as the man glanced around. Seeing Adam, the man motioned over his shoulder and directed a question at the bartender. Adam saw the barman say something and shrug his shoulders. The man took a long drink from the mug and then stood up and walked towards Adam's table, mug in one hand, hat in the other.

"May I join you?" he enquired with a small bow.

"Sure, I guess so," replied Adam, eyes wide.

"The bartender tells me you are here on your own. What's your name?"

"Adam."

"Where are you from, Adam?"

"Just a little village. Close to Budapest."

"Well, you are very brave to be travelling alone. Where are you headed?" The man took a long drink of his beer, watching Adam over the top of the mug.

"I'm just looking for work."

"Where are your mother and father?"

"They died."

"Oh, I'm sorry to hear that. Have you ever been to this part of Hungary before?"

"No sir. I was headed towards the mountains."

"Well, that's a good choice. The mountains are beautiful. I've got a house a bit further up, and a forest where I love to hunt. Are you a hunter?"

"I've never hunted before."

"What's the name of the village you're from?"

Adam hesitated. Maybe the guy was going to try to send him home. "I don't remember."

"You don't remember?" The man drained his beer and set his mug down on the table, then stood up and settled his hat onto his head. "Well, perhaps you'd like to come home with me for a few days and have some good food and some new clothes. We need a strong young man like you around the stable. What do you think?"

"Okay," said Adam, with a big smile.

"Let's go then."

Jumping to his feet, Adam followed the man towards the door.

"Good day, Count," the tavern keeper called out as they left.

Count! Holy cow! thought Adam. *I'm going to work for a nobleman.*

As they rode through town, and then along a winding road up into the foothills, Adam sat tall beside the Count. This was much nicer than what any of the rich farmers in Elek drove! Wiggling a bit on the soft padded seat, Adam inspected the details of the carriage. The dark wood of the frame gleamed, and the seats were covered with a beautiful forest green fabric, thickly padded. It felt like he was sitting on a feather pillow! Trimmed with polished brass, the carriage looked like something a king would ride in, Adam thought. His glance fell on the Count's boots. They were the most beautiful leather Adam had ever seen, stretching right up to the Count's knees. He tucked his dirty feet as far as he could under the seat. The Count kept up a steady stream of conversation, telling Adam about his family, his farm, even his horses' names. Adam found himself laughing and talking easily with his new friend as they wound their way up into the forest.

Rounding a corner, the Count slowed the carriage and steered the horses left onto a cobblestone drive and through a large wooden gate decorated with carved animals. A minute later, they emerged from the trees into a vast, manicured yard. Adam scanned left and right, taking in the Count's estate. The house looked like a picture in one of his school books, all white with fancy dark trim criss-crossing the front, and not a pebble or a blade of grass out of place anywhere in the yard. As Adam stared, they continued past the house and stopped in front of a matching building, with a horse fence attached to the side of it.

"Here's the stable, Adam," said the Count as he hung the reins in the holder in front of the seat and began to climb down. Just then a man came out of the building, nicely dressed in matching shirt and trousers. "Hello, Yoska," said the Count. "This is Adam. I met him in the village. Adam is an orphan. He's going to stay with us for a few days, and he can help you with the horses."

"Of course, Sir," said Yoska.

"Adam, why don't you climb down and help Yoska unhitch the horses and give them a rub-down and then a good brushing?"

"Yes, Sir," said Adam, scrambling off the carriage.

The shadows had lengthened when the Count returned with an armload of clothes, and a pair of shoes.

"Yoska," he called from outside the stable. Adam and Yoska were inside stabling the horses after their brushing. "Would you please light a fire and heat some water so that Adam can have a bath? I'll come back in an hour and get him. He's going to have supper with us tonight." He smiled warmly at Adam. "Once you're cleaned up, see if these fit you."

Sitting on a bale of hay after his bath, waiting for the Count to return, Adam chewed on a piece of hay and admired the beautiful horses he'd brushed earlier. Then he admired his clothes some more. They were similar to what Yoska was wearing, nice and new, and store-bought from head to toe!

"Yooohooo," a young female voice called out. "I am here to help a boy called Adam set up his bed and come in for supper."

As Adam jumped up, a pretty young woman stuck her head into the barn. "Oh, there you are. My name is Kata. Count says you can sleep in the manger at the far end. That'll be comfortable, he says. This turns into a bed," she said, holding up the end of what looked like a huge cloth bag. "See the gap here? You shove the whole thing full of straw and then you can move it wherever you want if you want to sleep somewhere different. But Count says you are to sleep right down here by this end of the manger," Kata repeated. After placing the bed thing and a blanket in the hay, she turned around and headed back towards the door. "Okay, follow me. Count says you're eating with the family, on account that you're so young."

Adam followed Kata across the cobblestones to the house.

"Come on in," she said, lifting the heavy iron latch and pushing open the tall door. Stepping across the threshold behind Kata, Adam breathed in the rich smell of roast meat. A wood fire crackled somewhere down the hall. Walking a few steps down the hall, the maid entered a room and stood formally off to the side until Adam walked in cautiously, looking around with wide eyes. Colourful draperies adorned one wall. Opposite, a rich guy on a throne gazed down from a huge painting framed in gold. A stag's head hung on the end wall. The Count was seated at the head of a thick wooden table that filled the room. A handsome woman sat at the other end, and between them was a little girl, looking at Adam through her lashes.

The Count rose when he saw Adam. "Adam, you look good! May I present my wife, and our daughter Irene."

"Hello, Adam. Welcome," the Count's wife said warmly, rising and taking both of Adam's hands in hers for a moment. "I'm so glad those clothes fit you. We had them for a young stable hand that worked here a while back. Say hello to Adam, Irene."

All eyes in the room turned expectantly to the little girl. She looked about seven or eight, close to George's age. Dwarfed in a heavy wooden chair decorated with brightly painted hearts and flowers carved into the high back, Irene smiled shyly and said hello.

"Sit here, Adam," said the Count, dragging a similar chair out from the table for Adam.

Four steaming silver pots lined the centre of the lacy tablecloth. Near the Count's plate was a roast of something. Adam's mouth watered as he gazed at the meat.

"That will be all, Kata," said the Count's wife, turning to address the maid who had been busily lighting candles and pulling the heavy draperies shut. "See you after supper."

"Yes, M'Lady," said the maid, and quietly left the room.

"Now, Adam, let me fill your plate while you tell me all about yourself," the Count's wife continued, scooping piles of mashed potatoes, shiny looking carrots, and green beans onto his plate, and then waiting while the Count sliced the meat and added some to Adam's plate before she poured gravy over top of it all.

"Yes, M'Lady," Adam mimicked the maid. "Except there's not much to tell. My parents are dead. I was looking for work in the area because I want to live close to the mountains."

"Is that a German accent?" she enquired casually.

"Ye-es," Adam replied hesitantly. Everyone he knew spoke German at home, but it had never occurred to him that he spoke Hungarian with a German accent.

"Where did you say you were from?"

"A small village outside of Budapest. My parents spoke German, but they died a long time ago. I ran away from the orphanage because they were beating me."

He'd been thinking. If they thought he was an orphan, they might try to make him live in one of those homes for orphans. Best to make them think that wasn't a good idea. As they all ate their fill, the Count and his wife chatted casually with Adam, alternating between telling him about the area, and asking him questions. Adam worried that his lies weren't all lining up, but he couldn't tell them the truth. They would send him straight home.

"You're a happy boy," Yoska commented the next morning as Adam shovelled out the horse stalls, whistling a lively tune.

"The Count and his family seem like very nice people. It's good to have steady work," Adam smiled at Yoska and continued shovelling.

With a full belly and a warm bed, he'd slept soundly, and after a hot breakfast in the dining room, the Count had confirmed he could stay for a while.

CHAPTER TWENTY-TWO

"Adam, come on out here," the Count called from outside the stable. Adam was busy cleaning the horse tackle, washing the sweat and grime off and then greasing the leather parts and shining the silver buckles with some special stuff that Yoska showed him. The Count had been out touring his property and meeting with his tenants several times in the week since Adam had arrived. Each time, he'd invited Adam to come along. The Count's property was huge! When they visited a tenant, they went into the house for tea and then walked through the barns and out to the fields to check the crops. The Count knew his farms well and quizzed the farmers on the yield they were getting, and how the various livestock were doing.

Adam hung the harness on the hook where it belonged and headed out the door of the stable.

"Hello, Sir," he greeted the Count.

"I don't think there's anything urgent happening out on the farms today. Let's go hunting!" the Count said, grinning from ear to ear.

"Okay!" replied Adam.

"We'll be going on some of the rough roads through the forest so we'll take the old wagon, and the black team is best for hunting. They are accustomed to gunfire and the smell of blood. Yoska can show you how to hook them up. Bring them around to the house when they're ready."

As Adam drove the wagon across the yard a few minutes later, wheels clattering on the cobblestones, the front door opened and the Count appeared. Drawing the horses to a standstill, Adam slid across to the passenger seat. The Count placed his shiny rifle into the back of the wagon before climbing up into the driver's seat. *Wow!* thought Adam. Special hunting boots with fresh black polish, and hunting clothes. No fancy gold stitching, just beautiful dark green pants and a matching jacket.

"We'll start in the field and see if we can scare up some pheasants," said the Count, flicking the reins lightly on the horses' backs. "Let's go, boys!"

"Here it is!" Adam yelled out gleefully from the field. Grabbing the dead bird by a leg and holding it up as high as he could for the Count to see, he jogged back to the edge of the field where the Count stood with the rifle over his shoulder and added the pheasant to the pile. Four! The Count was a good shot.

"Throw those into the wagon and we'll head up the road a bit. Kata would be happy with us if we brought back a hare for the stew pot," the Count said as he strode back to the wagon and stowed his gun.

"Does your dad like hunting?" the Count asked casually as Adam climbed onto the wagon, pheasants safely loaded on the back.

"I don't think anybody in . . . ," Adam stopped abruptly and looked at the Count, who was studying him closely. "I don't think there was much hunting around there. I don't remember him hunting before he died."

"Oh, that's too bad. It's a good sport," the Count said lightly, looking forward at the horses, and clicking his tongue. "Okay, fellas, let's go."

CHAPTER TWENTY-THREE

The days grew shorter and cooler, and Adam settled into a happy routine, brushing the beautiful horses until they gleamed, and keeping the stables clean and tidy the way the Count liked them. He could tell that Yoska appreciated his help, and there was always something new and interesting to do on the estate. Like climbing up the ladder to the pigeon cages in the loft above the cattle barn to look for baby pigeons for the soup that Kata sometimes made for supper. She needed at least four to make enough soup for the four of them and explained how to tell if the babies were the right size. Not yet flying but almost ready to learn. She called them squabs. The Count kept his partridges in another building closer to the house. They were just for show.

Most afternoons, after Adam had done some work in the stables or mucked out the cattle barn or pigsty, the Count came looking for him. Soon Adam knew the tenants by name and understood which ones the Count trusted to produce efficiently and which ones needed to be watched more closely and checked on more often. He learned how to sneak up on a flock of pheasants hiding in the tall grass and flush them out at just the right time when the Count had the rifle aimed above them so he could get in the most shots. And he developed a good sense for how to circle a deer and get it to turn its head without bolting so that the Count could get a clear shot. Once a week they went into the village, where Adam sat proudly in the carriage, watching the horses while the Count completed his business at the bank, the post office, and whatever other stops he needed to make.

One morning, Adam was greeted by a skiff of snow as he came out of the stable. A sudden wave of homesickness washed over him. Less than a month until Christmas, he thought to himself as he slowly headed towards the house for breakfast. What did his mom think had happened to him when he'd disappeared? Guiltily, he wondered how George and Theresa were coping with the chores.

After breakfast, Adam harnessed the fawn-coloured team to the fancy carriage. It was Sunday. The Count and his family would spend the morning at church, and the rest of the day visiting friends. He couldn't get his mom off his mind. In a couple of weeks, she would make cookies to hang on the Christmas bough. And by now she would have made presents for each of them. Last year she'd sewn him two new shirts from some coloured fabric she got at the Jewish store. She wouldn't need to make him a present this year. Tears welled up in Adam's eyes.

When the rattle of the carriage had faded away down the drive, Adam loaded up the wheelbarrow with firewood and headed for the house. After piling the wood neatly in the box beside the big stone fireplace and sweeping up the bits that had dropped on the floor, he stopped and listened. Silence. Kata normally left and visited her family on Sundays, so he was pretty sure the house was empty. Walking softly, he headed down the hallway in the opposite direction of the front door. The library, where the Count had his writing desk was the third door on the right. He'd called Adam in there once to show him the big map he had on the wall to see if it would help Adam remember the village he came from.

Adam pushed the door open slowly and peeked inside. The eyes of the mounted deer heads and stuffed birds that decorated the walls stared back at him. As he tiptoed over to the desk, he spotted the writing paper immediately. Good. He'd need a pen too. The only one he could find was a very fancy fountain pen. It would be better to write the letter here, so he didn't have to come back in and return the pen. It didn't need to be very long, he thought, sitting down. He just wanted to tell his mom he was okay and say Merry Christmas.

When he'd finished, he folded the sheet of paper neatly and slid it into an envelope that he pulled from one of the small shelves lining the front of the Count's massive wooden desk, then wrote the address across the front: BAUMANN, 12 GRAPE STREET, ELEK. He pushed back the big leather chair and stood up. There were stamps next to the writing paper. He'd sneak the letter into the mail box on their next trip into town.

A week and a half later, Adam's dad knocked on the door of the manor.

CHAPTER TWENTY-FOUR

Adam's dad had arrived during supper. Gracious as always, the Count and Countess had welcomed him to the table and filled a plate for him. Adam stared down at his own plate as the adults began a stilted conversation. Talk flowed more easily as they ate and drank. Every so often, Adam glanced across at his dad apprehensively, wondering what his punishment for running away would be. Oddly, his dad seemed more relieved than angry. God, how he missed his mom. He didn't want to go home though. At the Count's estate he did new, exciting things every day. The Count praised him for his work and his help when they hunted. And he hadn't been spanked even once.

While he sat watching his dad out of the corner of his eye, the adults discussed how different the countryside was where the Baumanns were from. So much flatter than here. The Count explained that they were in the foothills of the Alps, close to the border with Austria. His dad told them about his work looking after all of the vineyards in Elek. As the mood became more relaxed, the Count asked about the Baumann family. Adam was quiet. He knew the Count was trying to understand why he'd run away and stayed away so long. He'd told so many lies to the Count, and now he'd never have a chance to explain.

"Adam, it's a bit naughty of you to have pretended to be an orphan, don't you think?" the Count asked as they neared the end of the meal. Adam looked at him. He was trying to sound stern but there was a twinkle in his eye.

"Yes, Sir," Adam replied, looking down at his plate.

"I can't imagine the worry you've caused your family," said the Countess in a very serious tone.

"I know, M'Lady. That's why I wrote the letter," he answered quietly.

"Well, I'd like to make a toast to the resurrection of Adam's family," interjected the Count, lightening the mood back up.

"Hear, hear," said his wife.

"Hear, hear," echoed Adam's dad quietly.

"Will you have some pie and clotted cream?" said the Countess, carrying the pie from the sideboard where Kata had left it for them.

"Yes, ma'am," Adam and his dad answered together. Their eyes met and they exchanged a slight smile.

"Adam's been a very good worker," said the Count. "He's been working in the stables every day, helping our master horseman, and doing many other jobs around here as well. And he's been the main groomer for my prize team of horses."

"Adam does good work when he puts his mind to it," his dad said to the Count. "He's a quick learner too. Gets straight A's in school. And he's in the Hungarian Youth Movement. This year they asked him to recite the Hungarian anthem on St. Stephen's Day. Memorized the whole thing. And he learned to play the mouth organ in a day. Played as good as anyone in Elek by the time he was eleven."

Hearing the pride in his dad's voice, Adam had a sudden urge to go home.

"Yes, he plays for us sometimes," the Count responded. "We'll miss that. And he's a smart hunter too. In fact, we got this boar just a few days ago."

His dad was quiet as the Count regaled how they'd missed the first three, and finally got a shot at the fourth one, right between the eyes as it charged at him.

"Tell him about the big buck we got before that," Adam said with a big grin when the Count had finished his story.

"Yes, that was another good day." The Count smiled a little wistfully before launching into the story. When he was done, he grinned over at Adam.

Adam's dad looked quietly back and forth between the Count and his son.

The Count's wife broke the silence. "Adam has a nice warm spot to sleep with the horses. Perhaps we could make you a bed in the porch for tonight."

"No, I'll be fine in the barn with my son," his dad answered quickly. "We'll get an early start tomorrow."

"We'll have a hot breakfast together and then I'll give you a lift to the train station," said the Count. "Let me show you to the barn then."

There was fresh snow on the ground when they drove to the station the next morning. The Count insisted on paying for their train tickets, and shortly after dawn they began their journey east, towards home. There was lots of time for conversation on the long train ride, but Adam wasn't sure what to talk about. His dad kept asking him to explain how he got all the way across the country on his own. Adam tried to explain, wondering when his dad's anger would come, but as they rolled along he seemed more curious than anything.

Snow drifted down on them during the six kilometre walk from Kétegyháza to Elek, and they were relieved to reach the warmth of the house. As they walked into the kitchen where the smell of supper just eaten hung in the air, four sets of eyes turned towards Adam.

"Adam! Oh, thank the Lord, you're really safe." His mom was across the room in an instant, her arms around him so tight he could hardly breathe. As her familiar, comfortable scent filled his nostrils, he forgot everything else.

"Adam!" At the sound of his little sister's voice, he pulled away from his mom.

"Hi, Anni." She was looking at him with big eyes, her old rag doll under her arm. "Have you been a good girl? You've grown taller." He lifted her high in the air and then squeezed her tight before putting her down.

"Hi, Resi," Adam said, striding over to where his older sister stood in the doorway, smiling from ear to ear, to give her a quick hug.

Adam could see his brother, George, in the kitchen doorway behind Theresa. He had a curious look on his face.

"Hi, George," he greeted his eight-year-old brother, reaching past Theresa to slap his brother's shoulder.

"Where were you?" George asked, expressionless.

"I was living with a Count in the Alps, near Austria," Adam declared proudly.

"Well, you're in big trouble for running away," George informed him.

"You're a bad boy, Adam," Anni chimed in from where she'd climbed onto a kitchen chair.

"Never mind, everyone," Adam's mom interjected. "We are glad that Adam is safe and that is all that will be said about it. And now move out of my way while I fix your dad and your brother some supper. They must be starving, not to mention freezing from the walk."

There were lots of questions as Adam and his father ate their supper, but there was no more talk of trouble.

The next day and the one after that, Adam waited for a punishment that didn't come. Maybe his dad really was just happy to have him back safe. And even though he missed the Count a little and missed their adventures a lot, it was good to be home.

CHAPTER TWENTY-FIVE

That Christmas was the nicest they'd had in years. Everyone was happy. Even Adam's dad was softer than usual, at least for a few weeks. In January, Adam returned to school. With the war in its third year, the school was even more short staffed, but when Adam appeared in the doorway of the classroom early on his first morning back, Mr. Post put down his pen and asked to hear the whole story before they moved on to the topic of school work.

Through January, Adam spent his evenings completing the work Mr. Post gave him to catch up with the other grade seven students. By the middle of February, he was getting bored. Then he heard the youth brass band playing in the town square. It was fantastic! Just like on the radio, only better. All those shiny horns blaring out the notes. Ooom, pah, pah, oom, pah, pah!

Asking around, he learned that the band practiced at the school on Wednesday nights. The next week he crept down the empty hallway and sat on the floor outside the room the music was coming from. The band director was teaching them a new song. His ear against the door, Adam listened intently to the instructions and how each instrument sounded as they ran through the song over and over. He'd slipped quietly out of the house after supper when the radio broadcast started rather than explain where he was off to, so he couldn't stay out long. Best to get back before the broadcast ended and avoid an argument.

The next week he wasn't as cautious, and the house was quiet by the time he let himself in the front gate.

"Where have you been?" his dad's voice demanded from the darkness of the porch. Startled, Adam looked in the direction the voice had come from. A dark shape moved slightly and then a red glow lit up his dad's face as he took a long pull on his cigarette.

Adam stood at the bottom of the steps, his skin slightly chilled by the early spring air, weighing his options. His dad loved music too. He decided to tell the truth. "I was at the school, listening to the youth brass band," he replied. When his dad didn't respond, Adam walked up the steps and past him into the house.

Slipping off his muddy shoes in the entrance, he went into the kitchen. His mom glanced over from where she was working at the counter and smiled. She was cutting up the rabbits he'd butchered after school. George sat at the kitchen table, peering down at a book. Walking past his brother, Adam sat down on his bed.

"Adam, know what, Adam?" Anni slid off of Theresa's bed where she'd been sitting with their older sister, and climbed up with Adam, holding a corn cob. "When I'm big like Resi, I'm going to make pretty curls in my hair. See, like this," she said, grabbing a piece of her blonde hair and wrapping it awkwardly around the cob. She grinned up at Adam. Just then, their dad stomped into the kitchen, slamming the door behind him. Anni grew silent.

"I guess you think it's okay to wear the leather soles off your shoes walking around town at night?" his dad asked across the room, his voice low and angry.

Adam looked at his dad and answered calmly. "I'm planning to play the trumpet in that band when I'm old enough, so I wanted to hear what songs they practice."

His dad's face darkened. "That's a bunch of nonsense. You've got chores to do. Your responsibility is to this family. And I won't be paying for new shoes for you just so you can walk wherever you want at all hours and listen to music."

"No problem, I'll go in bare feet," Adam answered with a barely detectable note of defiance.

"Adam, you can't walk outside in bare feet. It's only March," his mom admonished quietly from the counter without turning around.

His dad strode over to her in three steps. *Whap!* His hand connected with the side of his wife's head. She stopped cutting but didn't turn around. George looked up, then quickly cast his eyes back down at his book and shrunk down a bit in his chair.

"Didn't you hear me? I just told him not to wear out his goddammed shoes!" he roared, then reached for the leather belt hanging in the doorframe and turned back to Adam. "And if you're going to be a smart ass, then you'll get a lesson in respect."

CHAPTER TWENTY-SIX

A month and a half later, Adam was accepted into the band. It hadn't been difficult to come up with fibs about going out to help the neighbours with various chores after supper, and after listening to a couple more practices from the hallway, he'd decided he didn't want to wait two more years until he was old enough.

The band leader's first response had been 'no'. Looking him in the eye, Adam promised he could play at the required level. The leader had given him a challenge, one he'd assured Adam it would take two years to meet, especially as Adam didn't own a trumpet. He was to learn a complex song and a series of advanced scales. The leader demonstrated both. When Adam could play these competently, he could join the band.

Each day after school, instead of hanging out with his friends, Adam exchanged a half-hour of barnyard labour for a half-hour lesson with one of the trumpet players in the band. When he showed up and performed the song and the scales a month later, the leader had clapped him on the back and welcomed him to the band on the spot.

Adam explained to his dad that he'd been asked to play trumpet as part of his duties to the Hitler Youth Group. He was confident his dad would support his trumpet playing under this pretext and hoping he didn't know enough about the band or the youth group to detect the lie. He was right on both counts.

CHAPTER TWENTY-SEVEN

Summer 1942

Band practice was Adam's favourite time of the week. But all too soon, summer break loomed and with it, the end of practices and the beginning of long days in the fields and vineyards with his dad. The need to escape dominated Adam's thoughts.

Wracking his brain, he came up with an obvious solution. Franz's dad needed someone to help his tenants out on the farm for the summer. It was easy work and he usually hired a kid. Adam walked home with Franz after school to talk to Herr Wittman about it. Within a few minutes, they shook on the deal. Even his own dad was in favour. The responsibility would be good for Adam and the extra money would be helpful. The best part of all, as far as Adam was concerned, was that the farm was too far out of town to walk back and forth every day, so he'd be sleeping out at the farm in the hay loft. Two long, hot summer months of freedom!

Herr Wittman picked him up to take him out to the farm and introduce him to the tenants on his first day. "Mr. and Mrs. Sommer, this is Adam Baumann. He'll be helping out this summer. I'll pick him up on Saturdays when I'm finished my rounds and give him a lift home, and he can walk back out on Sunday afternoon. Show him around and explain what you need him to do. Good day. See you Saturday, Adam." Herr Wittman flicked the reins against the horses' backs and drove the wagon out of the dusty yard into the road, back the way they'd come.

Mr. Sommer didn't have to explain anything twice. The job was simple. Make sure the cows got out to graze in the morning, back into the small corral for the afternoon to build up the manure pile for fertilizing the crops, and then into the barn for the night with clean water to drink.

Mrs. Sommer was a good cook and usually sent Adam out to the barn after supper with a bit of cake or a cookie to munch on. Adam loved his nights in the barn, especially the quiet time just after he settled into the nest he'd made for himself in the loft above the cows. He could hear the cows shifting around in their stalls below as they settled into the silence of sleep. It was then that he thought about everything he'd seen and done last year when he'd run away, about the Count's beautiful carriage and the manor house, and about all the places he was going to see someday. The guys that came home from the war on furlough had been to Yugoslavia and Russia. And his Aunt Louise was in America. And Germany sounded incredible from the radio broadcasts. So many places to see. One more year of school and then he'd set out and see the world. Somehow.

CHAPTER TWENTY-EIGHT

The last cow meandered lazily into the corral, flicking her tail at the flies on her haunches. Locking the gate, Adam climbed up onto the fence and balanced on the middle rail, oblivious to the pungent stink of the growing manure pile cooking in the mid-July sun. A piece of straw dangled from the corner of his mouth. Afternoons were a little boring. He could see Mrs. Sommer across the yard digging potatoes. The bull that Mr. Sommer had put in with the herd a few days ago was standing nearby facing the other direction. He was ornery, as Adam had seen that morning out in the field when he poked him between the back legs with a stick. Adam climbed down from the fence and climbed back up again closer to the bull. He looked over. Mrs. Sommer couldn't see him from here and Mr. Sommer was nowhere in sight. Grabbing the bull's tail, Adam pulled it to one side and twisted hard. Whoa! Laughing out loud, Adam jumped backwards off the fence as the bull leapt ahead and kicked his back legs high in the air. Then the massive bovine turned and trotted towards his tormentor, stopping with his huge face a few inches from the fence. After staring at Adam for a minute or so, he snorted a breath of hot air out his nostrils and walked back to the herd.

Adam decided to shovel out the stalls. After that he could mix up the feed for that night, and then it wouldn't be much longer until supper. *Might just add a little to the manure pile myself before I start shovelling*, Adam thought as he jumped into the corral. Pulling down his shorts, he squatted near the edge of the herd. The manure was squishy between his toes. He scratched idly at the mosquito bites on his arms and legs and looked around at the cows. He watched as the bull looked up from where he was standing on the other side of the corral. Slowly, the bull walked towards him and stopped in the middle of the corral, staring at him.

"What are you looking at?" Adam called out to him. "Get outta here."

The bull didn't even blink. He just kept staring. Adam stuck out his tongue.

The bull lowered his head and scraped his front hoof against the ground. Suddenly he was thundering towards Adam.

"GET BACK!" Adam yelled at the top of his lungs, turning and stumbling, tugging on his shorts. Then the bull's head was under him, and he was launched into the air.

"AAAHHHHHH!" he screamed. Adam's body slammed against the barn and he fell heavily to the ground.

Dazed from the impact, Adam strained to open his eyes. The bull was still there, head down, scraping his feet on the ground. He was going to charge again!

"Get back!" Mr. Sommer's voice boomed from the edge of the barn. The bull looked at where the voice had come from and looked back at Adam. "Get back, I said!" Mr. Sommer appeared in Adam's peripheral vision, ducking through the fence. He was waving a pitchfork at the bull and driving him back.

"Open the gate to the field!" the farmer yelled to his wife who had come running from the garden. Adam watched from the ground while Mr. Sommer drove the bull back and forth a few times until the animal finally trotted through the open gate at the opposite side of the corral.

Mr. and Mrs. Sommer knelt down beside him at the base of the barn wall.

"He's conscious," said Mr. Sommer.

"What's hurting, Adam? Is anything broken?" his wife asked gently.

"I don't know," whispered Adam. His right side hurt. And his head.

"Let's get him in the house," he heard Mr. Sommer say. "Can you walk between us?"

The sound of linen tearing startled Adam and he opened his eyes a crack. He was lying on the kitchen table. Mrs. Sommer was tearing a bedsheet into strips beside him.

"Thank the Lord you were on your way to the barn," she said to Mr. Sommer, who was standing on the other side of the table, looking down at Adam with a worried expression.

"Owwww!" Adam cried out and looked down to where the pain came from. Mrs. Sommer had a bowl of water and a cloth. She had started wiping his leg. The water in the bowl was turning red.

An hour later, they were in the old wagon Mr. Sommer used in the fields, headed for town. Adam's entire right leg and his torso and head were wrapped in white bandages. The scrapes that ran from his ribs to his foot burned, and his head throbbed with the jostling.

"Okay, here we are," said Mr. Sommer, drawing the horses to a stop in front of the Baumann house. "Do you think you can walk?"

"Yeah, I think so."

"Hold on, I'll come around and help you down."

Adam saw Theresa come down the steps to see who was at the gate.

"Adam! What happened?" Theresa exclaimed. "Mom!" she called over her shoulder.

"I'm okay," Adam insisted weakly as his mom and sister crowded around while Mr. Sommer helped him down from the wagon.

"We got a pretty nasty bull out there. Can't be trusted obviously. I'm so sorry about this, Mrs. Baumann."

"I'm sure it wasn't your fault," his mom replied.

"He was thrown against the barn wall pretty hard. I don't think anything's broken, but he's got pretty bad scrapes all down his right side. His head's pretty bruised and scraped up too. My wife cleaned it up best she could. Thank the Lord the bull didn't gore him. He'll be pretty sore for a while though. I'll talk to the landlord about getting someone else out for the rest of the summer while your boy recuperates."

"Thank you for bringing him home," his mom said graciously. "Adam, can you walk from here?"

"Yeah, I'm okay, Mom." He turned to the farmer. "Thanks Mr. Sommer. I'm sure glad you came with that pitchfork as fast as you did."

"All the best, Adam. Good day, Mrs. Baumann." Mr. Sommer turned and walked back to his side of the wagon, as Theresa opened the gate and his mom steered him through.

Adam walked gingerly to the front step and looked up at where Anni stood on the porch, her little fists planted firmly on her hips in consternation.

"Oh, Adam," her blonde hair swung back and forth as she shook her head at her big brother, tut-tutting. "What are we going to do with you?" she said with a heavy sigh.

Adam laughed at his four-year-old sister. "Owww, Anni, don't make me laugh, it hurts. I don't know what you're going to do with me. I guess you'll just have to keep me for a while longer."

CHAPTER TWENTY-NINE

Autumn 1942

The scrapes and bruises from his run-in with the bull healed quickly, and soon Adam was back at the usual routines, working in the fields with his dad when he had to, and escaping to hang out with Franz and Tony when he could. Finally, eighth grade started, his last year of mandatory schooling. The following year he'd be at home and working full time. His dad talked about it often, how they'd start asking around soon for more vineyard contracts and other jobs that Adam could do, and how the family would use the extra money. A veil of impending doom hung over Adam.

"My brother is coming home on furlough," Franz said as they left the schoolyard one warm Friday afternoon. Franz was still in school this year too. Even though grade nine wasn't compulsory, his parents wanted him to get an education. Franz's brother had joined the German army a couple of years ago and been promoted to officer. Franz talked about him all the time, and all the exciting places he described in his letters.

Just then, on the corner up ahead, a town crier started ringing his bell. The boys stopped to listen.

"*Achtung,* citizens! This is an important announcement! One week from tomorrow, on the 24th of October at precisely 2 p.m., the esteemed Heinrich Huber, envoy from the office of the Honourable Joseph Goebbels, Minister of Public Enlightenment and Propaganda serving the Third Reich, will be speaking in the Town Square, giving an official report on the progress of the German Army Group South B in the Battle of Stalingrad. Attendance of all citizens is mandatory! It is *verboten* to miss this rally!" The little man turned and faced the other direction, holding his bell above his head and ringing it vigorously a few times before repeating his announcement. "*Achtung,* citizens! This is an important announcement. . . "

For Adam, the rallies added some excitement to the monotony of life in Elek. Not only had he been selected from the youth group to deliver the speeches that the organizers provided, but he'd volunteered to play one of the big, long, shiny heralding trumpets the Nazis had provided for the events. At their practices, he'd become the de facto leader, marching at the head of the little group, keeping time.

"Well, now I know what I'll be doing next week," said Adam when the crier had finished the announcement. "It's a good thing Miss Krause will be back at work."

Miss Krause, the grade one and two teacher, had been away sick the previous few weeks and there wasn't another teacher to fill in, so Mr. Post had asked Adam to help out. Each day, Mr. Post gave him materials he'd prepared the evening before, and then checked in through the day as Adam delivered the lessons to the kids. Adam's own lessons had to wait until the evenings, but he didn't mind. The little kids were fun, sitting in rapt attention hanging on his every word when he read out loud or made up stories for them.

"I bet they'll ask my brother to do a speech," Franz grinned.

"They sure should. An SS officer from right here in Elek!"

It would be years before Adam, or the world at large, understood what Hitler's master plan had been, and the role that one particular top-secret division of the SS had played in it. It would be even longer before people realized that much of the German military, including most of the SS, had no awareness of the atrocities while they were occurring. Standing on the street that day, Adam and Franz believed, as most did, the simple propaganda – the SS was Germany's top-notch military force, and only the best and the strongest were allowed the honour of being a part of it.

Sure enough, the leader of the youth group approached Adam the following day and handed him his speech. Adam glanced at it. *"Official Speech of the Hitler Youth, October 1942, from Office of Joseph Goebbels, Minister of Public Enlightenment and Propaganda, Third Reich."*

It was pretty long this time. A new poem and some familiar stuff about the strength of the motherland and the evils that sought to destroy the superior German race. Adam didn't mind. Memorizing was easy and speaking on the stage was exciting. He loved the crowds that gathered for the rallies.

"How do you remember all that?" his mom asked, glancing over his shoulder later that evening. Adam knew she couldn't read many of the words, but whenever he was asked to speak, she looked at his script with interest and listened with a smile when he practiced.

"I put it under my pillow at night so that it gets absorbed into my brain," he said, grinning up at her.

On Saturday, Adam was ready around the corner from the town square at a quarter to two sharp. Although the morning had been frosty, the sun that shone down from the cloudless blue sky warmed the waiting boys. Adam had dressed in his brown Hitler Youth shirt that morning after chores and left early so they could practice the horns a bit more before the event started.

The organizer at the front of the procession waved his arm, and Adam began to march. The other six boys fell into step behind him, two rows of three. And behind them, the rest of the youth group members in their crisply pressed Nazi shirts. As they rounded the corner and approached the entrance to the square, they stopped in unison and raised the long horns in one coordinated movement. *Bah, bah, baahh!* Their timing was perfect. Adam resumed marching. *Bah, bah, bah!* Into the square and in front of the stage, playing the whole way.

The square was packed to overflowing, a sea of faces smiling in the sunshine, happily waving the swastika flags the organizers had handed out. As the seven horn players lined up in front of the stage, the rest of the brown shirts filed to the rows of chairs and took their seats. The officials from Berlin climbed the steps onto the stage and sat down on the chairs. When they were seated, Adam and his team blasted out the final few notes, then the seven horns went silent before they were lowered simultaneously to the boys' sides.

"Good afternoon Volksbund of Elek!" the master of ceremonies cried out. After some opening remarks, he asked Adam and one of the League of German Girls to come up onto the stage.

As he delivered his opening lines, Adam spotted his mom and dad. They were near the front of the crowd, beaming up at him with Theresa, George, and Anni beside them. The lines of the speech came easily and he glanced around the crowd as he spoke. At the end, he paused a moment for effect, then stepped back from the podium as the crowd applauded loudly. The energy of the crowd was building. Next was the girl's speech. Then Franz's brother was going to speak, and finally the dignitary from Berlin. By that time, the crowd would be jubilant. Looking back to his family he smiled and gave Anni a wink where she now sat atop of his dad's shoulders clapping as hard as she could.

When the rally had finished an hour or more later, and the final applause had subsided, the elated crowd filed noisily out of the square, talking of the grand things they'd heard. Behind the stage, Adam put the long trumpet carefully into its case and handed it to the leader, then called out goodbye to the other kids before taking off for Franz's house.

Franz sat on the front steps, waiting for him. "My brother has to leave tonight. He rushed home from the rally and got into the bath, so we can't talk to him right now. But his uniform and pistol are inside," he said in a hushed whisper. "And Mom and Dad aren't home yet. Come on." The two boys walked softly through the house and up the stairs into a bedroom.

"Wow, look at that," Adam whispered in awe when he saw the uniform laid out on the bed. He'd never seen an SS officer uniform before. It was jet black, with a shiny row of brass buttons down the front, and an SS motif on each side of the collar. The shoulders were decorated with gold embossed insignia. Adam could hear an occasional muffled splash from down the hall.

Franz picked up the jacket and held it up to his chest in front of the mirror. "My brother says the SS soldiers get superior training and better weapons than the regular army. The Russians turn and run when they see the SS coming." Gingerly, Franz slid his arms into the sleeves. "What do you think?"

"It's too big on you. Let me try it."

Carefully taking the jacket as Franz shrugged out of it, Adam slid it on and did up the buttons, then turned to face the mirror. He'd never worn anything so fancy. "Heil Hitler!" he saluted the mirror in a whisper. Franz snickered and thrust out his arm.

In front of Adam on the dresser was a revolver. "Look at this, Franz!"

"I know. I already held it. You can pick it up."

Adam lifted the weapon and turned it over in his hands a few times. It was heavy. Placing it back down carefully, he looked into the mirror again and gave himself a big smile.

CHAPTER THIRTY

When the weather turned cold, the work in the fields gave way to butchering season. Although it was hard work, butchering was a social activity that always involved a group of relatives and neighbours. Adam enjoyed it. Most weekends from late November until February, someone had a pig to kill, and with so many men gone to war or working in Germany, this year was busier than ever. The camaraderie of butchering days punctuated the winter with warmth.

The work started early. First someone would lure the pig out of his shelter with the scrap bucket. Then one of the men would daze the poor bugger with a sledgehammer. Another guy would jump in with a long pointy knife and go for a quick, clean cut of the throat, holding a bucket in place to catch the spurting blood as it was pumped out by the pig's still-beating heart. The tangy smell of fresh, hot blood filled the air and hung over the yard until it was replaced by cooking smells later in the morning.

When the blood had drained, the insides were quickly removed and handed over to the women, their dresses protected by aprons stained from butchering days gone by. By this time, Adam would have filled the big copper pot with water and built a fire under it to begin cooking down the head and other scraps as they were removed from the carcass. In a few hours, the copper pot would be filled with that delicious broth called "kredel."

A high proportion of body fat made the Hungarian Mangalitsa Pig a popular breed in those days, as the lard kept well and was treasured for cooking and baking. Unfortunately, the breed also has a thick coat of curly hair, all of which had to be removed before they could begin the meat cutting. Piles of straw and wood shavings were placed on the hairy carcass and set alight to burn off the hair. It was a finicky business. If the fire burned out too quickly, the job wouldn't be complete and the spot would have to be burned again. And if the fire burned too long, the skin would char, creating waste.

Once the pig was burned bald, the carcass was cut into sections. Adam's dad knew just how to get the most meat out of a pig and make nice hams, bacon slabs, pork roast, and sausage meat. Adam held the meat steady while his dad made the cuts. He'd watched it so many times, he was pretty sure he'd be able to do it just as well.

After a couple of hours, one of the women would slice up the liver, coat it in flour and fry it up with some onions and fresh pig fat. Everyone sat down for a quick break and dug in.

Then Adam's mom and the other women prepared the blood sausage, liver sausage, and head cheese, chatting and laughing amongst themselves all the while. The fat was scraped off the skin and set aside for lard. The skin was chopped up along with the kidneys, tongue, and various other parts, and mixed into the pig's blood. The mixture, seasoned with salt and spices, was then stuffed into the cleaned out large intestine and boiled in the kredel. The pig's stomach was carefully cleaned out and stuffed with a chopped-up mixture containing the pig's nose, ears, meat picked off the cooked head, and various other fatty trimmings from the pile Adam and his dad accumulated as they trimmed the meat. After the stomach was sewn shut, it was tossed into the kredel and cooked through, ready to be smoked.

For lunch, the women ladled some of the kredel into a smaller pot, threw in some salt and homemade noodles, and called everyone to sit.

Sausage making was the main act of the afternoon. His dad preferred Aunt Maria, Mom's youngest sister, to help with the sausage. She had a gentle hand and did the best job of scraping the film from the intestines with the back of a knife without tearing the delicate material. Then the intestines had to be washed several times before they were ready to be stuffed with freshly ground and seasoned meat. Everyone took a turn at cranking the handle of the meat grinder, and when the first batch was ground, it was time to season and mix. With a reputation for delicious sausage to uphold, Adam's dad concentrated on getting the seasoning of the sausage meat just right, adding salt, pepper, a variety of other spices, and of course paprika for colour, while the nominated mixer mixed and mixed and mixed.

When he was satisfied with the seasoning, Adam's dad would call him over to start stuffing the sausages. While his Aunt Maria carefully slid the intestinal casing onto the end of the sausage tube, Adam filled the tube with the seasoned meat and placed one end of the wooden shaft into the end of the full tube, pressing his stomach against the other end for leverage. Pushing the meat through at the perfect speed was important, so that the sausage would be packed just right, not too loose, making floppy sausages that would fall apart, and not too tight as to tear the casing. Aunt Maria watched like a hawk as the casing filled with meat, pricking any air pockets with a needle she kept handily stuck into her apron for this purpose.

Drawn by the smell of the kredel, neighbours dropped by in the afternoon, most with a pot in hand. The cooling broth was always shared generously, and for the next week, delicious soups and stews flavoured with the kredel would be enjoyed around the neighbourhood.

As the afternoon wound down, the last big job was smoking the meat. Adam, Uchie, and the younger cousins headed to the yard across town where wagons and wheelbarrows were built, to collect shavings and sawdust to burn in the smokehouse. By the time they got back, the racks in the smokehouse would be filled with fresh meat and boiled sausage. Almost everything was smoked – hams, bacon, reams of sausages, and countless bones from which the meat had been cut away to grind for sausage. In the cold winter months, the smoked bones would make their way, one by one, into the soup pot or into a meal of baked beans.

With the smokehouse filled and the fire burning just right to produce the amount of smoke needed, the men's work was finished. In the fading light, they washed up and sat down to relax over a cup of wine while the women roasted meat for supper and yelled to the kids to fetch vegetables from the root cellar.

"This tastes better than last year George, you must have remembered the salt this time," someone jested as they ate, triggering a burst of laughter around the big wooden table.

"He may have remembered the salt, but I think he forgot the paprika. The sausage looks a bit pale," someone down at the other end quipped.

"You just want my recipe," Adam's dad responded with a laugh.

"No, we don't, then we'd have to make the sausage ourselves," the heckler answered without missing a beat.

One by one, people pushed back their chairs from the table, praising the food for the umpteenth time. Soon the gramophone was out, and as the wine jug was passed around for refills, the adults took turns dancing. Eventually the yawning would start and good-byes were said amongst conversation about whose pig would be next.

CHAPTER THIRTY-ONE

Christmas 1942

"*I call all women Baaaby,*" crooned little Anni as she twirled around beside the kitchen table, holding the worn hem of her dress out like a ballerina.

"Why are you singing that?" laughed Theresa from where she was leaning over the kitchen table rolling out cookie dough. Shadows from the light of the lantern danced on the walls, and the smell of ham soup filled the warm little kitchen. They'd helped the Mahlers butcher a small pig that morning and Dad was still there, finishing up the sausage.

"It's Horst Winter! Haven't you heard him on the radio?" Adam asked Theresa from where he sat on his bed cross-legged, his back against the wall, reading a book about explorers he'd borrowed from Mr. Post.

"We should sing a Christmas carol, Anni," his older sister suggested, ignoring him. "These cookies will be ready to paint after supper and put threads through for hanging. You're going to help paint them, right?"

"Yes!" Anni exclaimed, as she stopped twirling and came over to peer onto the table at the shapes Theresa was making with the little tin cookie cutters that their mom had used every Christmas as long as Adam could remember.

"Anni, what's wrong with your neck? Come here for a minute," their mom interrupted from where she sat at the end of the table darning a pile of socks. "It's a bit red. Does it hurt?"

"No," said Anni.

Their mom lifted her five-year-old's hair and inspected her neck more closely. "Have you been scratching it?" Anni shook her head as her mom placed the back of her hand against Anni's neck. "It's puffy and warm," she said.

"It's okay, Mama," said Anni, pulling away gently to return to Theresa and the cookies. "Can I make one?"

"Sure," said Theresa, handing Anni the little horse-shaped cookie cutter.

Anni carefully pressed out the shape, then held the cookie cutter out to the room. "Adam and George should make one," she said.

"The swelling looks worse this morning," Adam heard his mom say as he drifted awake the next morning. His parents were talking quietly at the table. The house was dark. The sun wouldn't be up for another hour. Adam lay still, eyes closed. He loved the Christmas holidays. Everything was covered in snow, which meant no garden, no grape vines, and no crops to tend. Over the winter they kept only a few animals, and chores didn't take long. He had time to wake up slowly and savour a few minutes in bed listening to his mom rustling around in the kitchen fixing breakfast.

"There's a little red spot on her shoulder, like a little bug bite," his mom continued. "That's all I can see. But her whole arm is swollen and her shoulder and neck. I think you should get the doctor."

"It's only a bug bite. It will go down," his dad answered.

The swelling worsened through the day, and when their dad fetched the doctor, his best guess was an insect bite too, but he wasn't sure how to treat it. The following morning, Anni was listless as their parents bundled her up and climbed into the Mahler's wagon to drive to the hospital in Gyula. Hopefully the doctors there would have medicine to treat the swelling and the fever Anni had developed overnight.

When they returned a few hours later, Anni wasn't with them. There hadn't been any doctors on duty due to the holiday season and the nurses had insisted on keeping her until a doctor could examine her. Staying with Anni hadn't been an option either. Against the rules, the nurses had said. Uncle Florian had promised to check in at the hospital regularly and bring Anni home when she was ready, or at least come and give them an update if she had to stay longer.

The next day was Christmas Eve. All day they waited anxiously for news, and when none came, they went through the motions of hanging the cookies and lighting the candles. But no one's heart was in it. Anni should have been there to enjoy it. Christmas Day passed similarly.

Early the day after, there was a knock on the door.

"Florian, it's about time. It's been three days," said Adam's dad as he opened the door wide to let his older brother in. "Come in so I can shut the door."

As the two men walked into the kitchen, Uncle Florian took off his hat. His face was drawn and his eyes brimmed with tears. Adam felt his chest tighten. His uncle just stood there, his hat against his chest.

"What's wrong, Florian?" Adam's mom demanded sharply, standing up when she saw her brother-in-law's face.

"What the hell is going on, Florian?" his dad repeated the question, his voice rising.

"A nurse from the hospital came to the house very early this morning." Uncle Florian stopped talking for a moment, still not raising his eyes. Adam held his breath. Uncle Florian looked up at the family around the kitchen table in front of him. "Anni died last night."

Adam's mom let out a guttural sound, like someone had slammed a fist into her stomach, forcing all her breath out.

"What?" Adam's dad said, confused. "She just has a bug bite."

Adam jumped up, knocking his chair over backwards, and strode around the table towards the men. "No! That's not true! Why did they say that?!" he yelled at his uncle.

"What are you saying, Florian?" his dad interrupted in a low voice, shaking his head as if to clear up the misunderstanding.

Adam's mom had dropped back into her chair, and sat there silently, her hand still over her mouth. George sat still, his eyes big. Theresa was beside him, tears already streaming silently down her face.

"I don't know much more," Uncle Florian said in a desperate, apologetic tone. "The nurse came and knocked at the door, and said that she died last night, and could I notify you. She said there was too much infection. I'm so sorry, Anna." He walked over and put his hand on his sister-in-law's shoulder. At his touch, she made a strangled sobbing sound and closed her eyes, tears overflowing down her cheeks.

"She just has a goddammed bug bite!" their dad yelled, startling everyone. "A goddammed bug bite! You can't die from a bug bite!" He turned and strode out the front door, slamming it so hard the house shook. A moment later, he strode back in. "It's gotta be a mistake, Florian.

They said not to worry. They said they would look after her!"

Uncle Florian looked at Adam's dad silently, his cheeks wet with tears.

"Goddammed useless Hungarian nurses! Useless, all of them!" his dad roared as he strode back out the door onto the porch.

Adam sat down on the edge of his bed, dazed. He shook his head. This didn't make any sense. Anni. Perfect little Anni. How could she just die? Around him the noise continued. Theresa had started sobbing loudly, and Adam was vaguely aware of similar noises coming from his little brother.

"I should have stayed with her." His mom's words came out all broken. "I shouldn't have left her. They wouldn't let me stay. I should have stayed." Her words trailed off, replaced by a low, primal wailing sound. She began to rock forward and backward on her chair, arms around herself like a straitjacket.

Adam's dad stormed back into the house, sobbing as he hurled profanities about the doctors and the nurses and that it was crazy to say someone could die from a little bug bite. Adam sat on the edge of the bed, cradling his head in his hands as the noises ran together around him.

CHAPTER THIRTY-TWO

A week later, Adam sat wedged in between the rabbit cages and the house. The sky was heavy with dark grey clouds. It was snowing lightly, but he didn't feel cold. He didn't feel anything. People were still coming in the gate every few minutes. Inside the front door they would turn right and go into his parents' room to look at Anni, lying there in her little coffin. He'd been in there with her when people started showing up. Everyone loved Anni. They all cried as soon as they saw her sweet little face. Theresa had curled her hair. He kept remembering what the nurses had told Uncle Florian about the night she died. How she had been crying for her mama and repeating the same few words over and over until she lost consciousness. None of the nurses on duty spoke any German, but they remembered the words and repeated them to Uncle Florian. She'd been crying for a drink of water.

When his dad wasn't sobbing, he was in a rage. He raged about having to beg for money to pay the government fee to have Anni's body released to him, and five minutes later he sat at the table wracked with grief, sobbing about buying a nice coffin for his baby. The coffin he got had a little window in the top, where you could see Anni's face. She looked like she was sleeping.

After a while, Adam could hear people coming back out of the house and down the front steps. He stood up and looked around the corner of the house. Everyone was walking across the street to the cemetery. His dad and his Uncle Florian came last, except for his mom. They carried Anni down the steps and out the front gate, his dad leading the way and his uncle carrying the back end of the little box where Anni's feet were. Finally, his mom came out, wearing the black dress one of her sisters had brought over, and followed them across the road, the tears that hadn't stopped since that awful morning still streaming down her cheeks.

Adam crossed the road and stood beside his mom as they placed the little coffin beside the frozen hole. He'd heard the caretaker chipping and scraping at the frozen ground all day yesterday and again this morning.

Now the man carefully attached ropes to the handles on the ends of the box and then stepped back so that the priest could start. Adam didn't want to hear anything the priest had to say. God was a bunch of lies. If he could really create the world, then he could have saved Anni.

From where he stood, Adam could see the corner of Anni's face through the little window. Love and loss filled his 13-year-old body to the brim, so big and aching, he thought he would split open. He'd never forget how she looked when she stood with her fists planted on her hips, scolding him. She knew when their dad was in a bad mood, and when a licking for Adam was likely to come. And she knew how to soften Dad up. Since she'd figured this out, as often as not, her chiding would put a smile on their dad's face and Adam would be off the hook. Five years old and she had it all figured out.

The droning of the priest's voice had stopped and been replaced by music. It was Anni's farewell song. Fresh tears warmed Adam's cheeks as the man's voice rose and fell. He had a beautiful singing voice. They were lowering Anni into the frozen hole. His mom buried her face in her hands and shook with sobs. Someone grabbed a handful of dirt and threw it down onto the coffin. Another followed suit, then another. When the song ended, people began to drift away. Adam bent down and picked up a handful of frozen mud. He held it a minute and then let it fall from his hand back down beside his feet.

The priest was going to talk again.

"I'm going," he croaked and turned away. He didn't want to hear it.

CHAPTER THIRTY-THREE

Christmas holidays ended a few days after the funeral. Adam walked a different way to school so he wouldn't run into Franz. He didn't want to talk to anyone. A lot of kids knew about Anni, so no one really wanted to talk to him anyway. As he sat at his desk, staring at the chalkboard, Adam was glad to be away from home. He tried to concentrate on what Mr. Post was saying, but Anni swirled around in his head, twirling like a ballerina, scolding, giggling, and then lying dead under a little glass window. He swallowed hard every few minutes, trying not to cry. He had to hold back his tears until he got home.

The next day wasn't any better, nor the next.

"Adam, can you stay for a minute please?" Mr. Post called out a few days later, as the kids filed out at the end of the day.

Adam sat back down in his desk as the room emptied. Mr. Post came over and perched on the desk in front of Adam's, concern on his face.

"You're not yourself this week, Adam. Do you want to talk about it?"

Adam shook his head, suffocated by the lump of tears in this throat. He had to get out of there. Standing, he headed for the door.

As he walked through the schoolyard and into the street, he regained his composure and stopped. He wanted to tell Mr. Post. Turning around, he walked back across the yard and up the steps, breathing deeply as he walked back into his class. Mr. Post had his back to the door, cleaning the chalkboard. He turned when he heard Adam come in.

"Mr. Post, my little sister died. She was five."

"I'm sorry to hear that, Adam," Mr. Post said after a moment. "Thank you for telling me."

Spinning on his heel, Adam left again. This time he let the tears run down his face as he walked home, staring straight ahead, not caring who saw him.

CHAPTER THIRTY-FOUR

The days passed. Slowly, very slowly, it got a little easier to stay composed through the day, but the pain arose unexpectedly, stabbing him in the chest. Going home after school was the worst part. Anni wasn't there to greet him, just the gaping hole she'd left. Adam's mom stood at the counter and cried silently while she cooked, and while she mended, and while she washed up after supper. Theresa cried through whatever she was doing. A suffocating silence filled every inch of the house while they ate. George was quiet, maybe quieter than usual. And when his dad wasn't cussing and yelling, he sat, his shoulders heaving with silent sobs.

CHAPTER THIRTY-FIVE

1943

Anni had been gone a couple of months when Mr. Post approached Adam with a request. Would he be willing to help Mr. Post in the evenings for a while, marking grade six and seven papers? He could do the work at Mr. Post's house in the evenings, at a spare desk in his study. Adam's heart leapt at the idea. It was the first time he'd felt anything other than grief or emptiness since Christmas.

With a resigned shrug, Adam's dad agreed.

Carefully, Adam read through the assignments in the stack Mr. Post placed in front of him each evening, using a red pencil to mark answers that didn't match the answer key. As he completed the stacks night after night, Mr. Post's quiet companionship a salve to his raw, broken heart, slowly he began to feel a stirring of his old self. He thought about returning to band practice and wondered vaguely what Franz and Tony had been up to.

"Adam, what are your plans when school finishes for the summer?" Mr. Post asked casually one night as the two of them sat in comfortable silence, each busy with their work.

"The usual. Work in the vineyards, then wheat harvest and corn harvest. And I guess I need to start thinking about getting a job of my own." Thinking about the future invariably reminded him that Anni wouldn't be in it, and so far he'd managed to avoid it.

"The principal was asking me the other day how I was managing to keep up teaching three grades. I explained how you've been helping me and also how you led the primary class last year when Miss Krause was sick. He thinks, and I agree, that you should consider going to college. You're a smart young man, Adam. You should get an education. If you want one that is."

Adam looked at his teacher solemnly for a moment before he answered. "I didn't take the academic stream so I don't think I can, and we wouldn't have the money for it anyway."

"I thought you might say that. The principal and I would like to speak to your father about this, if it's okay with you. We also took the liberty of speaking to the local leader of The Party, since he knows you from the youth group. We thought that if the three of us met with your father together, we might convince him. You'd have a lot of work to do to make up your academic courses and complete the grade nine and ten requirement. As for costs, sometimes there are scholarships available for bright students. What do you think?"

Adam stared at Mr. Post again. "That would be great, Mr. Post," he said finally. "Thank you." He turned back to the paper he was marking to hide his tears. Mr. Post was definitely the best teacher anyone could ever have.

Adam listened quietly while the visitors complimented his parents for raising a fine boy and went on to explain the purpose of their visit. With Adam's potential, it would be a shame if he didn't get a college education. Mr. Post and Miss Krause were willing to tutor him through the necessary studies and assist with scholarship applications. If he worked hard he would be ready for college in a year. The college was in Budapest, so living arrangements would have to be made. As they spoke, the party leader nodded his agreement.

When the visitors finished explaining, Adam held his breath. His dad was hesitant, but in the end, there were too many important people in the room who obviously thought this was a good idea, for him to disagree. Mr. Post's strategy had worked.

That summer was different than any other in Adam's short life so far. Lessons in Mr. Post's study and completing assignments at the kitchen table at home filled his days, while his dad, mom, Theresa, and George worked in the fields as usual. Often his dad grumbled that Adam was wasting his time with his nose in a book while the rest of them did his work. But when the neighbours and relatives teased Adam about being a big shot, too important for normal work, his dad was quick to jump in. "I told you," he would say. "They said he's smart enough to finish up two years in one and then go to college. He's going to get a college education. My son's got a good brain."

As everyone else got busy with the wheat harvest, Adam started his first term at the academic high school, meeting with Mr. Post or Miss Krause several evenings a week for extra tutoring. One evening a week he saved for band practice. It didn't occur to Adam to doubt that he could complete two years of study in one. His mind delighted in the fascinating things he was learning. Advanced math, introductory physics, ancient history, geography of the world. And living in Budapest.

When he had a spare minute, the pain of missing Anni sometimes caught him unaware, but thankfully, spare minutes were few and far between. And with an exciting new life to look forward to, the moments of grief passed more quickly than they had.

CHAPTER THIRTY-SIX

Autumn 1943

A couple of months passed.

The crispness of the air spoke of winter, but Adam was warmed from the inside by beer and schnapps. At 14, he shouldn't have been drinking. Nor should he have been out until the middle of the night. And he had a stack of school assignments to do. But at the moment he wasn't worried about these things, nor had he thought about Anni the whole evening. A hiccup escaped his throat as he wove his way down the street, running his fingers through the coins in his pocket.

That night, playing with the band at the harvest dance that the rich farmers put on every year, had been the most fun he'd had since he could remember. He wasn't really old enough to be at the dance, but the other trumpet player had left to fight and they needed a trumpet to perform the songs properly. When he'd explained that he'd be getting his share of the tips, his dad had agreed, as long as he was home by midnight.

The dance was just like he'd always heard. Farmers' daughters showing off their new dresses trying to catch the eye of some young bachelor, and drunk farmers everywhere, buying beer for the band and throwing money into the hat at the edge of the stage. Polka, tango, waltz, polka, waltz, polka, foxtrot, waltz, polka, polka, fox trot. The evening had passed in a blur as the frequency of requests increased and the hat got fuller and fuller.

As he neared the gate, Adam's thoughts shifted from the fun of the evening to what might be waiting for him at home. It was after two. The house was dark. Hallelujah. Walking softly into the yard, he tiptoed up the porch steps, slipped through the front door ever so slowly, and shut it silently behind him.

"Who the hell do you think you are?" his father's voice filled the darkness. "You are two hours late!"

"I'm sorry, Dad. It was supposed to end at midnight, but they wouldn't stop dancing! I wanted to come home, but they just kept dancing," swore Adam. *Should have known it wouldn't be that easy.*

"You're going to turn out to be nothing but a bum! You're never going to learn to earn a living, staying out all night with those musicians and rich kids! What are you going to amount to?" A string of Romanian cuss words followed.

"What's wrong, George?" said his mom softly, appearing in the bedroom doorway in her nightdress, reaching up to smooth her hair.

"I'm going to throttle this snotty-nosed kid! He thinks he doesn't have to listen to me anymore. He's a big shot now, staying out all night with the rich kids!"

"Adam, you promised to be home at midnight," his mother admonished softly in the darkness. Agreeing with his dad was one of the ways she tried to calm him down. She struck a match and reached towards the lantern above the kitchen table. As the soft light filled the room, Adam saw Theresa and George staring silently out from under their covers.

He made another attempt at defending himself. "I couldn't leave. Everybody was still dancing and requesting songs and throwing coins in the basket. I couldn't just stop playing and walk out!" Then he remembered the money. "Look at this!" he said as he emptied his pockets onto the table.

His dad's eyes grew wide. "Where did you get that?"

"It's my share of the money the farmers paid for the music," Adam said, doing his best to hold back a smirk.

"What in the hell did they give you all this for? That's a couple weeks' pay!" For a moment his dad looked confused, and Adam felt a moment of satisfaction. That had shut him up!

Struggling to keep his face straight, Adam tried to explain. "Every time one of them wants to hear a specific song, he throws money into a hat on the stage. And when they all finally stopped throwing money and went home, I got my share." He let his smile show through just a bit. "That's why I couldn't leave. I had to wait and get the money. All the guys got this much! You should have seen these farmers, falling around drunk, talking louder than the next guy, showing off who could pay more for a song."

"Playing the damn trumpet is not work." His dad looked from him to his mom, willing her to agree. "What the hell is wrong with those fools, throwing their money away like that?"

"You know those foolish landowners, George," his mom said sooth-ingly, laying her hand on his father's arm. "They had too much to drink."

"I break my back for them every damn day and they pay me almost nothing, but they throw it around for a kid to blow a trumpet? No son of mine is going to earn money being a fool for those guys. You have to work for a living. Do respectable work." The fury had gone out of his dad's voice, and he sat down heavily, one arm on the table beside the money.

The house was quiet for a few moments.

"That's enough to buy us a couple of extra weaner pigs," his dad said, not looking at anyone. "You'd better damn well never do that again." He looked at Adam, making a half-hearted attempt to rekindle his anger.

"I won't. I promise," said Adam.

"Get the hell to bed." His dad stood up and walked slowly into the bedroom, shaking his head.

His mom opened the cupboard door and took down the money jar. Scooping up the coins, she dropped them in as quietly as she could.

"Good night, Adam." She smiled softly at him, squeezing his shoulder, and followed his father into the bedroom.

CHAPTER THIRTY-SEVEN

Soon fall was winter, marked by a solemn Christmas that reminded them that Anni had been gone a whole year. It wasn't just their family that was solemn. Others had lost sons in the fighting, and far more were missing their boys and wondering where they were spending Christmas.

After more long months of evenings and weekends crammed with studying and homework assignments, spring approached, and with it, some of the optimism that came with sunshine and warmth. Thoughts of college consumed Adam. After college, maybe he would move even further away than Budapest to get a job. He didn't talk about this to anyone other than Franz. His family wouldn't be happy. But Adam was getting more excited with every passing week. He'd be a college student, living in the city. Just a few more months.

"Okay, Mr. Post, I think this is the last one," Adam grinned at his teacher as he handed him a folder full of papers. "Unless you've found more for me."

"No, that was indeed the last assignment in the grade ten curriculum. And Miss Krause tells me you have finished everything in her subjects and your marks have been exemplary. Your exam marks were excellent too. I have them all here for you to have a look at. So I just need to mark this paper, and you will officially be a high school graduate. Congratulations Adam." Mr. Post smiled warmly at Adam and clapped him across the shoulder. Then his face got serious. "I had a letter from the college yesterday and I have some news. It seems that they don't have enough staff left to open in September, so you may have to wait a year. But as soon as the war is over, things will get back to normal and you can start college. You'll be ready when the time comes, my boy."

Adam stared at Mr. Post, not understanding. He felt disoriented. "What?"

"I'm sorry, Adam. It's just a temporary setback. You've had an incredible year, and now you'll be able to have a break before you hit the books again in college."

"Thank you, Mr. Post," Adam mumbled. Turning, he walked out of the room, and then out into the street. The war had been going on since he was ten years old. It could be years before it ended.

Standing on the street, Adam wasn't sure which way he wanted to go. He'd been planning to go and see Franz and announce that he was done. Turning in the opposite direction, he started to run. He didn't feel the tears that streamed down his cheeks. He just kept running.

"The college is shutting down. Teachers all gone to fight," Adam announced in a monotone voice at supper that night. He'd spent the afternoon slowly walking back from outside of town where he'd finally stopped running.

"Oh, Adam, after all your hard work!" his mom exclaimed.

"What are you going to do now?" Theresa asked, her eyes full of compassion for her brother. Adam's eyes filled with tears as he stared at his plate.

"So all this has been a waste of time?" his dad asked, dropping his fork onto his plate. "A whole year sitting around studying and taking fancy classes while everyone else in this house worked to keep food on the table, and now you can't go to college anyway?"

"It's not Adam's fault the college is shutting down," his mom said softly.

"Well, I will tell you all one thing. Adam will not be getting out of another year's work. Starting tomorrow, he will be pulling his weight again. And it's just in time. The Mahlers' cornfields need weeding and we can start tomorrow."

Yep, that's for sure, thought Adam as he pushed his food around his plate. The year had been a complete waste of time. Just like the rest of his life would be if he stuck around here.

PART TWO
A World at War

"Life is either a great adventure or nothing."

HELEN KELLER

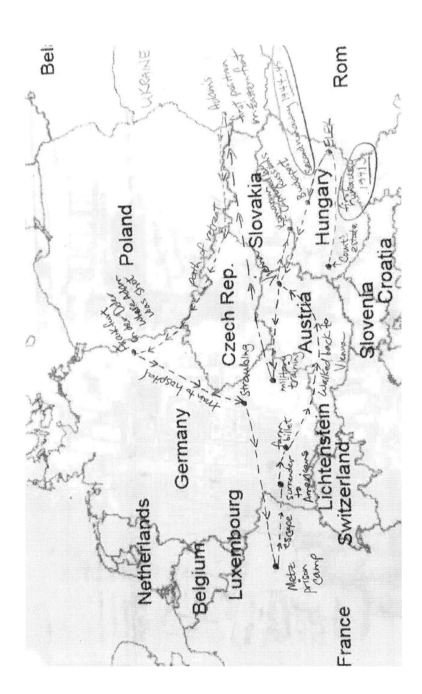

CHAPTER THIRTY-EIGHT

Summer 1944

Adam and Uchie sat side-by-side, gazing out the window at the rows of young corn and wheat speeding by as the train rolled towards Budapest. It had been a couple of weeks since he'd found out about the college. Summer was still young and harvest season was a couple of months away. By then they'd be far away.

"I wonder when we'll get our uniforms?" Adam mused out loud.

"Dunno," said his cousin. "I'm hungry." Just then the train began to slow.

"Here we are, Budapest. Let's figure out when our next train leaves and then have something to eat," said Adam as the train pulled to a stop. The boys got off and looked around. The station was deserted. As he thought back, a few things seemed familiar to Adam, but they'd looked different through the crack in the boxcar door. And that had been almost three years ago.

They walked over and read the schedule posted on the wall. Plenty of time. At the side of the platform, Adam lowered his lanky frame to the ground, untied his bundle, and pulled out his pocketknife. It was quite a big hunk of bacon he'd grabbed off the kitchen counter in the dark last night. His dad would probably be mad about that.

"Do you really think this is a good idea, Adam?"

"Of course it is. I'm not planning on rotting in Elek," Adam snapped, his voice cracking on the last word. Annoyed, he cleared his throat. He was 15. His voice still cracked regularly. "What are we going to do, prune grapevines for the rest of our lives? German soldiers get to go everywhere. France, Italy, Russia, England, you name it." Adam cut a slice of raw onion as he spoke, then leaned back against the fence and popped it in his mouth with a bite of the smoky bacon.

"It'll be dangerous," Uchie continued.

Adam swallowed. "Of course it'll be a bit dangerous. But Germany has superior weapons and very good strategies. They know how to fight and come out on top. It won't be like the Hungarian army. We'll get ourselves into Hitler's elite army, where we'll get the good stuff. We already talked about all this. Don't you wanna help chase the Russians back to Siberia?" Adam said enthusiastically.

Uchie looked doubtful.

The boys stopped talking as a train approached and stopped. A tall soldier carrying a filthy duffel bag stepped down from a car at the far end of the platform. Vacant eyes stared forward from his weary face as he walked in their direction. A long rip down the left side of his dirty overcoat flapped in the breeze. On his collar, the SS insignia was barely visible.

"Halt!"

The boys started as the command rang out. They hadn't noticed the young officer striding from the opposite direction, his crisp uniform with its gleaming buttons and newly polished boots a stark contrast to the soldier they'd been watching.

"Don't you know an officer when you see one?" the younger man barked loudly as he drew up to his full height in front of the soldier, who was taller by several inches. "You must salute an officer! Heil Hitler!" The young officer's arm flew up and locked in place in the Nazi salute, clearly expecting the weary soldier to follow suit.

The boys watched in fascination as the tired soldier met the young officer's gaze. As their eyes locked, the soldier pulled back the lapel of his filthy overcoat, and the officer's eyes dropped to the German cross that was pinned to the worn uniform underneath.

The soldier let his coat fall shut over the bravery medal. "Du Arschloch," he growled as he resumed walking.

Turning to watch the soldier walk away, the officer stood speechless, his arm hanging limp at his side where he'd let it drop. As the soldier disappeared, the officer regained his composure, spun on his heel and continued his brisk pace down the platform and out of sight in the opposite direction.

Uchie broke the silence. "We shouldn't go, Adam. Let's go home."

Adam looked at his cousin sitting beside him. Although Uchie was two years older than him, Adam was a head taller. Uchie's eyes were brimming with tears.

"I'm going." Adam was resolute. "I'm not going back. If you want to go back, you go, Uchie, no problem. But I'm going. I'm going to find where you sign up, and I'm going to do it. I'm not going back to Elek."

Uchie sat quietly for a few minutes and then stood up. "I don't want to go. Keep my food." He held out his bundle to his younger cousin. "Good luck."

Adam watched as Uchie walked back toward the platform they'd arrived at, then he got to his feet. His train was pulling in.

"Okay, see you when I get back," he yelled.

Uchie turned and lifted his hand in a half-hearted wave. "See you, Adam."

Adam turned and boarded. The sign hanging from the side of the train said Vienna.

CHAPTER THIRTY-NINE

"Vienna!" came the voice of the ticket collector over the noise of the train. "Vienna!" The voice was right outside the bathroom door now. Adam held his breath and pushed his body up against the wall behind the door as hard as he could. The door didn't open. "Vienna!" The voice was moving farther away. As Adam let out his breath, he felt the train begin to slow. Opening the door, he peeked out, then turned and checked the other direction before letting himself out into the empty corridor and casually joining the crowd preparing to disembark.

For a minute or two he stood and watched the crowd of people on the street outside the station, rushing home after work. Then he settled on a stout, older woman to ask. She hesitated, looking him up and down before meeting his gaze. Her eyes were sad. Adam wished he'd asked someone else.

"You still have to be 17 to sign up," she had finally answered.

Adam had heard all about it on the radio, how Germany had lowered the fighting age to 17 to support the last big push. With battles raging on so many fronts, Hitler needed more men.

"Yes ma'am. I just turned 17," he lied, smiling down at her politely.

The woman sighed heavily and then turned to point back in the direction she'd come from. "It's on Gloriette Strasse. Back that way."

Gloriette Strasse was easy to find. Adam stood there, facing a rather plain door like all the others on the street that opened into any manner of offices. This one had a number six painted on it. The sign hanging above read "Schutzstaffeln Headquarters and Recruitment." He'd made it this far. He just needed to convince them that he was 17 and worthy of being a part of the top military force in the world. He cleared his throat and reached for the doorknob.

Thirty minutes later, Adam walked back out the door. Out on the street, he squinted into the brightness of late afternoon sun pouring between two buildings opposite where he stood. *Grenadier Baumann! He was in!* He had to get moving. The recruitment officer had said the train to the training camp was leaving within the hour. Spinning on his heel the way they did when they practiced at Hitler Youth meetings, he turned in the direction of the station and marched jauntily down the street, whistling a happy tune.

CHAPTER FORTY

Adam sat on the edge of his cot after supper. He'd been at the training camp over two months, and the excitement he'd felt on arrival was
long since forgotten, replaced with a blur of yelling, marching, aching
muscles, and blisters. But he was getting stronger. He didn't notice the
weight of his boots anymore, even when they marched all night. Until
a blister broke open mid-march. Thankfully, callouses were forming and
there weren't many spots left to blister. And his shoulders and back weren't
as raw from his rucksack anymore. They still ached, but he was sleeping
through it now. In recent weeks the training officer had even asked him
to play his harmonica on their marches while the other recruits sang army
songs to pass the time.

Absently, Adam rubbed the scabbed-over tattoo under his left arm.
It was an A. His blood type. If he needed a transfusion while unconscious
in the field, they'd know what type to give him. And all the needles the
nurses had stuck in his rear end would protect him from getting sick.
Thank God he hadn't passed out with his pants down around his knees
like the guy in front of him in line. Adam grinned inwardly at the memory. How embarrassing. He hadn't enjoyed the needles or the tattooing,
but after one of the officers had explained that none of the other armies
had this kind of scientific smarts, he was grateful for them. Even the regular German army didn't get all these privileges. Although his feelings
about the SS and the war itself would soon change, that evening Adam
was still thankful he'd been accepted into Hitler's elite force and determined to make the most of the adventure ahead.

The gas mask drill earlier in the day had darn near killed him though.
By the time he'd reached the top of the hill wearing that stupid mask, with
his rucksack jammed full of rocks, his lungs had been burning so badly
from the lack of oxygen that he'd almost passed out. The next day they
would be doing the drill again. He looked around. Most of the recruits
were already sleeping. Four-thirty came early. Quickly, he unscrewed the
filter from his gas mask, then pulled a wooden match out of his pocket,

keeping an eye on the door. Breaking off a little piece, he shoved it carefully into the threads and screwed the filter back over top of it. He quickly looked at it from every angle. You couldn't tell. Tucking his mask under his bed, he stretched out. A moment later, he was asleep.

As he reached the top of the hill the next morning, Adam congratulated himself. He'd made it up the hill easily. He stumbled a bit to feign fatigue, and leaned over, pretending to catch his breath.

"Baumann, is there something wrong with your mask?" Adam froze. The officer was striding over to him.

Adam pulled off his mask. "No, sir!" he responded quickly.

"Then why is the lens fogged up? Give it to me." As the officer grabbed the mask, Adam looked around. Everyone else's mask was clear. His stomach rose into his throat as the officer unscrewed the filter. The bit of matchstick fell to the ground in plain sight.

"Are you trying to be a smart-ass, Baumann? Do you think you know better than me? Do you think you don't need to know how to survive with a gas mask?"

"No, sir, I don't think that," Adam said briskly, looking the commander in the eye.

"How did this bit of wood get into the threads of your mask then Baumann?"

"I don't know, sir."

"Get down on the ground this minute, Baumann, and give me a hundred. The other men will be having a well-deserved rest while you entertain us with your feeble push-ups. And after that you will put this mask on and you will run down this hill and back up, then down again and up again while we wait right here."

A week later they shipped out.

CHAPTER FORTY-ONE

WWII Eastern Front, Late 1944

The company they joined was stationed at a tent camp in the western part of the Ukraine. Their new commander gave them a speech about being ready to lay their lives down for the Führer and the future of the Aryan race. Then he assigned them to a rotating night watch. A week into it, none of the new recruits had been sent to the front to fight. No one knew what was happening. The bunkhouse crackled with tension as they rehashed the rumours they'd heard. Some were saying that the Russians were retreating, scared off by the arrival of additional troops. Others thought the enemy was lying low waiting for reinforcements. Adam had also heard that they were waiting for reinforcements themselves and then they'd be launching a surprise attack on the Russians. The commander didn't seem to have much information either, ignoring them or giving only vague answers when they asked.

Night watch was four hours at a time. Nervously, Adam patrolled back and forth well out in front of the camp as the commander had instructed, watching for activity to the east. The moon was bright. A couple more days and it would be full, and although Adam didn't know it, by then everything would be very different.

But for tonight, the bright moonlight on the space between the German and Russian lines that they called "no man's land" showed a barren, strangely serene landscape. The noises that were drifting to him across the expanse as he stared out towards the Russian side sounded almost like a party. Gripping the guard rifle, Adam wondered what they were celebrating.

The next instant he froze. There was something out there. He peered into the darkness. Maybe he'd imagined it. No, there it was again, a dark shadow moving towards him. Holding his breath, he squinted harder, trying to make out what it was. It wasn't moving very quickly. Was it a man? Several men? Frozen to the spot, Adam watched as the dark shape came closer. His mind was racing. Should he shoot? Maybe he should call for his superior. What the hell should he do? He should take cover. Darting behind a tree, he fumbled with his rifle, checking that it was ready to fire, and then peered out through the branches to where the shadow was still moving towards him. As he clenched and unclenched his sweaty hands on his rifle, the shadow got closer until Adam was pretty sure it was just one man.

He's looking for the guard, thought Adam, his heart pounding in his ears. *He'll kill me and then they'll start a surprise attack!*

"Nemetskiy."

Adam jumped as the Russian word reached his ears. The guy was closer than he'd thought.

"Nemetskiy," the Russian called softly again.

Adam had heard that word before. It was Russian for "German." He closed his eyes for a second, trying to swallow the bile that was rising up his throat. He was going to have to shoot first. Raising his rifle to aim, he tried to steady his shaking hands as he peered down the barrel of the gun. But something wasn't right. The Russian wasn't carrying a weapon. Maybe he wanted to surrender! Adam had heard of that happening. Sometimes they would sneak over at night to surrender rather than be gunned down in the daily fighting. Or to avoid starvation in their own camp. If he wanted to surrender, Adam would have to capture him and take him to his superior. Taking a deep breath, he stepped out from behind the tree, and clumsily pointed his rifle at the Russian.

"Stop!" Adam commanded. Horrified at the nervous croak that came from his lips, he cleared his throat, stood tall, and tried again. "Stop!"

Only a few metres away now, the Russian stopped and stood there swaying like a sapling on a breezy day. Adam could see his face clearly. This guy wasn't much older than him! Then the gaunt face broke into a boyish smile, revealing a couple of missing teeth. The stream of Russian words that followed was incomprehensible to Adam. Why was he smiling like that?

Adam summoned his courage and barked, "Are you here to surrender?" in the deepest voice he could muster.

The Russian laughed and waved at Adam. "Hallo, Nemetskiy! Cigarettes? Cigarettes pozhaluysta?" Now the guy was making smoking motions. Then he pointed to a bottle Adam hadn't noticed in his other hand. "Cigarettes pozhaluysta?" he repeated.

Not sure what else to do, Adam fumbled in his pocket and awkwardly threw his packet of smokes to the Russian, trying to keep his rifle aimed with his other hand. He'd only just learned to smoke a few weeks ago.

"Spasibo comrade!" the soldier said in a happy voice as he bent to pick up the package, nearly toppling forward. As he regained his balance, he stood up and lifted his prize above his head. "Cigarettes!" he cheered and smiled widely at Adam again. Stooping, he gently tossed his bottle towards Adam's feet. "Vodka!"

Incredulous, Adam watched as the drunken soldier spun on his heel and did a little jig as he headed back to his outfit waving the cigarettes and singing quietly in a slurred voice. The sound blended into the hooting and bursts of laughter coming from the distance across the field.

Adam exhaled. What should he do now? He'd given cigarettes to an enemy soldier and then let him escape. Was that punishable? Adam looked around behind him nervously. There was no movement in the direction of his own camp. Nothing. Shivering violently under the dampness of his cooling sweat, he picked up the bottle, unscrewed the lid and sniffed it, then shuddered involuntarily. Tipping it up, he swallowed once, twice, three times. As the fire travelled down his throat and began to warm his insides, he recapped the bottle and set it down beside the tree. Had he known what was coming, he might have sat down and tried harder to enjoy it.

CHAPTER FORTY-TWO

"UP, NOW!"

Adam jumped to his feet, looking around desperately in the semi-darkness, his mind jarred by the screaming of the officer near the foot of his bunk.

"We got 15 minutes of dark left! They're launching an attack and I guarantee they're not going to wait until full daylight! MEN! Get your gear and get to the front and dig in!"

The bunkhouse was in chaos. Adam fumbled with the clip on the handle of his spade. His fingers weren't cooperating. Finally he got it clipped on, then threw his gas mask strap over his head and around one shoulder, picked up his machine gun and the bag with the tripod and extra barrel, and ran for the door. A cook stood at the door, shoving something at the soldiers running past. Adam grabbed one and stuffed it in his pocket.

Joining the line of dark forms jogging up the gentle slope towards the front line, Adam shook his head, still waking up, and adjusted the load he was carrying. The moon had set. It was darker than it had been when he'd finished his watch a few hours ago. Everything was covered in white frost. At the top of the slope, the commander and a couple of officers were rushing around calling out orders in hushed voices. Adam dropped his gear where the officer pointed, a few metres to the right of the gunner he'd been following, and unclipped his spade. Cold sweat ran down his back as he worked frantically to make an indent in the ground, alternately scraping and trying to push his shovel into the frozen earth to scoop out the dirt. Every second or two he glanced forward anxiously, towards the Russian line. He couldn't see any movement. Glancing sideways, he tried to see if the other holes were growing any faster than his. A minute or two later, a group of ammo carriers came running up from behind, fanning out to deliver boxes of bullets to each gunner. The ammo boxes were heavy, and the guys assigned to run ammo had to be strong enough to carry two at once and run like hell.

When his hole was big enough, Adam threw down his spade and lay flat, catching his breath. He could hear the hushed voice of the commander telling them to ready their weapons, and the muffled banging of ammo box lids. He fumbled to screw the tripod onto his gun, and clumsily fed the end of the ammo strip into the carriage. Then he lay still again, staring through the sight on the barrel of his gun, heart hammering in his chest.

"Here they come!" the commander called out quietly. Sure enough, the line out in front of them that had looked deserted a few moments earlier, was alive with movement. Adam strained to hear the next command. "Take aim, but don't fire until you hear the command. We need to let them get close so we can kill as many of the bastards as possible. And don't forget to change your barrel after every other round, or you'll lose accuracy."

Shaking with terror, Adam stared through the first hint of grey light as hordes of Russian soldiers surged towards them, holding rifles aimed clumsily towards the German line as they ran. Second by second they got closer. Finally, when he thought he couldn't wait any longer without being seen, the commander barked out the order to fire. Adam pulled the trigger and held it in, moving his gun left and right. Still running, the Russians began to shoot. Then they were falling, all up and down the line, falling. Behind them, the wall of bodies kept coming. The air stank of gunpowder. Adam kept shooting.

At some point, he became aware of the bombardment of noise all around him. The staccato of machine gunfire punctuated by rifle fire, almost drowning out the tortured screams of the wounded. Every now and then, there was enough space in the noise to make out the lower pitched moans of the dying. It came from every direction. He'd changed his barrel so many times. How long had he been shooting?

The onslaught continued for most of the day, each new surge of Russian soldiers coming at them minutes after the last. At some point in the afternoon, the intensity began to lessen. Adam dug in his pocket for the rations he'd shoved there that morning and swallowed a few bites. As the sun approached the horizon, the fighting became sporadic, and by the time full darkness fell, the field was eerily quiet. Adam watched as guys crawled out of their holes and crept back to camp. Shaking with cold and shock, he joined them.

Back in camp, he counted for a while as stretchers and bodies draped in canvas tarps were loaded into trucks. Then he stopped counting, went to his bunk, and lay down with his gun.

CHAPTER FORTY-THREE

From that day on, time was a confused blur of terror and exhaustion. Adam's eardrums rang at night, tortured by the constant explosions and hammering of gunfire. His eyes burned from lack of sleep and staring down the barrel of his gun. When he was given a few hours to rest, he slept like the dead. When he was awake, he followed orders. When to return to the front line, when to fire, when to stop firing, when to dig a new hole, when to return to camp. The most important thing was to stay covered, and hence alive. A close second was to stay warm, or at least avoid freezing to death.

Every day or two they moved, usually backward. Sometimes they retreated on foot at a run, other times they loaded hastily into tanks with truck tires on the front, called half-tracks, where at least they were safe from light artillery fire. When there was time, a camp was hastily set up in a new location. But as winter set in, the pace of their retreat increased, and if they didn't find a deserted building to hole up in, their foxholes were their only shelter.

Nighttime in the foxhole was the worst, when darkness fed his fear. Curled up in a ball, his musty-smelling blanket wrapped tightly around him, Adam shook with cold, terror, and in his darkest hours, silent sobs. His brief snatches of sleep were blissful relief when they brought dreams of home and his mom or Franz and Tony. Other times he thrashed himself awake in a cold sweat, heart racing, willing his growing nightmares to fade.

CHAPTER FORTY-FOUR

Things had been quiet for two whole nights and the day in between, almost like the Russians hadn't followed them when they'd run this time. Without the noise of combat, Adam had slept deeply, curled in the fetal position in his hole. Before dawn, new orders came down the line, hole to hole. At daybreak they would be advancing to the northeast, reclaiming some ground. As the horizon turned from black to grey, Adam watched the white plumes of his breath against the sky for a while, then pulled out his harmonica. The notes, even as quiet as they were, helped to lessen his desperation for a few minutes. Advancing. Reclaiming ground. Who were they trying to kid? The result was the same every time. Try to advance and get pushed back even further, leaving more dead behind.

After loading their bedrolls onto the trucks and eating a little can of some kind of gelatinous meat, they crept forward through a sparse stand of bare trees. Adam peered around nervously. The fighting had obviously been heavy here, and he tried not to look at the stiff corpses on the ground around him. Most were face up, knocked backward by the impact of the shots that had killed them. Some stared skyward with open eyes intact, faces frozen by winter and death. Others were mangled by bullets they had taken to the face and chest. Limbs and torn bodies marked the spots where grenades had found their targets.

Suddenly the rattle of machine gun fire shattered the quiet. Adam threw himself to the ground, landing hard on his gas mask canister. The breath driven from his lungs, he rolled onto his side and fumbled for his spade, gasping desperately for air while he scraped at the frozen ground. *Goddammit all to hell!* Adam thought, filled with rage. They hadn't been advancing more than half an hour.

The German riflemen positioned at regular intervals behind the line began a counter attack to distract the Russians while the gunners dug in. Rolling into position in the pitiful indent he'd made, Adam flung his tripod and machine gun into position and opened fire. Not far in front of him, Russians were pouring out of some kind of trench and swarming towards them. Gunners up and down the German line had given up digging and begun firing into the oncoming horde. Bullets ripped into the bodies, knocking them backwards or spinning them sideways as they fell. *What the hell?* thought Adam as he watched the swarm in front of him. Some of those bastards were waving handguns. Fools. They'd never make it close enough to get a decent shot at a German with a handgun. Suddenly, an explosion deafened him. A dozen or more Russians flew through the air like rag dolls directly in front of him. In a matter of seconds, the gap was filled with more enemy soldiers running forward over top of their mangled comrades. From the corner of his eye, he saw another explosion of bodies at the far-right end of the Russian line. The roar of the grenade came a split second later.

Adam stared at the enemy soldier running directly towards him through the chaos and let off the trigger of his machine gun. The soldier was empty handed. A moment later, the Russian jerked violently backwards, eyes wide with surprise as machine gun fire tore up his chest and belly. Someone else had got him. Adam swallowed hard, watching the spot where the unarmed soldier had fallen, until a series of bullets struck the frozen ground beside him, peppering his helmet and shoulders with frozen mud and rocks. Refocusing on the swarm running towards the German line, Adam put his finger back on the trigger.

"Where's Schubert?" Adam yelled at the ammo carrier who slid in beside him a while later. Schubert had been running ammo for this section for the last several days.

"Over there," the guy motioned with his head. "Dead."

He heard the scream of the artillery shell, but before he could move, he was thrown sideways by the force of the explosion, and the world disappeared.

Adam's right ear was deaf as he lay on his left side, struggling to open his eyes and take a breath while debris rained down on him. He'd felt the heat of the hot metal on his face. Scrambling desperately back into position, he squinted and scanned the area to his right. He could see at least three motionless bodies and a couple who were writhing and scream-ing in agony. One or more guys who had taken a direct hit lay in pieces, torn apart by the grenade. *Where the hell had it come from?* Keeping his head as low as he could, he scanned frantically, his eyes darting across the torn up earth. *How did a grenade launcher get that close?* As he continued to search desperately, he knew they would be racing to reload.

"There!" screamed Adam, pointing wildly to a pair of Russians crouched in a crater slightly north of his position, scrambling to reload the weapon. Hoping at least one or two others had seen them, Adam looked down the barrel of his gun and began to fire. An instant later both of the Russians fell backwards. Adam let out his breath. With any luck, at least one shot had hit their weapon and damaged it too.

"Medics coming in! Cover!" he heard the head of the medical unit scream close behind him, over the gunfire.

Focusing on the section of the Russian line directly in front of him, Adam sprayed bullets at the fastest rate. Others were doing the same. They couldn't afford to lose any of the medical staff. Out of the corner of his eye he could see the medics running from body to body, crouched low, checking for pulses. The last team heaved a wounded soldier onto their stretcher and jogged away, heads down. When they'd reached cover, Adam slowed his firing pace slightly. Moments later, the last of Adam's ammo strips dropped out of his gun, spent.

Dammit, where was the ammo carrier? Looking desperately back over one shoulder and then the other, he couldn't see anyone coming. *What the hell?* The gunner to his left was still shooting, but a couple on his right looked like they were out of ammo as well. Suddenly Adam heard the explanation.

"Retreat! Out of ammo! Rifles, cover the retreat!"

CHAPTER FORTY-FIVE

From what he could see, Adam figured the enemy was suffering a half-dozen casualties or more for every German they were lucky enough to hit. But as Christmas came and went, the flow of Russians showed no signs of lessening. Week after week, the shrinking German force retreated, first through northern Hungary and before long, into the hills of Czecho-slovakia, areas more populous than the barren landscapes of the Ukraine.

Old men and women carrying ragged bundles or pulling little carts that carried what was left of their lives streamed in both directions along the roadways, seemingly not knowing which way would be better, or worse. Often they had little children in tow. Hatred flashed in the eyes of many as they stared at the Germans. These people believed the Russians were coming soon to liberate them. From what Adam had heard, life un-der Russian occupation wasn't going to be much of a liberation.

Winter had already been endless and it was only January. Then came the news that they would be billeted to local homes for the next while, near their latest line of defence. The prospect of sleeping indoors in a warm space occupied by other humans, lifted their spirits a little.

A few mornings after setting up in the little Czech village, the com-mander barked out an address to Adam, with an order to take two colleagues and locate three of their men who had missed roll call. The trio headed for the billet address. The front door was wide open. Inside, the missing soldiers lay face-down in pools of their own blood. Throats slit. The air in the room was thick with the stench of warm blood. Adam gagged as he worked to keep his footing in the slippery mess while they dragged the bodies out.

New orders came not long after. Rumour was that the enemy coa-lition had launched aggressive attacks from all sides. They were to fight when necessary, slow down the Russian advance when possible, and make their way north towards Berlin for a military regrouping.

Similar orders had been issued across the Eastern Front, and as they crossed onto German soil, disorganized fragments of units converged, joining the masses of terrorized civilians fleeing in all directions. The roadways became sloughs of mud and slush, torn up by the wheels and tracks of hundreds of tanks and trucks, while the allied forces rained destruction down on the miserable scene, determined to eradicate Hitler's weakened armies once and for all. Where there was any sign of troops or military vehicles, low flying planes attacked, dropping explosives and indiscriminately mowing down anyone in their path with sprays of bullets. Ditches and roadsides were littered with corpses of elderly people, women, young children, and soldiers alike. Dead horses blocked the roads in places, the wagons they'd been pulling now deserted or laden with bullet riddled bodies, depending on whether the family they had been carrying had lived to flee on foot or been cut down.

As the troops did their best to survive the relentless onslaught, this horrific collateral damage – the suffering of defenceless, innocent people caught in the clash – became the most disturbing of the vast collection of indelible wartime memories that Adam would carry around for the rest of his days.

CHAPTER FORTY-SIX

Early 1945

The sun continued to rise and set over the scenes of carnage across Europe, as what was left of Adam's unit alternately retreated and futilely attempted to establish a defensible position. The shortage of ammunition and food was a constant problem.

"The road ahead is bombed out. We can't get any further. But there's a unit with an operational field kitchen about ten kilometres from here. We're going to unload and march to the camp for some hot food and a bed while the trucks find a way around and catch up."

A surge of simple, childlike joy rose in Adam's chest as he heard the officer's words. It had been at least a week since they'd had anything other than stale bread and a few mouthfuls of canned fish each day. The only things he could imagine that would be better than a hot meal, were getting away from the horrors on the road, and having a place to sleep for a whole night.

Peering ahead, Adam craned his neck to see what was being ladled into each soldier's mess tin. It smelled heavenly. He closed his eyes to the camp around him and sniffed onions, maybe potatoes, some sort of meat? It almost smelled like home. Suddenly he jerked his eyes open as he swayed and stumbled. He had to eat and then he could sleep. Only a few more in line ahead of him now. Looking towards the stew pot again, Adam's eyes rose to the cook ladling out the food, who was looking back at him intently. A moment later the cook looked away and focused on the dish he was filling. Curiously, Adam studied him. Maybe a bit familiar. Maybe not. He'd seen so many thousands of unknown faces since leaving home six months ago. As Adam reached the front of the line, the cook dug deep into the huge pot. The ladle came up heaped with chunks of meat and a couple of potatoes. Adam grinned. Digging in again, he filled Adam's tin bowl right to the brim, then smiled at him briefly before shifting his attention to the next soldier. Adam carried the hot dish gingerly. He didn't want to spill a drop. Setting it down beside the closest tree, he lowered his lanky frame to the wet ground and lifted the bowl onto his lap, then leaned against the tree for a moment before digging in. As he shovelled the stew into his mouth, he glanced up over his spoon towards the front of the serving line. The cook who was ladling out the food was looking over at him. *Why is he staring at me?* Adam wondered as he continued spooning the meat and gravy into his mouth.

As he scraped the last few drops from his bowl a few minutes later, Adam looked up. The cook was headed over.

"What's your name, kid?" the cook asked with a smile, looking down at Adam.

"Adam Baumann."

"Where are you from?"

"Hungary."

"Hungary's a big place. What town?"

"Small town on the Romanian border. You probably don't know it. It's called Elek. E-L-E-K."

"What part of Elek?" The cook was grinning.

"By the cemetery. Why?"

"Grape Street, right? And I bet your dad's name is George," he responded, grinning even wider as he lowered himself to the ground beside Adam. "It's sure good to see a familiar face, Adam Baumann. Name's Henry Kuhn, from Elek. I've worked with your dad a few times, harvesting wheat."

"Wow. I haven't seen a single person I know since I left home last summer. Not even anyone from eastern Hungary," said Adam.

"So you've been out here since last summer? It's going on two years for me, since early '43. You ever get a chance to make contact with your family? You know, let them know you're ok?" Henry asked as darkness settled on the camp.

"Nope, not once. I asked about writing a couple of times, but they say there's no more mail service into Hungary now since the Russians took it over." Adam's voice cracked when he mentioned the Russians occupying Hungary. So many nights he'd lain on his cot, or in his foxhole looking up at the sky, wondering what was happening in Elek.

"I heard about a way to get letters in, and I've arranged to send one. You've heard of Marika Rokk, the actress, right? She's financing a smuggling operation that takes letters into Hungary to Budapest, and then the letters get mailed from an address she holds there. Apparently, the local mail is still running, so if they mail my letter from Budapest, it will be delivered to Elek. I'll write that I saw you, and then my mom can let yours know that you're okay. I don't know if it will actually get there, but I'm going to try." Henry smiled warmly at Adam.

"That would be great. That would be really great." Adam looked away for a minute, blinking back his tears.

The command to prepare to head out came as the sun was peeking over the horizon the next morning. The half-tracks had found a way through and caught up with them. Adam hadn't seen Henry while they were having their hasty breakfast. He hoped the Eleker would appear soon. He'd hate to leave without talking to him again.

"There you are, Adam." Adam spun around to see Henry walking towards him from the kitchen supply shed.

"Load up, men!" the assistant commander yelled out from where he stood near the row of half-tracks.

Henry stuck his hand into the sack he was carrying. "Looks like you're moving out right away. Here, put this in your bag." He handed Adam a chunk of something wrapped in brown paper and a smaller square package. "Just a little extra ration of salami and cheese. Better than what we've had for quite a while."

"Wow! Can you really give me that?" Adam asked disbelievingly. He was always hungry!

"Think of it as a Christmas present. Probably didn't have much of a Christmas out there, fighting for the Führer. So Merry belated Christmas, Adam Baumann. Keep your head down. I'll see you in Elek after a victorious end to this war." Henry raised his arm in a mock Heil Hitler salute, and grinned. "And I'll tell my mom I met you here."

"Baumann!" the assistant commander barked. Adam looked around and realized he was the only guy that wasn't loaded.

"See you, Henry. Thank you!" As Adam jogged to the convoy and climbed aboard the last vehicle, he felt less miserable than he had in some time. Imagine, someone from Elek. And he was going to get a message to Mom!

CHAPTER FORTY-SEVEN

The commander had said that morning that they were close to the Oder River, and that they'd have some shelter if they could cross and get to Frankfurt on the Oder. And after that, Berlin wasn't far. They were going to make it.

Crack, crack, crack! Adam jerked his head up. How long had he been dozing? Peering over the edge of the hole, he spotted them immediately, streaming out from behind the knoll almost directly in front of his position, firing off rifle shots in his general direction. Adam cursed and pulled viciously on the butt end of his gun to swivel it on the tripod. One or two other gunners began firing on them too, and most of the Russians didn't get far. After a couple dozen, the stream of soldiers stopped. That knoll was the same place the grenades had come from a couple of hours ago. How many more were back there?

Adam looked around. He needed a better view. There were a few trees and a sizeable boulder about fifty or sixty metres to the right. If he could shelter behind that, he might have enough of an angle to fire on whoever was back there. *Crack!* The same time he heard the shot, Adam felt a spray of dirt from the ground beside his foxhole. They had him sighted! Desperately, his eyes searched the knoll and the areas to the left and right of it. Where was the shooter? *Crack!* He pulled his head back down below the top edge of his cover as a bigger spray of frozen mud hit him. The shot was closer. He had to move.

"I need cover!" he screamed. The crack of rifle fire immediately filled the air to his left as he picked up his gear and stared for a moment at where he was going. Then he was up. *Run!. . . Run!. . .* The stupid spade banged the side of his knee with every step. He reached down to try to hold it still as he ran, his other arm wrapped around his machine gun and the attached tripod.

Almost there. Only another ten metres.

Dammit, his leg hit something, and he stumbled. Don't fall. Don't fall! The frozen mud exploded ahead of him. They were firing at him!

He stumbled again. Dammit, just a few more steps! Suddenly, his left leg kicked something, hard. Falling forward onto his chest, he clawed at the icy ground, and pushed himself forward over the frozen mud with his right leg. Where was his left leg?! Push! Push!

Almost there! A bullet exploded to his left, then another and another, each one closer. Flying ice and rocks stung his face. Push!

A final heave with his arms and right leg and he was behind the boulder. Adam squeezed his eyes shut and gritted his teeth. Pain seared down his left leg. He gasped for air as the ground spun underneath him. The twang of the bullets striking the boulder and the thud of those that hit the ground on either side of his shelter reached him through the swirling blackness, then faded.

Suddenly, his eyes flew open as the crack of gunfire penetrated his consciousness. He was on the ground. He looked wildly around, his breath ragged. Where was his weapon? As he scrambled to his hands and knees, a hot knife of pain shot through his leg, and he collapsed onto his right side. Taking a deep breath, he opened his eyes a crack and looked down to figure out where the red-hot pain was coming from. Blood. His leg was soaked in blood. He shut his eyes tight again. He needed to get his weapon. The machine gun fire that had roused him was close. Gritting his teeth, he opened his eyes once more. His gun was beside him. Reaching for it, he looked around. No bullets. He needed an ammo carrier.

He squinted and tried to focus on his surroundings. To his left he could make out another machine gunner, crouched behind a mound of frozen mud and roots, firing aggressively towards the Russian line. Then he saw more machine gunners. More than they'd had earlier. Another unit must have joined them. Lying back, Adam closed his eyes. He needed bullets. Where was his ammo guy? No, he'd been shot. He reached down to feel his leg. It was sticky. Where were the medics?

Sometime later, he regained consciousness. His leg was on fire. After a few breaths, he opened his eyes a crack. Snow was drifting down onto him through the dusk. The gunfire was further away than it had been. He shivered and peered out to where the line had been, but there were no gunners out there. Scanning towards the Russian line, he spotted movement in the distance to the north. The fighting had moved slightly. His mouth was gritty. He ran his tongue around his gums and spat. Where were the medics? Adam couldn't see anyone near him. The makeshift camp was a few hundred metres back, if it was still there. He was shivering violently. Clenching his jaw, he rolled onto his front and let out an anguished cry as the pain tore up his leg. Waiting a moment to catch his breath while the pain subsided a fraction, he turned towards where the camp should be, and began to drag himself through the snow and muck.

CHAPTER FORTY-EIGHT

Adam groaned. A few seconds later, his eyes flew open. It was dark. He must have fallen asleep in his hole. Where was his gun? He pushed himself up on one elbow, then gasped and fell back as pain shot through his left leg. That's right. He'd been shot. Where was he now? That noise was train wheels, he thought, staring at the ceiling. Turning his head, Adam realized with a start there was someone lying close alongside him. The guy's eyes were closed.

"I see you're awake." Adam heard a voice come from his other side and turned in that direction. The speaker was crouched beside him, holding a metal cup. A red cross decorated his shoulder.

"Where are we going?" croaked Adam.

"To Straubing. Have a drink." The medic held a cup to Adam's lips and helped him lift his head. Adam took a few swallows and then laid his head back down as the medic continued. "There's a hospital there that's still operational. They'll put your leg back together. It's slow going though. We already stopped twice today for bomb damage on the tracks. Luckily, it wasn't bad and we were able to patch it up and get the train moving again. So I'm not sure how long it will be before we reach the hospital. Go back to sleep if you can."

"Baumann... Baumann...."

Adam rose slowly through the layers of fog and opened his eyes. It was the medic. Now he was holding a tin bowl and a spoon.

"Hungry? I'm going to feed you some broth." The medic put the soup on the floor next to Adam, then gently lifted his head and put a rolled-up blanket under it.

Adam opened his mouth and closed his eyes. So tired. The liquid was warm and a bit salty. Soup? Hungry.

"Baumann...

"Adam...

"Baumann. . . ," The voice was familiar now. His eyes felt strange, like they were stuck shut. He tried harder and slowly got them open.

"You need to eat a bit more and drink some water. You're dehydrated. Here." The medic stuck the blanket under his head again, then held the cup of water to Adam's lips.

The next thing he was aware of was hot pain ripping through his leg.

"Owwwww!" he yelled, opening his eyes and struggling to sit up. The sun was too bright. He squeezed his eyes shut again, as hands pressed firmly against his shoulders, pushing him back down onto the stretcher.

"Sorry, soldier, you can't get up. We need to get you onto the truck and over to the hospital."

CHAPTER FORTY-NINE

After carrying him in through the large wooden doors of the hospital, the medics had transferred him onto one of the metal beds that lined both sides of the big room. His was the first bed on the right and he had a good view of the vast room without having to move much. All of the beds were full.

A lot of them look worse off than me, Adam told himself, clenching his teeth against the pain as he scanned the two long rows of bandaged heads and torsos, casted limbs, and bandaged stumps where arms and legs used to be. I hope they're not out of morphine, he thought next as he closed his eyes.

"Adam Baumann, I presume?" a soft female voice asked a few minutes later. When he opened his eyes, a pretty girl wearing a white hat was looking down at him.

"That's right," he croaked, and tried to clear his throat.

"Have a drink," she said, filling a tin cup from the jug on the table beside the bed, and passing it to him. "My name is Helen. I'm going to give you something for the pain," she continued, smiling sweetly as she lifted Adam's blanket. "I know it hurts, but I need you to roll onto your side if you can, so I can get at your backside."

"What's the date?" he asked when she'd finished giving him the shot.

"Sunday, February 11, 1945."

"My birthday," he smiled weakly at the nurse.

"Well, happy birthday! " she said brightly. "How old are you today?"

"Sixteen." Adam answered without thinking.

Helen looked down at Adam, her eyes filled with sadness and a hint of anger. A moment later, her warm smile returned. "I need to clean up your leg so the doctor can have a look before they take you into the operating room."

Two nights later, Adam lay in the dim room, gazing at the trough-like device that was supporting his leg, then followed the string with his eyes from the trough up to the ceiling. Turning his head, he looked out the window into the blackness, and tried to block out the night sounds of the room, the moans, the snoring, and whimpers of pain when someone tried to shift position. A moment later, soft shoes moved quickly across the floor as a nurse rushed to comfort a wounded soldier whose terrified cry told something of what was in his dreams. Outside the window, a bit of dawn light began to seep through the darkness. Big flakes of snow were drifting down, piling up on the window frame, softening the world a bit, if only temporarily.

Helen had brought him a little cupcake yesterday afternoon. She and two other nurses had gathered around his bed to sing happy birthday. For a few minutes, he'd felt almost happy. He closed his eyes and thought about home. Years seemed to have passed in the eight months he'd been gone. His mom would have been thinking about him on his birthday. He wondered if Henry had managed to get a letter through to Elek. The Russians were still occupying Hungary as far as he knew. Tears filled his eyes as he stared at the ceiling. He would pray if he believed in God. Pray that his mom was alright, standing by the stove, stirring a pot of stew, or maybe heating up some bacon fat to drizzle on warm bread. It was Monday. They'd probably be having bread, still be fresh from Saturday's baking. He was glad his mom and dad didn't know he was in the hospital. The last time one of them had been in the hospital was with Anni. She would have been seven now. A tear escaped from the corner of his eye and slid onto the pillow.

Oh Adam, he could hear her perfect little voice saying. *What are we going to do with you?*

"Good morning," a soft voice interrupted his thoughts.

Adam opened his eyes and blinked a couple of times before turning his head to look at the nurse. "Good morning."

"That was a good long sleep. Let's get you propped up for breakfast." Helen spoke quietly in the stillness of the morning. Her sweet smell filled Adam's nostrils as she straightened out his pillow.

"Is this a church?" he asked, thinking of the nuns who had walked through the previous evening, stopping to talk to a couple of the wounded soldiers.

"It was a church before the war. But it's been a hospital for a few years now. The nuns run it," she answered as she chopped a boiled egg onto the toast she'd brought for his breakfast.

Later that day, the doctor came by to check on Adam. He was pleased with how the surgery had gone, and assured Adam his leg would be fully functional again after it healed. It would need to hang in this contraption for a few weeks while the shattered bone regenerated, and then he would be on crutches for another month before he could put any weight on it. Adam laid his head back on the pillow as the doctor's words sank in. He had at least two months of reprieve.

CHAPTER FIFTY

The first month passed quickly, and before he knew it, Adam was up on crutches. There wasn't really anywhere to go, but he didn't mind at all. The hospital was a paradise. As busy as Helen and the other nurses were, they chatted with him whenever they could. At 16, the attentions of pretty, young nurses made Adam warm and happy like few other things could. On the days that Helen leaned down to give him a kiss on the cheek, he knew the hospital was the best place on earth.

"You look a little like my brother," Helen said softly one day. Her eyes were moist as she spoke. "I pray that he's at home with Mother. I haven't seen them in months. Father's been away fighting for over four years now, but I'm sure my brother is taking good care of everything at home." Her family lived close to the Polish border.

Almost all the soldiers who had been in the other beds when Adam had arrived were gone and replaced, sometimes twice, when the doctor came with the dreaded news. It was time to start walking without crutches. And once he'd done that for a few days, they were going to release him. The doctor explained that soldiers discharged from hospital in a condition deemed fit for duty, which Adam certainly would be, were to report directly to the military office in town for new orders. Adam's stomach churned. At least it wasn't cold outside anymore, he told himself as he looked out the window at the trees covered in bright springtime green leaves. Maybe it wouldn't be as bad.

CHAPTER FIFTY-ONE

April 1945

"Western Front," the officer said as he handed Adam some papers. A new company and unit to join. Hitler was consolidating in the west to push the Allied Forces out of Germany, back into Belgium and France. With a forced *Heil Hitler* Adam left the office and headed for the train station.

He wasn't travelling alone for long. The next day he met up with another soldier around his own age who had the same orders. Within a week, their little band was five strong, all heading for the Belgian border to join the front line there. One of the men had been the sole survivor when his unit had come under heavy fire just east of Berlin. Like Adam, the others had recently been released from hospital. Those who'd had a bit of reprieve while recovering from injuries looked to be in slightly better health. Then an officer joined them, making six. He'd escaped Berlin just as the Russians broke through the last defence line and poured into the city.

A couple of weeks later, they'd had no luck finding the front. With rail lines bombed out, and many roads impassable for the same reason, their only option was walking. The officer, who had taken charge of the little group, was determined to get back to fighting. Every day he spoke of pushing the enemy out of Germany. Adam hoped they never found the front, and he was pretty sure most of the others felt the same. Wandering around the countryside enjoying the spring air suited him just fine.

Sitting on the damp ground against a tree, Adam gazed up through the leaves. He'd just finished the last of his share of the sausage and bread from the farm they'd visited the previous day. It wasn't enough to fill him up. Hopefully they'd find some more food today. He missed the food at the hospital. It hadn't always been enough either, but they'd generally had at least two meals a day. Even more than the food, he missed the nurses.

A shaft of sunlight streamed down through a space in the canopy and warmed Adam's legs. He could straighten his left leg more every day.

The walking was doing him good. A plane droned in the distance. The Americans must be doing some kind of air raid in the area. Adam scanned the sky above them, happy for the cover of the trees.

"We made good time yesterday. I'd estimate we're here now," said the officer, jabbing his finger at the map that was spread out on the grass where they could all see it. "So, if that farmer was right, and the fighting is here," he jabbed again, "then we continue on the road we were on this morning, connect to this road here, and try to get a ride to the front and find someone in charge."

The farmer from whom they'd gotten the food had relayed what he'd heard a week or so earlier, before the radio broadcasts had stopped.

"Listen," said one of the guys. Adam could hear the rattle of tracks.

"Tanks!" said the officer excitedly. "They're coming from the west. They'll have the latest intelligence. Come on men, let's get down there."

They picked up their meagre belongings and jogged down the slippery hillside towards the sound. Adam limped along at the back and jumped out onto the road with the others just as the tank came around the corner.

It had a white star on it. The American white star. *What the hell?*

The soldiers riding on top of the tank lifted their weapons, aiming at the Germans and yelling.

The German officer cursed and raised his hands above his head. The rest of them followed suit. Adam's mouth went dry. His worst nightmare. Facing an armed enemy with no weapon. Hands in the air, he closed his eyes and swallowed, waiting for the shots.

A second later, one of the Americans yelled again. Adam opened his eyes. The soldier yelling at them was waving his rifle towards a truck that was pulling up behind the tank. It had the same white star on the door. As the Germans reached the rear of the truck, the American motioned them to climb in, then waved two men over to guard them and strode out of sight. The seconds ticked by. As they sat on the benches that lined each side of the truck box, Adam could hear the murmur of conversation from up near the tank.

Finally, the American commander yelled something to the two guards. Adam braced himself again. But instead of shooting, the guards climbed into the truck with them and leaned against the cab to steady themselves as the truck reversed and headed west, back the way it had come.

The six Germans and two Americans rode along in silence. Sweat ran down between Adam's shoulder blades. From the corner of his eye he watched the Americans standing with their backs against the cab of the truck, weapons ready. One of them looked over at him, and their eyes met. The American offered a little smile, and looked away, watching the scenery along the roadside.

A few kilometres later, one of the guards pulled a package of cigarettes out of his pocket and offered it to the Germans. A couple of the guys took one hesitantly. The American held out a match to each of them, then lit his own cigarette.

Not long after the spent cigarette butts had been tossed out onto the road, the fields that had been rolling past changed to dirty streets lined with small, run-down houses. Men in American uniforms mingled with men in civilian clothing. Listening closely to the voices calling out greetings and shouting commands, Adam couldn't recognize any of the words. The movement of a curtain caught Adam's eye, and as he watched more closely, he discerned faces peering out of the gloom behind many of the windows they were passing.

The truck slowed to a stop beside a little town square that was milling with activity. The soldiers and officers striding this way and that wore American uniforms. Their guards, still standing sentry at the front of the truck box, seemed to be waiting for something. A few minutes later, the American commander appeared at the back of the truck with two civilians wearing berets on their heads and semiautomatic rifles slung over their shoulders. Their eyes flashed angrily at the Germans. Pointing at the captives, the American officer said something, then turned and walked away. The men in berets barked some sort of command at them and beckoned angrily with their rifles for them to climb out of the truck.

"French freedom fighters," the German officer murmured quietly as he raised his hands into the air and climbed slowly down to the ground. They followed one by one until all six stood behind the truck. The engine started and the truck roared away. Adam turned his head and watched the two American soldiers who still stood in the back of the truck for a few seconds until they disappeared around a corner. Filled with dread, he turned to face their new captors.

CHAPTER FIFTY-TWO

At gunpoint, they marched southwest. As the light began to fade, the partisans herded the six Germans into an old barn, slamming and barring the doors behind them. The barn was set up as a crude prison of some sort, but it was vacant of other prisoners. They could hear a sentry moving around outside. Every now and then there were voices. The officer, his eye swollen shut from a blow across the side of his head with the butt of a rifle, said it was French they were speaking.

As the minutes ticked by, the little group talked quietly, trying to make sense of the situation. The front should be at least another 100 kilometres west.

But it was mid-May and unbeknownst to the captives, Hitler had been found dead a couple of weeks earlier. Germany had surrendered. The war was over.

Adam slept fitfully that night, listening to the others tossing and turning, jumping at every noise. The next morning, still at gunpoint and heavy with trepidation, the group boarded a train.

M-E-T-Z, Adam read on the side of the little station building as the train came to a stop a while later. Outside, the sun glared down on them as the Frenchmen jabbed them in the ribs, yelling angrily and motioning them forward impatiently. They'd just passed through a bombed-out neighbourhood on the train, but these houses, though small and shabby, looked intact. An old man appeared in a doorway and scowled silently as they walked by. Adam pulled his eyes away from the man and looked straight ahead. A few doors along, a woman stepped out with a toddler balanced on her hip. Her eyes grew big when she spotted the German uniforms, and she began to shriek, her free hand balled into an angry fist. Although he'd never heard the words before, Adam knew they were hateful.

The ruckus quickly drew more onlookers. Doors opened and people appeared in second and third story windows. Some stood silently, cursing the Germans with their eyes. Others lashed out with vicious sounding words. The soldier in front of Adam stumbled as a frying pan glanced off his helmet. Suddenly Adam's shoulder seared with heat. He jerked his hand up and fumbled to pull the steaming wet fabric of his shirt away from his skin, then looked around to find the source. A woman leaned out from a window above him, waving an empty pot in one hand and shaking her other fist, her lips curled in distaste. Adam watched in horror and then ducked as she took a breath and spat with all her force. The gob fell short and splatted on the cobblestones beside him. On the other side of the street a potted plant smashed to the ground.

A sharp jab in the lower back and more angry words from behind forced Adam along. Lowering his head, he stumbled through the chaos, stomach churning with fear, eyes focused on the boots ahead of him until finally, at the edge of the village a makeshift gate opened and swallowed them up, leaving the mob behind.

CHAPTER FIFTY-THREE

The stench of feces and urine and fear hit Adam in the face as the gate shut, imprisoning them within a tall, ramshackle fence. Masses of German prisoners milled about the expanse of muddy ground, shivering. As that day passed, and that night, and then the next, Adam fell into the wretched routine of the prison camp. Twice a day the guards poured cold boiled potatoes through a gap that ran along one side of the fence into rough wooden troughs that lined the ground. At night, the emaciated prisoners leaned against each other in huddles, the threadbare blankets they'd been issued wrapped tightly around them, trying to sleep without collapsing onto the wet, muddy ground.

"If your unit was headed for Berlin, that bullet in your leg probably saved you," one of the men Adam was leaning against said in a soft voice one night when he'd been in the camp about a week. The guards had roughed them up and stripped them of everything when they'd arrived, even the contents of their pockets. In the chaos, he'd lost track of the men he'd been travelling west with. For the last few days he had been huddled with these three, a doctor and two officers. It was the doctor who was speaking.

Adam shivered and pulled the thin blanket tighter around his shoulders, leaving the end he'd dropped in the mud hanging. The muscles in his back ached painfully from standing so long.

"They butchered everyone in the hospital," the doctor continued quietly. He'd been searching for supplies in a basement storeroom when the Russians had stormed the hospital in Berlin where he'd been working. "We'd heard that they were killing every soldier and every civilian they found anywhere in the city. But we assumed they would spare the hospitals." He was silent for a few minutes. "I stayed in the basement for hours after they left. Finally, I crept out. No one was alive. All my patients' throats had been cut. I suppose they didn't want to waste ammunition. The street was quiet. I ran from one building to the next, hiding. Bodies were everywhere you looked. And the blood. Even the streets were slippery in places. I made it to the edge of the city, then hid in a ditch half submerged in water. I figured if anyone came along I'd lie there like a dead body. I still can't believe I made it out. There were thousands of them roaming around killing people long after the surrender.

"How old are you, son?" the doctor suddenly asked him. Adam thought he had forgotten that any of them were there.

"Sixteen."

They huddled against each other in silence for a few minutes. Adam looked up at the stars, his mind wandering to happier places. It was cold for May. Too cold to plant the garden. Mom wouldn't be pleased about that.

"I've been watching how they guard at night," said one of the officers in a very low voice. "They don't have enough men or enough light to see the whole yard. And there are a couple of spots where the gap underneath the fence is pretty big."

CHAPTER FIFTY-FOUR

Adam scraped his toes in the mud, fumbling around for something to push against. He felt the doctor shoving hard on the soles of his boots. He was almost under. The push was what he needed and a moment later he was through.

"Run, Adam. Go!" the doctor whispered urgently as Adam stumbled to his feet on the other side and then crouched low. "Follow the other two. I'll be right behind you."

Disregarding his new friend's order, Adam turned and waited while the doctor clawed his way under the fence. The doctor was the biggest of the four of them and the gap was narrow. They'd planned it in this order so that if the doctor got stuck, Adam and the two officers could still get away. When the doctor's shoulders were through, Adam grabbed him under the arms and pulled with all his strength.

"Come on!" he grunted under his breath as he leaned backwards, straining until he thought he might pass out. An inch, and then another inch and another. It was taking forever. It was impossible to know what would happen if other prisoners realized what was going on. And the guard might get back to this side and hear them. Maybe he should have just run.

"Okay, let me go," the doctor panted. He was through. Heaving himself to his feet, he looked left and right up and down the fence. "Let's go."

They ran towards where the two officers had disappeared into the darkness.

"Here," Adam heard one of the other escapees whisper as they reached the first building. Quickly Adam and the doctor bent down and slipped off their boots. Boots in hand, the four moved silently across the cobblestones into the back streets of the village. Stopping every few minutes to listen for pursuers, they worked their way along the edge of the little town to the other side.

They'd agreed to head due east out of French territory, towards whatever might be left of Germany. The doctor had suggested they take

Adam. *He is just a boy*, Adam had heard him say to the officers.

They reached the eastern side of the town and stopped in the darkness at the edge of a field to put their boots back on.

"Let's move," whispered one of the officers.

The doctor paused, looking at Adam. "Are you okay to run on that leg?"

"Yep, fine." He still couldn't straighten it all the way and it was stiff from not moving in the prison camp, but he would run for days to get away from the French.

"Good," said the officer. "We've got a few hours before daybreak. They might not be organized enough to miss us or give chase, but who knows with these bastards. Let's just get as far away as possible. Be as quiet as you can."

For five nights they moved steadily east, staying well hidden during the day, as military vehicles raced back and forth and civilians wandered in both directions. Adam was slowly piecing it together. With Hitler dead, Germany had finally surrendered. The war was really over. Germany was under enemy control, which meant that all Germans citizens were officially under the control of the enemy. But which enemy?

After talking it over, they agreed to surrender themselves. They couldn't stay hidden forever. And based on their experience in Metz, France's plan for handling Germans wasn't very appealing. On the other hand, the four of them agreed vehemently that the Russians were worse. Much worse. That left the Americans and the British. They needed to keep going east and pray they found one of those before the Russians found them.

CHAPTER FIFTY-FIVE

"Now what?" The doctor stood at the edge of a wide river, hands on hips, contemplating their predicament. The water, high with spring runoff, slipped by quickly in the silvery moonlight. They could just make out the opposite bank.

The foursome headed north, hoping the river would narrow.

"A boat!" the doctor said excitedly from up ahead. They ran to catch up with him and helped turn over the wooden rowboat he'd stumbled upon.

Although the water was running quickly, it was smooth, and soon they were dragging the rowboat onto the opposite shore. There was enough time to make another fifteen or twenty kilometres before sunrise.

A few hours later, Adam looked out from behind the clump of trees where he and the others were hiding. They'd been watching the camp since first light. It looked like a temporary camp, just a few tents and some trucks with American markings.

"I'm pretty sure we're out of French territory," said one of the officers. "If we keep going, who knows how close the Russians might be? I say we approach them."

Everyone agreed with his logic.

"Okay, hands high in the air so they don't fire."

Raising their arms as high as they could, the four of them stepped out from behind the trees and walked slowly towards the camp.

Surrendering to the Americans had been a wise choice, thought Adam as he dug into the plate of noodles and meat sauce they'd been served when the Americans sat down for their midday meal. That night, after eating again, Adam smiled at the soldier who was guarding them and then drifted off to sleep under the warmth of a thick dry blanket and dreamed about his mom.

The next morning after breakfast, the four prisoners were motioned towards the back of a truck. Adam didn't move.

"This is what happened when they handed us over to the French,"

Adam said warily to the doctor. "They're going to drive us back."

The two German officers and the doctor stopped and stood with Adam. The American motioned again and said something in a friendly voice. The doctor stepped forward. Pointing west, he shook his head. "No. No Frankreich." Next, he pointed east. "No Russisch." Finally, he pointed to the four of them and then to the American. "Amerikanisch," he said.

Adam could see the soldier thinking, trying to sort out what the doctor meant. Then his eyes lit up with understanding.

"Amerikanisch?" he said, copying the German word for American and pointing to his own chest.

The doctor nodded enthusiastically. "Ja, ja, Amerikanisch."

"Amerikanisch," the American repeated in a reassuring voice, pointing down the road. With a smile, he walked over to the back of the truck and motioned gently for them to get in.

The drive was short. A large American military base had been established only a few kilometres away. The brightly lit room into which they were ushered smelled of fresh paint. Soon an officer came in and invited them to sit. Working through a translator, he asked their names and where they were each from, then explained that they would be issued identification papers that would allow them to return home and get on with rebuilding. They would stay in the camp until their paperwork was ready. Adam's case was a bit different. With Hungary under Russian control, he couldn't go home yet. The western allies had to negotiate a plan with the Russians. Until then, Adam would be billeted to a farm in Germany,

"You'll be staying here in the Youth section until we have a placement confirmed for you. It should only take a few days. Do you have any questions?" the American officer asked.

"No, I don't think so," said Adam.

"What is this Youth section you mentioned?" asked the doctor.

At this, the American officer sighed heavily. "Well," he began, "it seems that a significant portion of the German military are fifteen, sixteen, and seventeen-year-olds. Some even younger. We've set up a separate bunkhouse for the youths. That's what I was referring to. Giving them a bit of extra food, that type of thing. And in many cases, the kids don't have a home to go to. So there's some extra work to re-integrate them."

With wishes of good luck, the officers headed off. As Adam prepared to say good-bye to the doctor, tears blurred his vision.

"I can't thank you enough," he said in an unsteady voice. "I'd still be in Metz if it wasn't for you."

"I don't know. You're a bright boy. Maybe you'd have come up with your own escape plan." The doctor grinned at him. "And besides, without you, I might still be stuck under the fence."

In unison they reached for each other, and after a quick embrace, turned in opposite directions and headed off to their respective sections.

CHAPTER FIFTY-SIX

Summer 1945

Like so many, the farm in Bavaria where Adam was billeted had been neglected for years, with the husband, and later the teenage boys, off to war. Only one of the boys had come back. He and his mother were grateful for the help, even though it meant another mouth to feed. At first the mood during meals was sombre. No one wanted to talk about the war, and there was nothing else to talk about. But as they relaxed with each other, conversation became easier. His hosts were curious about Hungary, especially the German villages. When the subject did turn to the war, the woman and her son shared stories of Nazi raids that stripped them of their valuables and food, and spoke solemnly of Jewish friends who had disappeared.

The long summer days passed with relative comfort and ease and for once Adam enjoyed his chores, whistling while he worked the hardened fields and repaired collapsed fences. At night he savoured the privacy of the barn and the comforting sounds of the animals bedding down for the night.

But as July marched on, Adam began to get anxious. He wanted to get home. It was hard to believe that it had only been a year since he'd taken off without a word. It seemed like forever. His cousin would have told them where he'd gone, of course, and that would only have made his mom worry more. He hoped Henry's letter had gotten through. At least then she'd know he'd been alive six months earlier. The translator at the American army base had said it might take a couple of months before they were able to issue him with papers to travel to Hungary. It had been almost that since he'd arrived at the farm. Hopefully it wouldn't be much longer. Mr. Post would be glad to see him back. He wondered how long it would take to get the college up and running. If any professors had survived, that is.

"We're going to put the radio on for the news if you'd like to stay and listen," his hostess offered as she cleared plates after supper one evening. A new German radio station had been set up and news broadcasts about international post-war politics had become a regular part of their routine.

"Yes, thank you, I will." Maybe he'd hear some clue about how much longer he'd have to wait.

"Soviet leader Joseph Stalin, British Prime Minister Winston Churchill, and U.S. President Harry Truman have been in Potsdam since July 17 negotiating terms for the end of World War II," the broadcast began. *"In their first week, the Leaders have agreed on the implementation of a demilitarized and disarmed Germany, governed jointly by the western alliance and Russia. In the coming weeks, four zones of Allied occupation will be established - British, American, French, and Russian. And although Berlin will be within the Russian zone, the city itself will also be divided into four zones of allied occupation. Joint administration of Germany will take place from Berlin."*

Adam had heard this before. And they'd already announced a few days ago that all of Germany's military related factories and research centres were to be dismantled. Next the announcer explained that all of the anti-Jewish laws that had come into effect when he was a kid and during the war would be revoked. He'd heard that last week too. Adam pushed back his chair.

"I think we heard all this the other day. I'll check the gates and head to bed. Good night," said Adam.

"Okay, see you in the morning," the woman replied, not looking up from the hem she was stitching. As Adam got up to let himself out, the news continued.

"Soviet leader Joseph Stalin has recommended that those people identifying German as their mother tongue on the last census be returned to Germany. Much discussion has taken place on this question and the three leaders recognize that the transfer to Germany of German populations remaining in Poland, Czechoslovakia and Hungary, will have to be undertaken."

Adam froze, hand on the doorknob.

"The terms agreed to today also specify that the transfers of people of German heritage out of Hungary, Poland, and Czechoslovakia should be effected in an orderly and humane manner.

"The conference will continue tomorrow, as the leaders continue to deliberate on the Pacific War. . . "

Slowly Adam opened the door and stepped outside. Moving Germans out of Hungary? That would be almost everyone in Elek.

CHAPTER FIFTY-SEVEN

Adam stared up at the roof of the hayloft, unable to sleep. If they transferred his family out of Hungary before he got back, how would he find them? He needed to get home.

Adam couldn't have known the dangers of travelling in Russian-held territory, and even if he had, it probably wouldn't have changed his mind. All he knew was that he couldn't risk losing his family. He sat up, tempted to go right then, but as he looked around in the darkness of the loft, thought better of it. He'd be better off waiting a day so he could gather some supplies.

His plan formulated, Adam rolled onto his side and nestled into the hay. Through the opening at the end of the loft he could see a tiny sliver of moon. Tomorrow or the next night it would be gone completely. And by the time it was full again, he'd be home.

Twenty-four hours later, he opened the gate as quietly as he could and latched it carefully behind him. In the morning they would find the note he'd left. They knew he was anxious to see his family, so they would understand. He felt a bit guilty about the food he'd taken, but he had a long way to go and food was going to be scarce.

The darkness was thick. As he walked along, he listened to the wind brushing through the trees along the roadside. His footsteps were loud in his ears. Something snapped behind him. Jerking his head around he stopped and stared into the darkness. Nothing. A moment later a loud *Hooooo! Hoooo!* burst out of the night. He jumped sideways, then let out his breath and relaxed his shoulders. An owl. Relax, he lectured himself, the war is over. And this area is controlled by the Americans. Glancing around in the darkness one more time, he turned and resumed walking briskly into the night.

As the sun rose the next morning, Adam sat up between the rows of corn where he'd slept a couple of hours and yawned. After carving off a hunk of bread and cheese from his supply he stepped cautiously out onto the road, breakfast in one hand, sack in the other, and started walking. A few minutes later, he dove back into the sea of corn stalks. An old man driving an empty wagon came into view. When the wagon had passed, Adam ran out and strode alongside, smiling up at the farmer.

"Good morning, sir."

Startled, the old farmer pulled up the horses and stared at Adam. "Where did you come from?" he asked suspiciously.

"I was just sleeping in the field. I've been discharged from the army and am heading home." The farmer wouldn't ask to see his papers. "I was wondering if I could get a ride?"

"How come you talk funny?" the old man asked.

"I'm from Hungary, sir. I'm German, but my family lives in Hungary. I came to Germany to help in the war."

The old man stared at Adam silently for a moment before he responded. "If you came all the way from Hungary to fight for that demon, why would I give you a ride?"

Adam's smile vanished and he stared back at the man, his mouth open. "I. . . I don't know," he fumbled.

The farmer spoke again. "I'm headed to the next town to try to find some flour. Hitler's men came through a few months ago and cleaned us out again."

"I'm sorry to hear. . . It's terrible. . . by your own people. I don't really understand it. I was on the Eastern Front fighting the Russians until I was wounded. I'm sorry to have bothered you." Adam backed up a couple of steps and started to turn around. He stopped when the man started to speak again.

"Never mind. I don't think too many of us understand much about the last few years. The ones that came to our place said it was to feed the men at the front. Thing is, we needed to eat too. I trapped rabbits and squirrels. Made soup from a rat one time. Anyhow, we survived and so did you, and he's dead. I'll give you a ride. Climb up."

When Adam was seated beside him, the farmer clicked his tongue at the horses and continued. "Took everything but the radio, the one the Nazis issued. Only gets the one station. The one with all the stories about winning the war. Nobody will want it, but I thought maybe I could trade the parts for some flour or something."

CHAPTER FIFTY-EIGHT

In the hot dusty days that followed, Adam walked through the day and into the night, stopping only to hide when he heard someone coming, and to sleep a few hours in the darkest part of the night. He didn't know if the Americans would be looking for him and he didn't want to find out. Many of the fields he passed were ripped open by jagged craters and littered with toppled, scorched trees. Most of the human remains had been picked up, but skeletons of long-dead sheep and cattle lay in scorched pastures alongside various bits of deserted military equipment.

Most of the traffic on the road was American military. Petrol wasn't available to civilians, and with nothing to take to market, few farmers had reason to be out. Adam worried that he wouldn't make it back to Elek in time. When the occasional wagon did come by, he ran out and flagged it down. Stories of loss and abuse made for depressing conversation, but he was glad for any opportunity to get a little further east.

Hunger had once again become his daily companion. Gardens were sparsely planted if at all. Barns were empty and few yards had any chickens. The first door he knocked on was a farmhouse on a large acreage. They will have fared a bit better with so much land, Adam thought.

The door opened only a crack, showing a slice of a woman's face. A child cried inside.

"Hello. My name is Adam. I've been released from the army and I'm trying to get home to my family. I wondered if you could spare something to eat? Just something small?"

A bitter laugh escaped from the woman's mouth.

"Well, Adam," she said angrily, "if my husband or either of my half-grown sons had lived long enough to be released, we might have a few more animals around here and crops in these fields. When I figure out how to feed the three young ones I have left, you come back and we'll be sure to share our Sunday roast with you."

The door slammed shut.

He didn't try any more houses that day or the next, but eventually desperation propelled him up to another front door. The yard had a big garden space although much of it was lying fallow. He could hear chickens. Taking a deep breath, he knocked on the door.

When the door opened a crack, his words tumbled out. "I'm sorry to bother you, but I'm trying to make my way home before they deport my family. I've walked from Bavaria and I'm too hungry to walk anymore and I'm afraid I'm not going to get there in time and then I won't be able to find them. I wondered if you might have something I could eat. I don't have any money, but I could shovel out your chicken coop or do some other chores if it would help you. I only need something small. I'm very sorry to bother you. . . ," his voice trailed off as the door opened wider. Flooded with relief, he saw that the thin woman who had answered the door was looking at him kindly.

"Come in," she said, standing back from the doorway to let Adam pass. "Sit down."

Adam collapsed onto a chair beside the rough wooden table in the middle of the small, dimly lit kitchen.

"We can't let you starve, now can we? Let's see. . . I haven't looked for eggs yet today. Maybe we'll be lucky." Giving Adam another smile, the woman turned and let herself out a door at the back of the kitchen.

A couple of minutes later she returned, carrying two eggs in each hand. "Four chickens, four eggs," the woman said with another smile at Adam. "We are having a lucky day." She grabbed a bowl down from a shelf and began cracking the eggs into it. Disappearing again, this time through a curtain on the side of the kitchen, she reappeared with a jug in one hand and a small clay pot in the other.

"A bit of milk," she explained while she poured. "And we'll sweeten it up a bit," she continued, spooning in a little dab of honey from the pot. She stirred the contents of the bowl vigorously. "Here you go. This will fill you up and give you some strength. Drink it all," she said, placing the bowl in front of Adam before sitting down in the other chair.

With both hands, he lifted the bowl to his mouth, closed his eyes and drank until it was empty, feeling the raw eggs slide down his throat. Setting the bowl down on the table, he wiped his mouth with his sleeve.

"Thank you," he breathed, and then grinned.

"How far do you have to go?" she asked.

"Across to the other side of Hungary by the Romanian border."

"I've never been far from here, but it sounds like a long way. What are you doing so far from home?"

"Well," Adam sighed heavily, "I took off from home to fight for Germany, to help win the war. For years we heard the German news on our radio and it sounded good. Thought it would be exciting. I was pretty stupid."

The woman's smile had faded. She looked sadly at Adam for a few moments, then took a deep breath and put her smile back on. "Well, you're one of the lucky ones. And I'm sure you'll have some stories to tell your kids about Germany's great victory," she said, her last words tainted with sarcasm. Standing up, she disappeared behind the curtain for a moment and returned with the end of a loaf of bread.

"Now, you'd best be on your way if you're in a hurry to get there. Take this for a bit of supper tonight. No need to do any chores for me, I'm just happy to help you get back to your mother and father where you belong." Moving towards the door, she opened it wide. "Good luck to you," she said, grasping Adam's hands in both of hers for a moment as she smiled up into his face.

"Thank you again, ma'am. You're very kind," he said, returning her smile.

He thought about the woman at the farmhouse as he curled up in the corner of an empty barn that night. Her warmth had felt almost as good as that egg concoction in his belly. He couldn't wait to see his mom and sit down at the table with everybody. He wondered if they knew about the deportation plans yet. They'd probably heard it on the radio, he thought as he drifted off to sleep.

CHAPTER FIFTY-NINE

A couple of days later, Adam reached Vienna. From what he could gather, it was another four or five hundred kilometres to Elek. Anxiously, he walked through the streets of Vienna looking for the train station. Block after block, there were jagged smashed walls, partial floors suspended in mid-air, broken staircases that led nowhere, and empty, gaping windows. What if there were no trains? The occasional person he came across moved away or looked down as he passed.

Finally, he found the station, in a part of the city that had suffered less bombing. Pushing the door open, he peered nervously inside. Clerks stood behind a couple of the ticket windows that lined the front of the massive lobby, and a few people milled about. Stepping inside, Adam's scan of the waiting area stopped at the back of the big room where several rows of seats were filled with soldiers. Without moving, he looked them over, then let out his breath slowly. The uniforms were a mix of Hungarian and German, and a few were in civilian clothes. They looked at ease. Some chatted quietly. A couple were leaning against the wall smoking, staring into space. Here and there a soldier was slouched in his seat, legs stretched out in front of him, eyes closed. Cautiously, Adam headed in their direction.

A few of the soldiers glanced up as he approached. He lowered his tall, bony frame onto an empty seat at the end of the row, wincing slightly as he stretched out his left leg.

"Where are you headed?" he asked the soldier closest to him, speaking in Hungarian. Nervously, he glanced around the room every few seconds.

"Who wants to know?" the soldier answered after a few moments.

"Name's Adam Baumann. I was released by the Americans a couple months ago. I'm trying to get home to my family east of Budapest now, near the Romanian border. How are you getting across the border into Hungary?"

"We received our papers from the Americans yesterday. There's an agreement with the Russians allowing us to go home, and a train organized to take the whole lot of us to Budapest."

Hope stirred in the pit of Adam's stomach. If he rode with them, he could get to Budapest today and home tomorrow, or maybe even today if they left soon!

"Do you think I could get on that train?"

The soldier shrugged. "Don't see why not. They told us the train has been arranged to transport Hungarian soldiers back home."

As they rolled rhythmically towards the Hungarian border a couple of hours later, Adam closed his eyes, leaned his head back against the seat and thought about home. His mom and Theresa would cry when they saw him. George might be happy, but he wouldn't say much. His dad would probably yell and give him a licking for taking off in the first place. He smiled faintly as his head rocked gently back and forth with the swaying of the train. No more lonely nights in empty barns. No more begging for food or stealing from starving people. And no more walking.

Feeling the train begin to slow, Adam opened his eyes and unwound his legs from under the seat. It was too soon to be in Budapest. A sign for Komarom came into view. They were in Hungary. As the platform came alongside and the train lurched to a stop, Adam's thoughts of home vanished. There were too many uniforms rushing around on the platform. And too many guns.

"What the hell's going on?" One of the soldiers sitting near Adam voiced the question in everyone's mind.

"Hammer and sickle on the uniforms. Communist police," someone answered quietly. "Get your papers ready."

Adam looked around desperately for somewhere to hide, but before he could move, the door of the car slammed open. A uniformed man strode on board and glared at them menacingly.

"Inspection! Everyone off and line up outside!" He spit the words at them in Hungarian. Obediently, the soldiers disembarked in silence and formed a line. Hungarian and Russian voices shouted all around them. Adam's mouth had gone paper dry.

"March!" barked the commander who had ordered them off the train, motioning for them to follow a policeman waiting near the front of the line.

"We have papers from your American allies," one of the soldiers said loudly, holding the papers out to the commander.

The commander strode over to the soldier who had spoken, his eyes blazing. He lifted his rifle and pointed it at the soldier's forehead. "I SAID MARCH!" he roared.

"Yes, sir," replied the soldier, his eyes wide. The commander lowered his rifle and waved impatiently for his comrade at the front to proceed, then took up the rear.

Adam's stomach churned. The Russians didn't take prisoners. A few blocks down the street, a prison gate loomed ahead, open. Inside, the leader stopped and waved his rifle towards the centre of the yard, motioning the soldiers to keep moving as the gate clanged shut behind them.

The yard was in shadows, the sun already below the top of the high walls. Half a dozen guards in communist uniforms lined one wall. As the Hungarian soldiers filed in, the guards raised their rifles, keeping them trained on the incoming men. The commander strode back to the front of the line.

"Shirts off! Everybody! Now!" he roared, waving his rifle menacingly.

Adam fumbled for his buttons, his fingers paralyzed with fear.

"Approach the table, one by one!" the commander barked, motioning to a table at the side of the yard where an officer sat with a book open in front of him.

When no one moved immediately, the commander jabbed the soldier at the front of the line in the ribs with his rifle. "You! Move!"

As the first soldier got near, the officer at the table took over.

"Name?" he demanded.

"Becskei, Alpar," answered the soldier in a quavering voice.

The officer wrote it down, then looked up and barked another command. "Arms up!"

Dropping his bag and shirt on the ground, the soldier raised his hands above his head. The officer studied the underside of the soldier's raised arms.

"Papers?" the officer asked next.

Alpar Becskei lowered his arms and reached down to fumble in the pocket of the shirt he had dropped, then handed over his papers.

After unfolding and scanning the papers, the officer spoke to the commander. "Hungarian army."

"Approved for release," the commander announced, motioning towards the gate through which they'd entered. Several heads swivelled to look back at the gate as one of the guards swung the gate open partway. Alpar Becskei grabbed his shirt and bag from the ground, and walked nervously to the gate, glancing over his shoulder as he walked. When he'd slipped out, the gate clanged shut.

"Next!" called out the officer standing behind the table.

Several more soldiers who had served in the Hungarian army were processed and released. The ones still waiting shifted from foot to foot, waiting nervously for their turn. Adam swallowed repeatedly. He didn't have any damn papers.

"Name?" the officer demanded as a soldier in a German uniform approached the table.

"Lehmann, Heinrich."

"Arms up!" barked the other officer.

No sooner had Heinrich Lehmann lifted his arms than the officer yelled again. "Interrogate!"

Two of the guards along the wall sprang into action. Striding forward, they grabbed Lehmann and forced him towards the commander who had brought them from the train station.

"Lehmann, what position did you serve in the German army?" the commander demanded.

"Infantry, machine gunner," Lehmann responded clearly, standing tall and looking straight ahead.

"Were you a Nazi, Lehmann?"

"Yes, I was."

"That makes you an enemy of the State," the commander yelled, putting his face close to Lehmann's.

Lehmann didn't respond. The commander stared at him for a moment, then turned and spoke to the two guards who had led the soldier over to him. "Show Lehmann how we treat enemies."

Before Lehmann could move, one of the guards had both his arms held behind his back and the other had punched him hard in the stomach. Lehmann jerked forward, gasping for air. The officer held him firm, giving his comrade an easy target. The officer in front wound up and punched Lehmann again, then twice more. As Lehmann slumped forward, the officer punched him in the face. Lehmann's head snapped from side to side as the guard kept hitting. The yard was silent except for the sounds of fists connecting with Lehmann's body and face, and the soldier's corresponding grunts. Suddenly, the officer behind Lehmann let go of his arms and he crumpled forward onto the ground. The captives watched in horror as the guards wound up and began kicking their heavy boots into Lehmann's torso.

"Okay, enough for now," the commander said finally. "Take him downstairs."

Lehmann's head hung forward as they lifted him, one under each arm, and dragged him to a doorway on the opposite side of the yard, disappearing down a dark flight of stairs.

The next soldier was of German descent as well.

"Are you a Nazi, Gunther?" the commander barked into his face.

"No, sir!"

"Why are you lying to me, Gunther?" the commander's voice was low and ominous.

"I'm not lying, sir." Gunther's voice wavered.

"If you're not a stinking Nazi, Gunther, why do you have that tattoo under your arm?" Bile rose in Adam's throat. A few minutes later, the non-responsive Gunther was dragged across the yard and down the stairs.

The next captive was in civilian clothing. He had a German name.

"What position did you serve in the German army?" the commander began.

"Commanding officer."

Raising his rifle, the commander aimed at the German's head and pulled the trigger.

The watching soldiers gasped as the side of the man's head sprayed across the yard and his body slumped to the ground.

"Get rid of this piece of shit," spat the commander, kicking at the body before turning to listen to the next soldier's answers. A couple of the guards along the wall came running over and dragged the body away and through a different door at the side of the yard.

CHAPTER SIXTY

When Adam came to, he was lying on his side on the floor of a prison cell. Opening his eyes slowly, he looked around without moving his head. He could see four others. The guy directly in front of him was sitting against the wall crying softly, and somewhere behind him someone was praying fervently. *Holy Father, have mercy.* Loud footsteps interrupted the prayer. The door of the cell creaked open, and another soldier staggered in and fell to the floor.

Cautiously, Adam sat up. The side of his face was throbbing. Reaching up, he touched his cheek gingerly, then felt his blood-caked hair. His nose had stopped bleeding. He crawled to an open space along the wall and carefully maneuvered into a sitting position, then looked around again. There were eight of them in the cell. Adam looked sideways through the bars. The other cells stood open and empty. A stairwell, presumably the one they'd all been dragged down, and a tiny window at the other end of the short corridor that ran past the cells, were the only sources of light.

"Fucking communists!" one guy spat out. Adam looked at him and realized it was Lehmann. His swollen face was horribly discoloured. Blood had congealed where his distended lip was split wide open.

The unfortunate beside Lehmann crossed himself, his lips moving in a silent prayer.

Lehmann continued. "Who the hell do they think they are? They're breaking the treaty. The Americans promised us safe passage, said it was all agreed to in Potsdam. Stalin agreed that we could all be released and travel home safely. The fucking war is over!"

Adam put his head back against the cold wall. He hadn't thought it through well enough. A train to Budapest had sounded too good to pass up. But he should have stayed on his own, dammit! He'd been so close. Adam felt tears of frustration well up in his eyes. *Stupid! Stupid! Stupid!* A tear ran down each cheek. No one could see him anyway.

Suddenly a shot rang out, then another. The crying and praying stopped and the prisoners sat in silence. A couple of minutes later, the sound of boots clattered down the steps. The prisoner who'd been praying to be spared started up again, louder. The commander came into sight. Stopping in front of the cell, he stood with his hands behind his back and rocked on his heels for a moment, looking at them through the bars with narrowed eyes. Suddenly he leaned forward and jabbed his finger viciously between the bars.

"Did all you Nazis hear that?" he said in a low, menacing tone. "That was a couple more of your commanding officers. They were enemies of the State, and they deserved to die. Just like you." He spit out the last words, then spun on his heel and strode away.

CHAPTER SIXTY-ONE

When the weak light finally reappeared, the prisoners stirred. Those who had lain down sat up. Some stood up and peered towards the stairs, waiting.

All day they waited, praying, crying, swearing intermittently. Every now and then someone got up to relieve himself in the corner.

"I wish they'd fucking hurry up," muttered Lehmann.

A week passed. The only sign that anyone remembered they were there was a serving of watery broth delivered silently by a couple of guards each evening. Every now and then one of the captives talked a bit about where he was from, or about his family. But mostly they just sat, hungrily drifting in and out of sleep as the weak light in the corridor appeared and then eventually faded again, marking the days.

CHAPTER SIXTY-TWO

Adam sat in his usual spot, shivering. It was morning again. He hadn't moved much in the last day or two, except to grab a bowl of the watery soup when the guards came. The stink from the corner and the sour smell of filthy bodies were sickening.

Suddenly his ears perked up. There were boots coming down the stairs. It wasn't soup time. Maybe today was execution day. When the sound of the boots stopped in front of the cell, he opened his eyes a crack. It was the guards with more soup. He shook his head to clear it. *Had the day passed already?*

As the guards filled the bowls and passed them through the bars, the prisoners grabbed at them. They were filled with meat stew! Adam shovelled his portion hungrily into his mouth.

Later that day, the guards returned with another pot of stew, and twice a day for the next two days. On the fourth day, the prisoners were awoken at sunrise.

"Okay you stinking Nazis, let's go, we've got some work to do," said the guard as he unlocked the door. "Follow me."

Several horse-drawn wagons filled with long wooden boxes waited in the street outside. A farmer sat in each driver's seat, watching the scene apprehensively. Two men in uniforms with red crosses on the sleeves sat beside one of the drivers. Behind the men sat two large dogs who gazed around calmly at the activity in the street. At an order from the commander, a couple of guards stepped forward and herded the prisoners onto an empty wagon, then climbed in with them.

The wagons moved slowly with their heavy loads. The early morning sun hinted at a warm autumn day, but cold sweat ran down Adam's back. The guy beside him stank. Adam looked out at the wheat fields rolling past, golden under the bright blue sky. It would have been beautiful in other circumstances. That day he just stared at it numbly. A couple of kilometres further, the wheat gave way to rough, unplanted fields. Adam turned and looked in the direction they were driving. Fallow fields as far as he could see.

The wagons turned off the road. As they bumped along through the field, Adam realized why it wasn't planted. The holes they were driving through and around were foxholes and craters from explosives. A bit further, a faint odour of death wafted through the air. Adam tried to breathe through his mouth.

The wagons stopped beside a stand of trees a kilometre or more from the road, and the men in Red Cross uniforms climbed down with their dogs. The guards joined them for a hushed conversation, then one of the guards walked back and addressed the prisoners.

"We have orders to clean up the bodies from these fields to prevent sickness," he barked. "The dogs will help find them. Each body goes into a box. Grab a shovel and get to work."

Adam shuddered, thinking back to the previous winter. The medics had tried to get the bodies back to the camp to be hauled away, but when the Russians were coming fast, they couldn't get them all. As the war had progressed, the commander had sometimes ordered them to dig mass graves. They'd scraped as far down as they could and then covered the bodies with as much mud and rocks as possible before they had to move on or get back to fighting. But sometimes there wasn't even time to do that. At least it had been winter then. Now, in the heat of summer, the stench of rot hung over the entire area.

As the dogs sniffed the ground eagerly, the Red Cross workers explained how to dig around the area the dog indicated, disturbing the corpse as little as possible. They would be checking each body for identification tags, and then taking them away for burial. Any weapons or personal effects were to be gathered up as well.

Within a minute or two, the dog nearest Adam began to bark excitedly at a spot on the ground. Adam and his assigned partner began tentatively removing shovelfuls of damp earth from the area, while the others followed the other dog. Sure enough, after only a few shovelfuls of dirt had been removed, a ragged edge of cloth appeared. Adam stopped and stared down at it. A uniform. There was someone under the ground right here in front of him. Someone who'd been alive last year, but now would never see his family again. The other prisoner had stopped digging at the same time. Adam looked up and their eyes met for a moment. Swallowing hard, he refocused on the shovel and the ground in front of him and began to scrape away the earth along the edge of the uniform. A pant leg by the look of it. A few minutes later, they had exposed the long-dead soldier. His head lay at an unnatural angle above his sunken torso, eye sockets filled with decay staring up at a sharp angle off to the side. The soft flesh of his cheeks had rotted away, revealing his white jawbone and teeth below the matted hair that stuck out from under his helmet. The Red Cross worker squatted down and pulled back the collar of the uniform. The dog tag was there. He backed away while the prisoners brought a box alongside the body. Pulling on edges of pant legs and other bits of the soldier's uniform and pushing gingerly with their shovels, they slid the decomposed corpse onto a sheet of canvas and then lifted it into the box. Adam picked up a boot that had come off and placed it in the remains. Scraping around in the hole left by the body, he unearthed a gas mask.

Box after box, they repeated the gruesome task. Many of the bodies were relatively complete, killed by gunfire. Other spots that the dogs led them to revealed the aftermath of a grenade blast, limbs, torsos, and other fragments of soldiers lying where they'd landed. Finally, as the sun neared the horizon, the guards ordered them back into the wagon. Adam slumped to a seat inside the wagon and closed his eyes, drifting in and out of sleep as the wagon lurched back through the field and onto the road.

The next day passed much the same.

As they rode through another field on the third morning, Adam stared off into the distance towards the sunrise. Elek was out there somewhere.

"Get moving!" the guard yelled at them as they climbed off the wagon and stretched their aching bodies. "Work this direction along the ridge. Our information says the fighting started here and continued across the plateau." The sound of a gurgling creek drifted up to them from somewhere over the ridge.

Mid-morning one of the dogs started barking from somewhere over the bank by the creek. Adam had just finished shovelling some personal effects into a box beside their erstwhile owner, while his partner started on the next spot. He wiped the sweat from his forehead with his sleeve as he watched the guard stride to the ridge and look down at the dog.

"We got one down there by the look of it," he called back to the group. He sounded annoyed. "Come here," he barked, seeing Adam idle. "Move it!"

As Adam jogged over to him, the guard turned and headed down the slope towards the barking, beckoning Adam to follow. Reaching the edge of the ridge, Adam glanced down the hill in front of him and across the creek. Corn. Almost ready to harvest, as far as the eye could see.

Halfway down the hill, the dog came into view, barking excitedly between the creek bank and a small stand of trees. The guard stopped walking and looked back up the hill over his shoulder. Adam looked in the same direction. They couldn't see the wagon or the rest of the crew from here.

"Get down there and dig," the guard said after a moment, waving his rifle down the hill.

Adam strode down to the dog and waved it back. Giving the spot a tentative scrape he couldn't see anything on the surface. Backing up a foot or two from where the dog had been focused, he positioned the shovel and stepped on it to push it gently into the ground.

Out of the corner of his eye, Adam saw the guard turn and head back up the hill. Slowly he lifted the shovelful of mud and emptied it off to the side, his attention trained on his peripheral vision where the guard was disappearing out of sight. Was fate handing him another chance? His breath quickened. He placed the shovel again, pushed down again, emptied another shovelful of mud off to the side. The dog was moving away, nose skimming the dirt as she crisscrossed her way a bit further along the creek and then headed up the bank at an angle. Adam kept the shovel moving slowly as his mind raced. How long would the guard be out of sight? Looking furtively around, Adam considered the options. He could hide in the stand of trees that started a couple hundred metres downstream. Or maybe across the creek. Yes, across the creek! His scent would be lost in the water. Otherwise the dogs would find him right away. The corn on the other side of the creek was tall. Taller than him. How long had the guard been out of sight? Another shovelful, then another, then another. Movement at the top of the hill. The guard was coming back to check on him. *Don't look up.* Adam swallowed. His mouth was so dry.

Keep shovelling. Look focused on finding what the dog had smelled. The guard stood, watching. *Place the shovel, push it into the ground, lift the mud and dump it. Bend down as if something has been uncovered, stand up, place the shovel, push it in, lift the shovelful out.* The guard turned away. He was walking away. He was gone!

Dropping the shovel, Adam dashed into the creek. Quick, quick, quick! His boots slipped here and there on the big rocks that lined the creek bottom, and the knee-deep water felt like molasses. He headed towards the opposite bank at a downstream angle. He needed to come out as far away from where he went in as possible. A little further. A few more feet. Okay, far enough, no more time. Stumbling onto the opposite bank, Adam glanced back over his shoulder. No movement on the hill. Diving into the cornfield, Adam ran blindly forward down the row in front of him. His arms flailed wildly, knocking the leaning corn stalks out of his path, waiting for the sound of shots to ring out behind him. Sharp leaves slashed at his face. *Further, further, further.* Try not to move the corn so much, he thought suddenly. What if they could see it moving from up the hill on the other side. Concentrating on his legs, he pumped them as fast as he could, keeping arms at his sides, and his head down.

Run! ... Run! ... Run!

The blood roared in his ears. His legs began to slow. The strength he'd regained from a few days of stew wasn't enough. But he had to keep going. He concentrated. Keep running. One leg in front of the other. Faltering, he stumbled, then regained his feet and ran on. The corn ended, and he ran across a narrow wagon track and a small open field. Reaching the next corn crop on the opposite side of the open field, he leapt in and kept running, terror trumping the burn of his legs and the sweat in his eyes. Looking up, he saw the end of the row ahead. He'd reached the edge of another field.

Stopping just before the edge, he stood for a second, gasping for air, still hidden in the corn. Desperately, he tried to quiet his ragged breathing so he could hear the sounds around him. Turning in circles, he peered wildly into the sea of corn. The communists with their rifles and dogs couldn't be far behind, but he didn't detect any movement. Turning nervously back towards the edge of the corn, he crept forward and peered out, looking quickly from side to side. A small road. In the distance to the right he could see houses. He swallowed. What next? Where could he hide? He had to keep moving. Deciding to stay behind the cover of the corn, he turned to the right and ran in parallel with the road towards the houses. At the corner of the field, he stopped and studied the houses. The road was empty. Stepping out from the corn, he jumped over the dry ditch onto the road and walked quickly towards the village. What if communists lived here, he wondered, glancing from side to side as he strode between the first few houses. Which house? Which house? Someone was going to see a stranger walking through town and report him. Fixing his gaze on a small house ahead, he made a beeline for the front door. Heart pounding, he knocked rapidly half a dozen times, paused for a split second and rapped again. *Hurry up! Open the door!*

As he raised his hand to bang again, the door opened a few inches. A wrinkled face topped with a few wisps of white hair peered up at him.

"What do you want?" the face croaked.

"I need your help," Adam said urgently in Hungarian, looking over his shoulder and then back at the face in the crack of the door. "I've run away from the communist police in Komarom. They were going to shoot us. Please. I don't know if they are still chasing me, or if I've lost them, but I need a place to hide. Please!"

After an eternity, the door opened. The old man stepped aside to let Adam into the tiny kitchen and shut the door quickly behind him. A thin, elderly woman stood with her back to the kitchen counter, twisting her apron in her hands, her eyes wide and her lips pressed together.

"Who are you and why are you running from the police? We will report you." The man raised his chin and gave Adam a challenging look.

Adam looked from the man to his wife and back again. Surely they wouldn't. Oh my God, had he made another mistake? He closed his eyes for a moment, and wished there was a God to pray to. Taking a deep breath, he started to explain as rapidly as he could.

"My name is Adam Baumann. I am from a small village near the Romanian border called Elek. I was fighting in the war and now I can't go home to my mom and dad because of the communists. I walked from Bavaria to Vienna because they are going to deport my family and I need to get there before they do that and then the police stopped the train in Komarom and took us to the prison and they shot some of us. And they kept some of us and we've been doing forced labour to dig bodies from the fields. And I ran away just now when the guard wasn't looking. I ran across the creek into the cornfield. . . " He stopped talking, his throat too tight for any more words to get out.

The old man and his wife looked at each other. Then the man spoke decisively.

"I can hide him in the hay stacks across the creek."

"Okay, I'll fix some food," his wife responded.

"Be quick. If they find him here, we'll have hell to pay."

The old woman turned to the counter, pulled the cloth from a loaf of bread it was covering and started to saw slices from it. Smearing something onto one of the slices, she handed it to Adam.

"Here, eat this and I'll wrap up a couple more." She watched for a moment as he bit into the bread covered with bacon fat, chewed a couple of times, then took another bite before even swallowing the first. Her eyes brimming with tears, the old woman turned back to the counter and smeared bacon fat on the other slices.

"We lost two grandsons in the war," her husband said quietly. "They were too young to be fighting, like you. We would have wanted someone to help them." Grabbing the small bundle his wife handed him, he quickly opened the door and checked the street. "Okay, follow me."

A couple of chickens scattered off the path as they rounded the house and headed towards a gate at the back of the yard. Through the gate, they hurried along a path into the trees. Adam's eyes darted around as they jogged along. The trees had begun to shed their leaves and didn't provide good cover. The path was leading them down a hill towards the sound of water. It dawned on Adam that this was probably the same creek he'd run through earlier. An hour ago? Longer? Judging by the lengthening shadows it had been longer.

Ahead of him the old man was wrestling a raft into the water. The creek was deeper here, and a bit wider, but moving slowly. Just as the raft began to float, the man clambered on and picked up an oar that had been laying on it. Wading into the water, Adam jumped on, giving a final push as the man started to paddle. A few minutes later, they jumped off and dragged the raft up onto the other shore.

"Up here," said the man, heading up the hill along a well-worn path through the brush and low bushes. The fenced hay field at the top had been cut recently, and the hand-tied bales were stacked under a roof at the side of a small barn a little way inside the fence.

As they climbed through the fence rails and headed towards the haystack, the man explained. "I work for the farmer who owns this land, and I keep a cow of my own and a couple of goats over here. His animals are in a bigger field down the road. Me or the wife come over most days to feed and check on things. Let's rearrange this stack of hay with a space in the middle where you can stay."

When they'd finished, Adam had a tiny den inside the stack, big enough to sit up and lie down in a curled up position. He could crawl out to go to the bathroom.

"But other than that, you stay in here all day. Stay completely out of sight," the man ordered Adam in a kind voice. "I'll come back tomorrow and bring some food. And maybe a blanket." The man paused, looking earnestly at Adam. "Promise me you will stay inside the haystack and out of sight."

CHAPTER SIXTY-THREE

Over the next couple of weeks, the old man came almost every day with food, water, and news about the search for escapees. In the first few days, a wagon carrying half a dozen armed communist police had come through the village a number of times, questioning people in the street and forcing their way into houses to search for "dangerous escaped prisoners." But since then, the man and his wife hadn't heard anything more.

Adam ate heartily. He was sure food must be in short supply here, the same as everywhere else, but somehow the man always managed to bring a good meal. Bread, a vegetable or two, some days a couple of boiled eggs, or even a bit of cheese or meat. It was peaceful in the field, and when it seemed the police had stopped looking for him, Adam began to sleep well at night. He often slept through the afternoon as well and, day by day, he began to feel stronger.

In the third week, Adam peeked out as he heard the old farmer coming across the field. The man had a bundle under his arm.

"Hi," said Adam, pushing aside the bale that covered the entrance to his den, and smiling happily at the man as he crawled out into the sunshine and stood up.

"Hello," the man said cheerily, handing Adam the bundle. "Good news. Got some of my grandsons' clothes here for you. A real good shirt and pants, and a coat, and I brought a pair of boots too. Almost new. They belonged to my younger grandson. He only wore them a few times. You should have new boots to go home in after what you've been through to get there."

Adam looked at the man, humbled. He swallowed hard so he could speak.

"That's very kind of you. I don't know how I can ever repay this kindness."

"No need to repay anything. It's good to put this stuff to use. The boys' things have been just sitting there since they left. Even when we knew they weren't coming back, nobody wanted to let it go. But we all talked about it, my son and his wife, and my wife, and we all want to give it to you. And the best part is that we think it's safe enough now for you to leave and head home. I'm going to get the wagon ready early tomorrow. And then I'll bring the raft over and get you. I'll take you to the train station."

After the old man left, Adam sat down on a bale of hay and untied the bundle. At the sight of the boots, he grinned. Brown leather, and a thick sole! And they laced up past his ankles. He'd never had boots this nice. He slipped on the socks that were stuffed inside the boots and pulled the boots onto his feet. Perfect fit! Next, he inspected the clothes. He put the new shirt to his face and inhaled. . . clean. . . and soft. He closed his eyes and savoured the smell and the feel for a moment. The clothes that the woman had given him at the farm in Bavaria almost three months ago were filthy. Stripping them off, he pulled on the pants and shirt. Looking down at his new clothes, he grinned. They hung on his frame, but he didn't care. He was going home tomorrow!

CHAPTER SIXTY-FOUR
Autumn 1945

Adam turned up the collar of his new coat and sank down in his seat as the rhythm of the train wheels began to slow. They were approaching Budapest. The tickets that the man had bought him were in his pocket, the one for Budapest, which he'd already used, and the one from Budapest to Kétegyháza. Although he would never set eyes on the old farmer or his wife again, or find any trace of them when he searched years later, their immeasurable kindness was present in a corner of Adam's mind for decades after that day.

As the train eased into the Budapest station, Adam's eyes darted back and forth looking for police. His mouth paper dry, he stood and filed out the door with the crowd. Outside the train, he walked nervously into the station, looking around desperately for something that would tell him where to board the next train. His stomach felt watery.

The next train was easy to find. Climbing into the first car, Adam settled into a seat in the back corner and waited impatiently for the train to move. So far, so good. No one at the busy station had even glanced at him. As they rolled away from the platform, he looked around cautiously at the other passengers. An older couple sat across from him, backs straight, eyes forward. The man's coat might have been blue once. Now it was worn thin and a pocket had been removed and used to patch the elbow. A couple of rows ahead of them sat a mother facing in their direction. Her two young daughters peered out the window silently, noses against the glass. They were about Anni's age, the age Anni would have been now. Their mother's lifeless eyes stared forward at nothing. Another woman sat near the front of the car on Adam's side, her back to him. Beside her Adam could see the top of a boy's head. The woman's bright red coat and fashionable red hat, trimmed with a pretty black band, were a jarring contrast to the other passengers. But she sat with her face turned to the window, and in the reflection her expression was forlorn.

Adam looked out at the fields, away from the sadness that filled the train. He'd been gone almost a year and a half. Closing his eyes, he leaned his head back, wondering what he was going to find at home.

George was twelve now. He'd have grown, probably a lot. And Theresa was nineteen. A woman. His mom and his grandma would both hug him hard. He smiled at their faces inside his eyelids. A couple of weeks ago, he'd asked the old man what he knew about the Russian occupation in eastern Hungary. He hadn't known anything specific about the area around Elek. Adam had tried not to think about it. His dad would have kept them all safe and fed anyway. If anyone could, it was his dad.

CHAPTER SIXTY-FIVE

Kétegyháza. They'd arrived. Adam was waiting at the train door to pull it open as soon as they pulled even with the platform. Sticking his head out, he glanced left and right. No uniforms.

Jumping off, he dashed through the handful of people waiting for the train, and around the end of the station building to the road. They might be checking papers here before the train headed over the border, and he wanted to get far away from the train station as quickly as he could just in case. In the street, he turned towards Elek and forced himself to walk. Running through town would draw too much attention. Houses soon gave way to dry brown fields, the wheat long since cut and hauled away for milling. Unable to resist any longer, he broke into a run. The crisp air filled his lungs as he raced towards home.

The strength to run was short-lived, however, and soon he slowed to a walk to catch his breath. The autumn sun warmed his back as he trekked along, and as the sights on either side of the road grew increasingly familiar, he found himself whistling an old tune.

But as he turned the last corner, Adam stopped dead. A gate across the road. A checkpoint. Right there on the road a hundred metres in front of him. Behind it in the distance the Elek church tower rose through the trees. Two policemen stood in a little wooden booth beside the gate. Adam watched as one of them stepped out onto the road and took a couple of paces in his direction, a rifle swinging from his right hand. Adam's mind raced. He had to walk forward. Run and he'd be shot. Stand here and they'd know something was wrong. He had to walk towards the policemen and their guns. His mind cast around for a story. Another thirty seconds and they would be questioning him.

"Hello," Adam called out in Hungarian as he approached the officer who was facing his direction.

At that moment, the second policeman picked up his rifle and slung it onto his back as he stepped out of the booth to stop a little girl coming from the opposite direction on her bicycle.

"Where are you going?" the second policeman barked at the girl, his back to Adam.

"To the farm to see my grandmother and grandfather," Adam heard her answer, just as the first policeman addressed him.

"Name," he demanded, staring coldly at Adam.

"Adam." His voice came out too quietly. "Baumann. Adam Baumann," he said more loudly. He swallowed. Would Komarom have alerted them?

"Papers," the policeman demanded.

"I have to apologize, sir. When I came around the corner and saw you here, I realized I forgot my papers at my uncle's home near Budapest. I was helping him with the wheat harvest, and now that it's all done and the milling is all done, he said I can come home. My family is here in Elek."

"By law you are required to carry your papers when you travel." The policeman's eyes narrowed. Adam's eyes went to the communist symbol on the collars of the officer's uniform.

"Yes, sir. I know that and I apologize. I am in the wrong. I was happy to be coming home and I stupidly forgot to bring my papers. They are sitting on the shelf in my uncle's kitchen."

"You are breaking the law by travelling without your papers," the officer repeated.

Adam swallowed. His mouth had gone dry. "I am very sorry, sir. It was very stupid of me to forget my papers when I caught the train," Adam said again, in a thin voice. Suddenly he remembered his train ticket. He fumbled in his pocket and drew it out.

"Here is my ticket from Budapest. I am very sorry that I forgot to bring my papers."

The officer took the ticket and studied it. Adam watched closely, trying to read his expression. Little red veins ran like spider webs across the surface of the officer's nose. His eyes shifted from the ticket to Adam's shiny boots, while the hand holding the ticket fell to his side. Adam looked down, then looked at the officer's feet. The sole was coming loose at the front of one of his grimy, worn shoes, and the other had a hole where his dirty sock showed through. When he looked back up, the officer was smiling at him triumphantly. Wordlessly, he pointed to Adam's boots with his rifle and motioned for him to take them off. His heart still beating against his ribs, Adam leaned down and unlaced the boots. Dammit! He wanted to keep these boots! When he had them both off, he picked them up and placed them on the ground in front of the policeman. The officer reached over to lean his rifle against the shack, then slipped his shoes off and picked up Adam's boots before sitting down on the little bench at the front of the shack.

Adam glanced over at the other policeman and the little girl. He'd missed what they'd been saying, but the officer was holding onto the handlebar of the girl's bicycle. She looked up at the man as she climbed off her bike, then over at the officer who was sliding his feet into Adam's boots. Her eyes brimming with tears, she glanced at Adam.

"Go ahead," the policeman said to the girl impatiently. "You can go and visit your grandmother and grandfather."

"No, I can't," she said through her tears. "It's too far to walk."

The policeman holding her bike ignored her and wheeled the bike towards the back of the little shack.

Adam shifted his eyes back to the first police officer who stood and took a few steps in the new boots, then picked his rifle up and came back to stand in front of Adam.

"I should report you for travelling without your papers," he said staring into Adam's face. Adam said nothing and willed his eyes not to well up. "Never mind. Go ahead, go home. Don't forget your shoes," he said, pointing towards his worn-out pair.

Wordlessly, Adam slipped his feet into the old shoes. They were still warm inside from the policeman's feet. Suppressing a shudder of disgust, he turned his back on the two policemen and walked around the end of the gate. As he walked past the little girl, he gave her a sympathetic smile.

Looking down the road, he focused on the church tower and started to walk.

CHAPTER SIXTY-SIX

He'd almost reached the edge of town when he heard a commotion behind him. Someone was yelling. Looking forward, he kept walking. Whatever was happening at the checkpoint, he didn't want to be part of it. He was almost home.

A woman was yelling behind him.

"Aaaaaaa!" came the voice again. *No, please,* he thought to himself. Leave me alone. I just want to go home.

"Aaaaaaadaaaaaaaaam!"

Was someone calling his name? Reluctantly, he stopped and turned around. Two women were hurrying towards him with the little girl, and one of the women was waving frantically. He stared at them, confused. Then suddenly, he realized who it was.

"Mom!" he yelled, and began sprinting back towards the gate. His mom left the other two behind and rushed towards him.

"Adam!" she cried out as they got closer together.

"Oh, my God, Adam," his mom gasped as she threw her arms around him and squeezed. He leaned down and hugged her back, as hard as he could. She was so much thinner than last time he'd hugged her. They stood there holding onto each other until the other woman and the little girl caught up.

"Look at you," said his mom, pulling back and looking up at him. Her cheeks were wet with tears. She laughed up at him and wiped her eyes with one hand. "Look at how tall you are!" she said before she wrapped both arms around him again.

"How did you find me?" he asked, still confused, as his mom let him go.

"Well, this beautiful little girl here," his mom smiled at the little girl who was grinning happily now, "was crying so sadly, we stopped to ask her what was wrong. And she told us that the police had taken her bicycle, and how they are stealing from everyone, they even stole some boots from a big boy named Adam Baumann, and she pointed to you up ahead. I couldn't believe my ears. And then you wouldn't stop!" she laughed. "Adam, this is Mrs. Kuhn. Her son is Henry. He was a cook in the German army. "

"We should walk," Adam said, looking back at the policemen who were watching them.

"Henry Kuhn," his mom said, as they started to walk towards town. "He wrote to his mother and said he had met up with you."

Henry! From the camp where they had the hot meal just after Christmas. So the mail smuggling operation had been real!

"Mrs. Kuhn came to see me when she got the letter a few days ago, and we went to Budapest to find you."

"But I met Henry in Germany and that was ten months ago," he said, looking at Mrs. Kuhn. "We were never in Budapest."

"Yes, we understand that now. We went to the address on the letter this morning, and they said it was just an address for forwarding mail from the front," his mom explained.

"You just got off the train from Budapest?" Adam said incredulously. "I was on the same train."

"It's been ten months since you saw Henry?" Mrs. Kuhn interjected anxiously.

"Yes." How could he tell Mrs. Kuhn that they were still capturing and torturing German soldiers? If Henry had even made it through the slaughter in Berlin.

"But he may still be in Germany. After the surrender, I was billeted to a farm in Bavaria to await my papers, and the Americans said that I would be able to use those papers to get into Hungary and get home. I left early, before the papers came, but Henry may still be working in Germany. The papers take a long time," he said, trying to sound convincing.

At the edge of town, Mrs. Kuhn and the little girl left them to head to their own homes. His mom was walking along beside him, her arm firmly around his waist.

"How is everyone?" Adam asked.

She stopped and turned to face him, her eyes filled with pain.

"The Russians took Resi. I don't know where she is." At his mom's words, panic clutched at Adam. "And your dad was drafted into the Hungarian army," she continued. "They said he was too old to fight, thank God, but he still had to go and drive supply wagons. He left over a year ago, not long after you. Resi left in January. I haven't heard from either of them since they left," she finished, her voice trembling.

"You and George have been alone all this time?"

"Yes, but we've been fine. George is a big boy now, and of course Uncle Florian has been a big help. There hasn't really been any serious trouble here since they transported everyone to work in Russia. They steal whatever they want, like your boots, but nothing really bad now. Never mind, let's get home so you can see George, and I'll fix supper. You're so thin!"

CHAPTER SIXTY-SEVEN

They divided a bit of leftover stew and polenta onto three dishes. With only three of six chairs filled, the kitchen felt lonely. While they ate, George told Adam how he had looked after the family home all year. He'd made sure the pens in the backyard were in good repair, the way their dad liked to see them, and helped some of the farmers with their vineyards. The rich farmers had really appreciated his help, George explained with pride.

Adam listened attentively. His little brother had been only ten when Adam had run off. He must have been terrified after their dad had gone, being the only male in the house. He'd had to grow up quickly. Adam felt a pang of guilt.

"You did a great job of everything, George. Dad will be really happy," he said warmly when George had finished.

He had wanted to believe everyone was safe at home while he'd been away, but as he talked with his mom that night, he learned the truth. In August the previous year, not long after he'd left, Romania had become a Russian ally, making the nearby border into an enemy line. The Russians had entered Hungary in late September. For two weeks, the fighting had raged, first at the edge of town as the Hungarian troops strove to hold the enemy out, and then in the streets of Elek among the houses. Families had clung together behind locked doors, trying desperately to hide as gunfire riddled the walls and explosions shook the ground. Before long the Hungarian losses were too great, and Elek fell. Adam shut his eyes while his mom talked, imagining the terrifying events happening right there in Elek while he'd been in the training camp.

For the next three months, there was no rule of law, and chaos had reigned. Russian soldiers, long desensitized, roamed the streets looting and raping. Thankfully, the cemetery caretaker had devised a plan to protect his three daughters, and he'd thoughtfully invited Theresa to join them. A pile of bricks in his yard was cleverly rearranged with a space in the centre to hide the girls. The ruse had worked.

Just before Christmas, the Russian officials arrived to organize the occupation. While the most flagrant abuses were brought to a halt, a more devastating plan was in the works. Gates were erected at all entry and exit points. Leaving was punishable by death. Within days a terrifying notice was posted on the street corners. All women aged 17-35, and men aged 16-45 were to assemble at prescribed locations around town with warm clothing and bedding, and enough food to last three weeks. Stories were circulated by the Russians. They would be going to Russia by train, where their help was needed to rebuild war-damaged areas. Some would be working in sugar factories.

Theresa's assembly point was the movie theatre. After everyone had dutifully arrived, the doors were locked behind them. In the following days, while the men and women were held captive, the remaining food stores of the people staying behind were collected and loaded into boxcars. A final order was issued for relatives to bring nice clothes and jewellery to the meeting points for the labourers, as they would have opportunities to go to the theatre and the opera, and enjoy other entertainment in Russia.

In mid-January, a long line of cattle cars departed, carrying Elek's young men and women, almost a thousand in total. Theresa, Aunt Maria, Franz and Stumpf, Michel and Tony Pender, and Uchie were all on board. Uchie, who only a few months earlier had left the train platform in Budapest in tears, opting to stay safe at home.

A few weeks before Adam's return, a single rail car full of people too sick to work had arrived back in Elek. Relatives waiting at home learned that the transport had gone to a place in Russia called Krivoy Rog, the passengers nearly freezing to death on the way. The Russian soldiers had cut holes in the side of each car and used gutters ripped from nearby houses to create makeshift chimneys. Each car had been provided with a pile of firewood and a metal jerry can to use as a stove. Another hole was cut in the floor of each car for a toilet. On arrival in Krivoy Rog, they'd been sorted by strength and sent to different camps.

On arrival, the women were injected with an experimental drug the Russians were developing, in order to avoid the inconvenience of menstruation and pregnancy. Although temperatures of -35 to -40 degrees

Celsius were common in winter, the bunkhouses lacked heat. Nor did they have toilets or washing facilities, and guards were soon shaving heads as treatment for the rampant head lice. It was hard for Adam to imagine a woman from Elek having a haircut, never mind having her head shaved. They grew their hair for their whole lives according to tradition, braiding it modestly but proudly. It was part of them.

With workdays of ten hours or more, seven days per week, and a lack of food, the workers began succumbing to the conditions. People averted their eyes when they passed by the shed where rats fed on the growing pile of bodies.

But no one on the returning rail car had had any news of Theresa.

When his mom finished talking, Adam sat silently, staring into the darkness, his cheeks wet with tears. His sister. His beautiful sister. She was strong. But was she strong enough?

CHAPTER SIXTY-EIGHT

The blood pounded in Adam's ears as he climbed the steps of the Elek town hall a few days later. He'd argued with his mom, but he was convinced it was the right thing to do. Without papers it was just a matter of time before the communists threw him back in jail.

Pulling the heavy door open, he slipped inside and stood quietly at the back of the familiar room. A few clerks sat at desks over to the right. As Adam watched, one of the doors along the back wall opened, revealing an office filled with a large desk. His heart missed a beat. The portly man who sat at the desk studying a stack of papers was wearing a communist uniform. The woman who had opened the door from inside walked out, closing the door behind her. She paused, looking directly at Adam, then begin walking briskly towards him. Adam turned and pushed the door open and let himself back out onto the step. A second later, the door opened again and the woman slipped out beside him.

"Adam, what are you doing here?" she asked nervously, glancing up and down the street.

"Miss Krause! I got home a couple of days ago and I don't have any papers."

"Get out of here. Go straight home and hide. Tonight, after dark, come to my house and I'll explain. But stay hidden until then."

That evening, as Adam sat in the room where she had tutored him through his expedited high school studies, Miss Krause explained. She had learned a few words of the language from her Russian father, and when the Russian officials had arrived, she had been ordered to serve as secretary to the commander in charge of Elek. Only days earlier, a letter from the Komarom prison had arrived, asking if Adam Baumann had been seen. The letter was still on her desk, hidden under a stack of other papers.

Adam quickly explained what had led up to his escape from Komarom, and the two of them devised a plan. Since he wasn't on the census that the Russians had conducted earlier that year, they would say he'd been living with a relative in Budapest. Miss Krause would answer the letter from Komaron, saying Adam hadn't been seen, and then destroy it. Then she'd fill in the forms required to issue his official identification papers.

According to the papers that were issued a few days later, ultimately forming part of the archived records of World War II, Adam had never been out of Hungary and had certainly never served in any military.

CHAPTER SIXTY-NINE

No one in Elek knew much about the upcoming deportation, but as autumn deepened into winter, more and more rumours began to circulate. People were saying that the new communist government, controlled by the Soviets behind the scenes, planned to seize all property owned by anyone of German descent and send the owners back to Germany. The Germans were "enemies of the State," just like the commander at Komarom had said. The property rightfully belonged to Hungarians. All property, from family homes on small plots like the Baumanns' to the largest properties owned by the rich farmers, would be seized.

At first, people laughed and dismissed the rumours as nonsense. Their ancestors had settled this area over two hundred years ago. It had taken generations of hard work to transform it into the productive farmland it was now. It had never belonged to anyone other than them. How could it be the rightful property of someone else? And how could they be sent *back* to Germany, since they'd never been there? If the Germans left, the town would be empty. No, they reassured each other, it was nonsense.

Most of the radios in Elek had been stolen or smashed. They couldn't have heard the official news release about the Deportation Act that was passed just after Christmas making the deportation of German descendants from Hungary and several other countries into law. The stories that were reaching them were getting more substantial though, corroborated by sources at town hall. Slowly it sank in. Anger began to replace the disbelief of the previous months, and any gathering of family or friends was dominated with heated discussions about the outrage of it all. As the spring thaw began, the anger gave way begrudgingly to acceptance. They were being deported.

Soon after, the parties started. "Better to eat every morsel and drink every drop than leave it for the communists," the people of Elek told each other. So they celebrated not needing to do any planting that year since they wouldn't be there to harvest, and they celebrated not needing to ration since they wouldn't be here later to eat what they saved. They threw caution to the wind. Eating and drinking with abandon intoxicated the town. Families with one pig shared it with their neighbours, and land-owners with quantities of livestock threw parties and invited everyone in town. They even invited the people who wouldn't be leaving. After all, the unfair decisions of the politicians were hardly the fault of the people they'd lived alongside as friends and neighbours their whole lives.

Free from his dad's scrutiny and temper, Adam submersed himself in the festivities, assisting at butchering parties nearly daily, and blowing polkas and foxtrots on his harmonica and trumpet into the wee hours night after night. Throughout those reckless months, he did his best to keep his fears about Theresa out of his mind and, despite everything, he enjoyed the heady mood that pervaded Elek that winter.

In the midst of the merriment, news arrived that Adam's dad was in a holding camp in Budapest awaiting his papers. He needed tobacco, the man who delivered the message added. Seeing his mom's tears of joy and the grin on his brother's face, Adam couldn't help being happy about the news.

The next day Adam and a cousin travelled to Budapest, traded a bit of bacon for some tobacco and delivered it to the prison. As he rode the train home, Adam whistled a tune quietly to himself. The guards had promised to deliver the tobacco. His mom would be pleased. Then he thought of Theresa and stopped whistling.

CHAPTER SEVENTY

Spring 1946

The Deportation Act was officially announced in Elek in April. The town criers and the posters at town hall explained that weekly transports would begin leaving soon. There would be six transports in total to clear all of the Germans out of Elek, departing from the livestock shipping station at the south edge of town, near Adam's grandparents' house. The Baumanns and the Bambachs were slated for the third transport.

The following week, Adam stood in the dirt beside the train station with his mom and George, watching. The first transport was almost finished loading. For the last several hours, wagons had been pulling up in front of the building that had been converted to a depot to process the deportees. People climbed down with their bundles and clung to friends who were staying or scheduled for a later transport, before being herded inside for inspection. Helplessness and despair hung over the crowd like a cold, wet fog, chilling everyone to the bone. As Adam watched through the station window, the policemen ripped open carefully tied bundles, rifling through the contents before gathering them up loosely and placing them on the scale. When a bundle was too heavy, the policemen shook their heads and watched while the owner decided what to surrender to lighten the load. Adam watched in disbelief as a policeman ripped his bayonet through a feather pillow and stirred the blade around, searching for hidden valuables.

The crowd at the station consisted mainly of old men and women, as well as children. The few young adults he could see were Hungarian. A handful of times he spotted a German man or woman who had obviously returned from Russia, emaciated or disfigured from a labour camp accident. His eyes settled on a young woman seated on a bench waiting for her father to carry her to the train. She'd been a few years ahead of him in school. The sharp points of her collarbone stuck out through her dress, and blank eyes stared out from her gaunt face. A kerchief covered her shorn head. Still, at least she was home.

Car by car, the heavy doors were slammed shut and barred. As the wheels began to turn, pulling the line of boxcars away, a chorus of good-byes and good wishes arose from the throng of tear-streaked faces lining the platform.

"They have robbed you. This is not right," a female voice called out from the crowd in Hungarian.

A Romanian man chimed in. "Come back to your home someday, friends."

"We will search for you in Germany. May God keep us all safe," said a German voice.

The next day strangers began to appear in town, filling the empty houses and rifling through the belongings left behind.

CHAPTER SEVENTY-ONE

The squeak of bicycle brakes in the street made Adam look up from where he was sitting on the porch with his mom. One of the local policemen who had patrolled Elek for years slowly leaned his bike against the fence and opened the front gate. At the sound of the policeman's arrival, George came in from the back yard and stood protectively on the porch beside their mom.

"Good afternoon, Mrs. Baumann," the policeman said in Hungarian, touching his fingers to the brim of his new communist police hat. "I'm sorry, but I have the details of your transport here."

Adam stood up and took the paper the policeman was holding out. They hadn't gone to watch the second transport depart.

The policeman stood at the bottom of the step, his arms at his side, then cleared his throat and continued. "Transport Three leaves the day after tomorrow. A wagon will come by to pick you up. And I'm supposed to remind you about the 20-kilogram limit, and any gold or valuables you own are to be surrendered at town hall before you leave. It's all on the paper. . . ," he trailed off and looked down at his feet. He was silent for a moment, then looked back up at the three of them. "Well, I guess that's it. Best of luck to you. May God keep you safe," he said, then turned and let himself out of the gate.

"And you," Adam's mom called out softly as he took hold of the handlebars of his bicycle. At the sound of her voice, the policeman stopped and met his mom's eye, then touched his hat again before riding away.

CHAPTER SEVENTY-TWO

The boxcar smelled of manure and animal sweat. It had already gotten stuffy since they'd shut the doors. Forty people and just one small window on each side, eye level for Adam if he stood on his tiptoes. Most others wouldn't be able to see out at all. He could see Uncle Florian through the little window, standing beside the station with his wife. She was Hungarian, so they would be staying. Adam's throat ached from saying good-bye to his uncle. The rest of his relatives were in the boxcar with him. Adam had helped everyone climb on board, passing up the heavy bundles, the pots filled with roast meat covered in lard to keep it fresh, and various other food items. His grandma and grandpa had been the last of his family to load, shuffling out of the station with their bundles. Now his grandma sat awkwardly, balanced on a bundle of bedding, glancing around nervously as people talked quietly.

The process was slow. Another hour or more had passed and as far as Adam could tell there were still another dozen or so cars to load to make up the 1,000 people scheduled for Transport Three. Idly, he pulled on the handle of the door he was standing next to, on the opposite side of the train from the one they'd loaded through. It moved. They hadn't locked it! He didn't speak for a moment, thinking about how best to take advantage of the open door. No point in escaping. He couldn't leave his family now. And where would he go anyway? He scanned the view through the little window on the side of the unlocked door. Everything was quiet. A small field and then forest. He couldn't see any movement. Everybody was busy on the other side, inspecting, directing, and saying good-bye. His grandma and grandpa's house wasn't far from here.

"Adam, no," said his mom when he whispered his plan. "They'll catch you and who knows what they'll do to you?"

"I'll be fine, I promise," he said, smiling down at his mom reassuringly.

Quietly Adam explained to the others in the boxcar that he had to go back for something, slipped out the door and eased it shut behind him. Crouching down, he looked around and ran across the grass into the trees, then scanned behind him. No sign that anyone had noticed.

When he got back, the train had moved forward to load the next bunch of cars. Even better, Adam thought to himself. Now there was less chance they'd spot him through the gap under the train. Running to the car number his family was in, he eased the door open a couple of feet and passed up the pillow cases he'd filled at his grandparents' and neighbouring houses, then turned and took off once more.

On his third trip, he handed his grandma's rocking chair up through the open door, then climbed in and pulled the door shut. They were loading the last couple of cars. He couldn't risk another trip. He grinned and wiped the sweat off of his forehead as he rearranged a few bundles so he could place the chair in the corner, then waved at his grandma to come over.

"Adam, you're cheeky, but you're a good boy," she said as she sat down with a sigh and a weak smile.

Not long after, the train began to move. This time it didn't stop. They were on their way. Calls of good luck and good-bye could be heard in the distance. Adam peered out the little window, trying to catch a final glimpse of Uncle Florian, but they were too far from the station already.

Air from the little windows cooled the inside of the car a little as the train clattered along. The women dabbed handkerchiefs at the tears rolling down their cheeks. Someone was sobbing out loud. Suddenly one of the men that had been leaning quietly against the wall turned around and threw a vicious kick at the wall.

"Goddammed Russians. First they kill your son, then they take your home." He kicked again and then fell silent, slumping down to the floor with his back to the wall.

A few minutes later one of Adam's aunts spoke quietly from where she sat on the coat she had spread out on the floor near his mom. "Where do you think they are really taking us?"

The boxcar was quiet for a moment. Then Adam answered loudly.

"We're going to Germany, and it's going to be nice there. The flowers will all be in bloom this time of year, and the crops will be growing, and it'll be beautiful. Nicer than Elek. Any place will be nicer than Elek," he laughed, "where the meat's all been eaten and the wine's all gone. And fewer mosquitoes. There's sure to be fewer mosquitoes in Germany." A few people smiled. "And there won't be any Russians there," Adam continued.

"Or communists!" one of his uncles piped up.

The sobbing had subsided and the silence that followed was slightly more comfortable.

"What do you see outside, Adam?" one of his cousins asked a little while later.

Adam stretched and looked out the vent.

"We're on the route to Budapest. I recognize it. And the fields are all empty, just like Elek. No crops planted. Wait, what's that over there? It's a communist trying to plough the field, but he's got it attached to the wrong end of the ox team. Guess these fields are going to be empty for a long time." Adam smiled broadly as a few people chuckled at his silly joke.

As the afternoon wore on, the occupants of the boxcar intermittently chatted and rode in silence.

"I'm sorry, everyone. I'm so sorry. But I can't wait any longer, I have to relieve myself," one of the older ladies near the middle of the car said after a couple of hours, as she stood up from the bundle of blankets she'd been perched on. "I'm sorry. . . I'm very sorry." Wringing her hands, she glanced toward the back corner of the car, where a large tin bucket sat.

"That's nothing to be sorry about," Adam responded quickly. "Heck, I bet half the people in here have to go, and the other half will definitely have to go before we get to Germany." Once again, he was rewarded with smiles and a few laughs. "Let's all turn and face towards the front when someone has to use the bucket, to give them some privacy. Go ahead, Mrs. Klassen," he said, turning to face the front wall of the boxcar himself.

They'd passed through Budapest without slowing down when the light in the boxcar began to fade. Someone lit a lantern. Soon women began opening bundles of food and carving off small helpings for each family member. The mood had turned sombre again.

Adam peered through the little window, looking for clues about their location. 'Tata Banya,' he read silently from a big sign as they rolled past it. Some sort of mine. Then more fields, some forest, more fields, a little village, more fields.

"I wonder how long this food really has to last," asked a woman who had lived on their street.

At that prompt, one of Adam's aunts voiced the fear that he guessed was in most people's minds. "I bet they're taking us to a labour camp in Russia."

Adam scanned out the window again for a clue to reassure her. "I can see the sunset up ahead in the direction we're going. That proves we're still going west." With that he pulled his harmonica out of his pocket and began to play. After a few minutes one voice, and then a few more, began singing the words to the old song.

Later, when people began spreading their coats and blankets on the floor, preparing for sleep, he stopped playing and tucked his harmonica away.

PART THREE

Germany

"Some changes look negative on the surface but you will soon realize that space is being created in your life for something new to emerge."

ECKHART TOLLE

CHAPTER SEVENTY-THREE

Summer 1946

As the early radio broadcasts had described, Germany had been divided into four zones, American, French, British, and Russian. Until the countries that had defeated her judged Germany ready to function effectively again, they would each govern a zone and support the rebuilding process while ensuring no chance of a Nazi resurgence. Fortune smiled on Transport Three. They were assigned to the American Zone.

The journey in the cattle car took nine days, with frequent stops to let higher priority trains pass. Next was a week in a tent camp in Hockenheim, and then another short train ride to Laudenbach, where residents of the relatively undamaged town had been required to identify rooms they could spare to house the displaced Germans from Hungary.

Summer in Laudenbach was almost as hot as in Elek. It was late July and Adam had settled into a routine centred around finding enough food for the three of them and their relatives. The rooms assigned to him, George, and their mom were comfortable enough. Two army style cots in the back room of one house for the boys, and across the street and down a block, the summer kitchen of another house, with a bed squeezed in against the end wall, where their mom could sleep and cook for the three of them. The authorities had organized for accommodation for the deportees to be rent-free until they were working.

"Get up, George. Mom will be waiting for us," Adam said, sitting on the edge of his cot. He swung a foot forward and kicked at the canvas under George, making his little brother grunt.

"Don't," came George's sleepy voice.

"I'm going." Adam stood and walked out into the kitchen of the house where he and George slept.

The post-war coalition that had unilaterally decided to move all German descendants back to the motherland might have thought they belonged there, but the locals couldn't have disagreed more. Already struggling with the post-war conditions of their country, and now forced to share their homes and the meagre food supply, the people of Laudenbach were bitter. Of course, there were exceptions. Adam's life so far had been blessed with many exceptions and now he was blessed with one more.

"Good morning, Mrs. Pope."

"Good morning Adam. And I already told you, call me Anna. We're practically living like family. Here's a bit of bacon you can take over to your mom. It's not much, but she'll make good use of it."

"Thank you, Mrs. . . Anna." Adam's mouth watered as he took the little chunk of bacon from her and thought again how lucky they were. He'd heard the snide remarks as he walked past people in the streets. Hungarian Gypsies the locals were calling them. "*You think we like it any better than you?*" he wanted to yell in their faces.

A half-hour later, Adam ignored the hollow feeling in his stomach as he and George headed out to check the shops. The half slice of bread with a little drizzle of bacon fat had just made him hungry. The shop shelves were almost always bare. Hopefully today he'd find something to buy with the ration cards tucked in his pocket. He had to. The bread had been the last thing in the house to eat.

The low-grade desperation that was constant in the back of Adam's mind didn't let up as he led George from shop to shop. Everyone was counting on him to find food. It wasn't the only thing they relied on him for. None of the relatives could read or write enough to complete the various paperwork needed to keep the ration cards coming. They didn't have enough furniture to sit on. No one knew what to do with themselves from day to day in this new place where they weren't wanted. These thoughts churned through Adam's mind as they walked out of one empty shop after another.

When the last door closed behind them, all they had to show for the morning was a few puny turnips. They needed to look elsewhere. A little way out of town they found a garden they hadn't visited before. As George stood guard, Adam ducked in between the potato plants and pulled one up. He only had time to stuff five potatoes into his pockets before George's whistle prompted him to duck back under the fence and run down the street in the other direction before circling back to meet his brother. They stopped to leave a potato and a turnip with their grandma and grandpa, then headed for their mom's room.

"Oh, thank goodness you're here. A man dropped this off today," his mom said, thrusting a letter at Adam. She'd already opened it and pulled it out of the envelope for him. "Does it say anything about Resi or your dad?"

Adam scanned the letter.

"No. It's about me and George. There's a job for me at a brush factory on the east side of Laudenbach, starting Monday. And the name of a school where George is to start attending next month."

"I want a job too," said George. "I already told you I'm not going to school here."

Adam and his mom looked at George and said nothing. He'd only finished grade six before the schools in Elek had shut. He was 13 now. The local German kids wouldn't be kind to a refugee kid who was behind and spoke the Eleker dialect. But still, he belonged in school.

"They'll make you go, George. The American soldiers will come and get you if you don't go," Adam threatened.

"I said no! I hate you, Adam, I hate you! You're not the boss. I wish you had never come back from the war! You're not my dad, and you can't boss me!" Running out the door, George slammed it behind him and took off.

Adam sat down on the bed. No need to chase him. The only place he'd go alone was back to their room.

"Poor George," said his mom. She carried the potatoes to the little sink and began washing them. "And a job for you. That's good, Adam. You'll be able to earn some of that new money the Americans are making."

The Allied Occupation Marks that Adam earned weren't particularly useful, with nothing in the shops to buy. Summer trudged by, day after hungry day. Adam yearned not only for food, but for some sort of news of his sister. In between, he ached for relief from the boredom of being a 17-year-old in a place where he knew no one and no one knew him.

CHAPTER SEVENTY-FOUR

That autumn, Adam struck up a friendship with a neighbour, Martin Edam. Martin had a garden and small vineyard just outside of town, and soon Adam was helping him out after work and on weekends. Martin showed his appreciation in the most valuable currency, food, bringing them bags of damaged noodles from the noodle factory where he worked, and sharing a few vegetables. Basic food items like milk and eggs were still nowhere to be found, and what they had was rarely enough to satisfy the bellies around their own table and the tables of the relatives. But still, it helped, and by the time Adam's father reached Laudenbach in late October, the constant gnaw of hunger had lessened somewhat.

"Some stranger living in our family house! And a German woman if you can believe it! Says she's the new owner of the house, and who was I? Hungarian husband killed in the fighting, so she decides she's a communist, and gets a free house. My house!" Adam's dad stopped and pulled a rolling paper out of the pack on the table where he sat with one of Adam's uncles, and filled it with tobacco from the little bag.

His dad had arrived unannounced the night before. It had been a joyful reunion until he'd asked where Theresa was. They still had no idea whether she was alive or where she might be.

Adam sat at the table, with his dad and uncle, working on the forms to register his dad and apply for his ration cards. He'd lost track of how many times he'd heard about the new owner of their house in Elek and how his dad had managed to locate them in Laudenbach. And worst of all, he was missing choir practice. When Martin had first invited him to join the choir, he'd been hesitant, but once he'd seen all the pretty girls in the group, Adam had quickly forgotten that he'd sworn off church.

"Our father was born in that house, just like we were. And little Anni was born there." Adam's dad spoke a little more softly when he mentioned Anni, rolling the cigarette between his fingers before licking it. "And, goddammit, Adam's kids should be born in that house." He sat back, stuck the freshly rolled smoke in his mouth and struck a match.

Touching the end of the cigarette with the match, he inhaled deeply before he continued. "I walked all the goddammed way to Gyula after I heard that woman's story. Figured if she got to stay because she had a Hungarian husband, maybe Florian was still there too."

Uncle Florian had helped Adam's dad find out where they'd been assigned to live and bought him a train ticket.

Interrupted by a tap on the door, everyone stopped and waited to see who it was. An aunt appeared when the door opened.

"George! Oh, thank the Lord, it's true! Maria came over and told us you were here. How did you find us?"

Adam sighed and looked back down at the papers.

CHAPTER SEVENTY-FIVE

"Hello, Adam," his landlady said, as he came in from work a few days later. She looked up from the pot she was stirring to smile warmly at him.

His dad was sitting at the kitchen table with the landlord, having a smoke.

"We've met your father. You must be so relieved to have him with you finally. And what a terrible story, the way they've given your house away," she said, shaking her head. "Your mom brought some noodles over today. It's so good of her to share. She was telling me how grateful that fellow has been for your help with his grape vines."

"Well, I'm glad to hear that, son," his dad interrupted, and then spoke to the landlords. "I taught Adam how to look after grape vines in Elek when he was a young boy. I looked after the grape vines for every farmer in town. They all wanted me. And I showed Adam how to prune the vines to get the best crop. Adam's a smart learner." His dad smiled at the room.

"Yes, you have a smart son, Mr. Baumann," the landlady responded. "We are enjoying having him and George here. Adam plays a bit of music for us once in a while too. It's a pretty gloomy world these days. Between the sharing and the music, it cheers us up a bit."

"We're happy we can help you, Anna," said Adam. "You've been so good to us. Not everybody in Laudenbach was welcoming, but you were kind from the start. . . ," Adam's voice trailed off as he noticed his dad scowling at him.

"A pleasure to meet you both," his dad said, standing abruptly. "I'm grateful to you for giving my sons a bed. I'm sure they are grateful as well, and I want you to know that we raised them to be respectful." He walked out the front door and pulled it shut hard behind him.

Adam looked at his landlords in the silence that followed. "I guess I should wash up and get over there."

A few minutes later, Adam pushed open the door of his mom's room and stepped in.

SLAP! His dad's open hand connected hard with the side of Adam's face. Adam felt his anger rise as he put his hand to his reddening cheek.

"What was that for?" he said.

His dad yelled into Adam's face, "You know what it's for! Who the hell do you think you are? A smartass kid is what you are. Is that how we raised you? I'm ashamed of you."

"What the hell are you talking about?" Adam asked, his throat tight.

His mom walked softly over to the door and shut it so that his dad's yelling wouldn't be so easily heard in the street. George cowered on the bed.

"The generous woman who is allowing you and your brother to sleep in her back room is your senior and she's a respectable woman. What the hell are you doing using her first name? She's Mrs. Pope to you, and you will show her respect! A good licking will beat some respect into you!"

"She asked me to call her by her first name long ago." Adam's voice was controlled. "She insisted. I wasn't being disrespectful."

"No son of mine is going to talk to his seniors that way." His dad turned to pull the leather razor strap down from where his mom had hung it beside the stove when she'd first moved into the room.

Adam stood perfectly still, his fists clenched at his sides and his eyes trained on his dad. He spoke in a low voice, emphasizing each word. "Dad, I was doing as I was asked. A licking will not be necessary."

His dad stopped and slowly lowered his arm, leaving the strap hanging on the nail. Turning, he met Adam's gaze. Neither moved. A few moments later, he strode around Adam and out the door. The windows along the front of the summer kitchen shook with the force of his slam.

CHAPTER SEVENTY-SIX

The attempted spanking was never mentioned again. To the casual observer, the relationship between Adam and his dad seemed back to normal. But something had shifted. The fierce control his dad had always tried to exercise over him was gone. The continuous demands to do this or that, listen, pay attention, and come straight home so that his dad would always know where he was no longer dominated their interactions.

While his dad worked hard digging ditches and unloading trucks all day, and raged about the injustices of the situation in the evenings, Adam's social life was taking off. He'd struck up easy friendships with the kids in the choir, and once he'd found the nerve to ask girls out, he was rarely at a loss for pretty female company at the dances and parties they all frequented on weekends. The absence of Theresa and any word of her was a dark cloud in Adam's world, but when he wasn't thinking about that, he was happier than he'd been since before the war.

"A man from city hall brought it this morning," said his mom, handing Adam an envelope when he arrived for supper one night in February. "Can you read it please?" His dad was sitting at the table smoking quietly, an apprehensive look on his face.

Adam took the envelope and shut the door behind him. His heart sped up. A Red Cross logo. Good news or bad? Tearing it open, he pulled out the single sheet of paper inside, unfolded it and began to read quickly.

"She's alive. . . ," he continued to scan, ". . . and she's fine!"

His mom clapped her hands over her mouth. "Oh, thank God," she said, tears welling up in her eyes.

"What else does it say?" said his dad, bumping the table as he jumped up, scattering his tobacco.

"Where is she?" said his mom.

"Is she released?" his dad said at the same time.

"Hang on, hang on, let me read it properly," said Adam, studying the paper as he walked to the table and sat down.

"Resi's alive and she's fine," his mom repeated, looking into his dad's face as he wrapped his arms around her, his own tears of joy wet on his cheeks.

"Is that letter from Russia?" George said from where he sat on their parents' bed, his back against the wall.

Adam read quietly for a few moments, digesting what the letter said as melting snow puddled around his boots.

"At the labour camp in Russia she became ill. They transported her to a place called Bittstadt, just outside of Arnstadt in the eastern part of Germany, in the Russian zone. She's living with a family, working on their farm." Adam lowered the paper to his lap and grinned as tears slipped down his cheeks.

"I've got to go tell Grandma and Grandpa," said his mom a few minutes later, laughing as she wiped at her eyes with the heel of her hand. Untying her apron, she hung it over a chair and threw on her coat. "I won't be long," she said over her shoulder as she left.

CHAPTER SEVENTY-SEVEN

February 1947

Pedalling along on the rickety old bicycle he'd bought for almost nothing from a boy in the choir, Adam pulled up in front of the farmhouse where Petra lived. She was waiting on the front porch.

He'd met Petra at a dance. She was a pretty girl, but oddly no one had been asking her to dance. When she got up to use the washroom, he understood. She had a limp. One short leg, like Metzla back in Elek. When she'd returned from the bathroom, he'd swooped in and asked for a dance, then another, and another. They'd become good friends since that night.

"Did you find out anything about when the labour camp victims will be able to come home?" Adam asked. Petra worked at city hall, in charge of ration cards.

"I talked to the manager of that department," Petra responded as she climbed onto the cross bar in front of Adam. "He said the negotiations with Russia are taking a long time. He's not sure when it will be. Maybe another year. But he said not to worry, they will be bringing them home and reuniting them with their families."

With Petra balanced on the crossbar, steadied by Adam's arms on either side of her, they pedalled into Hemsbach, a little village near Laudenbach that had re-opened its theatre. The old bicycle clattered along the bumpy road and then over the slush-covered cobblestones until they came to a stop in front of the movie theatre. Once they'd settled into their seats, Petra opened the bag she was carrying. Biting into the sandwich she'd handed him in the dark, he let out an appreciative *mmmmmmmmm*. Ham on schinkenbrot, same as last week. He chewed slowly, savouring the delicious bread and the smoky taste of the ham, thinking about what Petra had found out.

After supper that night, Adam pushed back his plate and looked at his mom and dad. They weren't going to like this.

"I'm going to get Resi."

Everyone stared at him, uncomprehending.

His dad broke the silence. "What the hell are you talking about?"

"I'm going to get Resi and bring her home."

His mom was studying his face, her eyes narrowed. "You can't go to the Russian zone. It's not permitted."

"I'll sneak in and get her and bring her home. I've thought about it and I'm going. We don't know how they are treating her and we can't leave her there. I'm not waiting another year, not knowing."

"You want to go back to jail?" his dad asked, a hint of anger in his voice.

"No, I don't. And I won't. I won't get caught."

His mom tried logic. "Adam, it's the Russian zone. If they catch you, they'll see your tattoo. Like at Komarom. You will be sent to prison."

"Or shot," his dad added, taking a hard pull from the cigarette he'd just lit.

His mom got up and began clearing the table. His dad smoked in silence. George got up and moved from the table to sit on the bed.

When she'd wiped and put away the last of the dishes, his mom came and stood in front of him. "Adam, please. They shoot anyone who tries to cross the border. Do you want Resi to get shot after all she's been through? I can't lose you both."

Adam didn't respond.

The topic wasn't raised again that night.

The next afternoon, Adam stopped by his grandma and grandpa's rooms to drop off a half loaf of bread and an onion. He'd been trying to find a second chair for their room, to replace the wooden crate his grandpa sat on, but no luck so far.

"Not to worry," his grandma had said, giving him a hug. "You're such a good boy, Adam, bringing us food every day." He'd keep looking for a chair.

Back at his mom and dad's room, Adam went to the sink to wash up. His dad and George were already there. The kitchen was quiet as his mom divided up the last of the cabbage soup.

"I'm sorry, there's not much tonight," she said, placing a bowl in front of each of them. Adam looked down at his supper. A little bowl of soup.

"I think the bakery by the station might have some bread tomorrow, Mom. And Martin hasn't brought any noodles in a while. Maybe he'll have some soon," he said, smiling up at her.

As she sat down with them, conversation turned back to Adam's plans.

"I think it would be better to wait until the people are all released from the Russian zone officially. The letter said she's fine," said his mom.

"Mom," he looked at her gently. "I've decided."

"You're not allowed to go, Adam! Mom and Dad said 'no,'" said George, his confusion and annoyance evident.

They continued eating in silence.

"I'll leave on Friday," Adam said as they finished eating.

"Adam, can't you hear? Your mother and I said you're not going. That tattoo under your arm makes you a target for the Russians. I'm not going to have my goddammed son walking straight into their stinking red hands. It's ridiculous!"

Adam looked at his dad and took a deep breath. "Listen to me carefully everyone. I . . . am . . . going."

Standing up, his dad pushed his empty bowl away, knocking it over. As it rolled across the table, he sat down heavily on the bed and lit a cigarette.

His mom cleared up and did the dishes in silence. When she returned to the table and sat down, her cheeks were wet. She looked at his dad.

"He's run away twice and didn't tell us he was going. He's 18 now. Almost a man. Do you really think we can stop him? At least this time he told us, so we'll know where he's gone when he disappears." Her voice cracked. "Do we want him to go with our blessing or without?"

"Fine," his dad said, standing up from the bed. "Do whatever the hell you want." He strode over to the sink and stared out the window for a few moments, then turned and walked out the front door, slamming it shut behind him.

CHAPTER SEVENTY-EIGHT

Adam's stomach twisted in knots as he got off the train at the last stop and walked out onto the road with the handful of other passengers. A border policeman was watching them. This was the end of the line in the American zone. The communists had torn up the section of the rail line that connected the two zones and built a fence of sorts the length of the border.

It had taken him several hours to get here from Laudenbach. In another hour or so he would have the cover of darkness. He patted the pocket where his papers were, listening for the comforting crinkle, then lifted his collar around his neck and headed south along the little road. Based on the map in his other pocket, Bittstadt was about sixty kilometres east of the border and a little south.

He kept his head down and kept walking as he heard a wagon approaching behind him. He hadn't been walking long. Did the police patrol with wagons? He quickly rehearsed his story. His uncle had a farm south of here, and they hadn't seen him in a few months, since before Christmas, so his mom had sent Adam to check on him.

"Hello, there," a friendly voice called. Adam looked up.

"It'll be dark soon," the farmer said from the driver's seat. "I'm going a few more kilometres if you'd like a ride."

Adam thought for a split second. He looked harmless. And some local intelligence wouldn't hurt. "That's kind of you," he said as he climbed up beside the farmer.

"Where you headed?" the farmer asked as he flicked the reins to start the horses moving again.

When Adam had explained about visiting his uncle, the farmer studied him for a moment and then gave him some advice. "Best to be careful in these parts. The police are suspicious of everybody. The ones on this side aren't too bad. Lock you up and question you, but I've heard they're mostly reasonable to deal with. It's the Russians and communist Germans patrolling the other side you really have to watch for. They'll shoot you just for being near the fence. We've been farming this land for generations. Hard to believe how things are now."

Adam was glad for the early winter nightfall as he lay behind a bush a little later in what was left of the early March snow. If this warm spell kept up, there wouldn't be much snow left in a few days. Already the low-lying parts of the fields and the pathways were bare.

After hearing the farmer's first bit of advice, he'd decided to tell him the truth so he could ask some detailed questions to help him plan his crossing. The farmer had explained what he knew about how they patrolled the fence, and they'd discussed where he'd find the best cover for hiding. The barbed-wire fence, about twenty metres in front of him, was easy to make out in the light of the three quarter moon. The farmer didn't think the police on the west side of the fence guarded this area at all, and so far, Adam hadn't seen anything that looked like a patrol on this side. But the guard on the other side paced back and forth at regular intervals, a rifle slung over his back. If he had a flashlight of any kind, he wasn't using it.

Adam counted the seconds and calculated the minutes that it took the guard to return each time he walked north and south. He re-counted several times and concluded that it took the guard longer to return each time he walked to the south. Counting silently until he thought the guard would be at his further point south, Adam jumped up and ran towards where the gap underneath the bottom wire was the biggest. Throwing himself onto the ground, he pushed the wire up and wriggled under it through the slushy mud. He was clear. Scrambling to his feet, he ran for the cover of the low bushes on the other side and continued into the woods.

Wet snow began to fall softly. There should be a road a few kilometres ahead, based on the map and the farmer's recollection. He would need a ride if he hoped to get to Bittstadt and find the farm that night. And if he didn't get one he'd follow the road until he found a barn with some animals he could sleep near for some heat.

The snow was falling more heavily now, making it hard to see where he was running. Slowing to a walk, he focused on keeping to a straight path in what he hoped was the right direction. Before long he heard the sound of an engine somewhere up ahead and began to run again. Slowing as he neared the edge of the trees, he could see headlights in the distance to the north. He crouched down and waited, squinting into the blinding glare of the driving snow in the headlights as the truck got closer. Peering as it pulled alongside his hiding spot, he couldn't see any symbols or anything that looked military or communist. Just a beat up old truck. Taking a deep breath, Adam stood up and ran alongside the truck, waving for the driver to stop. The truck halted and the window opened a crack.

"What do you want?" yelled a gruff voice through the darkness. He was German!

"I'm trying to get to my relatives' farm and was hoping for a ride."

After a few moments of silence, the truck driver responded. "Okay, get in."

It was a bit warmer in the cab, and after shaking the snow off his hat and mitts, and putting them on the floor by his feet, Adam rubbed his hands together over the weak flow of warm air blowing out of the dash.

The driver was hauling a load of coal to a town about a hundred kilometres east. He asked where Adam was headed. When Adam hesitated, he understood.

"I'm not going to turn you in to the Russians if that's what you're afraid of," said the driver.

"I'm just over from the west for a few days," Adam said warily. "I have my papers."

"Don't worry, son. There's hardly any German communists, other than maybe a few with cushy office jobs in the city. We're captive over on this side of the fence. Not allowed to leave. If we try, chances are we'll get shot. And unless the whole family can run like hell, you'd have to leave them behind if you wanted any chance of getting across the fence. So we're captives of the goddammed Russians. Nobody's ever got enough to eat, no matter how much you produce. They take everything we grow. Only difference between this and being a prisoner of war is that we can see our families and sleep in our own beds. And that's worth everything."

The driver knew the area, and as they continued to talk, he was pretty sure he knew where the farm was.

CHAPTER SEVENTY-NINE

Adam crept closer and peered out from behind a shed. This must be the place. It matched how the driver had described it. They'd have finished supper some time ago. It had stopped snowing and what had fallen was melting quickly. He didn't see any movement in the yard. Opening his packsack, he stripped off his wet, muddy clothes and replaced them with his good shirt and trousers. Putting on a good coat and cap he'd borrowed from Petra's father, he shoved the bag under the shed, pulled a pencil and notepad out of his pocket and crept back out onto the road so he could walk in through the gate.

His heart threatening to burst out of his chest, Adam pulled himself up to his tallest and knocked on the front door of the house. It opened a second later.

"Good evening, ma'am," he said to the woman holding the door, touching his fingers to his cap. "I'm sorry to bother you. I'm Adam Schmitt from the office that handles the placement of workers by the Soviet Administration. We're getting caught up on our paperwork. Do you have a . . .," he paused and looked down at his notepad, "Theresa Baumann living here?"

"Yes, we do." The woman's eyes were wide as she looked up at him.

Her husband appeared behind her in the doorway. "Is there something I can help you with?" he asked.

"I need to ask Miss Baumann a few questions to update our records. Where might I find her?"

"I believe she's still out in the barn. With the warm weather, the runoff barrels have overflowed, and we've had a bit of a flood. She was going to go out and clean up some of the water," the husband explained. "Would you like me to show you the way?"

"No, no, that won't be necessary. I assume that's the barn there. I'll just head over there and speak with Miss Baumann. It shouldn't take long. Thank you for your help. Good evening." Touching his cap again, Adam dipped his head at the couple and turned towards the barn, his heart racing. Resi was really here.

He heard the door shut behind him and forced himself not to run across the yard to the barn. Pulling open the barn door, he walked inside and shut it softly behind him.

A figure in gumboots and brown quilted Russian army pants and jacket was scooping water out of the manger on the opposite wall by the light of an oil lantern. Her back was to Adam. Moving a bit closer, he cleared his throat. Turning, she let out a little yelp of surprise.

"Good evening," she said, her eyes fearful as she took in his nice clothing.

He cleared his throat again and tried to swallow the lump in his throat. She'd always been small, but she looked even tinier than he remembered.

"Good evening," he said in his deepest voice. Raising his notebook, he began to question her.

"Are you Theresa Baumann?"

"Yes."

"Where are you from?"

"Elek, Hungary."

Adam made a note in his notepad. "And would you like to go home and see your family?"

Theresa's eyes welled up. "Yes, of course. Very much. But I think that the Germans have been deported out of Hungary, so I don't know where they are."

"How long have you been working here?"

"A little over a year. Since January 1946."

He made another note.

"And you live here as well?"

"Yes."

"Can you tell me a bit about your work here please?" Adam continued, keeping his eyes on his notepad. It was getting difficult to keep his face straight.

"I feed the animals and do the milking, collect the eggs, shovel out the stalls, mix the feed, that type of thing."

Despite his effort, Adam's face began to curve into a smile. Suddenly, Theresa's mouth dropped open, but no sound came out immediately.

"Adam? Oh my Lord!" The bucket clattered to the ground as Theresa's hands flew up to cover her mouth. "Adam, is it you?"

No longer trying to hold back his joy, Adam laughed out loud. "You better believe it," he said as Theresa flew across the barn and flung her arms around him. "It's good to see you, Resi." He picked her up off her feet for a moment.

"Oh, Adam," she sobbed into his shoulder. "I didn't know if you were alive." A few moments later, she pulled away. "Look at how tall you are! You've grown a head taller, or more. And I can't believe you fooled me like that." She swatted at him, smiling through her tears. "That was mean."

"It was great," he replied, laughing. "You should have seen the look on your face. And anyway, you should know your own brother. But before we talk more, what are the people in the house like? They know I'm here and if there's any chance they will call the police or turn us in, we should make a run for it now. I know the way back across the border."

"Uh uh, we'd be shot trying to cross the border. And, the people here are wonderful. I was so sick at the labour camp. I was sure I was going to die. But God was looking after me when they sent me to work here. They're kind and generous. Let's go into the house. I want to introduce you!"

Adam couldn't stop grinning as his sister linked her arm through his and led him to the house.

CHAPTER EIGHTY

"May God keep you safe, my children," the farmer's wife said, hugging Theresa for the umpteenth time outside of the Arnstadt train station, her cheeks wet with tears. After several days of talking to various locals and planning their route back to the fence, Theresa had hesitantly agreed to the crossing.

But when the train pulled in, Adam's heart fell. It was so packed, people struggled to avoid being jostled out the door when it opened. There were only two trains a day and if they missed that one, they wouldn't make it to the fence in time to cross that night. Taking a deep breath, he hoisted Theresa into the air, and handed her onto the shoulders of a group of young men jammed together just inside the door.

"Would you mind holding my sister," he said to the guys, with a grin, as he wedged onto the train and pulled the door shut. "Thank God she's small. I'm so sorry, but we really need to be on this train." The guys grinned back good-naturedly.

At a tiny station about 15 kilometres before the border, they disembarked and walked north, the snow falling lightly around them, until they found the village where they planned to wait out the evening in a dank little pub that one of the neighbours in Bittstadt had recalled. The light snow had turned into heavy flurries, and they watched out the window with dread as it accumulated deeper and deeper every hour.

At twilight, they set out, trudging further north along the snow-filled road. If anyone asked, they had agreed to say they were on their way home to their farm a few kilometres north. A couple of kilometres out of the little village, when they were confident no one was following them, they turned off the road. The middle of the night would be the safest time to cross the fence. If the maps they'd studied were right, they had about ten kilometres or so to walk to the place people had said was poorly guarded at night. And with the snow now past Theresa's knees, going would be slow.

Turning to his sister, Adam explained one more idea he'd had to help keep them safe.

"Resi, we're going to make it look like only one person, a tall man, walked across these fields. That way, if they're looking for the two of us, or for a woman, they might not follow these tracks. So I'm going to go first and take large steps. You step in my footprints okay?"

Every few steps, Adam stopped to listen and to see how Theresa was doing. He watched as she strained to stretch her short legs into the deep holes he had left. Within minutes, their pants were soaked through and caked with icy snow, but Adam was warm from the exertion.

They'd been labouring through the drifts for a couple of hours when he turned to his sister and motioned for her to be still. The snow had finally stopped, and the moon was peeking out between the clouds.

"Shhhhhh," he said softly. There were faint voices ahead in the distance and to the left. The plan was to cross at least a kilometre north of the last guard tower that was manned at night. Turning north, they continued for what they judged would be far enough, then resumed their westward trek towards the border. When they could just make out the fence ahead, they squatted in the snow, huddled close together, to watch and wait. His mom's words were running through Adam's mind. He couldn't get his sister shot after all she'd been through.

They shivered as the warmth from their trek dissipated. Adam opened his coat and did his best to wrap Theresa inside of it with him. When it felt like it must be well after midnight, they stood up to go. They hadn't seen any guards at all since they'd been watching, and hopefully the ones at the closest manned post would be sleeping by now. Adam grabbed Theresa's hand and pulled her along the last few hundred metres as fast as he could manage.

The fence was wooden here. Reaching up, Adam could just get his hands over the top. The Russians weren't allowed to shoot at anyone on the western side. It was common knowledge that they didn't always respect that law, but being on the other side would surely be safer than being this close to the fence on the eastern side.

Motioning to Theresa, Adam bent and laced his fingers together into a stirrup. She stepped on, and he lifted with all his strength, pushing her as high as he could. Straining to hold her full weight in his hands, he peered up past her bottom to see what she was doing.

"Go," he whispered. She hesitated a moment more and then pulled herself onto the top of the wall, where she paused.

"Jump." His voice was too loud in the silent night. "Jump!" he whispered. She wasn't moving. "Jump or I'm going to push you. And do not scream whatever you do."

Grasping the top of the fence a little to the left of his sister, Adam pulled with every ounce of strength, scraping against the fence with his feet. Slowly he inched high enough to get one hand placed flat on top of the fence and grunted as he lifted his body weight up. Flinging one leg over, he straddled the fence, panting.

"I'm going to push you now. Stay quiet," he whispered to Theresa who still sat atop the fence. Giving her a firm push, he watched her land silently in the deep snow on the western side of the fence. Leaping down beside her, Adam grabbed her arm and put his lips close to her ear.

"Are you okay?" he whispered.

She nodded, her eyes as big as saucers.

"We did it," he said and squeezed her arm. "Let's go."

Crack! Adam flung himself flat beside Theresa. A gun shot. *Crack!*

He raised his head and looked over at his sister's terrified face. Leaning closer, he squeezed her arm again and whispered, "It's okay, they're not shooting at us. Those shots are a long way away. Let's get moving and get away from this fence." As they rushed through the deep snow, Adam wondered if the bullets had found their target.

It was good to be moving and warm again. When the fence had been out of sight for a while, they turned south. Somewhere up ahead there was a raised pathway where the tracks had been. It would be easier walking than on the open field. There was only one train a day heading west from the border and it left in the morning. They couldn't afford to miss it.

The station came into view as the night began to fade to grey. Adam could see light coming through the dim windows, but they weren't clear enough to see inside. The one daily departure was around nine in the morning from what people had said. It would be best to stay hidden until closer to departure time and then he could go in first and get the tickets. That way, any border police that patrolled the station would be less likely to ask Theresa for papers. She should be safe now that we're on this side, thought Adam, but who really knew? Maybe they'd send her back.

As they sat watching the station, he heard his sister's teeth chatter and looked over. Crouched down beside him with her arms wrapped around herself, she was shivering uncontrollably. He looked back at the station. He'd seen several people with luggage or parcels go in. He hadn't seen any sign of any uniforms.

"Let's wait inside," he said, changing his mind. "We'll just have to keep a good eye out."

It was wonderfully warm in the station. After buying their tickets, Adam sat down beside Theresa towards the back of the waiting area.

"We're almost there. The train leaves in an hour," he said, smiling at her. "Tonight you'll see Mom and Dad and George."

"I can't believe it, Adam. I still can't believe you crossed over the fence to the Russian side to get me," she whispered, leaning her head on his shoulder.

As they sat quietly, Adam focused on staying awake, watching nervously each time the station door opened. As the departure time approached, the crowd in the station grew. Families with children swinging their legs from their seats, young couples holding hands, farmers with gunny sacks, young guys puffing on cigarettes. Suitcases, satchels, pillowcases, parcels, each packed for someone's journey, were strewn along the space at their feet, between the rows of seats that faced each other. Adam and Theresa moved down to the end of their row to make room for a mother and her three children. As they were settling into their new seats, the door opened again. Adam's head jerked up. A young guy with a backpack was coming in. Pulling the door shut behind him, he jerked his thumb towards the street. Adam strained to hear what he was saying. A second later, the word *police* rippled through the crowd, each person turning to the people next to him or her to share the warning.

Adam looked around wildly. Nowhere to go.

"Hey, excuse me, excuse me," he said, addressing everyone in the vicinity. Several heads turned in his direction as he rushed on. "We just got my sister over the fence. She has no papers yet." He turned and spoke to Theresa. "Lie down on the floor." Then to the crowd, he said "Please don't mind me. I'm not stealing anything. Resi, lie down right here, hurry, lie down." Scrambling to grab suitcases and parcels, he piled them around and on top of her, forming a row of luggage that ran between the two rows of seats. A few people reached over and handed him their bags to add to the pile. Everyone watched the door nervously.

"Hurry up!" someone hissed.

Shrugging out of his coat, Adam tossed it casually over the end of the pile where Theresa was concealed, then sat back down in his seat as the station door creaked open.

"Papers!" the police officer called out to the room.

Ten minutes later, Adam sighed in relief and slumped down in his chair. The door had closed behind the policeman. He hadn't given the luggage pile a second glance.

"Thank you," he said with a grin to the people nearby.

"Best to wait a few more minutes," a man across from Adam suggested. "Sometimes they come back. The train will be here pretty soon. She can get up and get straight on when it arrives."

Adam nodded. Good idea.

"Did you hear that, Resi?" he leaned forward and asked the pile, keeping his eyes on the door.

"Yes," came the muffled response.

A few minutes later, the train pulled in.

"The train is here, Resi, and there's no police," Adam called down into the pile as people began grabbing their belongings. Theresa sat up, knocking the last couple of bags off. Her hair was plastered around her face with sweat.

"Oh my, it was hot under there," she said laughing shyly at the small crowd watching to see the girl who had escaped from the east.

CHAPTER EIGHTY-ONE

Adam and Theresa settled into a seat in the corner of the train and watched in silence as the snowy landscape slid by. Adam leaned back and closed his eyes. He'd done it. Theresa was safe. The family was back together. Except for Anni. He needed to find a way to get more food for everyone, and he'd have to apply for bigger accommodation, but those things were minor. Resi was safe, and they were all back together. Feeling himself drifting into sleep, Adam sat up and shook his head. Theresa was watching him, a soft smile on her face.

"Thank God you ran away to war, Adam," Theresa said, her eyes glistening with unshed tears. "Thank God. The women who guarded us had these big guns. They were animals. They were so angry. I can only imagine what the men's camps must have been like. I didn't know people could be like that. I didn't know they were capable of such cruelty to each other."

Adam nodded. He'd had no idea either, before.

"There's something else I need to tell you," Theresa continued a few minutes later. She spoke slowly, pausing between sentences. "Your friend Franz was in my camp. We were on a bricklaying crew. Me and Aunt Maria were assigned to the same crew, thank God. We had to carry bricks to the bricklayers and mix mud for them. They woke us up to start work at six in the morning and let us go back to our rooms at six in the evening. Every day. At first it was mostly women on the crew. It was considered lighter work and the men were assigned to another camp doing harder work.

"Anyway, a few months after we got there, Franz came onto our crew. He was sick. He was so skinny. We were all skinny by then, but he was worse. He had dysentery. The Russians didn't care. There were no doctors or anything like that. After a few weeks he couldn't work anymore. I saw him once after that. He was looking through the fence. He could hardly stand. Then I didn't see him again. I'm so sorry, Adam. But I thought you'd want to know."

Tears slid down Adam's cheeks as he listened and imagined his best friend's last days. When Theresa finished, he stared out the window, not seeing anything. He and Franz had had a lot of fun together. Teasing that kid with the white suit, building forts, ice-skating, watching the stallions and the mares. Glancing over, he watched as his sister gave in to the exhaustion and let her eyelids close.

A while later, she stirred.

"You know, I always thought Germany would be such a grand place," she said, watching the destroyed buildings and piles of rubble sliding past outside. "Remember how everyone talked about it when we were kids? And now it's a wasteland. Just ruins. Everything is broken. And everyone looks sad."

"Yes, there's a lot of sadness. And everyone's hungry. There's nothing to buy in the shops most days. And hardly anything at the market. Almost every day I have to hunt for food for everyone." A few minutes later, he spoke again. "Just two more stops and we'll be there," he said.

As the train slowed for the second stop, Theresa got up and looked back at Adam. "Well?"

"I was just kidding. This isn't our stop," he grinned. "It's the next one."

The train rolled along for another quarter of an hour before it began to slow for the next stop. Theresa was grinning from ear to ear as she stood up and moved into the aisle, joining the queue to get off the train.

"I can't wait to see Grandma," she said over her shoulder to where Adam was standing behind her.

"Me too. But this isn't really our stop." Adam burst out laughing and sat back down.

"What? Really, Adam?" she said turning around. When she'd sat back down, she leaned forward and kicked his shin.

"Ow!"

"Okay, this is it," Adam said as the train slowed for the Laudenbach stop.

"Is it now?" Theresa looked at him, her arms folded across her chest.

"Yes, this is really our stop," he said, laughing as he stood up and moved towards the door. "Come on."

Theresa sat, unmoving.

"Resi, get up." Adam was at the door now. Everyone else had already climbed off. The oncoming passengers were elbowing past him. "Resi, this train is going to take off in a minute and go to Weinheim. Get up!"

The conductor's whistle blew and Adam felt the train inch forward. Running back, he grabbed his sister's arm and pulled her to her feet. Tugging the door back open, Adam jumped out, dragging Theresa out of the moving train with him.

When they reached their mom and dad's door, Adam reached up and turned the knob, then pushed it open and motioned for Theresa to go in. It was supper time. Their mom, dad, and George all looked towards the sound of the door.

"Oh, my girl!" his mom's chair fell over backwards as she jumped up and threw her arms around Theresa. "Oh, my girl, my precious girl," she mumbled into Theresa's hair, holding her tight, as their dad wrapped his arms around them both.

"George, look at you," Theresa said when she'd unravelled herself from her mom's arms. "Come here." George got up shyly and walked into Theresa's outstretched arms. "Oh, my God, you were just a boy when I saw you last. You're so grown up."

"I've got a job now," George said, looking at his big sister from under his lashes.

Their mom and Theresa burst into laughter, as everyone mopped at their eyes.

"George is working with me," said their dad. "He's. . . "

"Oh, Adam, I was so worried about you," Adam's mom turned towards him where he was watching from the doorway, a satisfied smile on his face. Walking over, she hugged him hard and then let him go and turned back into the room. "Oh, my God, Resi, you're really here. Now we're all here. We all made it. We're all alive and we're together." A smile radiated from her face.

And then suddenly, the smile vanished and fresh tears filled her eyes.

"I didn't save anything for the two of you to eat. My girl is back with us after two years, and I have nothing to feed you. After everything you've been through. Oh, Resi, I'm sorry."

"It's okay, Mom. There was food on the train, and we're really not hungry," Theresa lied.

"Let's go and tell Grandma and Grandpa you're both home safe. They might have a bite left. They've been waiting for news every day. And tomorrow, we'll have a proper meal," their mom said, turning to grab her coat.

CHAPTER EIGHTY-TWO

That weekend, all the relatives pooled their food items for a celebration dinner to welcome Theresa home. The evening passed in a happy glow as Adam and Theresa sat in the centre of the crowded little room, regaling everyone with their tales of getting in and out of the Russian zone. The room exploded into laughter as Theresa recapped how a mysterious stranger came to the barn and began questioning her.

Not long after, a job came up at the noodle factory where Martin worked, and soon Theresa was contentedly heading to work each day, contributing her weekly pay to the family kitty. As the days began to warm, Adam whistled his favourite tunes and often pulled out his harmonica on his way to and from work. His mom was even starting to gain some weight. He was pleased. Another good sign.

"I guess you're not so grown up as you think you are, Adam," Mrs. Pope laughed at him when he mentioned his mom's good health one morning. "You can't recognize a pregnant woman yet. How long has your dad been back?" She smiled at Adam, eyebrows raised.

Adam felt his face go red. How dare his dad do this? Hadn't his mom been through enough already? Now to have to go through childbirth at her age. It was dangerous. And to have another mouth to feed. For weeks Adam stomped around, silently raging at his dad.

Little Frank arrived in late July, the first Baumann to be born in a hospital. The joy on his mom's face as she gazed down at her newborn dispelled what remained of Adam's anger. With a book of contraband ration cards from Petra, he set about finding baby clothes and a pram for his baby brother. That way at least his mom wouldn't have to carry him everywhere.

"Wow, Adam, you work fast," called out a female voice from a window above the street, as Adam strolled home from the train station in the sunshine pushing a shiny new pram and whistling a tune. He looked up. Two of the girls he knew from the choir were leaning out a window, giggling. "We didn't even know you were married."

Adam laughed up at the girls. "It's for my baby brother who was born last week."

"Pretty fancy," said the other girl. "Lucky baby. See you at the dance tomorrow night."

"You sure will," said Adam, with a wink up at the girls before continuing toward the farmhouse at the edge of town where they'd all moved after Theresa's return. He couldn't wait to see the look on his mom and dad's faces. First Baumann baby to have a pram too.

CHAPTER EIGHTY-THREE

Adam had seen the old man from Elek on his way to and from work many times, ambling along the pleasant little road that was flanked by wheat fields and apple trees, hands clasped behind him, a smile on his face. But that day, the man shuffled along, his weathered face solemn, his eyes downcast.

Adam stopped his bike.

"Hello, there. How are you today, sir?" he asked.

After a bit of prodding, the old man explained what had happened.

The conviction that the stronger members of the community should always help the weaker ones had been a part of Adam's belief system since he was a child. What had happened to the old man was wrong.

"It was Hans, I'm sure of it. He lives in the main street in Laudenbach," Adam said to his friends a few days later, "in that fancy house with the blue shutters. The old guy described him perfectly, and I've seen him along that road before. I think his family has a garden along there. He called the old man a dirty Hungarian Gypsy and made him drop the apples he'd picked up from the ditch." They were standing in the street outside the movie theatre. "Hans has a girlfriend here in Hemsbach. He often takes her to see a movie on Saturday. I've seen them in there lots of times. I came and waited across the street before the show started and saw them go in. When this show finishes in a few minutes, I'll bet you anything he'll be dropping her off and then riding home. We need to teach him a lesson."

His friends looked uneasy. After a moment, one of them spoke up. "Adam, you know it's always us that gets in trouble. Did you hear about the latest brawl? At the soccer game in Weinheim last night? It was Hans and his buddies who started it, but the police hauled away a couple of kids from Elek and a couple of Czech Germans instead. Just kids, younger and smaller than Hans and his friends. And the police didn't say a word to the locals. It's the same every time."

"I know, but I got an idea from that new western movie we watched the other day. No one will know it was us," said Adam, leaning in to explain his plan.

A half-hour later, the three of them crouched down in the bushes waiting for Hans.

"Shhhh, there he is," said Adam, his voice a bit muffled.

When Hans was a couple of bike lengths away, out they jumped.

"What the hell?" said Hans, slamming on his brakes.

"Off your bike and hands in the air," said Adam through the handkerchief tied over his nose and mouth, western style. He spoke in an extra deep voice.

"You've got to be kidding," said Hans, looking at the three bandits in front of him.

"Off your bike now, or you'll be sorry," said another one of the bandits, raising his fists in front of him.

"He's not kidding," said the third. Still Hans didn't move.

"I guess he needs some help," growled Adam.

Wrestling Hans off the bike, one guy pinned his arms behind his back so that the others could get in a few punches.

"That's enough," Adam said to his friends as blood dribbled out of Hans' nose. Then he spoke to Hans. "Now take off your clothes."

"What?" said Hans, incredulous.

"Do you want some more?"

"No," said Hans quickly.

"Then undress . . . right. . . now. Everything off," Adam repeated in his stage voice. Slowly, Hans unbuttoned his shirt.

When all of Hans' clothes were on the ground, including his socks and underwear, Adam wheeled the bike over to him.

"You'd best be getting home," he said.

Speechless, Hans climbed onto his bike, and pedalled away cursing. When he was out of sight the three guys pulled the handkerchiefs off their faces, howling with laughter.

"That was great, Adam," said one of his buddies, breathless from laughing.

Adam piled up the clothes on the ground and knotted the sleeves of the sweater tightly around the bundle, then stood up, grinning at his friends. "Maybe Hans will pull his head in for a while. We should get out of here before he sends the police to find the masked bandits. And I need to find a pen and a piece of paper."

"Why?"

"We're gonna write a note explaining what the licking was for, attach it to this bundle, throw it over his front gate. Hopefully his parents will find it."

CHAPTER EIGHTY-FOUR

1948

With their biggest problems solved, and nothing new to tackle, Adam became restless. He'd already left the brush factory and found a new job at a shoe factory, but the boredom there had become intolerable too. Despite his mother's protests, one day in early spring a year after his trip into the Russian zone to rescue Theresa, Adam quit his job, confident he'd find something better.

Fortunately for Adam, his father had been thinking about his son's prospects for a while. He needed a real job. Not nailing heels onto boots. Adam needed a trade. Based on the destruction all over Germany, Adam's dad surmised that bricklaying was a trade that would feed a family well for many years, and had quietly broached his idea with the boss of the construction company he was working for, describing his eldest son's capabilities. Before long, Adam was apprenticing as a bricklayer.

He took to the new work with his usual energy and enthusiasm, and progressed quickly, perfecting the basics of working with the mud, lining up the bricks, and making flawless joins. The work was interesting because each job was a little different.

A couple of months into his apprenticeship, an incident occurred that would start a new era in the post-war economics of the Baumann family. Assigned to patch bullet holes in the American barracks, Adam stumbled upon a soldier who'd been away from home for some time. The young man, lonely for his wife, had decided to stay in his bunk that morning with a girlie magazine for company. Thinking the barracks empty for the day, Adam went over to investigate the noise coming from one of the bunks. Realizing what he was seeing, he beat a hasty retreat but the red-faced young soldier followed him, beseeching Adam with gestures not to tell anyone. Over the next couple of weeks, the soldier plied Adam with goods he'd stolen from the base, holding his finger to his lips in a shushing motion each time they met.

Adam and his family savoured the food items around the supper table at night, but the cartons of cigarettes the soldier had given him, he kept from sight. American cigarettes were a hot item on Germany's burgeoning black market. He and his dad could smoke hand-rolled cigarettes like they always had.

As he put his mind to the black market, Adam spotted another opportunity. The electronics factories hadn't re-opened since the post-war closures, and demand was growing. Asking around, he found a couple of local guys with jobs on the American military base who were happy to smuggle parts out of the warehouse for him in exchange for black market food items. Next, he searched out someone who knew how to build radios and offered him a deal where he could keep every fourth one in exchange for his services. In the evenings, Adam re-finished scrap wood to make boxes and carefully cut and sanded little holes for the knobs. The radios sold faster than they could produce them.

With all the extras coming in, it wasn't long until the family found a place to rent that would give them each a bit more privacy and a back yard of their own.

CHAPTER EIGHTY-FIVE

The warmth of springtime on his shoulders and the world by the tail, Adam strolled towards their new home whistling a cheery tune. On his head, at a jaunty angle, was his new fedora. It was a hat that the well-to-do wore, and he knew it looked good on him. He'd been eyeing it for weeks. It had taken a lot of persuasion to convince the shopkeeper to sell it to him. She wanted to keep it for the display. More accurately, she didn't want to accept Reichsmarks for it. That day Adam had gone to the shop with a couple of pounds of butter and a little bag of flour, and now he was wearing the best-looking hat in Laudenbach.

"Hi, Franz," he said as he opened the front gate, tipping his hat to the guy sitting on the step.

While Adam had been studying bricklaying and working the black market, a fellow Theresa had known back in Elek had been searching for her. Franz and Theresa had been seeing each other before the war had interrupted. Finally, nearly five years later, he'd found her again. Theresa's beau had been at the house several times since, taking the train from where his family lived in Bavaria.

"I want to marry your sister," Franz said after they'd chatted a few minutes. "I was hoping you'd put in a good word for me with your parents and Theresa."

By the following weekend a date had been set. The wedding would be on the first of May.

Theresa and Franz's wedding would be the first Eleker wedding in Laudenbach, and Adam was determined to make it a grand affair. With cartons of American cigarettes, a roll of white linen stolen from the military warehouse during a wall repair job, and a variety of other hot commodities, he set to work.

But the ability to pay was only half the battle in post-war Germany. The other half was finding the goods you wanted to buy.

Lacking neither creativity nor determination, Adam found what he needed, and when morning broke on the day before the wedding, everything was lined up. Veal from an unexpected twin calf that a lucky farmer hadn't reported to the authorities would make a big Hungarian goulash, a barrel of wine had been brought from the mountains of what would later become the Pfalz wine region, and a five-piece band that he'd enticed with the promise of a spectacular meal and a package of cigarettes would play dance music.

The only task left was to say his confession so that he could take the sacrament with the rest of the family during the wedding ceremony.

Adam looked up at the priest who was looking back at him expectantly where he knelt. What was he supposed to say? He couldn't remember any of it. In fact, he couldn't remember the last time he'd been to confession.

"Go on, son, say your prayers and then I will hear your confession," the priest said quietly. Adam began mumbling in Hungarian, saying whatever nonsense came into his head.

"I can't understand you," the priest interrupted.

"I'm sorry, Father. Back in Hungary, before we returned to the motherland, our church required that we pray in Hungarian. It's the only way I know." Adam looked up at the priest apologetically.

"Oh, that's fine, son. The Lord understands all languages."

CHAPTER EIGHTY-SIX

The wedding was everything Adam had wanted it to be, and as his new brother-in-law settled in with them, the Baumann household had a contented air about it. His parents had their routines, George was enjoying the painter apprenticeship their dad had arranged, and little Frankie was doted on by all. Even when Theresa caught her new husband escorting a strange girl to a movie to cover for Adam because he'd double booked himself yet again, she couldn't be angry. With so much to be grateful for, the family basked happily, if somewhat tentatively, in their newfound ease as the summer waltzed by.

Just before Christmas, despite his father's certainty that he'd never pass after only nine months of a three-year apprenticeship, Adam successfully challenged the bricklayer's exam. With Class One Journeyman papers in his pocket, he started the new year with optimism. But before long, the jobs developed a certain sameness. Routine had set in. Despite the spring air that cheered others, to Adam, Laudenbach seemed to be shrinking. He was ready for something new. Something exciting.

"Aunt Louise is so thoughtful," said his mom as she pulled a dress out of the box and held it up, then handed it to Theresa. Packages arrived a couple of times a year from New York where his dad's youngest sister had settled. "Here's the letter," his mom continued, pulling an envelope out of the bottom of the box and handing it to Adam. "Can you read it to us please?"

Adam tore open the envelope and began reading out loud. Her husband had started a new job and he was making more money now, so they'd moved into a big house outside the city. Their son was doing well in school. The next paragraph was addressed to Adam. He stopped reading out loud and scanned it. Aunt Louise wanted to know if he would be interested in moving to the United States. For a moment, the bedtime stories Aunt Louise had told him when they'd first moved into the family home, about all the grand things she'd do when she left Elek, popped into

Adam's head. The letter said that if he was interested, she'd go to the immigration office and look into what would be involved in sponsoring him.

"What else does she say?" his mom asked as he read silently.

"She says she'll help me immigrate to the United States. I'm going to write back right away and tell her I'm interested," he said, jumping up.

His mom looked startled. "Oh," she said dropping the pants she'd been holding up back into the box.

For the next month, Adam checked the mail every day after work. Finally, there was another small parcel from Aunt Louise. Tearing it open at the post office, he pulled out the letter. She had been to the German Embassy in New York, and to the United States Immigration Office, and submitted all the paperwork. They'd cautioned her that there was a long waiting list and it would take three to six months. She would let him know as soon as she heard anything. He turned over the page. *I've included a suit for you to wear when you arrive in New York. I hope it fits,* she'd written.

Grabbing the parcel, he had a quick look inside and then stuck it under his arm and headed home to try on his new suit. He was emigrating to the United States!

When several months passed, and Christmas came and went with no news from Aunt Louise, his excitement began to dissipate, replaced by irritation and impatience. His mom invited a local girl for supper, and spent the evening rambling on about the girl's cooking skills and all the linens and household items she'd accumulated to set up her own home someday. Adam felt like he was suffocating.

Keeping his ear to the ground, Adam got wind of a six-month contract, doing brick work on a large construction job in France. *Finally, something a bit different,* he thought as the train chugged south, *even if it is in France.* As luck would have it, news on his US immigration finally came when he'd been in France only a couple of weeks. Leaving a note of apology for his boss, he jumped on the next train back to Germany, and a handful of days later, he was en route to an interview at the American embassy in Frankfurt.

The appointment was going well. His sponsorship had been approved. The visa was ready to go. The last step was the physical, which the fellow assured him would be a mere formality for a healthy young man like Adam.

Vitals checked, reflexes checked, temperature checked.

"I need to listen to your lungs," said the doctor. He waited while Adam unbuttoned his shirt and threw it over the back of a chair. "Take a deep breath," he said next, pressing the cold stethoscope against one side of Adam's chest. He moved the stethoscope to the other side. "And again. .. now turn around... another deep breath. And again... Okay, now lift your arm a bit so I can listen from the side. Deep breath." As he moved around to Adam's left side, Adam automatically lifted his other arm and took a deep breath. The doctor listened, then scratched a few notes.

"Okay, I think that's it. You can put your shirt back on and wait in the lobby."

A few minutes later, the first man he'd met with came back out into the lobby.

"Can you come into my office, Mr. Baumann?" The doctor was in the office too.

"Sit down," the man continued when he'd shut the door behind Adam and taken his own seat behind his desk. "It appears we have a problem. How old were you when the war ended, Adam?"

"Sixteen. What's the problem?"

"Why do you have a tattoo of your blood type under your arm? Were you member of the Schutzstaffel?"

Adam looked at the two men silently. "Yes, I was," he responded after a few moments. "Why do you ask?"

"Because the immigration policies of the United States do not permit entry of former members of the SS. But based on your age we thought perhaps we were mistaken and the tattoo was for something else. Why were you in the SS at 16?"

Taking a deep breath Adam explained.

". . . and now I live in Laudenbach. I'm a Class One Journeyman Bricklayer," he finished.

The two men had listened quietly. When Adam stopped talking the three of them sat in silence for a few moments.

Then the man behind the desk cleared his throat and spoke. "I'm sorry, Adam. I'm sure your involvement in the SS was no more ominous than any soldier on the front line in any army. But former members of the SS are not allowed to immigrate to the United States."

CHAPTER EIGHTY-SEVEN
1951

Adam's relatives sympathized and expressed their dismay at the outcome of his interview at the embassy, but Adam knew they were relieved. He was their problem solver, their security blanket. No one wanted him to leave. The company where he'd apprenticed was glad to have him back, and his social life picked up where it had left off, but Adam went through the motions listlessly.

The days and weeks plodded by. Summer came and went, and Adam filled his time with picnics, dances, and playing music for his friends and relatives. He took little Frankie to festivals and on hikes with his friends on the weekends, carrying his four-year-old brother on his shoulders. He began dating a pretty girl that he'd known for a while, until her father took him aside to explain that, although he liked Adam, he'd never allow his daughter to marry a refugee. He was sure Adam would understand. No problem, he assured the girl's father. It was the last time Adam asked her out. In the fall, Adam bought a little red weaner pig and built a shelter for it in the back yard. Everyone would enjoy having fresh meat and eating his father's sausages again.

All the hard times seemed to be behind them, but Adam lay awake in bed at night, wondering what to do with himself. He toyed with the idea of moving to one of the big cities in Germany, but they didn't hold much appeal. He wanted something new and exciting. Further afield in Europe might be interesting, he thought, except he knew that being German would plague him. Six years hadn't dulled people's memories much.

He still hadn't come up with a plan as he headed home from work one day in early autumn. Grabbing a magazine from the station kiosk, he jumped on the train and sat down beside his brother-in-law, stretching his long legs out into the aisle beside the seat in front of him. Half way through the magazine, an ad caught his eye.

Tradesmen Wanted in Canada, the title read.

Adam sat up. This could be interesting. They wanted all sorts of tradesmen including the building trades. They would organize work visas and find jobs for qualified men. And they would even arrange the ocean crossing, and loan you the money for the fare. The next few pages had similar ads for Australia and Argentina. Three different countries, far from Europe, looking for tradesmen. And they were advertising in a German magazine. This was promising. Except, of course, for his tattoo. But he had to try. That night after supper Adam wrote three short, identical letters and addressed them to the embassies shown in each of the ads.

CHAPTER EIGHTY-EIGHT

"BOO!" said little Frankie, jumping out from the alcove in the wall of the train station where he often hid as their train approached the platform at the end of the workday. Adam, George, their brother-in-law, and their dad all pretended to be startled, making little Frankie giggle.

"Hello, Frankie," said Adam, as he reached in his pocket for a coin. "Why don't you go get yourself an ice cream?"

Grabbing the coin, little Frankie raced away past the line of horse-drawn wagons lumbering up the hill now that the railway-crossing arm had lifted.

There was a letter waiting for Adam when they reached the house. His heart pounded as he grabbed the envelope off the table. It was from the Canadian Embassy in Karlsruhe. He hadn't expected a response so quickly. He hadn't told anyone about the ads. Taking the letter into his room, he ripped it open. An interview next week. Sitting on the edge of the bed, he remembered the snow-covered mountains pictured in the ad.

"But, Adam, we don't know anyone in Canada," his mom said when he announced the interview at supper.

"I'd meet people. It probably won't happen anyway. They'll find my tattoo."

"You can't just pick up and move to a country where you've got no job and no family," his dad said, matter-of-factly, as he helped himself to another slice of bread. "Your family is here."

"Well, I'm going to the interview next week and then we'll see what happens."

The first interview went well. They reviewed his citizenship papers and his bricklaying qualifications and filled in several forms. Adam listened intently as the official told him a bit about the geography of Canada and asked where he planned to settle. Most immigrants settled in Ontario, but British Columbia, out west, was mountainous and beautiful and that's where the future was, the man said.

His medical examination was scheduled for the following week.

Adam sat nervously in the waiting room, tapping his foot on the floor.

"Adam Baumann?" said the man who stuck his head into the waiting room.

"Yes."

"Come in."

The first part of the medical was the same as at the US Embassy. Poking here and there, and looking down his throat, and into his ears and eyes. Then it was time to listen to his lungs. Adam swallowed hard as he unbuttoned his shirt and took it off. Slowly, the doctor listened to his chest and his back, and then asked him to lift his arms.

"I see you've got one of those SS tattoos. Another deep breath please. . . that was a good idea, identifying a soldier's blood type with a tattoo. Bet it saved a few lives. Not the prettiest tattoo though," the doctor chuckled. "Other side. . . deep breath."

"Is the tattoo a problem?" Adam asked when the doctor put down the stethoscope.

"No. There was a policy previously that disallowed former SS members, but it's been lifted. It's no problem."

Adam's heart leapt.

Two weeks later, his tickets arrived in the mail, along with his visa to work in Canada. He would be sailing on a ship called The Fair Sea, leaving from the port in Bremerhafen in early November. Ten days later, he would be in Quebec City.

PART FOUR
Canada

"It is not the critic who counts; not the man who points out how the strong man stumbles, or where the doer of deeds could have done them better. The credit belongs to the man who is actually in the arena, whose face is marred by dust and sweat and blood; who strives valiantly; who errs, who comes short again and again, because there is no effort without error and shortcoming; but who does actually strive to do the deeds; who knows great enthusiasms, the great devotions; who spends himself in a worthy cause; who at the best knows in the end the triumph of high achievement, and who at the worst, if he fails, at least fails while daring greatly..."

THEODORE ROOSEVELT, APRIL 23, 1910

CHAPTER EIGHTY-NINE

The small crowd of relatives on the platform looked forlorn as the train rolled away. Aunts, uncles, cousins, his grandma and grandpa, his mom and dad, Theresa and her husband, George, and of course little Frankie. They were all there. '*Good luck!*' they'd all called out as he'd climbed the steps into the train. Their eyes were anxious. Although no one had said it out loud, he was sure everyone wondered if they'd ever see him again. They thought he was crazy heading off into the unknown, and besides, what would they do without him in Laudenbach? He'd thought this through countless times. Everyone would be fine. They all had jobs and no one was going hungry any more. And Theresa's husband could read and write as well as Adam could, so he'd be able to step in and help with what they couldn't do themselves. They would all be fine. His mom had come up with the suggestion to have his photo taken before he left. He'd put one in a little frame for her to keep by her bed and gotten a few extra copies for his relatives.

Fields patchy with early snow slipped past the window of the train for most of the day, interrupted occasionally by a dreary grey town. Eventually, the light began to fade into dusk.

Near Bremerhafen, the train slowed as they rolled into a beehive of port activity. He strained to read the names of the ships they were passing. When they came to a halt, Adam stood and lifted his hat and his cardboard suitcase down from the luggage rack as the conductor announced, "Bremerhafen—end of the line—everyone off!"

This is the beginning of the line, thought Adam as he stepped down off the train, grinning to himself.

For a few moments, he stood transfixed. People of all descriptions were rushing in every direction. Mothers holding onto small children, old couples shuffling along, young women and young men on their own dressed in their best travelling clothes. Suitcases and heavy trunks on dollies were everywhere. Dock workers were heaving cargo off and on vessels of all sizes, captains and other men in uniform were rushing on and off boats, and immigration officials scanned lists and directed traffic. Adam stood and took it all in.

It didn't take long to find The Fair Sea, even amidst the throngs of people. She was the biggest ship in port, by far. The official standing at the bottom of the gangplank ran his finger down the passenger list. "Baumann, Adam, disembarking in Quebec City with onward passage by train to Vancouver," he read out loud, looking at Adam for confirmation. Adam nodded.

"How many does this ship hold?" Adam asked, gazing at the massive ship while the man marked him off the list and hunted through some papers.

"Eighteen hundred. She was built for carrying troops, but now she transports immigrants from Europe to North America and Australia. We got 1,800 Germans on this trip, headed for Canada." He handed Adam a small bundle of papers. "Here's your papers for when we dock in Quebec City. Men's quarters are in the bow."

CHAPTER NINETY

Most of the passengers were close to Adam's age. Friendships were struck up easily as they speculated about what Canada would be like, and what they would do when they arrived. Everyone he talked to was headed for Ontario, other than Willy Fleischmann, a guy he met the first afternoon at sea. Willy's wife had run off and taken their young son, and he wanted to get as far away from Germany as possible. Vancouver, the wild west of Canada, would be perfect, he explained to Adam.

"Play another!" a pretty blonde girl called out a couple of evenings later, as the clapping died away. Adam had eaten his supper in the second sitting, as per the posted schedule. When they'd finished eating, he and Willy had come out to the deck to find a place to sit near the back of the ship out of the wind, and Adam had pulled out his harmonica. Before he finished the first song a small crowd had gathered, sitting on the deck cross-legged or perched on the large wooden storage boxes that lined the walls of the ship.

As he was considering what to play next, a young male voice called out, "How about a polka?"

"As long as you get up and dance," laughed Adam and put his mouth organ to his lips. With that, the young man who had requested the song hopped up and pulled the girl beside him to her feet. Soon the deck was full of merriment as couples crisscrossed the makeshift dance floor to the music. While he played, Adam scanned the people who remained sitting. It was almost all girls. There were a lot of young women on the ship on their way to join men who had gone ahead of them to get established. Adam looked at the pretty girl who had asked him to play another. She was standing off to the side of the group, tall, with long sexy legs and high boots. She smiled brightly as she clapped to the music.

After a few more songs, he tucked the mouth organ back into his pocket. "That's all I got for tonight," he said to the group. As he stood up to go and talk to the pretty blonde where she'd settled with her back against the ship's wall, a couple of girls started singing a lively German folk song. Adam joined in as he tipped his hat to the blonde girl and lowered himself to the deck beside her. As the last line of the song ended, another started up. Looking at one another and laughing, Adam and the blonde girl joined in again. A slower song followed, and the crowd swayed as they sang the romantic lines. Finally, no one could think of another song, and a few people stood up to leave.

"I'm Adam," Adam smiled at the girl.

"I'm Beatrice. Pleased to meet you. I loved your music," she said, smiling prettily at him.

"Would you like to go for a stroll around the deck before turning in for the night?"

Beatrice was bound for Toronto to join her fiancé. He'd written lots about Canada in his letters. They would be married soon after she arrived, Beatrice explained as they walked. After strolling a full lap around the ship, Adam said good night and left Beatrice at the entrance to the women's quarters.

As the shipload of immigrants journeyed across the Atlantic away from their homeland, a carefree mood prevailed. Laughter could often be heard as groups passed the time playing games and swapping stories.

Adam often joined one of the many card games that took place in the afternoons. In the evenings, he was scarcely seen without Beatrice by his side, dancing in the ship's refurbished ballroom or strolling arm in arm under the stars. They compared notes on Germany and their families, and wondered what it would be like to live in Canada, if it would really be as cold as they'd heard, and if bears really roamed through towns attacking people. Willy often tagged along, but when they wanted some privacy, it wasn't hard to give him the slip.

A week into the voyage, The Fair Sea hit rough water. Within hours, the air below deck reeked of vomit. For three days, Adam and others not affected by the rolling seas, spent part of each morning and each afternoon carrying babies and toddlers from the women's quarters up to the dining hall, feeding and entertaining them to give their mothers a break.

Then, the day before they were due to dock in Quebec City, the morning dawned bright and blue, the seas hospitably calm. Anticipation had been growing. Talk among the passengers was that they would sight land before dark. From early afternoon, Adam stood at the rail with his eyes on the horizon, whistling one tune after another. He didn't want to miss the first glimpse of Canada.

"Hi, Adam," a soft voice beside him interrupted his thoughts. It was Beatrice. She wasn't her usual smiley self.

"Where's Willy?" she asked.

"In the loo, I think. His stomach isn't used to the calm water," Adam joked.

"Good. I wanted to talk to you alone," she hesitated and looked down.

"Okay, go ahead, we're alone," said Adam.

She raised her eyes to meet Adam's and hesitated. Then her words came in a rush. "I want to go to Vancouver with you."

"But you're meeting your fiancé in Ontario, aren't you?"

"Yes, but you said the future is in the west, and I haven't seen Karl in ages and sometimes I feel like I hardly remember him, and I'd like to go with you instead. Wouldn't you like that?" she batted her lashes and smiled.

"Of course I'd like that, Beatrice," said Adam, putting his arm around her shoulder, "and I'm very flattered. But I can't take another man's fiancée from him. And besides that, I only have seven dollars and no job. I'm expecting a lot of hard times ahead, and your fiancé already has that good job and everything all set up so you can enjoy Canada like you should." Adam's voice was gentle, but he saw Beatrice's eyes fill with tears. "I'm really, really flattered, but I'm not established like your man is, and I can't take responsibility for someone else right now. Even if she is the prettiest girl on the ship."

Beatrice smiled a tiny smile through her tears at the compliment. He didn't want to hurt her feelings, but the last thing he needed was a girlfriend or a wife.

"Okay, well, that was just awfully embarrassing then," Beatrice said, turning to stare at the horizon.

"Nonsense, forget about it. And your fiancé is the luckiest guy in

Canada. I bet he'll have a nice house set up, and in no time, you'll be starting a family and your kids will be Canadian." Adam continued his pep talk as Willy came up and leaned on the rail on the other side of him.

"What's that, Adam?" Willy asked.

"Nothing. Beatrice is just excited to see her fiancé after all this time," he said, winking at her.

Early the next morning, passengers filed up onto the deck with their luggage to watch as they cruised up the St. Lawrence River, into the gulf, and approached Quebec City. The air nearly crackled with the crowd's nervous anticipation. Everyone strained to get a closer look.

"All the best, Adam," the guy who'd slept in the bunk above him called out over the heads of the people between them.

"You too. Stay warm."

"Bye, Adam," yelled a voice on the other side of him.

"All the best!"

The handshaking, backslapping, and hugging continued as the ship docked and the immigrants began to file off and disperse into line-ups according to their final destination.

On the dock, Adam and Willy pumped the hands of the last of their new friends, and stood for a few minutes, laughing at how the ground swayed under their feet.

"Come on, let's find the line-up for Vancouver." Adjusting his hat to a jaunty angle, Adam turned towards the crowded building, Willy right behind him.

CHAPTER NINETY-ONE

It turned out Willy and Adam really were the only passengers from The Fair Sea going all the way to the west coast of Canada. Adam couldn't understand a word of the strange-sounding conversations all around them on the train. And all he could see out the window was snow-covered forest, devoid of colour. It went on forever. A day later, the scenery hadn't changed. Canada was bigger than he could ever have imagined, and, my God, the distances between the towns.

When they did slow down to pass through a town he stared at the buildings.

"I'm not sure I'm going to be able to get work as a bricklayer in Canada, Willy," he finally said.

"What do you mean?"

"Look closely at these walls." The train had slowed right down to pass through a little town. He and Willy put their faces close to the glass and Adam pointed as they went by the next building. "The joins between the bricks are so fine you can't really even see them. Look at how smooth the whole wall is."

Willy squinted and tried to see what Adam meant.

"I don't know how they do it." Adam sat back against his seat again as the train resumed its speed and the scenery changed back to snow covered trees.

Climbing down onto the platform the next morning, Adam looked for the conductor. The train was stopped at a little station, and they needed to restock on food. Using sign language and pointing at the face of the clock on the station, they determined that the train would be stopped for about twenty minutes.

It didn't take long to find what they were looking for in the little shop across the street, and soon they were back on the platform with time to spare. Adam wandered over to the building at the end of the platform to have a closer look at the brickwork. He knocked his knuckle against the wall and listened.

"Well, I'll be damned. It's not brick. It's a thick sheet of some kind of tar paper made with sand or something, covering a wall made of wood. Unbelievable."

Adam inspected the wall and the structure of the building for a few more minutes, until the conductor stepped down from the train and motioned for them to board. As the train eased out of the station, he became even more apprehensive. They didn't need bricklayers in this country if that's how they built. They needed carpenters.

"Isn't this bread the strangest thing you've seen?" Willy said as he folded a slice around a chunk of Spam.

"Yep," said Adam. "I've been wondering about that too. First of all, how do they get it so white, *and* how do they get it full of air? They must use some kind of an air compressor, which seems like an awfully big expense for a bakery."

The next morning, Adam and Willy were feeling groggy when the train slowed to a stop. Three nights sleeping sitting upright on a hard train seat was taking its toll, and Adam's legs were stiff. It had been snowing lightly since first light. The sign on the platform said Winnipeg. It looked like a fairly big town. They watched silently as people filed off and a new crowd filed on, reaching up to stow bags and then hats, scarves, and heavy coats, shedding their winter layers and settling into their seats. Some even had fur hats and wraps, and everyone was wearing big, thick boots.

"I wonder what the temperature is out there," Adam mused out loud.

"German?" a young man sitting opposite enquired when he heard Adam speak.

Adam and Willy both nodded.

"Do you have a Leica camera? I will buy it from you," the young man spoke slowly and rubbed his fingers together as if he was talking about money, but Adam and Willy didn't understand.

"Leica camera," he said even more slowly, and made a motion like taking a picture.

Fishing in his coat pocket, Adam pulled out the little Agfa camera he'd splurged on just before leaving Laudenbach.

"No, this is an Agfa," said the man, pointing to the brand printed on the top of the camera. "I want Leica."

"No Leica," said Adam, putting the camera back in his pocket. He sat quietly, thinking. Canadians obviously had disposable money. He just had to pay attention and figure out where the opportunities were.

The forest had disappeared and the land was flat as far as they could see. Nothing but white snowy expanse, and an occasional small town. The next afternoon, they rolled into a place called Jasper, the last stop before Vancouver.

"I'm not getting off. I've got enough food for tonight and can't afford to spend any more money anyway," Adam was saying to Willy just as a German voice interrupted from the front of the car.

"Adam Baumann und Willy Fleischmann?"

"Yes," they said in unison. A tall, uniformed man strode towards them, speaking German.

"I am from the immigration office and have been contacted by my colleagues in Vancouver. They have been reviewing the files of the German immigration program of which you are a part," the man explained. "I understand you are both planning to go to Vancouver to seek work. Do you have any relatives or friends in Vancouver to stay with until you find work?" He glanced back and forth between Adam and Willy.

"No, neither of us knows anyone in Vancouver," said Adam hesitantly.

"Because it is winter time now, they say it is unlikely that you will find work in Vancouver. Labourer jobs typically become available in Vancouver in the spring and summer. Perhaps you have enough savings with you to live on over the winter if you can't find work?"

"No, sir, I don't," replied Adam. This was serious. Willy said nothing.

"There is another option," the immigration official said. "There is a place called Prince George, in the northern part of British Columbia. It's a booming area. There are almost 5,000 people in the town now, and a lot of work in the winter. Hundreds of sawmills and they all need men.

The jobs are out in the bush, working in camps. They give you room and board. It's pretty basic, mind you. But they're willing to teach guys the ropes as long as you work hard and don't mind the cold."

Adam and Willy looked at each other and back at the officer. After a moment, Adam shrugged.

"If there's work, I'll go to this place. I'm out of money and I need to work."

Willy interrupted him. "I don't know, Adam. I was hoping to see Vancouver and I'm not sure about living in a camp in the bush. I've got my savings. Let's keep going."

Adam looked at Willy impatiently. "I need work. And if this guy says there's no work in Vancouver . . . No, I'm going to go to the other place." Adam turned back to the immigration guy. "How do I get to this other place?"

"There's a train at the next platform, leaving in about ten minutes, same time that this one leaves for Vancouver. The town is called Prince George and you'll arrive at four tomorrow morning."

Adam stood up and reached into the rack above his head for his suitcase and hat. Willy stayed sitting.

"Are you coming?" Adam looked down at his friend and asked.

Willy hesitated a moment more. "No. I don't want to go north and live in the bush. There's gotta be one job in all of Vancouver. It's the land of opportunity, remember?" Willy smiled as he quoted what Adam had said on the ship.

Adam settled his hat onto his head and reached out his hand. "All the best to you then. I'll look you up when I get to Vancouver in the spring – if I don't freeze to death over the winter."

CHAPTER NINETY-TWO

November 1951

Adam stepped down from the train tentatively. His Sunday shoes had seemed like the best choice when he left Germany nearly three weeks earlier, a fact that was by now almost comical. Crossing the icy ground precariously, he breathed a sigh of relief as the door of the small dark station building opened with a gentle pull. Inside, he stoked the little potbelly stove from the pile of wood beside it, relishing the surrealness of the situation, and sat down to wait.

For whom or what he waited, Adam wasn't quite sure, but a little past nine, when it had been daylight for nearly an hour, the arrival of an immigration official with a translator in tow ended his wondering. The two men stamped the snow from their heavy winter boots before joining Adam beside the stove to warm their hands and introduce themselves. The fellow in Jasper had telephoned first thing, they explained, and they had a job lined up for him starting Monday. Adam beamed at the news.

Down the street, they helped Adam check into The Europe Hotel where Immigration Canada had an account. He could pay it back later with the rest of what he owed for the trip. Next, they showed him where he could get a meal at the Mason Café, and where to find the unemployment office on Monday to catch his ride out to the sawmill.

With nowhere to be for the next three days, Adam walked the streets of Prince George, peering into shop windows and studying the buildings, returning frequently to the hotel or stopping at the café to warm up. All weekend the snow fell. And each day the snowbanks grew several inches. Elek and Laudenbach had snow on the ground all winter, but not like this.

'Cutlet' was the only word on the menu of the Mason Café that Adam recognized. The third time he ordered it, the waitress laughed and spoke to him in German. Her family had immigrated here before the war, so she knew all about living in Canada and happily answered Adam's questions. He'd seen police hauling people away from the dance hall across from the hotel late at night and didn't understand why. The reason, she explained, was that Canadians had a lot of rules about how much fun you are allowed to have in public places. Adam shook his head. Strange.

Making his way to the unemployment office on Monday morning, Adam wondered how he would survive in the bush at those temperatures until payday in the clothes he'd brought. Once again, the immigration official ended his wondering. The translator was nowhere to be seen, but the official had no problem making himself understood. Looking Adam up and down with raised eyebrows, he hugged himself and rubbed his arms, the international motion for cold, then pointed at a logger walking down the street outside the window, and at the department store across the street. Reaching in his pocket he pulled out a 50 dollar bill and handed it to Adam.

An hour later, clad in his new winter work clothes and boots, Adam climbed into a pickup truck with his new boss, Archie.

CHAPTER NINETY-THREE

It was the end of his second week at camp. Adam scraped the snow off of the last couple of feet of the log, grabbed one of the chokers from over his shoulder, looped it around the log and fastened it, then ran over to the next hump of snow and repeated the process. He could hear the skidder coming back already. Chokerman was a far cry from bricklayer, but it was a pay cheque.

"Lunch," yelled the skidder operator, when the load was all hooked up, motioning Adam to climb aboard.

The cookhouse was boisterous with rowdy conversation and laughter. Adam moved close to the wood stove and held out his hands to the shimmering heat while he waited for the food to come out, careful not to get too close and burn himself. He was starving. Lunch smelled pretty good. *It's no wonder that the only warm place here and in the bunkhouse is within ten or 15 feet of the stove,* Adam mused, lost in thought among the loud conversations going on around him in English. It wasn't noticeable at breakfast or supper because it was too dark outside, but at lunchtime you could see daylight through the walls where boards were warped or cracked and the tar paper was coming off.

Laughter erupted at the long table and Adam looked over.

"Adam, come sit," yelled one of the fallers over the din. He patted the bench beside him, then waited until Adam was seated. "When the cook brings lunch," he motioned towards the kitchen and the plates on the table, "you go down to the mill," he pointed at Adam and then waved his arm in the direction of the mill, "and tell the big boss it's time to eat, okay?" He made an eating motion.

Adam knew a few of the words. 'Boss' was Archie, the guy who'd picked him up in town and brought him out to start the job last week.

"You talk English to the boss, okay? Good English," the faller continued. "Say this *'Archie, you dirty rotten son of a bitch, I want to kick your ass.'* Okay, now you say it 'you dirty rotten . . .'" He waited while Adam practiced a few times, and then coached him through the rest of the sentence.

"Lunch is served!" the cook bellowed from the doorway of the kitchen.

Adam repeated his message one more time as the guys grinned and nodded encouragement, then headed for the door.

He could see the big boss on the roof of the sawmill down by the frozen lake, repairing a sheet of roofing tin that had torn loose in a strong wind a couple of days ago.

"You dirty rotten son of a bitch, I want kick your ass," Adam repeated over and over under his breath as he headed down the hill. "Hallo, Archie!" he yelled up at the boss when he reached the mill. The boss stopped hammering and looked down at Adam and grinned.

"Hello, Adam."

"You dirty rotten son a bitch, I kick your ass."

Archie stood upright and stared down at Adam. "What did you say?"

Just then a noise carried down the hill, and they both turned. A crowd of guys was standing outside the door of the cookhouse, hooting and whooping as they slapped each other on the back, some bending over double with laughter.

Adam looked back up at Archie, not sure what was going on.

Archie's grin was back. "Bastards," he said as he swung his legs over the side of the roof and jumped down to the snowbank and then down to the ground. He threw his arm over Adam's shoulders. "Come on, let's go eat lunch."

When they finished eating, the guys were still laughing.

"You're still gonna play us a few songs tonight, right Adam?" one of the guys asked, pausing to mimic a harmonica, as he got geared up to head back out into the snow. "Tonight?" he repeated.

"Maybe yes, maybe no," Adam said with a grin as another guy gave him a slap on the back on his way out the door.

CHAPTER NINETY-FOUR

A few weeks later, Willy Fleischmann climbed out of a taxi outside of the cookhouse during lunch. The usual mealtime ruckus had gone silent as the crew stared out the window.

"Hallo, Adam," Willy said with a grin when he walked outside, confused. "Vancouver wasn't so great so I decided to come and work here with you. I told the unemployment office I travelled from Germany with you and got waylaid in Vancouver. They called the boss here and he hired me!"

Twenty minutes later, Archie came over to where Adam and Willy were sitting at the end of one of the long tables. "Okay Willy, let's go. I'll show you where the horses are," Archie said to Willy when they'd finished eating. Willy just looked at him blankly. "Adam, come along and help me explain to your buddy. At least you know a half-dozen words."

At the crest of the hill they could see the log yard in one direction with a team of horses standing under a shelter nearby, and the mill down the slope the other way. "Willy is horseman, okay?" He looked at them both until Adam nodded. "With the horses, you pull them logs down to the mill, from where the skidders drop them over there." Archie pointed as he explained.

Adam turned to Willy and spoke in German. "Did you catch any of that? I've seen the other guy doing it. You hook the logs up behind the horses over there, then drive them over there and unhook, so that the sawyers can feed them into the mill."

"Oh sure, I can do that. No problem," Willy said to Adam and Archie in German, nodding enthusiastically.

"Adam, show Willy the bunkhouse, then you both get to work. I'll be back around quitting time to drop off the supplies and see how things are going." Archie turned and headed to his pickup truck parked beside the cookhouse.

After showing Willy the bunkhouse and helping him harness the horses, Adam hurried back to the trim saw and began carefully feeding two by fours through the saw, cutting them to ten feet. He'd been moved up to the trim saw a week earlier. He'd done shorter lengths so far, and that day, he was learning to do ten-foot lengths. It was a little harder to get a straight cut on a longer board.

When he reached the bunkhouse after work, Willy was already there, lying on his bunk. He sat up when Adam sat down on the next bed.

"I don't know if I can be a horseman Adam. The horses don't listen to me."

No sooner had Willy finished speaking than the door opened and Archie came in and towered over them, hands on his hips.

"Adam, listen. When I got back from town and checked on Willy, he was standing there talking German to the damned horses. Not one damned log was moved. *No logs moved,*" he shouted, as if Adam and Willy were deaf. "Looks to me like your friend lied about being a horseman. He doesn't know a goddammed thing about horses."

Archie was obviously angry, but Adam couldn't follow everything he was saying. Archie tried again. "Willy," he jabbed his finger towards Willy. "No good with horses." He shook his head to emphasize the *no good* part. Everyone was quiet for a moment. Then Archie spoke again. "How about you? Are you good with horses?" Archie pointed at Adam as he asked his question.

"Yes, no problem." Working with horses wasn't difficult, he thought. You just tell them where to go and when to stop and that's about it.

"I'll tell you what. Willy can stay as long as the work gets done. Two guys, two jobs. You figure out how to get both done, okay?" He repeated and re-explained until he was satisfied that Adam understood him, then got up and stomped out, slamming the bunkhouse door behind him.

The next morning, Adam lined up the six-foot boards and taught Willy how to run the trim saw. Then he rushed down to the horses and moved logs as fast as he could. At lunch and after work, he coached Willy on handling the horses. For the next few days, they repeated this, working until long after the rest of the crew had finished for the day.

"Remember, show 'em who's boss," Adam said a week later. He couldn't keep this up. Willy better be ready.

Willy grinned at Adam as grabbed the harness. "Giddyup!" he shouted, and looked over at Adam proudly as the horses began to move. "Giddyup, heeya," he yelled, slapping the horses lightly with the reins and grinning at Adam again as they sped up.

CHAPTER NINETY-FIVE

Not long after Willy had been trained, Archie moved Adam up to a slasher job, working alongside a faller named Jim. The new job came with a raise of 15 cents per hour.

A month later, Jim was injured and Adam became a faller. Falling was the most dangerous job in the bush, but he had watched Jim carefully and he figured he could do it. First, you had a good look at the tree to see if it was leaning at all and studied what the wind was doing up near the tops. Then, you made sure there was a clear path to lay it down. Sometimes you used a wedge to force a tree to fall in a particular direction, so that the butts were all lined up pointing the same way. The money Adam had saved so far was just enough to buy Jim's chainsaw. It was an investment, he figured. Fallers got paid by the tree and if he was fast he could make 30 or even 35 dollars a day.

Willy, on the other hand, didn't adjust so well to life in the bush. A couple of weeks in, Adam found him huddled out behind the bunkhouse, tears frozen on his cheeks. The poor guy was frozen half to death, mumbling that he couldn't stand it anymore. The next day Archie hauled him into town and dropped him off at the bus station.

One evening in February, Adam lay down on his bed after supper to read a letter from Laudenbach that Archie had picked up in town that day.

Little Frankie had loved the cowboy suit Adam had sent for Christmas. It made him look just like the guys in the movies. And George wanted to come to Canada. Adam stopped reading and wondered if he'd done the right thing only telling them the good parts about Canada in his letters.

The next day Adam wrote back to George. Canada was great like he'd said before, he explained, but there was more that George needed to know. After describing the weather and the realities of camp life in harsh detail, he assured George that if he still wanted to come, he'd help him get it arranged.

CHAPTER NINETY-SIX

Although he didn't frequent the beer parlour like most of the guys did, that's where Adam was when he met Freddy Brandel. He'd been killing time while his clothes were drying at the laundromat, and thinking about how to find a room in town, for weekends. Camp was bad enough all week and worse on weekends when most of the guys were off, including the cook. Brandel was sitting by himself at a table off to the side of the beer parlour, watching the usual Saturday afternoon shenanigans from a distance, which was where Adam preferred to watch them from as well. After a few pleasantries, Adam realized that Brandel was German and soon they had struck up a conversation. By the time Adam left to fold his clothes, they had shaken hands on a deal for Adam to stay in the little room in Brandel's attic on weekends, share Sunday dinner with Brandel and his young Canadian wife, and have his clothes laundered each weekend.

The Brandels had invited him to join them and a couple of friends for supper one Saturday evening, a few weeks after Adam moved into the attic. Afterward, they would take him to a house party. With Freddy helping when he couldn't think of the right words in English, Adam had just finished telling the little group a story about the night he'd spent in the drunk tank a while back. It had all started because a swig of brandy a couple of times a day helped Adam stay warm out in the bush. He'd picked up a fresh mickey, and the cops had spotted it sticking out of his back pocket. For some reason which Adam still couldn't grasp, they had manhandled him into the back of the police car, and then into a jail cell for the night, with a crowd of stinking, noisy drunks. And he hadn't even opened the bottle yet! He'd lain awake most of the night, fuming. The boss had come in the morning, knowing where most of his guys were when they didn't show up back in camp on schedule, and advanced Adam the ten dollars to pay the fine. And the cops had kept the mickey!

"More, Adam?" Adam's new landlady asked when they'd all had a laugh at Adam's story.

"Yes, ma'am, you cook very good," he complimented her in English.

"Oh, this isn't anything special. Just a bit better than camp food, I imagine," she said, scooping more chili into Adam's bowl. "Tomorrow night, for Sunday dinner we'll be having roast beef with mashed potatoes and gravy. How was work last week? You said you were going to be doing a different job than usual?"

Archie had asked him to fill in on the green chain. It was the hardest job he'd done at the mill so far. You had to be fast to get the boards off the chain as they came down, and onto the right stack based on their size. Otherwise they piled up and made a big mess.

"Very good. Yes, very good. But it is sometimes too much of the fucking lumber coming so fucking fast," he responded calmly before putting a forkful of food into his mouth. As he chewed his food, he looked around. Everybody was looking at him silently. One of the women stifled a giggle behind her hand. After a long pause, conversation started up again.

After supper, the women went upstairs to fix their faces.

"Do you know what you said in there about the lumber coming too fast?" Freddy asked Adam, raising his beer to his lips. His buddy let out a laugh.

"I say something wrong?"

Both guys laughed at Adam's question.

"Well, Adam, that word. . . "

Adam's face was hot with embarrassment when the women returned, lips bright with lipstick.

"I am sorry, ladies. I say bad swearing. Very sorry. English is little difficult sometimes."

"Oh, Adam, don't worry, it's no problem. You're just learning." They smiled sweetly.

"Now let's get going to that party!" The landlord jumped to his feet and downed his beer.

"Okay, one minute, I take music." Adam headed for the stairs to grab his mouth organ from the attic.

"Sure, we'll get our boots on," the landlord said as Adam took the stairs two at a time.

Quickly, Adam changed to a fresh shirt and slipped his harmonica into his pocket.

"Adam, hurry up! Come down!" someone called out from downstairs as he pulled the door of his little room shut behind him.

"Something more?" he asked over the railing.

"No, just hurry up," repeated one of the guys.

Confused, Adam went downstairs.

"I should go up?" Adam asked when he reached them.

"What?" the wife said, looking up at Adam.

"You want I should 'hurry up'?" Adam said again, motioning with his thumb towards the stairs.

The foursome burst into laughter.

"No. 'Hurry up' is just a way that we say 'hurry.' Up doesn't really mean up. It just means hurry more I guess."

"Oh... Okay," he said, shaking his head as he followed the group out the front door.

CHAPTER NINETY-SEVEN

Spring 1952

When the ice on the sidewalks had disappeared and patches of mud began to show through on the sides of the road, the sawmill shut down for the season. Much to Adam's delight, the unemployment office lined up a bricklaying job for him, starting the following week. It was the only bricklaying work in town, but it was a big project, a year, maybe more. George was due to arrive from Germany in a couple of weeks, so the timing was perfect. That weekend, Adam found an unfinished basement suite he could afford on the bricklayer wages. Next, he lugged a used, double mattress home from the Salvation Army and borrowed a hot plate from the landlady.

Monday morning, he showed up at the job site a few minutes early, proudly carrying the bricklayer's tools he'd purchased at the hardware store. They were different from the ones he'd used in Germany, but the man at the store had assured him he was buying the right stuff.

By morning coffee, he was in trouble. Desperately, he tried again to clean up the join he'd just done and get the block to lay straight. He'd been a top bricklayer on every job site he'd worked on in Germany. He wiped the sweat from his forehead and tried again. It was a mess. He couldn't make the oddly shaped trowel move the mud the way it should.

"Sorry, Baumann." Startled, Adam looked up over his shoulder at the boss. "No time to train new guys on this job. Pick up your pay cheque for this morning and get out of here." The boss motioned over his shoulder with his thumb. Fired? He was a Class One Journeyman!

Adam opened his mouth to protest. "I am a Journeyman, boss."

The boss looked at him and shook his head. "Sorry Baumann. Your story doesn't cut it. You're done."

Adam looked down at the mess he'd been making all morning. Dejectedly, he picked up his tools and then his laughable little pay cheque. It didn't even pay for the tools.

Back at the basement suite, Adam sat on his bed. He'd come all the way to Canada to work as a bricklayer. Now what? He lay down and stared at the ceiling. That was the only bricklaying job in town. All his training was no good now. Class One Journeyman. Highest qualification in the trade, and the boss fired him for having no experience. And in a couple of weeks, he'd have two mouths to feed.

CHAPTER NINETY-EIGHT

"Hi, George! Welcome to Canada!" George looked relieved to see him. "How did you like the trip? Was the crossing rough? Big country, eh?" He put his arm around his younger brother. "I got us a little place to live for a while. Let's go and relax a bit and then I'll show you around the town."

Seeing how George was dressed, he thought back to his own arrival at four in the morning in the dead of winter. Lucky for George the spring air had the first breath of summer in it.

He was proud of George. His younger brother had never been as reckless as him. Barely nineteen, it would have taken some real guts for George to leave home and come all this way.

"Adam, I'm really sorry about this, but I gotta tell you something," George said as they walked. His tone alarmed Adam. "Mom really wanted you to have some meat from that red-haired pig that you got us last year. She packed two jars in my suitcase—a liver sausage and a blood sausage. And she made me promise not to eat it before I got here. Did those goddam immigration guys in Quebec City make you open your suitcase and dig through it?"

Adam breathed a sigh of relief and laughed. "Yep."

"Well they saw those jars and they said there was no food allowed and they took them. I tried to explain that they were for you, but they just ignored me. Mom is gonna be upset about this. She really wanted you to have a taste.""

"Don't worry about it, George," said Adam, unlocking the side door of the house and letting his brother into the basement. "I would have loved to taste it, but it's water under the bridge now. You can have a shower, and I'll make us a bite to eat. Then we'll go out and have a look around. I want to introduce you to the landlord too. He and his wife are good people. He owns a construction outfit and he's given me a bit of day labour. I want him to meet you and remind him we both need work."

Over the spring and summer, the landlord came downstairs often to offer a day or two of work. When Adam and George didn't have anything lined up with him, they walked the streets of Prince George, picks and shovels over their shoulders. The small town was growing fast, and work digging holes and trenches for septic systems was plentiful.

"What's wrong with your hand?" asked the landlady at the supper table one evening later that summer. Once or twice a week they invited the boys for a meal, a welcome break from what they could cook on their hot plate downstairs.

"It's nothing," said Adam. "Just got a small cut from the shovel, digging a septic hole last week." Truthfully, the wound had been increasingly painful.

"Well it looks very infected to me," said the landlady. "I'm taking you to the hospital in the morning to have it looked at."

The next morning Adam was admitted to the hospital for intense antibiotic therapy.

"You won't be digging any holes with that hand for some time," said the doctor as he wrapped up the examination.

CHAPTER NINETY-NINE

"There's nothing here worth anything," Adam said quietly to George. They were a couple of hours hike up a mountain side in the lower mainland of British Columbia. "And he's not looking too good," Adam continued, motioning at the old man sitting on a stump nearby, who, until 18 hours earlier, had been in the bed next to Adam in the Prince George Hospital.

At the old man's urging, they had taken the Greyhound from Prince George and then trekked up the mountainside to have a look at a gold-mine claim he'd staked years ago. He was ill, very ill, he'd explained as they'd lain there in the hospital, and with no children of his own, he thought the claim would be perfect for Adam and George. *Finally*, Adam had thought. The break he'd been looking for in Canada. Something with a future.

What they'd found was an old rotting log cabin, quickly returning to mother earth, and faint signs of a small mineshaft that had long ago caved in and been reclaimed by the rugged hillside.

"Adam," the old man called out suddenly, his breathing ragged. "I need to get back to the hospital." Adam looked at the man's bloated mid-section and sickly grey pallor.

"Walking up here was too much," Adam said to George. "Wait here with him."

An hour later, Adam returned in a pickup truck with a farmer who lived partway down the mountain. They loaded the old man into the back and headed down the overgrown track towards the bus stop.

For months, Adam and George turned over stone after stone.

Their next stop was Vancouver, where the job situation wasn't encouraging. Their savings were nearly depleted by the time, a few weeks later, Adam got a tip that a mining company called Bralorne was hiring. When the interviewer clarified that they were hiring experienced miners only and asked him about the last mine he'd worked at, he froze for a second. Then the sign he'd seen from the little window of the deportation train five year earlier flashed in front of his eyes, and the words 'Tata Banya' came out of his mouth. Fortunately, that was all the proof they needed of his mining experience. Before accepting the job, Adam insisted they find work for his brother. Soon they were packing their meagre belongings back into their ratty suitcases and setting off to another unknown destination.

Bralorne Mine was a full day's travel out of Vancouver. The first leg of the trip was by boat, up an inlet flanked by soaring mountains. A ship travelling along the other side of the inlet looked like a toy against the backdrop as Adam and George stood at the railing in the salty air, gazing around awestruck. Most of the other passengers sat inside on the benches sleeping, heads lolled to the side. They were all headed to the mine.

That night, he lay in the Bralorne bunkhouse, listening to the silence. It was more comfortable than the bunkhouse at the sawmill. They had their own rooms and the walls were insulated. Boarding the boat at dawn that morning seemed like a week ago. They'd disembarked from the boat in a place called Squamish, taken a train to a crossroads called Shalalth, then climbed on to an old bus. As the bus navigated the switchbacks, taking them up the mountainside to Gold Bridge and then on to Bralorne, Adam chatted with the men in the seats around them as best he could. George had passed the miles quietly, watching out the window as they climbed up and up.

At the mine, a supervisor had shown them to the bunkhouse, then over to the company store. They needed mucking gear before going down the mine shaft early the next morning, he'd explained as he helped them pick out yellow waterproof pants and jackets, and rubber boots with steel toes. For light they each purchased a hard hat with an electric light mounted on the front and a cord hanging down the back to the battery that attached to a thick leather belt. Their first pay cheques would go to the company store to pay for their gear. This seemed like a big, solid operation, Adam thought to himself. A guy could work his way up and make a future at a place like Bralorne.

At first light, Adam and George followed a herd of guys into the room they called "The Dry" and put on their new mining gear like everyone else was doing. The supervisor they'd met the night before came in and sent George off to learn how to work the rail cars, then introduced Adam to a big Swede named Arnie.

"Arnie here will show you how we do things here at Bralorne. Next week we'll set you up in your own patch."

Adam could feel the big Swede scowling at him as they munched on their sandwiches a couple of hours later. It had been obvious that he was a fraud as soon as Arnie asked him for "a three-footer." He'd looked blankly at the Swede, then gazed at the row of tools and equipment until Arnie had come over and grabbed it himself. Adam couldn't finish his sandwich. If he got fired, George would get fired too. They needed these jobs. He put the half-eaten sandwich back into his lunch box on top of the other one.

"Arnie, you can see. Today for me, first mining. Me, my brother, we need work. You teach, I learn quick." The big Swede had stopped eating to listen. "You teach?"

Arnie looked at Adam for a minute more and reached down into his lunch box for his other sandwich. Neither of them spoke as Arnie finished his lunch. Adam was beginning to wonder if Arnie had understood him. When Arnie closed up his lunch box and moved to stand up, Adam did the same. As they turned to head back to the stope, Arnie threw his arm over Adam's shoulders.

"Okay, Adam. One week, Arnie makes you a miner." The big Swede grinned at him. Adam grinned back.

A week later, Adam was pulling on his rubber pants, getting ready to head down into the mine when the supervisor called out to him from the doorway. "Adam, you'll be starting on your own stope today," he announced. He was a miner! He looked past the supervisor, who was explaining how to find the stope he'd been assigned, and grinned at Arnie. Arnie smiled back and gave him a thumbs-up.

It wasn't long before Adam qualified for his blasting certificate as well, allowing him to set up his own fuses and blast his own holes. Without having to wait on the pace of someone else's blasting, he began collecting bonuses for exceeding the quota of ore each miner was expected to muck out in a week. Bralorne was working out well.

CHAPTER ONE HUNDRED

1953

"Anybody seen George?" Adam called out in the shower room one afternoon the following spring. It was the end of the shift and George typically beat Adam out of the shaft.

"Not since this morning."

"Nope."

When he'd dried off and put his regular clothes back on, Adam headed over to the bunkhouse to look for his brother. George wasn't there either.

"Adam, I've been looking for you," said the supervisor as he spotted Adam coming back out of the bunkhouse. "I think you'd better head over to the hospital. Your brother had an accident today. I'll drive you up." On the drive, the supervisor explained that a rail car had slipped off the track and pinned George against the wall of the tunnel. He'd been hauled out of the shaft and rushed over to the hospital. "I haven't heard how serious it is. But we got a real good doctor here," the supervisor assured Adam.

George wasn't conscious, so Adam went searching for the doctor.

"He's got a nasty cut about three inches long in his belly, but luckily it didn't puncture any organs," the doctor explained. "The wound is patched up and we've got him on some strong painkillers. He'll probably sleep the rest of today and through tonight."

The next afternoon his brother was awake when Adam rushed in after work. He paled as he told Adam how the rail car had come at him.

The following week, they moved George back to the bunkhouse with orders to stay in bed for another three or four days before going back down the shaft.

On the third day, Adam made a decision. He couldn't put his younger brother back in danger. "I got another bonus this week," he said to George. "We have enough to live on for a while. Let's get out of here and find something else to do." As they headed for the office to hand in their resignations, George looked happier than he had since they'd arrived.

CHAPTER ONE HUNDRED ONE

Next, they hitched a ride to a dam site they'd heard was hiring. Sure enough, the dam needed fallers for a short contract. Excavation was due to start three weeks later and the area had to be cleared by then.

The chainsaw wasn't anything like the one he'd used up north in Prince George. The blade was more than twice as long and there was a handle on the end of it for another guy to hang on to. When Adam saw the trees they were to fall, his jaw dropped open. The trees he'd fallen in Prince George had been 12, maybe 14 inches across. These were three or four feet!

As they approached the first tree, his mouth was dry. Using every bit of logic he could think of for how to fall a tree this big without killing himself, he took it slowly, thinking through each step. Then, sending George a safe distance away, he held his breath as the monstrous trunk began to lean slightly, and then to teeter. The old-growth giant crashed through the canopy, then cut through the air with an audible *whoosh*, before hitting the ground with a bone-shaking *whumpf*! The earth trembled as the massive tree bounced before becoming still. Adam and George were silent, staring at the felled giant for a few minutes before reluctantly looking around for the next tree.

Three weeks later they were on the road towards the big city once again, their wallets a little more cushioned against whatever might unfold next.

CHAPTER ONE HUNDRED TWO

Adam set the Vancouver map down on the bed beside him and stood up to stir the eggs and flip the slices of Spam. He'd walk further east tomorrow and see if there were any job sites out that way. Then, in the afternoon, he'd revisit neighbourhoods he hadn't been to in a few weeks. There had to be a construction site somewhere that didn't hire only from the union hall. He'd spent a few precious dollars when they'd arrived in Vancouver to buy some mud mix and a few bricks to practice with. He wasn't going to lose another bricklaying job.

"It's ready," said to his brother, who was napping soundly, face turned to the wall.

George rolled over and yawned. "I'm starving," he said as he shimmied off the end of the bed and sat down at the table.

As Adam flipped the hotplate switch to off, the landlady appeared in their doorway.

"Hello, boys. Vell, Georgie, do you like your new job?" Mrs. Kalanovich asked, her thin frame leaning against the door jam.

"Yes. Thank you," replied George. His brother hadn't picked up much English yet.

"He says it's a nice small crew and a good boss," said Adam. *And non-union*, he added under his breath.

"Zat ees good. You're lucky to have a bruzzer vis a job, Adam. Now he can pay zee rent and look after you, and you don't have to vorry." Mrs. Kalanovich turned to go.

Adam sullenly scraped the pan onto his plate, sat down and opened the bread bag. George looking after him. *Hmmmpf.* He didn't need looking after, he *did* the looking after.

The job site he found the next day looked like a pretty big project. The yard was filled with pallets of blocks and bricks. Adam took a deep breath and walked into the yard towards a guy who was standing idle, watching the crew work.

"My name is Adam Baumann," he said, holding out his hand.

"What can I do for you?" the man replied, shaking Adam's hand.

"I am a Class One Journeyman bricklayer and I see that you have a lot of blocks and bricks here, and I wonder if you need another bricklayer." As he spoke, Adam pulled his tradesman's certificate and the booklet listing his qualifications and skills out of his pocket and held them out to the guy.

After glancing at the papers, he looked back up at Adam.

"German?" he asked, handing them back. Adam nodded.

"Well, I can't read German," he continued, "but they look pretty official. I could use a good bricklayer. We're building a service station here, whole thing out of blocks and bricks. Hard to get good bricklayers. You a member of the union?"

Here we go, thought Adam. "No sir, I would like to maybe, but I don't know how to join this union."

"Well, you have to be a member of the union to lay bricks in this town. You're going to have to join."

"I will do what I need," Adam assured him.

"You got your own tools?"

"Yes, sir."

"You can start tomorrow. Let's see what you can do. We'll worry about the rest later. Name's Dave Pipe. See you at eight tomorrow morning."

"Yes, sir! Thank you, Mr. Pipe. I will see you in the morning." Adam smiled broadly and shook Dave Pipe's hand vigorously.

"Call me Dave."

"Thank you, Dave. See you tomorrow," said Adam as he turned on his heel, grinning.

Adam whistled as he strolled back towards West Georgia Street and the boarding house.

The practice paid off. His work on day one wasn't perfect, but he knew it was passable. The second day was better and by the third he was confident. This was his fourth day. Morning coffee break was almost over when Adam joined the crew of Danes and Swedes for a quick smoke. He'd been finishing up a section of the back wall and wanted to make sure his last joins were perfect. He was getting faster with the Canadian trowel.

"Hey, Baumann, I've been meaning to ask you something," a short Swede named Jimmy called out as Adam approached the group and lit his cigarette.

"Yes?" said Adam cautiously. He didn't get a good feeling from Jimmy.

"I haven't seen you around the union hall. You a member?"

Adam didn't answer right away. He didn't have a choice though. They'd find out if he lied.

"No."

Jimmy stood up and walked towards him, a scowl on his face. "You're working in a union job," Jimmy said in a low voice, standing close to Adam. "You can't work a union job unless you're a member of the union. You're taking a job from a union man."

Adam looked at Jimmy for a minute. No one else was saying anything. He took one more pull from his cigarette, dropped it and ground it out with his boot, then turned to go back to work.

"I'm gonna report you," Jimmy called after him.

"This is looking good, Adam. I like your work." Adam looked up to where Dave was standing over him a little later and wondered what was coming next. "Jimmy's all fired up about you not being in the union. He's a real union man, Jimmy. I'd like to keep you. But you're going to have to join the union or they'll be on my back. I'm not allowed to employ bricklayers who aren't members, so we gotta get this straightened out. No union, no job."

Adam finished the last bit of the join he was working on and stood up.

"I will join the union, no problem, but how do I do it?"

"Head down to the union hall on Broadway, and talk to the secretary, a guy by the name of Paget. It's almost quitting time. You should probably head over there now or Jimmy will beat you to it."

"I got bricklayers out of work, waiting for jobs," said Mr. Paget, looking up at Adam over the top of his wire-rimmed glasses. "I can't accept any more applications until the existing members have jobs. When they've all been placed, I can look at your application."

"But I have a job. I need just the union," said Adam, confused.

"That's right. A union member will take that job, since you can't do union work until you join." Mr. Paget turned his attention back to the document he'd been studying when Adam came in.

Clearly the discussion was over.

"If you take this job away from me, I can't get another job, because I'm not in the union," Adam said to the top of Paget's head.

"I've already explained it, Mr. Baumann. Now if you'll excuse me."

That evening, Adam gave his share of the dinner to George, and sat silently on his bed, his back against the wall. No other job site had even considered him after asking about his union membership. Now Dave Pipe couldn't keep him on. Running his hands through his hair, he sighed. He'd have to look for labourer work again.

Adam didn't sleep that night. Maybe it was time to consider going back to Germany. Or a different country. Or Ontario. The only things that he had succeeded at so far in Canada were working in the bush and down a mine shaft. He wasn't about to do either of those jobs for the rest of his life. Towards dawn, Adam dragged himself out of bed and went outside where he sat down heavily on the front step and lit a cigarette. At starting time, he would go to the job site and collect his cheque, he thought dejectedly. Hopefully Dave would pay him for the last few days.

CHAPTER ONE HUNDRED THREE

"Well, sure, that's the way it works," said Dave when Adam re-capped what had happened. "But there's a way. Paget just didn't want you to know because there are guys that are paying their dues with no work. A job going to a new guy in town makes him look bad. But there's a rule that says if a union contractor, such as myself, wants a particular worker and promises to keep him employed, the union has to accept you. I'm gonna write you a letter to take back to Paget."

Half an hour later, Adam headed back to the union office, letter in hand. He wasn't convinced. Paget had been adamant and he seemed to be in full control of the bricklaying job market in Vancouver.

Mr. Paget read the letter quickly, then looked up over his glasses and fixed Adam with an unfriendly stare. "There is a fee of $120 to join," he said, then held Adam's gaze silently for a moment. "Do you have $120?"

Adam didn't have anywhere close to $120. He hesitated.

"Not today, but I can get this money," he responded, holding Paget's gaze.

His annoyance clear, Paget reached into his desk drawer and slid some papers across the desk.

"The next union meeting is Thursday night. Come back with these papers filled out, and your $120," he said curtly, and resumed writing lit-tle numbers in the ledger spread open on the desk. As Adam was about to turn away, Paget looked up and added, "Don't come back without the money, and do not work until you are a member or I will bar you for life."

On Thursday, Adam was back in front of Paget's desk.

"Here it is," he said, placing the papers on the desk. "And I have the money."

He'd borrowed all of George's money and gotten loans from four other guys at the boarding house. He glanced in through the door to the big meeting hall while Mr. Paget reviewed his forms. A blue haze of ciga-rette smoke filled the room where the union members stood talking and laughing in small groups, waiting for Mr. Paget to come in so the meeting could start.

"Your forms aren't filled out correctly. You need signatures here from two union members in good standing, vouching that you're qualified and of good character. Come back next month, third Thursday." Paget jabbed a finger at the date on his wall calendar. "And remember what I said about not working until you're a member. I'll bar you and you will never work as a bricklayer in this town."

Mr. Paget stood up and walked into the meeting hall, shutting the door behind him before Adam could digest what he'd said.

Adam stood in the quiet of Mr. Paget's little office for a minute, then walked out into the hallway and sank into a chair. A month. Dave wouldn't wait a month. There went that job. Exasperated, he got up and paced the hallway a few times, then sat back down. The huge clock at the end of the hall ticked loudly. He wasn't going to let Paget win.

A quarter of an hour later, a string of curse words and a loud laugh echoed through the hall as the front door opened. Adam watched as two men stumbled in, one of them tripping on the door ledge and nearly falling. They walked towards Adam, a bit unsteadily.

"Has the meeting started?" one of the guys asked.

"Yes," Adam replied. They must have been waiting for the meeting time to roll around in the beer parlour across the street by the look and smell of them. And they must be union members if they were going to the meeting.

"Hey, fellas, maybe you will help me? I am trying to join the union and I need two good guys to sign the form," Adam explained as clearly as he could.

"Sure buddy, we'll vouch for ya!" the other fellow said and reached out to steady himself against the wall.

"Thank you!" said Adam. "Here and here," he pointed to the two signature lines and reached into his shirt pocket for his pen.

Adam was waiting at Mr. Paget's desk when the meeting finally finished.

"Here you go Mr. Paget, here is the form with the two signatures, and here is my money."

After scrutinizing the form, Mr. Paget put it down on his desk and sighed heavily, then scribbled his signature across the "Approved by:" line. He looked up at Adam. "Your union card will be mailed to you in the next week or so."

CHAPTER ONE HUNDRED FOUR

Over the summer, Adam got to know Dave and the crew. They were hard workers, good guys. Even Jimmy lightened up once he saw Adam's union card. When Dave began to understand the extent of Adam's training, he took to discussing the best approach to each phase of work with Adam and asking his opinion. They'd barely started the next job, a fancy church built from sandstone and Roman tile, when Dave took Adam aside to talk. He wanted Adam to be his superintendent.

Mrs. Kalanovich beamed when she heard the news. That weekend, Adam received the first of many invitations to join the family at the supper table. The oldest Kalanovich girl, Violet, would be finished high school next year, the landlady explained, and ready to move back to Saskatchewan with a husband, to farm the half section of prairie land they had there. Violet and her husband would inherit that land, Mrs. Kalanovich emphasized, looking directly at Adam. Although Violet was really just a child, he couldn't see any harm in taking part in the home cooked meals.

Letters arrived regularly from Germany, Theresa's husband having taken over the role of family secretary. Everyone was working steadily, and Adam tucked a few bills into the envelope each time he wrote back, so everyone at home had plenty. George's painting job was going well too, and Adam was sure his brother must have a nice little nest egg started. They'd run into Willy a month or so after settling in Vancouver, and the three of them explored the city on the weekends, usually finding a dance or some kind of party to go to. The immigration officer at the Canadian embassy in Frankfurt had been right. Vancouver was full of opportunity.

CHAPTER ONE HUNDRED FIVE

The sun was warm as Adam and Willy walked along Kingsway from one car lot to the next. Willy had asked him to come along and help him buy a car. It was no wonder Willy still needed a translator. Adam never heard him practice. Willy and George – German, German, German – they'd rather talk to each other and the other Germans in the boarding house than to any locals or immigrants from other places. Not Adam. If he was going to find real opportunity and be successful in Canada, he needed good English and he spoke it at every opportunity. It was paying off. Dave was letting him talk to suppliers now, and giving him more responsibility, even though he stopped in at the job site an awful lot to check up on things.

"Let's have a look in here," said Adam. The lot was crammed with used cars of every size and colour. Adam and Willy meandered through the rows, reading the prices scrawled on the windshields.

"There's one!" Willy pointed to a black Willys.

"*Take me home for $50!*" teased the bright yellow words scribbled across the windshield. Adam and Willy walked slowly around the car, sizing it up.

"Looks pretty good," said Adam. "Maybe it's Willy's Willys." The two young men chuckled.

The door of the showroom opened and a salesman headed towards them.

"Can I help you boys?"

"Yes sir, we like this car," Adam answered in his best English.

"That's a good-looking car and a very good price," the salesman said as he reached them. "Let me start it up for you." He climbed in and turned the key. After a couple of tries, the engine roared to life. Willy grinned.

"Is good," said Willy, when the salesman shut off the motor.

"Well then, let's write it up and get you boys on the road!" beamed the salesman.

"Your driver's licence please," said the salesman a few minutes later, not looking up from the paper he was filling out at the desk in the corner of the showroom.

"Do you have a driver's licence, Willy?" Adam asked in German.

Willy's face fell. "No, is it important?"

Adam turned back to the salesman. "My friend has no driver's licence, and I don't too."

The salesman put down his pen. "I'm afraid I have to see a driver's licence before I can sell you a car," he said.

There was a pregnant pause as the three men looked at each other.

"There is a driver's examination office on West Georgia where you can get a licence," offered the salesman finally.

Willy nodded enthusiastically as Adam translated. The salesman scribbled the address on a slip of paper and handed it to Adam.

"Good luck," he called after them as they headed out the door.

Twenty minutes later they were at the licensing counter.

"This is the written part of the test. Answer all the questions and bring it back to me when you are finished," said the clerk as she handed them each a form.

Adam and Willy sat at the table she'd directed them to and examined the paper.

"Well, what now, Willy?" whispered Adam. "I can't read this and I'm pretty sure you can't either. You got any ideas?"

"Nope."

Adam stared down at the paper in front of him, looking for anything he recognized. "It looks like they are all Yes/No questions. Maybe if we fill it all out and where I answer yes, you answer no, maybe one of us will get enough right."

The dejected look lifted from Willy's face. "That's a good idea Adam."

"Okay, I'll mark Yes for the first one and you mark No, see right there," Adam pointed to Willy's form to show him where to mark his answer.

It only took the clerk a few minutes to mark their tests.

"Willy Fleischmann," she called. Adam stood up and accompanied his friend to the desk.

"I'm afraid you have too many wrong answers. You can take the test again in two weeks if you wish."

"Are you Adam Baumann?"

"Yes, ma'am."

"You passed. Have a seat in the Driver Examination waiting area for your driving test. It's down the hall on the left."

"Yes, ma'am. Thank you."

When they were seated in the next waiting area, Adam leaned over and whispered, "Can you drive?"

"Sure. I drove my grandfather's tractor lots of times."

"Well, if you want to buy that car, when they call my name, you're going to have to go in there because I've never driven a car, or a tractor, in my life."

A half-hour later, Willy came back through the door, smiling from ear to ear, and sat down beside Adam.

"There were two tests. One for traffic lights and signs, and then a real driving test in a car. I think I did pretty good."

"Adam Baumann!" called a voice from a wicket to their left.

Adam nudged Willy to get up, and then followed him to the wicket.

"Your form please, and the cost will be five dollars," the clerk said to Willy. Willy pushed Adam's form towards the clerk, then fumbled in his pocket and pulled out a crumpled five-dollar bill. *Whap!* The clerk stamped the form, and slid it back to Willy.

"Okay, so this is your official driver's licence, Mr. Baumann," she said to Willy. "Make sure you have it with you when you drive."

Willy just looked at the clerk.

"Take it," Adam said quietly in German.

"Thank you, ma'am," Adam said to the clerk, then to Willy in his clearest English he said, "Let's go, Adam."

Back at the car lot, Adam held out the paper to the salesman. "We got a driver's licence," he said, then grinned at Willy.

"Now we buy the car," said Adam.

"That old Willys was such a good deal, I'm afraid it sold right after you left." The smile fell from Adam's face as the salesman spoke. "But we've got some other quality vehicles you boys should take a look at. The next best priced car I can offer you is showing for $150."

"No, thank you. That's too much money for my friend." Adam got up and shook the salesman's hand, then switched to German. "Come on Willy. They sold your car. We'll find one another day. And you don't have a driver's licence anyway," he said with a laugh.

CHAPTER ONE HUNDRED SIX

"I'm the boss on this yard, Dave, and I give the orders, not you," Adam announced loudly enough for the crew to hear. Dave had turned up at the site and was wandering around as usual, criticizing the work and giving the guys a hard time. He'd just ordered one of the guys to put out his cigarette while he worked. Adam had had enough.

"What? You're fired!" Dave yelled back in response.

Adam stared at him for a moment. "Okay," he replied, "you can do it all." He stomped off the site and went home, too mad to be worried about being out of work.

Dave telephoned the boarding house the next morning to ask him to come back. When Dave asked him, a few weeks later, if he would be interested in supervising some out-of-town work, Adam jumped at it. Being in another town, away from Dave, sounded like the perfect solution.

"You'll have to haul the equipment up to the job site in Clearwater, near Kamloops. It's a day's drive. You can take my two-ton. You have a driver's licence, right?" asked Dave.

"Of course," he replied. He had the paper with the stamp on it in his wallet.

When Dave left the job site that afternoon, Adam climbed hesitantly into the two-ton flatbed truck parked in the yard. He'd watched other guys drive. After a few failed attempts, he figured out he needed to push in the clutch to start the engine. Thankfully the site was big and he could practice out of sight of the crew. A couple of hours more and he was making it around the yard, stalling only occasionally.

By the time he finished navigating the truck full of scaffolding along the winding road that hugged the cliffside through the Fraser Canyon the following week, across narrow wooden bridges hundreds of feet above the river and sections of road built from planks cantilevered off the side of rock bluffs, he was shifting perfectly.

After the Clearwater job, Adam continued north almost as far as Prince George, supervising a series of small jobs for Dave throughout the summer and early fall, exploring the little towns dotted around the interior of British Columbia. In the fall, Dave called to discuss a big job he'd secured, building a hangar for the Canadian Air Force in Comox on Vancouver Island. Although Adam had only been a superintendent for a few months, Dave wanted Adam to run the hangar job and have full responsibility for the high-profile project.

Two weeks later, whistling a catchy polka he'd heard on the radio, Adam drove to Comox in the well-used, but newly painted, pickup truck he'd purchased. That Friday and every Friday after, he drove back to Vancouver to spend the weekend with George and Willy, looking for places to dance and girls to dance with. He'd found his rhythm on the work front. His personal life, on the other hand, felt empty. It was time for some sort of change.

CHAPTER ONE HUNDRED SEVEN

They'd heard there was a dance on at the Swedish Hall. It was a chilly Saturday evening in early December, Violet Kalanovich's 16th birthday as a matter of fact. After a bite to eat and a quick appearance at the birthday celebration in the Kalanovich living room, Adam left George mooning over his new girlfriend, and met Willy in the street outside the Hall.

The girls at the coat check giggled and batted their eyelashes when Adam handed his coat and hat across the counter with a wink, before heading into the dimly lit dance hall. A waltz was just ending. The next song was a polka. Tapping his foot to the music, he scanned the crowd for someone to dance with.

When he first saw the girl, she was dancing with a much older man. They danced well together. Her father? She threw back her head of short dark curls and laughed. Adam smiled. He watched patiently as they circled the dance floor, the petite girl gliding gracefully within the circle of her partner's arm. As the song began to fade, Adam stood up tall from where he'd been leaning. She was heading towards a table full of people on the other side of the hall.

"I'm going to dance." He tossed the words over his shoulder to Willy without taking his eyes off the girl. He'd only crossed half the distance when a young man swooped in from the other side and led her back out onto the dance floor. Adam turned and moved out of the way of the couples making their way onto the dance floor. He'd have to be faster next time. Looking around, he found an empty chair closer to the table she'd been heading for. He sat down and waited again, watching her dance.

On the last note of the song, he sprang to his feet and intercepted before she could reach her table.

"Hello. I am Adam Baumann. I'm pleased to meet you," he said in his clearest English.

Surprised, the girl drew back the tiniest bit, and looked up at Adam.

"Would you like to dance?" he continued, giving her his most charming smile. The first notes of a waltz filled the hall.

She hesitated another moment, then agreed.

"What is your name?" Adam asked as he took her left hand in his and put his other hand lightly on the small of her back.

"Jean Nordstrom," she replied as Adam began to guide her around the floor.

You smell nice, Jean Nordstrom, Adam thought.

They fell into silence as they weaved among the other couples.

"Do you come here with some friends?" Adam asked.

"My friend Mary and I are here with my father and stepmother who are celebrating their wedding anniversary. They are all sitting over there," Jean tipped her head in the direction of the table she'd been heading towards when Adam stopped her. "What about you? Are you here with your friends?"

"Yes, my friend Willy is here," Adam replied.

The conversation faltered and they went back to silence. He couldn't think of anything he wanted to say to her that he could say well enough in English.

At the end of the song, Jean smiled up at Adam, a pretty flush in her cheeks. "That was fun, thank you. I'd like to sit down now."

"Okay, yes." Adam placed his hand on the small of Jean's back and followed her partway back to her table.

Jean stopped and turned to him before they reached the table. "Thank you," she said with a polite smile, dismissing him.

A couple of songs later, Adam glanced over to where Jean was sitting, then looked away again. He and Willy had arrived well into the dance, so he didn't have much time. Jean had danced with two other men since him, a younger man who was sitting on the other side of the hall, and one older fellow from the same table as her. The older fellow must have been a friend of her father. Now she was talking with her girlfriend and laughing. The man across from her was the one she'd been dancing with when they first arrived. That must be her father. He said something and Jean leaned in a bit to hear him, then smiled warmly at him. The fat woman beside her father said something to both of them and laughed at her own joke. Jean looked away.

When the next song started, Adam stood up and walked over.

"Pardon me, Jean. Maybe I have another dance?"

Jean looked up at him from the conversation she'd been having with her girlfriend, a surprised look on her face.

"Who is this, Jean?" her friend asked with a wide smile, not taking her eyes off Adam.

"This is Adam Baumann. Adam, this is my friend Mary."

Adam shook Mary's outstretched hand gently. "Pleased to be meeting you," he said, and then looked back at Jean and held out his hand.

"All right," said Jean, standing up.

"You dance very good," Adam said a few minutes later. He wanted to make her smile.

"Well, thank you," she said politely with a hint of a smile. "You also dance very well. Where did you learn?"

What a lovely face, Adam thought as he watched her speak.

"In Hungary and in Germany," he replied. "And I played trumpet in a band at dance halls like here and at many parties I play my harmonica."

"That sounds like fun. You must be talented," she said, and her smile widened.

Just then the song ended. They stepped apart, their arms falling to their sides. Jean turned towards her table.

"Wait, maybe one more dance?"

She turned back towards him but hesitated. There was no music playing yet. A moment later, a polka started up.

"All right," she said, smiling.

Adam grinned down at her happily and held out his hand.

As the last note faded a few minutes later, Adam blurted out what he'd been working up his courage to say. "Can I give you a ride home?"

"No, you may not," she responded somewhat indignantly. "I arrived with my father and stepmother, and I will leave with them, thank you very much. Good night." She softened her words with a smile and turned to walk back to her parents' table.

Adam stood there for a moment, searching his brain for a plan. How was he going to get to see her again? Vancouver was a big place! The next song started.

"Can I have one more dance?" Adam asked, catching up to Jean.

She turned and laughed up at him. "I suppose."

"Where do you live?" Adam asked as he twirled Jean under his arm a few minutes later.

"Lulu Island," she said breathlessly. "Richmond."

"What if I ask your father if I can drive you home? If he says yes, will you ride home with me?"

She looked surprised for a moment.

"Be my guest. But he won't agree," she said, then twirled away.

Following Jean back to the table after the song, Adam took a deep breath and thought about his words. Jean leaned down and said something to the man Adam had suspected was her father, then stepped aside.

"Hello, sir. My name is Adam Baumann," he said to the man. "I like to ask if I can drive your daughter home after the dance."

The man stood and put out his hand. He was tall and well built. "Hello, Adam. I'm John Nordstrom. I've noticed you've had quite a few dances with my daughter tonight," he said as they shook hands. Mr. Nordstrom paused for a moment, sizing Adam up. "I suppose that would be all right. You can follow Kay and me. But your headlights better stay within view in my mirror all the way there."

Adam beamed. "Yes, sir."

CHAPTER ONE HUNDRED EIGHT

In the Nordstrom's driveway, Adam jumped out of the pickup truck and rushed around to the passenger's side to open Jean's door before she could escape.

"Okay, here we are," he said, offering his hand to help her down.

"Why don't you boys come in for a cup of coffee before you drive all the way back home?" Jean's stepmother called from the front step. Willy and Mary had ridden in the car with Jean's parents.

"Yes, okay," Adam responded immediately.

"What do you do for work, Adam?" Jean's father asked a few minutes later as he filled three beer glasses from unlabelled bottles. Kay had gone into the kitchen to make coffee. Mary and Willy sat on the sofa chatting, their heads close together, while Jean perched on the edge of a chair near where Adam stood chatting with her father.

"I am superintendent for Pipe Construction. We build many projects. We built a big church in Vancouver and a pumping station by Clearwater. Now we are building an aircraft hangar on Vancouver Island for the Canadian Air Force. On Monday mornings I go to the ferry and drive to Comox, and each Friday I drive back to Vancouver because I live in a boarding house on West Georgia with my brother. "

"Well, that is a good job for such a young man," said Mr. Nordstrom, smiling warmly. Adam liked Jean's father.

"Thank you, sir. I am a Class One Journeyman Bricklayer," Adam said proudly. Mary and Willy were talking quietly. Every so often Mary giggled.

"Adam is also a musician, he tells me," Jean interjected as Kay squeezed through the kitchen door carrying a tray of coffee and cake.

"Speaking of music, why don't I put some on?" her dad said, setting down his glass to thumb through the records on the shelf under the record player.

Conversation flowed easily and the time passed quickly.

"It is late. I think we will go home now," Adam said an hour later. He didn't want to wear out his welcome on his first visit. "Thank you for the beer and the music, Mr. Nordstrom." He stood and shook John's hand.

"Adam," said Kay, "why don't you come for dinner on Sunday, around five o'clock?"

Adam glanced at Jean, who was staring at Kay with a surprised look on her face.

"I would love this," he said, walking over to the door and bending to pull on his boots. "Thank you, Mrs. Nordstrom. It is a pleasure to meet everyone." He tipped his hat towards Jean and her dad. "See you on Sunday. Good night, Jean." He caught Jean's eye for a moment and then turned and let himself out the door behind Willy.

Sunday dinner was a success. Jean's father listened with interest as Adam explained how he had immigrated from Germany and worked in the north that first winter. Her stepmother doted on him, laughing gaily at his jokes. After dinner Adam pulled his harmonica from his pocket and blew the opening notes of a song he'd played often at dances in Germany. Soon Jean's dad was guiding his wife around the living room.

Adam had been thinking about the best way to ask Jean on a date. She was smart. He wanted to invite her out to do something interesting. There was a documentary on the John Phillips Sousa Band playing at the Granville Street Theatre. Sousa was his favourite type of music and learning about the life of John Sousa sounded interesting. As Jean walked him to the door at the end of the evening, he blurted out the invitation. She accepted with a pretty smile. Driving home that night, Adam whistled happily.

As they sat in a corner booth of a nearby diner after the movie the following weekend, Adam and Jean talked non-stop. Adam told Jean about learning the harmonica up in the cherry tree and about playing in the Youth Brass Band. Jean told Adam of her plans to travel the world when she'd saved enough money. The conversation continued as they drove back to Richmond, and before they reached Jean's house, Jean had agreed to see him again.

CHAPTER ONE HUNDRED NINE

1954

January was a cold, rainy month in Vancouver, but Adam was enjoying it regardless. Christmas had been wonderful. Jean had loved the little music box he'd given her. She'd surprised him with a gift too, a hairbrush with a beautiful wooden handle. He smiled every time he saw it lying on the little table in his room. He was seeing Jean regularly, and every Monday as he caught the ferry and drove north along the coast of Vancouver Island to the job site, he thought about what they could do the following weekend.

It was Friday, and he was planning to take Jean out for dinner at the Johann Strauss Building on Hornby Street. Dave said they served good German food and played dance music after dinner. Willy was going to ask Mary and the four of them would have dinner together. George hadn't been interested when Adam mentioned the fancy restaurant. He and his girlfriend would probably just eat something back at the room and go for a walk.

Adam was thinking about holding Jean close on the dance floor after dinner when he pulled up in front of the office where she worked. She normally came out, but this week he had to go in. Her boss, Mr. Elder, was putting on an "after Christmas" party, and had asked Jean to invite him.

"Well, hello. You must be Adam," Jean's boss said as he stuck his hand out to Adam a few minutes later. "Can I pour you a scotch?"

As Mr. Elder poured the drinks, Jean introduced the other men who had gathered around them.

"Jean tells us you're German," one of them commented.

"I lived in Germany for a few years, but I grew up in Hungary," responded Adam.

"And what brings you to Canada?" asked someone else.

"Canada was looking for tradesmen and I thought it would be an interesting place." Adam could feel the men looking at him intently.

"Are you planning to settle here in Vancouver for good?" asked Jean's boss, as he handed Adam a glass. Adam looked at him without speaking, and then looked around at the other guys. What was this about?

"I'm sorry," Mr. Elder continued. "We've been looking forward to meeting you. We're very fond of Jean around here."

Adam felt his face get hot. Were they implying he wasn't good enough for Jean? He looked over at her. She shrugged ever so slightly as if to say she didn't know what was going on either. "Well, let me tell you a bit about myself then. Maybe we sit down?"

Over the next 15 minutes, Adam proceeded to tell Jean's boss and co-workers about being raised in Hungary and deported to Germany after the war. He explained what it was like to live in Laudenbach, about bringing Theresa back from the Russian Zone, trading on the black market to get enough food for all his relatives, and challenging the Journeyman Bricklayer's exam. Then he suggested that he and Jean get going in order to be in time for their dinner reservation.

"It was good to meet you, Adam," said Mr. Elder, giving Adam's hand a hearty shake. "You kids have a good time tonight. You can usually find us in here on a Friday after work. Come in for a drink anytime."

CHAPTER ONE HUNDRED TEN

Between the Swedish Hall, the Hungarian Hall, and the various other dance halls that dotted downtown Vancouver, there was always a good band playing somewhere, and rarely a weekend passed without a night of dancing, for Adam and Jean both loved to dance. Willy and Mary, and George and his girlfriend often came along, and the six young people laughed gaily as they swirled around the dance floor to polkas and foxtrots, and moved close together when a waltz was played. When Adam wasn't guiding Jean around the dance floor, they went out to movies and spent quiet evenings away from everyone, talking late into the night. Sunday afternoons were spent at Jean's home in Richmond, as Sunday dinner with Jean's parents had become a weekly event.

Adam's birthday was approaching. On February 11, a Thursday that year, he would be 25. He'd saved his Christmas bonus, and planned a special date with Jean.

The evening had been perfect so far. They'd been to a new restaurant on Hastings Street. Afterwards, Adam had driven them to a viewpoint that looked out over the city.

As they sat gazing at the twinkling sea of lights, he cleared his throat. "Jean, there is something I want to ask you," he said, turning towards her on the seat. "I am so happy that I met you." He'd reached in his pocket while he was talking and pulled out a box. Jean gasped. He opened the box and held it out towards her. Jean looked at it and back up at Adam. Her eyes were big. "I want to spend the rest of my life with you, Jean Nordstrom. Will you marry me?"

Jean just stared at him. Then she shook her head. "Adam, I'm sorry if I've led you on. I can't marry you."

"Why not?" he asked, a confused look on his face.

Jean glanced at the ring and then looked into Adam's face. "I just don't want to get married."

Adam swallowed, and looked out over the city lights for a moment, then tried again. "I know it's not much of a ring. Think of it as a down payment. When I make my fortune, you will have a big diamond."

Jean laughed her beautiful laugh. "It's not that. It's a lovely ring. But we hardly know each other. We only met two months ago."

"I know enough and I love you. You are the woman for me."

She was silent again, looking down at her hands in her lap. Adam waited. Finally, she looked at him.

"Adam, I have no plans to get married any time soon. I've been working for almost two years now. I told you, I've been saving up to travel. Mary and I are going to see the world before we settle down."

Adam thought for a moment. "I can be your travel guide. I already speak three languages. I'm sure you want to see Europe. Well, I'm from Europe. I can show you around. I want to see the world too. Let's see it together."

She'd been watching him intently while he spoke. Now she looked out at the city lights, deep in thought.

A few minutes later, she laughed quietly, still looking out the windshield of the truck towards the city. "My boss called me into his office on the Monday morning after they interrogated you that night. He said you have rough edges and you'll need a lot of smoothing out. He said I was just the person to do it, and that we would be a very good match."

"You see?" Adam put his finger on Jean's chin and gently turned her face towards him. "Even Mr. Elder knows we should be together. Let me put this ring on your finger."

Adam held his breath. She wasn't saying no.

"You're crazy," she said finally, holding out her left hand.

CHAPTER ONE HUNDRED ELEVEN

Adam whistled as he climbed the front steps of the Nordstroms' house on Sunday afternoon. He hadn't seen Jean's father yet since Jean had accepted his proposal three nights earlier, and he was looking forward to it.

"Come on in, Adam," Jean's father said as he opened the door, smiling weakly.

"Hello, John," said Adam, shaking the offered hand, looking from Jean's dad to Kay and back again expectantly.

"I hear congratulations are in order," said Kay from where she was sitting in her favourite easy chair.

"Yes, thank you," Adam responded hesitantly, glancing back at Jean's father.

"Sit down," said John. "Jean is in the kitchen finishing up dinner." There was an awkward pause. John seemed distracted. Something wasn't right.

"It's wet outside today," Adam said finally. "It will be another wet week at work."

"Yes, likely," replied John.

Adam was relieved when Jean appeared in the kitchen doorway a few moments later.

"Hello, Adam," she said, flashing him her bright smile. "Dinner is served, everyone."

"Hello, Jean," he said as he got up and gave her a little kiss. "You look beautiful."

"Thank you," she said, looking up at him, then turned to her dad and Kay. "Come on, before it gets cold."

"This is delicious, Jean," said Adam, smiling at his fiancée as he helped himself to another slice of meatloaf. They'd been talking about what was new at Adam's job site and John seemed a bit more relaxed.

"When are you two thinking about getting married?" asked Kay. John stopped chewing.

"Oh, not until next year I expect," said Jean. She was watching her father as she spoke.

Adam swallowed his food and took a drink of water. "Well, we haven't discussed it. I was thinking it might be nice to get married in June on Jean's birthday, since we got engaged on mine."

No one spoke for a moment.

"What's the rush?" John asked.

"It's not a rush," Adam replied hesitantly. "Jean and I will have to talk about it and decide on the right date."

"What was that all about?" Adam asked Jean in the truck after dinner. He'd invited her to come for a drive so they could talk.

"I'm sorry, Adam," she said. "Dad was so happy when I told him Friday morning. He went to the Swedish Hall last night to tell his friends and celebrate. And one of the men, a guy who's been a friend of the family since before I was born, apparently said to him, *'You're going to let your only daughter marry a Nazi?'*"

Adam pulled over to the curb and shut off the engine.

"What?" he said finally.

"It's made him a bit unsure. And I couldn't answer his questions. We've never really talked about the war, Adam."

Adam sighed and slumped back in his seat for a minute, then turned in his seat to face Jean. "Okay, I'll tell you about the war. And then we'll go back to the house and I'll tell your father about it."

Jean listened quietly as Adam explained how the German propaganda had glorified the war and the SS, and how he'd run away from home to get away from his dad and have an adventure. He told her about being a 15-year-old boy freezing in a foxhole, and about going for days without food or sleep. Then he told her about being held captive, first by the French and then the Russians. And finally, about being loaded into a cattle car with his family and neighbours and transported to Germany as a refugee.

"Thank you, Adam," she said when he was done. "My father will feel better if you just talk to him. We just didn't know anything about it and his friend's reaction was a bit of a shock."

Jean's father was relieved after Adam talked to him, just as Jean guessed he would be, and offered Adam an apology. But when Adam left that night, he and Jean still hadn't addressed the question of a date. And he had no intention of waiting a year.

CHAPTER ONE HUNDRED TWELVE

A few more dates and long conversations, and the wedding date had been set for June, the weekend after Jean's birthday. In the weeks that followed, the gloomy wet blanket of Vancouver winter began lifting, allowing the light of spring to seep in. Hand in hand, Adam and Jean strolled the streets, and the seawall around Stanley Park, breathing in the sweetness of the blossom-laden trees that adorn Vancouver in springtime, and revelling in the promise of their future together.

A delay in the start date of the next construction project triggered an event that would steer the direction of that promise and set the course for decades to come. With a couple of weeks of down time coming up, Dave thought a pre-wedding vacation would be just the thing for Adam before he settled into married life. He said the Okanagan Valley was nice that time of year. Little did he know how the endless blue skies and the construction boom of the Okanagan would capture Adam's imagination.

With a road map spread open on the passenger seat of the new Volkswagen Beetle he'd purchased a month earlier, Adam set off. Each day he drove to another town, booked a room in a cheap motel, and strolled around, taking in the sights and enjoying the warm dry air that was so different from Vancouver. The night before he was due to head home, Adam pulled into a picturesque little town called Penticton, situated between two deep blue lakes. Before he'd even found a motel, he'd decided to stay more than one night.

When Adam left Penticton two days later, he'd introduced himself at several construction sites, a number of which needed bricklayers, and met a fellow who owned a block plant in a little town nearby. He said to get in touch if Adam was ever interested in living in the area.

At the top of the long hill just west of town, early on the third day, Adam pulled the Beetle over to have one more look before setting out for home. Gazing back over the little town, and the valley beyond, his mind whirled with possibilities.

On the morning of Adam and Jean's wedding day a few weeks later, George decorated Adam's Beetle with ribbons and bows, and drove out to Richmond to pick up the bride and her maid of honour. Adam's guest list was short, George and his girlfriend, Willy, and the Kalanovich family. But the little church was full enough. Jean's father was popular in the Swedish community, and of course there was Mr. Elder and the other men from Jean's office.

When Jean walked up the aisle on her father's arm, Adam couldn't take his eyes away. She was breathtaking. And she was finally going to be his wife. He was surprised at how short the ceremony was. Before he knew it, they were kissing in front of everyone and heading outside for pictures. Vancouver was beautiful in June, Adam thought as he looked around, and tonight there would be dancing. Dancing with his beautiful wife.

CHAPTER ONE HUNDRED THIRTEEN

"I'm going to be late for work again if that girl doesn't hurry up," Jean said impatiently. They'd been in their new apartment for a month. It was the cheapest one they'd seen, and it hadn't been Jean's first choice. The little cooktop didn't work properly and the bathroom, just outside their door, was shared with the girl across the hall and the couple that lived in the attic apartment.

Just then they heard the bathroom door open, and Jean rushed out before someone else got it. Adam had been getting up extra early to use the bathroom in privacy. Mornings were the worst.

"Remember that we're having dinner at Dad and Kay's tonight," Jean said as she returned. "George is coming too, isn't he?"

"I told him to come," replied Adam. George would enjoy something other than his own cooking. "Do you want me to pick you up after work?"

"Yes, please," said Jean as she pulled the curtain aside and looked out at the sky. "It doesn't look like the rain is going to let up. Are you going to be warm enough? Maybe you should wear your raincoat."

"I can't work in it. I'll be soaked by the end of the day like usual. See you tonight," he said as he kissed her goodbye.

That afternoon, George pulled into the Nordstroms' driveway a couple of minutes after Adam and Jean arrived. Jean's father and Kay weren't there, but there was a note to make themselves comfortable. They wouldn't be long.

"Do you want a beer, George?" said Adam. He'd already helped himself from the fridge.

"No. I want to talk to Jean," George sputtered as he came in and shut the front door behind himself.

"What's wrong?" asked Adam.

George turned and glared at Jean, where she was sitting on the sofa. "What business do you have telling my girlfriend that I'm seeing someone else at the same time?" he barked in German. Jean shrank back at his raised voice and looked at Adam for help.

When Adam had translated, she looked indignant. "Well, she asked me. And you *are* seeing someone else. What did you expect me to do, lie?"

"It's none of your business to tell my girlfriend what I am doing!"

"He says it's none of your business to tell his girlfriend what he is doing. Did you really do this?" Adam asked her.

"Of course I did, Adam. As I already said, she asked. And I do not lie." She enunciated each word.

"Well, nobody is saying anybody should lie, but what George does with his private life is not yours to interfere with."

Jean stood up, her eyes flashing. "I was not interfering. I simply answered a question truthfully. And I will not lie. Ever. And I expect the same from my husband." She walked to the door and began putting on her shoes.

"Where are you going?" demanded Adam.

"I am going home. I do not want to be in the same house as you right now. I am disappointed, Adam. If you aren't truthful, then what do we have?" She opened the door, and then stopped and turned back. "And another thing. I am your wife. And your wife comes first, always." She slammed the door behind her.

Adam and George didn't speak for a few minutes.

"You'd better go home, George," Adam said finally.

He sat for a while longer after George left. His mom would never have spoken to his dad like that. But Jean's strength was part of what made her so beautiful. And he sure wasn't planning on treating his wife like his dad did. He got up and headed out the door. He needed to find Jean and apologize.

CHAPTER ONE HUNDRED FOURTEEN

It never really rained hard enough in Vancouver to empty out the clouds. Just a constant, slow drizzle. Penticton popped into Adam's mind often. And it wasn't just the weather. Kay was stopping by and telephoning often. Too often. She seemed to enjoy stirring up trouble with her opinions and advice. What did she know about their finances and their goals?

"Jean, honey. I have an idea," Adam said after supper one evening, as he stood behind her at the kitchen sink, arms around her waist as he nuzzled her neck. "Let's move to Penticton where the sky is blue."

"Don't be silly, Adam," she said, immersing a pot into the dishwater. "What about our jobs?"

"We'll quit. The stadium is done, and Dave can find a new superintendent for the job we just started." Adam had been supervising the construction of Empire Stadium, the brand-new venue for the upcoming Commonwealth Games. It had been a high-profile job, and he wouldn't have wanted to leave Dave in a lurch. But he was out of patience. "I want to see green fields once in a while and hear the birds and be dry when I work."

"We can't just quit our jobs."

"We'll get new jobs. When I was in Penticton before the wedding, I stopped at some construction sites. Lots of bricklayers needed. And I met a guy who owns a block plant who said to call him if we ever want to live around there."

"But we'll be so far from family. My father will worry. I'm his only daughter, remember? He'll worry that we'll starve living in such a small town."

"I couldn't get much farther from my family than I already am. But we can drive here any time to visit your father and George. They can come visit us too. And we won't starve. Other people are making a living there. We can too."

"Okay," Jean said hesitantly. "If you think it's the right thing to do."

As Mr. Elder had predicted, Adam and Jean were a good match. Although they'd known each other only eight months at that point, the pillars of their partnership had been established. If Adam's fearless nature scared Jean a bit at first, her trust in his instincts already outweighed her fear. For his part, Adam's appreciation of Jean's strength and independence, as different as they were from the female culture he'd grown up with, continued to grow. Few men could be so fortunate.

CHAPTER ONE HUNDRED FIFTEEN

With his ratty suitcase and a couple of boxes loaded into the work truck he'd traded his Beetle in for, Adam hit the road. He was disappointed that Jean wasn't with him, but she had decided to stay for a month to train a replacement and ensure Mr. Elder was in good hands.

Penticton was continuing to enjoy the so-called "golden years" of post-war expansion and within a couple of days, Adam had several jobs lined up building brick fireplaces in new houses. Next, he rented a little two-bedroom house he thought Jean would like, then organized a meeting with the owner of the block plant.

The plant sold its relatively small production mainly to landscapers and plumbers. Talking to the supervisors at the building sites around town, he learned that the concrete blocks and bricks used in buildings were typically brought in by rail from Vancouver. To Adam, the opportunity was obvious. If the builders used blocks produced locally, there would be no shipping costs and they would save money. The growth potential for the block plant was significant. Excited by the opportunity he'd discovered, Adam made a proposal to the owners of the block plant. He was willing to invest his entire savings of three thousand dollars and manage the plant in exchange for one-third ownership. Without blinking, the two owners agreed.

When Jean arrived, Adam was splitting his time between the masonry contracting company he'd set up for the bricklaying work, and getting the block plant into shape.

Initially he'd overheard a few comments about not giving work to 'the German,' but word had spread that his fireplaces didn't smoke like the ones built by the other bricklayers in town. And as the builders in town got to know him, it grew beyond fireplaces, and for the first time in his life, Adam had more work than he could handle. Soon a hard-working German bricklayer from the crew in Vancouver named Andy Arnold was settled in the spare room of Adam and Jean's little house, and Adam's masonry contracting company had doubled its capacity.

The block plant was another story. The crew was competent and the plant seemed to operate all right. But Adam couldn't convince a single contractor to buy his blocks, even with the lower prices. Slowly, as Adam did the digging that he should have done before investing in the block plant, the pieces of the puzzle fell into place. For building construction, blocks needed a special certification. His blocks didn't have that certification because they didn't pass the "press test." Without it, no architect would recommend his blocks or sign off on a plan that listed them.

The salesman from the block plant equipment manufacturer confirmed Adam's suspicions. The plant would need all new equipment in order to produce certifiable products.

Carefully, he put a business case together and presented it to his partners. But no matter how compelling the numbers were, both owners were focused on retirement and investing in new equipment held no appeal. Adam drove home from the meeting fuming.

CHAPTER ONE HUNDRED SIXTEEN
Christmas 1954

"So I telephoned the salesman from the equipment manufacturer and asked him to come back up here and meet with me," said Adam. It was a few days before Christmas. Willy and Mary, newly married, had driven up from Vancouver for a visit. The men were enjoying a drink in the living room, while Jean and Mary fixed supper. "He came over for supper and we made a plan. The bigwigs at his company have agreed to finance me to buy the equipment that I need to produce certifiable blocks. Then I went to this bank called the Industrial Development Bank. They lend money to start-up businesses that they think have good potential. I told them my story and they agreed to finance the construction of a plant," Adam laughed. "Can you believe it?"

"Wow, so you're a big businessman in Canada now," said Willy.

"Not yet," Adam replied, refilling Willy's beer glass. "I still need land to put the equipment on. And I don't know how I'm going to afford that. Land is pretty expensive around here. But I talked to a guy named Sid Canyon who owns one of the big general contractors in town. He says that the city council is releasing some land for industrial use and selling it cheap. Just the cost of putting in the water and electricity and paving the road, which is peanuts compared to what it would cost on the open market. So I'm going to look into that when everything opens up again after the holidays."

"That sounds exciting, Adam," said Mary from the doorway where she'd been listening. She waddled back into the living room and sat down slowly. "Sorry, it seems like I'm bigger every day. Feels like I'm having triplets. Jean says to tell you supper is almost ready. And she told me the exciting news about this house too. Wow!"

Adam grinned. "The landlord agreed to half up front and the rest at five hundred dollars a year for the next four years. So with a couple of good months to end the year, and the room and board money from Andy, we were just able to do it. It makes a lot more sense than paying rent every month. The..."

BOOM! Suddenly the house shook with the force of an explosion.

"Jean!" Adam leapt up and ran for the kitchen.

Jean was standing in the middle of the kitchen with a terrified look on her face.

"Are you okay, honey?" Adam asked, grabbing her by the shoulders and looking down into her face.

"What happened?" said Willy from the doorway behind Adam.

"I don't know," said Jean, looking towards the stove. The stove top was lying on the floor beside an upended cooking pot. Food had splattered in all directions and was dripping down the wall. "The stove just exploded."

"Goddam oil stove," said Adam, his arm around Jean's shoulder. "How that thing works has been a mystery since we moved in here."

Mary had waddled back in from the living room and stuck her head in around Willy. "Look up," she said.

Jean was the first to start laughing as the four of them gazed up at the long black strands of tar dripping from the ceiling.

"Guess you can't call the landlord to come take care of this, hey?" said Willy.

CHAPTER ONE HUNDRED SEVENTEEN

1955

After Christmas, Sid Canyon offered to have his secretary write a letter for Adam to send to city council applying to purchase three acres of the newly released property. When it was ready, she read it out to Adam. It said that he, Adam Baumann, was going to build a block plant to supply the construction market in the Okanagan Valley, employing approximately seven men at first and increasing to about fifteen. Him. Adam Baumann.

The response from city council arrived a couple of weeks later. There were only three lots on offer, and Adam's application letter had the latest date stamp of the four they had received. Unfortunately, there was not enough land available to offer him any.

This was a serious problem. Without land to build on, he'd lose the financing he'd been approved for.

"I figured that would happen," Sid said when Adam showed him the letter. "I told you I was applying for one of the lots, and a lawyer by the name of Christianson applied for one. The third applicant is the owner of the drive-in theatre at the end of the street. He just wants that strip at the end to expand the space for cars to watch his movies. Christianson doesn't need the land. It's just too good a deal to not get in on. And like I already said, I got so many construction jobs on the go that a local block plant would be worth more to me than that land.

"Here's what I think you should do. Request to meet with the council and tell them that you plan to build your block plant right away, and therefore you will create employment immediately, and that if you are not allowed to buy one of the lots, you're going to make it publicly known that you have been refused land even though you are the only applicant that is planning to develop the property and create jobs."

Adam was hesitant. He'd been making good progress meeting the business people in town and showing them he was good to work with. Getting offside with the city council seemed risky. But he was pretty sure he could trust Sid, and he needed that land.

On the appointed day, Adam parked outside of City Hall and walked nervously into the building. The council had invited all four applicants to the meeting. Adam had only just sat down in the waiting area and said hello to Sid when they were summoned into the council chambers. Adam could see his letter lying in the middle of the boardroom table with three other letters. Nervously, he cleared his throat and explained his plans for the property, and his grounds for why his application should be granted.

"Mr. Baumann," the mayor said when Adam finished speaking, "next time we open up some land for development, we will ensure that you are notified and given first choice, but I'm afraid your application was the last one submitted and this offer was on a first come, first served basis."

Adam swallowed hard. He was new in town. He was the youngest in the room. And he was German. But he needed this land.

"Mayor," he said as clearly as he could. He'd been working hard on pronunciation. He cleared his throat. "Mayor, sir, I think that one or more of the other applicants has no plans to develop the land. However, I will be building my block plant and creating jobs immediately. As I said, my equipment is already purchased. I think that if I am not granted one of these lots, then it will be a shame for the town of Penticton that the land will sit empty, and the people of the town should know about this." Adam held the mayor's gaze while he delivered the speech he had practiced.

The mayor turned to the other applicants. "What are your plans for the land, gentlemen?"

One by one the other three applicants responded. None would be creating new employment.

"Well, councilmen," the mayor said to the men seated around the table, "you heard what the applicants have said. What do you think?"

"The rules are the rules, Mr. Mayor," said one of the councilmen.

"The fact is that Baumann's letter was last and the other applicants are long-standing members of this community and solid businessmen," said another.

"But the purpose of making the land available for development is to stimulate growth and jobs," said a third.

"That's true, but the process still has to be followed and this fourth applicant was not only last to submit, he has no track record in this community. He is a tradesman and an immigrant, and as such, how do we know he's going to succeed at such a significant undertaking?"

The conversation continued like a game of freestyle ping-pong around the boardroom table.

Finally, one of the councilmen interrupted the rally. "Mr. Mayor, can we ask these gentlemen to leave us for a few minutes?"

After ten minutes of small talk in the anteroom, Adam and the others were called back in.

"After further consideration, there is unanimous agreement from council," the mayor began. Then he addressed the owner of the drive-in theatre. "You will be permitted to purchase the piece you applied for to increase the parking space available for movie goers.

"Mr. Baumann, you can take your pick of which of the three-acre lots you want for your block plant. The remaining three-acre lot will be subdivided into two smaller parcels, which will be available for purchase by Mr. Canyon and Mr. Christianson."

The room was silent for a moment. Adam stole a glance at the faces of Sid and the Christianson guy. They didn't look upset.

Then Sid spoke. "Mr. Mayor, if I recall the shape of the parcels of land, subdividing will result in one lot with significantly more street frontage than the other. I would like to request the lot with the larger frontage."

The mayor sighed. "Which of the letters was postmarked earlier, Mr. Canyon's or Mr. Christianson's?" he asked the councilman closest to the letters.

After a moment's inspection, the guy answered. "Same date."

The mayor sat back in his chair, shaking his head. After a few moments he spoke. "All right, we're going to settle this, and then we're going to move on to other business," he said. Standing up and reaching into his pocket, he pulled out a coin and threw it up in the air. "What'll it be, Sid, heads or tails?" he said as he caught the coin and slapped it down onto the back of his other hand.

CHAPTER ONE HUNDRED EIGHTEEN

The year whizzed by. It had been a decade since the end of the war and Adam was in his mid-twenties. The past was over and Adam rarely thought about it. It was the future that excited him, and he dug into his two businesses with tremendous energy.

Construction of the block plant was complex, and Adam tackled it fearlessly, relying on the equipment supplier for technical expertise, and on his growing network of local business people for advice and support. Convinced that the two things most critical to his success were the respect of the community and a hardworking crew, Adam made two decisions that year. The first was to invest time in a Toastmasters course. Every day he focused on increasing his English vocabulary and eliminating his accent. The second was to hire a crew comprised of recent immigrants, guys who were willing to work as hard as they needed to never be hungry again.

With the booming economy and his good reputation, Adam's masonry company was winning bid after bid. The crew was up to three full-time guys now, including Andy Arnold's brother Hans, whom Adam had sponsored to immigrate from Germany. They were hard workers, pulling long days, week after week and month after month. Penticton was growing as a tourist destination, and Adam didn't know it yet, but within the next few years, the main streets would be lined with new motels, and his masonry company would have had a hand in building all of them.

Although the pace was hectic and Adam frequently worked much of the night on bids, often falling asleep at his desk, he and Jean managed to make time most weekends for an outing together. A picnic or a movie, or even just a drive around the lake. When Jean announced that she was pregnant, their world was complete. Adam began looking around for a lot to build a new house for his family. He would build it from concrete blocks and open it up to the public to show them how much more solid and luxurious it could be than a house built from wood.

When Jean's pregnancy began to show, she resigned from her secretarial job, as was proper. With the growing administrative needs of

Adam's entrepreneurial ventures, the timing was perfect. Seamlessly, Jean slipped into the role of managing the growing mountain of paperwork Adam dropped on her desk each evening, and quietly, when the mountain had been taken care of each day, she turned their new house into a home, ready to receive their first child.

CHAPTER ONE HUNDRED NINETEEN

1956

The jangle of the phone startled Adam. It was a Sunday morning in January. He was deep in thought about the blueprint he'd been studying. The customer wanted two fireplaces in rooms that shared a wall. There had to be a way to reduce the materials needed.

"Good morning, Adam. How's everything over there?" His brother-in-law's voice crackled over the line from Germany.

"We're fine, Schnube," Adam said warmly, using his brother-in-law's nickname. "Well, I'm fine and Jean's moving a little slower these days. Less than two months to go," he smiled at Jean standing in front of the stove, one hand resting on her belly. The slow boil of the porridge she was stirring made soft popping noises every couple of seconds as the air bubbles forced their way to the top.

"I have some bad news, Adam," his brother-in-law continued. "Your dad's in jail."

"What? What happened?"

"Some kind of misunderstanding. He was at work. Remember I said in my last letter that he's got a new job in the boiler room of the fancy new American apartment complex? Well, a little girl from some American family wandered down to the boiler room. He's there shovelling coal, stoking the boiler to keep the hot water heating system going, same as every day. And she comes in and, I don't know, I guess your dad stops to talk to her to figure out why she's there by herself and where she belongs. Anyway, pretty soon he hears the parents calling for her outside, all frantic, and he sends her out to them and goes back to shovelling. But the little girl's father comes in to see where she'd come out from and confronts your dad. The mother found coal dust on the little girl's underpants. She probably sat down on the floor, who knows? And what the hell was she doing wandering around in a little dress in the middle of winter? But anyway, you know your dad. Apparently, he chased them out with a shovel when he realized what they were suggesting. Next thing you know, the police show up and haul him away. What the hell do they think? She's only about three years old!"

"My God, that's ridiculous."

"I know. And I thought I would be able to straighten it out. I went down there to talk to him and tried to talk to the police, but nobody's listening. He's been in jail for a week now and he has to stay there until his court appearance next month. I thought I'd better give you a call."

A few minutes later, Adam hung up the phone and sat down at the table as Jean placed a bowl of steaming porridge in front of him.

"What's going on?" Jean asked, handing Adam his coffee and easing herself down onto her chair across the little table from him.

"Unbelievable," Adam started out, then quickly recapped what his sister's husband had just told him. Then he sighed. "This will be killing Mom. Imagine the rumours that are floating around town. I'm going to have to straighten this out. But I can't go anywhere right now. Look at you."

"Well. . . I have another seven or eight weeks to go. If this is a serious situation, which it sounds like it is, and your family needs you, then you have to go. I'm sure I'll be fine. Just get home before my due date," Jean replied matter-of-factly.

A week later, Adam pulled into the slushy yard of the little house in Laudenbach where his parents and little brother lived along with Theresa and her husband. Turning off the key of the rental car, he sat back and closed his eyes for a moment. The next morning, he would go to the post office and use the phone to call and check on Jean. He was exhausted after travelling for twenty-four hours, but it was certainly better than the two weeks it had taken four years earlier. The cost of the plane ticket meant slowing down the construction of their new home on Duncan Avenue until he could collect for a couple of more masonry jobs, but it had been the only option given the circumstances and, truthfully, he'd been excited to try flying.

As he climbed out of the big copper-coloured Chevy and stretched his legs, the front door of the house opened. His little brother, eight now, stood in the doorway, looking out at Adam shyly.

"Hi, Frankie," Adam said with a grin, taking the stairs two at a time. "You're sure a lot taller than you were last time I saw you."

A timid smile appeared on little Frankie's face as Adam picked him up for a moment, then set him down and tousled his hair.

"Hi, Mom," Adam said, looking past his brother as his mom appeared in the hall. Her eyes filled with tears as she stretched out her arms towards him.

"Oh, Adam, it is so good to see you." His mom's words were muffled by his collar. She smelled of baking. He gave her one more squeeze before letting go.

"Come in." She stepped aside so Adam could get past, then called out the door. "Frankie, come in the house and get a coat. It's freezing out there."

"Mom, can I go get Lutz and show him Adam's car?"

"I guess so, but put on your coat."

Adam looked out the window as Frankie slammed the front door and ran to where a bike was leaning against the fence. It was the old bike he'd left behind four years ago. Frankie bobbed up and down as he stood on the pedals to turn them, rattling down the street over the wet cobblestones. Looking back over his shoulder at the car, Frankie was all smiles. A couple of seconds later, he turned the corner and disappeared.

"Resi and Franz are still at work," said his mom as she followed Adam into the living room.

"Where did that come from?" Adam interrupted his mom as his gaze fell on the portrait hanging on the wall. It was him smiling out from behind the shiny glass, the fedora he'd been so proud of perched at a jaunty angle, his jacket and tie just so. It was the photograph he'd had taken for his mom before he left for Canada, enlarged and in a fancy frame.

"Your dad saw it every day in window of the photography shop in the train station and made a deal with the photographer to buy it when he was done displaying it. He saved a bit of money from his pay every week until he had enough and then when the photographer was finally ready to change his display, he brought it home. He had everyone in the neighbourhood come and take a look at it. It's been hanging here for a couple of years now."

Adam was quiet for a moment. "How is he?"

Later that night after little Frankie was in bed, Adam sat in the little living room with his mom, sister, and brother-in-law, talking quietly about what to do. Tomorrow he'd go and see his dad and the lawyer.

His dad looked relieved to see him when the guard led him into the windowless little room where Adam was waiting. Adam listened while his dad retold the story his brother-in-law had relayed.

"Goddammed Americans, what the hell do they think?" he said when he'd finished.

"I don't know, Dad. I'll figure it out. Oh, I almost forgot, I brought you some tobacco."

The lawyer didn't offer much hope. Since there were no witnesses, it would be his dad's word against the American officer's. Adam took down the officer's name and address. Maybe he could reason with the guy.

A beautifully dressed woman with a tall beehive hairdo opened the door when Adam rang the bell. After he'd introduced himself, she stepped aside and let him in, but only long enough for her husband to come down the stairs and kick him out. As Adam drove back to his parents' house that evening, he couldn't help but agree with his dad. Goddammed Americans! It wasn't just them though. Nothing had changed. The Baumanns were still refugees from Hungary. Second-class citizens. That's what this was really about. The officer had said it outright. *You think we're going to look the other way when some dirty old Hungarian refugee molests our baby? You must be out of your mind!*

All they could do now was wait until the court appearance. Maybe the judge would surprise them.

While he waited, Adam looked up his friends and caught up on who was doing what. Like most of the Elekers, Michel and Tony still lived nearby and worked at the same jobs as they had before he'd left. It was good to see them. On Sunday, he recapped his adventures in Canada for Joe Post over a schnapps, while snow fell outside the pub.

"Did you hear that guys?" Joe said to the other guys at the table whenever Adam paused to take a drink. He was a good guy, Joe.

When the court date came, Adam settled into the public gallery behind their lawyer while they led his dad in and sat him in the prisoner's box. As the two lawyers stated their cases, Adam's heart sank. It was just like their lawyer had predicted. The Hungarian German refugee's word against the American officer's. He knew what his dad would be thinking though – that the judge would see that the charges were ludicrous and throw the bloody American out of the courtroom.

"Guilty," said the judge. "Sentenced to six months in prison."

For a moment, his dad didn't understand what had just happened. Adam watched as the confused look on his dad's face changed to shock and then disbelief. His dad looked from the judge to Adam, his mouth hanging open, speechless. Adam wanted to look away, but he couldn't. Suddenly his dad looked small sitting there in the prisoner's box. Then, a policeman led him out of the box towards the side door. He looked back at Adam, a pleading look in his eyes. Adam met his dad's gaze and gave a helpless little shrug. I would help if there were anything I could do, he was trying to say.

After the door closed, Adam sat for a moment, holding his head in his hands. Six months in jail for child molestation. His mom was going to be heartbroken too.

Suddenly, the judge's voice reverberated into the room. "Is there an Adam Baumann in the courtroom?"

Adam's head jerked up. "Yes, Your Honour."

"Approach the bench."

How did they know his name or that he would be here?

"I understand you went to the residence of the plaintiff last Wednesday," the judge said when Adam stopped in front of him, "and that you attempted to discuss the case and persuade the plaintiff to drop the charges?"

"Yes, sir, that's correct."

"Are you aware that it is an offence to interfere with the justice system?"

Adam looked over to where the officer and his lawyer sat watching the conversation. The officer had a smirk on his face.

He turned back to the judge. "No sir, I was not aware of that," he said.

"Well, it is, and the plaintiff has filed a complaint. You are charged with Interference. Your case will be heard tomorrow." The judge looked towards the police officer standing at the side of the room. "Take Mr. Baumann to the cells please."

Adam stared at the judge, speechless, as the police officer walked over to usher him from the room. Turning in obedience with the policeman's hand on his elbow, he looked over at the officer. The smirk had grown to a grin.

Adam lay awake staring at the ceiling of the cell. He needed to pick up the boiler in Vancouver next week. And Jean's due date was now only three weeks away.

In the morning, when the judge asked Adam to explain himself, he knew what he had to do.

"I am very sorry for what has happened, Your Honour, and for wasting your time. My wife is expecting our first child in a couple of weeks. I left her alone in Canada to come to Germany to try to understand what has happened with my father. I am very sorry that I attempted to talk to the American officer and his wife. I did not know it was a problem, and of course now I know I should not have done this thing. I'm sure you can imagine how important it is for me to get home to my wife before she goes into the hospital to give birth to our child."

Five minutes later, the case dismissed, Adam was back in his car, driving towards Laudenbach. Everyone would be wondering where he'd been. And he had to tell his mom that his dad wouldn't be home for a while.

CHAPTER ONE HUNDRED TWENTY

His mom was distraught, as he'd known she would be, but Adam had to get home, and Theresa and Franz were there to support her.

Jean looked radiant when he strode in through the front door and stretched his arms around her, belly and all. A new crib and change table filled a corner of their room. She'd completed all the final touches. After a quick recap of what had happened back in Germany, Adam headed to the block plant to work on the final touches there.

A couple of days later, Adam set out for Vancouver well before dawn, navigating the icy roads cautiously as he wound his way up through the mountains and back down again into the Fraser Valley. Getting the heavy boiler positioned on the flatbed of his little truck and properly strapped down took longer than he'd planned. By the time he'd ascended back into the mountains with his load, the snow had started. Conditions deteriorated rapidly. Visibility was negligible, the accumulating snow obscuring the icy, winding road he'd driven earlier that day, rendering it nearly impassable by the time he reached the summit. Slowly, Adam inched his precious cargo down mile after mile of hairpin bends, gripping the wheel with all his might, until finally he reached the flats outside of town. Exhausted, he pulled the truck into the block plant yard, shut off the engine, and rested his head on the steering wheel.

Unaware of the fly about to land in the ointment, Adam followed the sour-faced inspector nervously around the site as the little man silently scribbled notes on his clipboard. It had taken a week to set up the boiler and train the crew. The inspection was the final step before they could fire up the plant and begin production. Every now and then the inspector looked at Adam, then looked away and continued his scrutiny.

"And who will be operating the boiler?" the inspector asked when they'd returned to the office.

"I will," Adam replied.

"I need to have a look at your boiler certificate please."

"My what?"

"Your boiler certificate. You require a certificate to operate a steam boiler."

"How do I get one?"

"You can apply at City Hall. But, of course, you must be a Canadian citizen or a British subject to apply."

"What?"

The inspector looked like he was enjoying this.

"You must be a British subject or a Canadian citizen. Is there a problem?"

Citizenship required five years of residency. He couldn't apply for another year.

"Yes, it is a problem. What are my other options?"

"Well, maybe one of your crew could operate the boiler?" The inspector raised his eyebrows and feigned a smile. Adam had introduced the crew to him during the inspection. He knew they were all recent immigrants.

Adam glared at him. "Get off my property."

"As you wish, Mr. Baumann," he said pleasantly, standing to leave.

"And go to hell."

Slamming the door after the inspector, Adam sat back down at his desk to think. Even if he could find someone with the certificate he needed, he wouldn't be able to afford him.

Ted Millington was at the counter when Adam walked into City Hall. He knew Ted from Kinsmen.

"It's true, Adam, that is the law," Ted said when Adam finished explaining what had just happened.

"I spent a year building the block plant, Ted. And when the City Council sold me the land, they knew exactly what it was for. I can't believe this hasn't come up before. And I'm in debt like crazy. What the hell am I going to do now?"

Ted thought in silence for a few moments, then made a quick phone call.

"Judge Washington is at the courthouse and he has time to see us," Ted said a minute later, beaming at Adam as he grabbed his coat.

The Judge sat behind a huge desk strewn with files, his large hands flat on the desk in front of him. "What can I do for you?" he said in a very proper British accent. His long bushy eyebrows lifted at the end of his question.

"Well, Your Honour," Adam started, "today I learned that I need a boiler's certificate to operate my block plant. I don't have one you see and I can't apply for one because I am a not a Canadian citizen yet. I have nine guys at the block plant waiting to work, and several customers who have said they will place orders with me as soon as I can produce some blocks, because the prices are better than shipping blocks from Vancouver. And I have a Canadian wife at home who is going to have a baby any day, our first child, and I need to make payments on the loans I have used to build the plant."

The Judge listened patiently, a kind smile on his weathered face.

"Yes, Ted mentioned this on the phone a few minutes ago. I've put a bit of thought into it. "I can understand that it is important that you get that plant open in order to create those jobs for which the land was made available." Adam nodded and the judge continued. "Are you intending to become a Canadian citizen?"

"Yes, most certainly."

"How long have you been in Canada now?"

"Four years, Your Honour."

The Judge addressed Ted, where he hung back near the door of the chambers. "Ted, take ten dollars from Mr. Baumann and fill out the Citizenship application form. Lodge the application today and bring it forward for processing when the five years are up. Then issue him a boiler certificate immediately, so he can start producing those blocks."

Three days later, Adam climbed into the forklift and moved the first pallet of blocks into the kiln to dry. The pallet sold the day it came out of the kiln, just like all the pallets that came out after it that day, and on the days that followed. By the time Adam and Jean's first daughter, Sue, arrived, a week overdue, Western Brick and Block was running at full capacity.

CHAPTER ONE HUNDRED TWENTY-ONE

The 1950s were exciting times in western Canada, times of rapid growth and development, a perfect environment for Adam's entrepreneurial mind. His assessment of the construction market couldn't have been better. Between the numerous general contractors in the area, and his own growing portfolio of projects, demand for blocks and bricks was through the roof. If he was going to keep his customers satisfied, he needed inventory.

With his credit fully maximized, Adam was desperate for cash when Dave Pipe drove into the block plant yard unexpectedly one afternoon. Dave was moving to Penticton to retire and looking for a business to invest in as a silent partner. It appeared as if fate had once again handed Adam a golden opportunity. In no time, he and Dave had reached an agreement, and production rapidly doubled. Local contractors were thrilled. Before long, shipments of blocks from Vancouver to the Okanagan Valley had ceased.

While Jean took on the routines and demands of motherhood, Adam, convinced that single-family home construction was an untapped market for his blocks, took out full page ads in the local paper, inviting people to visit "The Dream House" on weekends and see for themselves. All the while, both parents doted on the miracle of their baby daughter, amazed at the wonders of how she looked when she slept, how she smiled at them when she woke, how much she could eat, how many new things she did each day.

They hadn't had much time to enjoy their new rhythm before tragedy sought them out. Jean's father and stepmother had returned home from a visit to Penticton to meet their little granddaughter only a week or so earlier when their home on Lulu Island caught fire in the middle of the night, burning to the ground before the blaze could be contained. The fire department found Kay hiding in the blueberry fields nearby, reportedly in a delusional state related to her diabetes. Jean's father hadn't moved from his bed, asphyxiated where he lay. The loss hit Jean hard. After her mother's death when Jean was barely a teenager, her father had raised her and they'd been close. He was the only family she'd had.

The tragedy heightened the anxiety that had been growing in Adam's mind about his own parents. Thoughts of the continued discrimination he had witnessed on his visit to Germany were never far from his mind, and anyway, they should be enjoying a taste of what Canada offered. Reaching a decision, he submitted a sponsorship application to bring his parents and little Frankie to Canada.

A few weeks later, the first denial arrived. Scar tissue on his dad's lung had shown up during the medical exam, and Canada wasn't accepting immigrants that might become medical burdens. Over the next two years, Adam spun his wheels in a battle with the Canadian Immigration Department, resubmitting the application every few months. Each time, a denial letter arrived soon after.

On the business front, however, opportunities popped up everywhere Adam looked, perhaps more visible to his entrepreneurial eye than to most. Tirelessly, he tackled one venture after another. The Dream House, as he'd dubbed the house built from concrete blocks, hadn't turned public opinion towards block construction for the residential market as Adam had envisioned it would, regardless of the effort they'd put into hosting lavish open house events to show it off. So when he heard about another building lot for sale at a good price just down the street, and a double lot that was zoned for apartments, both of which he could afford if he sold the Dream House, he did just that. An apartment building would bring in good rental income, he explained to Jean.

Next, a magazine article about a tourist attraction that was becoming popular in the United States caught his attention. Although the masonry company, the apartment building, the new house he had under construction, and the block plant kept him on the move long hours each day, Adam set his sights on building a miniature golf course. Over the next six months, the mini-golf where Adam and Jean's children would spend their summers learning all manner of skills from making change to making cotton candy, and which would become a landmark in Penticton for the next 40 years, took shape. And just months before the grand opening of the place that would be so central to their family life, their second daughter, Sandy, was born.

Soon after, an advertisement in the local paper caught Adam's eye. The government was selling off a 77-acre parcel of land just north of town. Although he had no time or money to develop it, and both the sheer size of the property and the $28,000 bid he submitted were staggering, the land was being re-zoned and sold at less than market value. The siren of opportunity wailed once again. As always, Adam was compelled to respond, and soon he was the owner of a piece of land big enough to rival the richest of the rich farmers of Elek.

CHAPTER ONE HUNDRED TWENTY-TWO
1958

Adam had been at the mini-golf site all morning. He needed to get over to the block plant to organize the upcoming orders. But first, he wanted to stop and say hello to the Arnold brothers, and congratulate them on a new contract they'd won. For the cost of the tools, he'd sold the masonry business to Andy and Hans. They deserved it for all their hard work over the years, and besides, the fun had gone out of it for Adam. It was a well-oiled machine that really didn't need him anymore.

Adam was perplexed to see a truckload of small blocks driving out of the driveway as he pulled into the block plant a little later. He'd asked the foreman to hold all small block inventory for a new contract he'd just signed.

"Where's that truck headed?" Adam said to his foreman, getting out of his pickup.

"Dave brought in an urgent order he got this morning. Said to send two truckloads of those blocks over today."

Adam couldn't believe his ears. Dave had done it again! The last incident had been the week before.

"And how are we going to fill the big order that's due on Monday for that new contract?"

"He said they'd have to wait a couple of extra days."

"I told them they could have the full order on Monday. That's what they are expecting. So now I'll have to go and explain to them that we can't deliver what I promised." Adam was yelling by the time he finished.

"Sorry boss. I thought maybe you knew. Like maybe Dave had called you or something."

"Don't worry about it. This is between me and Dave."

Adam jumped into his truck and slammed the door, spraying rocks out from the tires as he roared out of the driveway.

"Well, you didn't tell me about the order for Monday!" Dave yelled back at Adam twenty minutes later.

"Why would I tell you? You're a silent partner. Silent partners don't need to know the daily details of operating a business! I don't know why you're out there selling when you are supposed to be retired, but from now on if you get an order, you talk to me! I'm running the plant, Dave, not you!"

The fight continued until Adam gave up and stomped out, slamming Dave's front door behind him. Next he had to go and apologize to the customer.

"What?" Adam bellowed at Dave a few days later. "You told them what?"

"I told them to switch over and produce more of these," said Dave, jabbing his finger at the stack of blocks they were standing beside, "because I was talking to a guy this morning and he said he'll need a big supply of them in the next couple of weeks if he wins the bid on the commercial building on the south end of town."

"And how are we going to fill our current orders for those?" yelled Adam in response, pointing at the pile across the forklift path.

"I talked to the crew about it and with what's in the kiln today, we've got enough for the current orders!"

"Well, the crew doesn't know about the big commercial project on the north end of town I signed on late yesterday!" Adam roared, his face inches from Dave's, then turned and stomped down the pathway between the stacks of blocks before turning and striding back. Putting his face close to Dave's again, he said in a low voice, "Look Dave, I've had it. You're no silent partner, and you're not retired, and this place isn't big enough for both of us." His voice began to rise again. "You've got more goddammed money than me, so you either buy me out, or I'm going to get a box of dynamite and I'm going to blow this place sky high!"

With that he turned and stormed out to his pickup and spun out of the driveway.

"I'm selling the block plant to Dave," Adam announced at supper that night, his jaw set in a stubborn line.

Jean put down her fork and looked at Adam. In the crook of her arm, Sandy was slurping hungrily on a bottle. "Selling the block plant? Why?"

"He's meddling, every day he's meddling. He's no silent partner. And there's no room for two bosses. Simple as that."

"But Adam, you built it and it's a very lucrative business. Maybe Dave should leave instead of you."

Adam shook his head stubbornly. "He won't leave. I know him. It's easy money now that it's up and running. I've got lots of other projects. Life's too short to have this kind of bullshit to deal with every day. We'll be fine." Adam looked down at his plate and resumed eating.

A few weeks later, the sale of Adam's half of Western Brick and Block was complete.

CHAPTER ONE HUNDRED TWENTY-THREE

Business at the mini-golf was booming. Weekends were busiest, since that was when the locals could come. But the tourist traffic was steady all week. Sometimes Adam joined customers for a hole or two and a few laughs. It helped him see ways he could improve things.

The apartment building, which they'd named Century Manor, had been open a few months now, and the units were starting to fill up. He was getting the hang of being a landlord and Jean had taken on the paperwork seamlessly.

One problem he still hadn't solved was his parents' immigration application. They'd been trying for over two years. When he heard one of the men at the Kinsmen meeting saying that the Minister of Immigration was coming to town to do a campaign speech for the upcoming election, Adam's ears perked up.

"I need to deliver these papers to Mr. Fulton," he said to the front desk clerk at the hotel where he'd heard the politician was staying, waving the envelope that contained an English, notarized version of his dad's test results. He'd requested the results a few months back, hoping he could use them to talk sense into the officials at the local immigration office, but it hadn't worked. "Can you give me his room number please?"

"Hello?" said Mr. Fulton, opening the door a crack.

"I'm sorry to bother you so late sir. My name is Adam Baumann. I am a businessman here in Penticton. I listened to your speech and thought it was very good. Since you are the Minister of Immigration, I was hoping I could talk to you about a problem I am having. You see, I've been trying to have my parents and little brother come to Canada to join me and my other brother and our wives here, under the family reunification program. For over two years now, the Canadian government has refused to allow them to come."

The door opened wide. "Come in, Mr. Baumann."

A couple of short weeks later, the application had been re-evaluated and approved.

CHAPTER ONE HUNDRED TWENTY-FOUR

A month had passed since they'd had the good news about his parents. Everything was organized. On the 8th of October they would be arriving at the train station in a town called Salmon Arm, a three-hour drive from Penticton. With the mini-golf shut down for the season and no block plant to manage, Adam had had a bit of time to plan.

Jean was sitting at the table, feeding baby Sandy, when Adam got home. As he sat down at the table after washing up, Jean set the squirming baby on the floor and turned to smile at Adam. "I'm pregnant again," she said.

"Wow, that was quick," he said, looking up from where Sandy was crawling rapidly away. "It's wonderful, honey," he continued, as Sue banged her spoon on the table of the highchair, her hair and face covered in orange goop. "When's the due date?"

"Early April."

"I sold the house today," said Adam.

"What?" Jean's smile dropped away. "I thought we agreed to stay in this house."

"Well, the purchaser I have lined up for the apartment building said he'd only buy it if he could have the house too. And the profit on the apartment building was too good to turn down. I'm sorry, hon."

"Adam, we have moved every year since we've been in this town. And this house is perfect. It's taken a lot of work to get it just right."

They finished eating in silence. As he pushed back his chair to head into the office, Adam broached the subject of housing again, since Jean hadn't asked.

"There's not enough time to build again before Mom and Dad get here," he said, "so I looked at a few places today. There's one at the corner of Eckhart and Government that has a basement suite. It's not as nice as this, but it's got lots of space. And now with a new baby coming too, we'll be able to use the space." He paused for a few moments. Jean didn't say anything so he continued with the rest of his news. "I'm driving to Kamloops tomorrow to look at a couple of side-by-side building lots zoned for apartments. If they look good, I can break ground right away. I'll have to be there during the week while the building is going up, but I'll be home weekends and probably a day or two most weeks, keeping an eye on things here," he finished up, unfazed by the fact that he had just informed his pregnant wife of another move with a baby and a toddler, and that she'd be on her own with live-in in-laws who couldn't speak English.

CHAPTER ONE HUNDRED TWENTY-FIVE

"There's the train!" Adam looked up at the sound of George's excited voice. George and his new wife Irene had driven up from Vancouver the night before their parents' arrival date so that Adam and George could leave early to meet the train.

George hadn't seen their parents or little brother in almost seven years. Adam had only seen them once himself.

"Right on time," said Adam as he crushed out his cigarette in the ashtray stand. He stood and strode over to the door as George stubbed out his own cigarette and hurried to join him. Stepping out into the crisp autumn air, the brothers stood side by side and waited as the train slowed and rolled to a stop.

Doors up and down the train began sliding open. Adam and George looked left and right, scanning the disembarking passengers.

"There they are." Adam pointed and headed towards where he'd spotted their dad.

"Dad! Mom!" he called out through the growing crowd. "Hi, Frank!" he added when he recognized the tall boy beside them.

At the sound of Adam's voice, Frank found his older brothers in the crowd and steered their parents towards them.

"Frankie, you're so tall, I hardly recognized you," Adam greeted his little brother in German and gave him a quick hug. The lanky preteen standing in front of them hardly resembled the shy eight-year-old Adam had last seen. They'd have plenty of time to get reacquainted. Adam beamed at his parents.

"How was the trip?"

At the sight of his dad's scowl and his mom's strained face, Adam's smile disappeared.

"Is everything okay?" he looked from one to the other and back. His dad grunted and looked away.

"You both look so good," his mom said, a bright smile pasted on her weary face as she hugged her sons. "Never mind. Everything is fine."

"Let's go then," said Adam, glancing at his dad's dark face. "It'll take us about three hours to get home from here, and Jean and Irene will have some supper ready for us." He grabbed the suitcase his mom had been carrying and led them through the station.

As they emerged out of the other side of the building into the parking lot, Adam strode over to his car and inserted the key to open the trunk.

"Is this *your* car?" Frank's tired face came alive with interest when he saw the big shiny Buick. Adam stood back and admired the red, black, and white three-tone paint job, and the white wall tires for the hundredth time. This would definitely be the nicest car either of his parents had ever seen, let alone ridden in.

"This is my car all right," Adam grinned proudly. "A '56 Buick Riviera, damn near new. You won't find a car like this in Germany."

"How the hell do you afford a car like this? And what the hell do you need it for?" his dad grumbled as Adam finished stowing the bags. Everything they'd brought to start a new life in Canada didn't even fill the trunk of his car.

"Hop in, everyone." Adam ignored his dad's questions and opened the back door for his mom.

Silence filled the inside of the car as Adam pulled out onto the street and headed south, but the silence was far from empty.

Finally, a few minutes into the drive, his dad explained. "I've broken my back all my life working to make a living and provide for my family, and what do I get? First, it's the goddammed Russians and the goddammed communists that take everything a man's got," his voice began the familiar rise. "So you start over and you break your back some more, digging ditches, piling bricks, shovelling coal for those lousy, lying Americans. And then your goddammed wife wastes it all! You might as well know now that we are riding in your fancy car and arriving on your doorstep with empty pockets, thanks to your mother," he ranted, glancing over his shoulder at his wife. "All the money for settling here is gone, wasted."

"Your father thinks there was money saved to bring to Canada and that I spent it. There was never as much as he thinks there was," Adam's mom defended herself from the back seat where she and George were settled on either side of Frank.

"Week after week I handed my pay over to you, from every god-dammed job I had, and where did it all go?"

"Food and rent cost money. And the clothes you're wearing. I've explained this to you already," Adam's mom answered quietly, but her tone, usually gentle, had an edge. She fell back into silence and looked out of the window.

As his dad opened his mouth to argue, Adam interrupted. "It doesn't matter. We have everything you need here. This is all water under the bridge now, and we don't need to hear any more about it."

He thought about Jean. They'd settled into the new house a couple of weeks earlier. She was still upset at him for selling the split-level, but she already had the new place looking great, and they'd set up rooms for his parents and Frank downstairs.

Adam looked at his little brother in the rear-view mirror. "Tell us about the ship and what you saw on the train ride, Frankie."

CHAPTER ONE HUNDRED TWENTY-SIX

When they reached the house, Adam climbed out of the car and glanced up at the front window as he stretched his legs. Jean was holding back the curtain, watching them. She'd been nervous when he'd left that morning. She and Irene had had their hair up in those big curlers, and Irene, who had herself come from a German village in Hungary, was teaching Jean to make a Hungarian dish for supper.

Adam opened the back door of the car and held out his hand to his mom, while his dad stood on the other side of the car, gazing around the neighbourhood. These houses, typical for Penticton, were bigger than any in Elek or Laudenbach. Grabbing a suitcase in each hand, Adam headed for the house.

"Here we are," he said with a smile at Jean as he pushed the front door open wide. Ushering his parents into the living room, he set down the bags. George and little Frank took up the rear with the remaining luggage. Switching to German, Adam presented his wife and his sister-in-law.

"Hello and welcome to Canada," said Jean to her mother and father in-law, using the German phrase she'd practiced. "And hello, Frank," she said with a warm smile at the 11-year-old, as everyone else carried on in German around her.

After receiving a handshake and a kiss on the cheek from each parent, Jean scooped Sandy up and balanced her on her hip and drew Susie in close. Jean had the girls in perfectly pressed little dresses with those little coloured clips in their hair. They were beautiful, all three of them, thought Adam, beaming.

"This is Sue," said Jean. "Say hello to Granny and Grandpa, Sue." Everyone waited patiently while the toddler looked at the floor silently.

Adam's dad stooped down and spoke softly in German. "Hello, Susie. It's nice to meet you. You're a pretty little thing. You look a bit like our little Anni."

Hearing his dad say Anni's name, Adam felt a slight pang. He could still see her beautiful little face in his mind's eye.

"And this is Sandy," Jean continued. She didn't know what her father-in-law had said, but his voice was kind.

Standing back up, Adam's dad reached for Sandy and settled her on his hip as he began speaking gently to her, smiling softly.

"You must be exhausted," Jean said brightly. "Would you like a cup of coffee or tea? And I've got some nice fruit juice for Frank, and then maybe Adam can show you downstairs so you can freshen up a bit? Adam, can you translate that please?"

After a quick exchange in German, Adam relayed their order. "They'll both have coffee with milk." The three new arrivals all nodded and smiled at Jean.

"Go ahead and sit down then. Irene and I will get the coffee."

A couple of hours later Jean ushered everyone into the dining room. It was cozy with this many people. "Dig in," she said in a cheery voice. "We've made Chicken Paprikash. I hope you like it." Jean smiled brightly at her mother-in-law as Adam translated.

"Did you find everything you needed downstairs?" Jean continued as she cut up a plate of food for Susie.

Adam's mom smiled graciously when she heard Jean's words translated to German. "Ja dankeschön," she replied. She smiled at Jean, but her face looked drawn.

Adam wondered how she was really feeling. He remembered vaguely how he'd felt after sitting on that train for almost a week.

He could see that Jean was doing her best to follow the conversation over dinner, quietly feeding Sandy and urging Susie to eat a bit more. She prompted him for translations when he forgot. As he looked around the table, everyone seemed to be enjoying the food, although his mom wasn't really eating much. His dad, on the other hand, ate heartily, and he saw Jean wink at Frank as she filled his plate for the third time.

"Because our money was all gone," Adam's dad tossed a scowl towards his wife and then continued, "we could not eat in the dining car on the train. The prices were goddammed ridiculous anyway! So when the train stopped at some little town for a few minutes, I would jump off and run down the street to find a shop for some bread and cheese, or some salami or whatever." He was smiling again. "There wasn't anything much good, but I always found something we could eat," he continued, talking a little louder until all other conversation stopped. "But this one time," he chuckled as he looked around at his audience, "I was buying some food just down the street from the station, not too far, and the goddammed train starts to move! I was already on my way back with the food, and I see it start to roll away. Well, holy cow! So I started to run and started hollering at the conductor standing there in the doorway of the last car. *Stop!* I yelled. *My family is on that train!* Of course, he didn't speak any German. But he disappeared and wouldn't you know it, the train starts to slow down. They stopped the goddammed train so I could get on! And they even lowered the stairs, so I didn't have to climb up. Amazing! If Canada treats a guy like that, it's pretty good." Smiling broadly at his own story, Adam's dad shovelled another large bite of chicken into his mouth and looked around the table while he chewed.

"Well, isn't that wonderful!" Jean exclaimed when Adam had relayed the high points. "You were very fortunate. I wouldn't have thought they would stop the train for one passenger. Wasn't that nice of them! And, Frank, what kinds of things did you see from the windows of the train?"

"Well," Frank began quietly, "we saw a lot of trees. Really a lot, all day long, trees. I never saw so many trees before. And we saw some black bears by a river. And at this one place, there were some animal skins hanging on these rack things." Frank's shyness dissipated as he recounted the strange sights he'd seen. "A man on the train said they were deer skins that the Indians were drying to use for clothes. I just couldn't believe how long the forest went on for. And not very many towns. And you wouldn't believe the colours of the trees that we could see from the ship when we got close to Montreal!" Adam smiled at his little brother's animation as he described his first impressions of Canada. And he hadn't even seen anything yet. Frank had so much to look forward to now. He was going to love Canada.

"And, George, do you and Irene live near here?" their mom asked at the next lull in the conversation.

"Not really, Mom. Vancouver is about 250 miles from here," replied George. George and Irene had tried Penticton, but it hadn't lasted long.

George was a good worker and Adam had enjoyed having his brother on the crew, especially for the fruit-packing house, which had been a huge job. But after a year, Irene had announced that she preferred Vancouver, and they'd packed up and headed back. "It takes about six hours to drive. We have to go home tomorrow so I can get back to work."

"You have a goddammed car too?" their dad interrupted through a mouthful of chicken. "How does everybody get a goddammed car in this country?"

At this, Adam jumped in. "He saved up, Dad. George has a good job in Vancouver. The pay is much better here. Everything is much better."

"Not very smart. You both should have bought houses first, for your families. You gotta make sure they're going to have a roof over their heads before wasting money on cars."

"I own this house, Dad, and George owns his house in Vancouver too."

His dad stopped chewing and stared at him, speechless for a moment.

"I break my back for ten years to buy my brothers' shares in the family home, so you can all have a good, respectable place to live. I tend the grapes for the whole goddammed town, I break my back, harvesting wheat for the goddammed rich farmers, I do day labour when I need to, I raise my animals and sell them for a profit when I can. And then the goddammed communists take it all and deport my family. And you young smart asses come to Canada and work for a few years and each have a house and a car?" The colour had risen in his dad's face as he spoke.

"It's different here, Dad," Adam repeated. "The economy is different. It's booming. And there was no war destruction to recover from. It's different."

"What's going on, Adam?" Jean asked before her father-in-law could resume his rant.

As Adam finished explaining to Jean what his dad was talking about, his mom pushed her chair back from the table and stood up. As she turned away, Adam saw her face crumble.

"What's wrong, Mom?" Adam said gently to his mom from where he'd followed her into the living room. Frank squeezed past him and sat down beside their mom on the sofa.

"Are you feeling sick again, Mom?" Frank asked. Both their parents had experienced sea-sickness on the ship, and their mom hadn't been able to keep food down until they'd been back on solid ground for a couple of days.

"No, no, it's nothing. I'm just a little tired. What time is it in Germany right now?"

"About three in the morning," Adam answered quickly. He could hear Jean and Irene clearing the table.

"Everyone will be sleeping now. We need to let my sisters and Resi know that we've arrived safely. I haven't spoken to any of them for almost two weeks," her voice caught in her throat. "What if something has happened and they can't reach us?" Her voice broke and trailed off, and Adam could see her shoulders shaking.

"Everybody is fine, Mom," Adam tried to reassure her.

"She's exhausted and probably homesick," Jean's quiet voice at his elbow startled Adam and he jumped. "I think it's time for everyone to hit the hay."

"You'll feel better after a good sleep, Mom. And tomorrow we can telephone Germany," Adam suggested in German. He heard Frank mumble something to their mom as he tried to wipe his eyes so his big brother wouldn't see his tears. Jean was right. They needed sleep.

CHAPTER ONE HUNDRED TWENTY-SEVEN

After her initial homesickness, Adam's mom settled in well. She and Jean overcame the language barrier with hand gestures. They were becoming fast friends. Gradually, the hand signals evolved into stilted conversations punctuated with laughter as Jean worked to learn the Elek dialect of German, and her mother-in-law began to pick up a few English words.

Frank adapted quickly too. He had looked terrified when Jean left him at the door of the classroom that first Monday after they arrived, but the principal said not to worry. Kids learned new languages at lightning speed through immersion and Frank would be fluent in English in no time.

Sure enough, the principal had been right.

About a month after Frank started school, Adam joined him at the kitchen table after supper, where he was bent over a book. It was a Thursday and Adam had been in Kamloops all week, arriving home in time for supper that evening. "How's school going, Frank?" he asked, speaking German to his little brother.

Frank looked up and beamed at Adam.

"I am reading in the grade three class now and next week I move up to grade four. The little kids in grade one follow me in the playground and ask me to come back and sit with them in their class," he laughed.

"They're both asleep," said Jean as she walked into the kitchen from the girls' bedroom down the hall. "Now Frank, let's go through that book." She sat down beside Adam's little brother and placed her hand on the bump of her belly. "Mr. Ellis says he's moving up quickly and making friends in each class," she added.

"Yes, that's what he just told me," Adam said, tousling his little brother's hair.

"Okay, Frank, go back to the start. Read it to me again." Jean stopped rubbing her back and bent over the reader with Frank.

Adam's dad wasn't adjusting as well.

Adam had invited him out for a drive the morning after they had arrived. He'd been eager to show his dad the mark he was making on Penticton, and he'd started the tour with pride. First the block plant, then the motels and the other buildings his masonry contracting company had done, then the three houses where they had lived the last four years, two of which he'd built.

The more they saw, the further downhill his dad's mood went. Realization began to dawn on Adam. Elek hadn't changed in his dad's lifetime, nor had Laudenbach. Here, on the other hand, there were construction projects every few blocks. Half the town had been built in the last few years. Adam loved the pace, the constant change. But it was completely foreign to his dad. He couldn't comprehend growth like this. And his dad had worked most of his life for a few pengoes a day, so how could he possibly grasp Adam's ability to buy and sell properties and finance these large projects.

Despite his dad's lack of enthusiasm, Adam took him to see the 77-acre parcel of land he'd purchased. Maybe he'd think owning land was a good thing. They parked at the bottom of the property and hiked up the rocky hill.

"Why would you throw all your hard-earned money away on land that can't be farmed?" his dad demanded, waving his arm at the craggy outcrops that overlooked the lake.

His family had been in Canada a week or more when Adam paused at the top of the basement stairwell on his way to bed one night. The door was open a crack.

"I don't know what's going to happen, Anna. Adam's got a lot of debt. He doesn't actually own a goddam thing. And now he's got three more mouths to feed, and another baby on the way. If he goes broke, we'll all starve. How the hell are we going to feed ourselves? No garden, no cow to milk, not even a pig. Nothing," his dad ranted. "And he doesn't work. He just drives around. I might not know much, but I do know that a man's got to work to keep his family fed."

His dad fell into a routine of sitting in a chair in the living room, playing with Susie and Sandy and not doing much else.

In late November, Adam invited him along to the construction site in Kamloops for the first time. The apartment building that was going up there was bigger than the one Adam had built in Penticton, twenty-four units, and the site more complex. But it was coming along well. His dad had wandered around the site and sat nearby smoking, not saying much.

"Another half-hour and we'll be home," Adam said on their drive home. Thick snow had been slicing through the beam of the headlights for most of the drive and they'd had to take it slowly. He hoped it didn't continue through the weekend. He had to be back in Kamloops at first light Monday morning.

"You know, Adam," his dad's words interrupted Adam's thoughts, "the girl you married, she's a nice girl. I like Jean. And she's a good cook. But she's going to make you broke."

"Why? Jean's good with money."

"Have you ever watched closely when she peels the potatoes?"

"No. . . ." As if I have time to stand around and watch potatoes being peeled, he thought.

"Half the potato goes into the garbage. Every time. You gotta tell her to cook them with the skins on, and if the skin's not good, then peel it very thin like paper. Like your mother does."

"Okay," Adam responded.

"She's too wasteful. You're never going to make it."

"Well, I'm going to try real hard, Dad."

His dad muttered something Adam couldn't make out.

It didn't stop there.

"What are you doing, Mom?" Adam asked one evening not long after.

"Mending some of your work socks. The darning I put into the heels has worn through, and I thought Frank could wear them to school this winter."

"You don't need to do that, Mom. They've already been mended once. They're not worn right through. I can wear them a bit longer before they are finished. And Frank can have new socks to wear to school. You don't need to mend the mending."

He and Jean watched their money carefully, but socks were not that expensive and business was good. He didn't want his little brother looking like a refugee. As soon as the words were out of his mouth though, he knew what was coming next.

"Buy another pair? Just like that?" his dad jumped in. "And what, throw these away? Perfectly good wool. Anna, you will not throw that away. It's good wool and it can be made into something else."

He'd been staring at the game show playing on the TV. Adam knew he didn't understand the words, and by the scowl on his face, he wasn't enjoying it.

"What are you going to do when things aren't so easy Adam? What's going to happen when you run out of fuel for that fancy heater? You won't be able to just turn up that thing on the wall then," his dad's voice had started to rise a little. "In Laudenbach we didn't have any goddammed fuel for our fire. Nothing to burn. And no money to buy wood at the outrageous prices they charged for those little bundles. I used to wait until the city workers finished cutting firewood and went home for the day, and then sneak in there and take some of it, and pick up any that they'd left behind when they were stacking it, and sometimes pull branches off the trees. They caught me one time. Hauled me in." His dad's voice calmed a bit, and Adam sensed the beginning of a story. Jean and Frank had given up trying to go through Frank's homework and were listening now, although Adam would have to translate the pieces that Jean missed. And his mom's hands were resting in her lap, eyes on her husband.

"I asked that goddammed German judge, sitting there like the king, if his family was ever cold, and if I could just pay two fines and get it over with, one for now and one for the next time I had to go out and get wood to keep my family warm. They never bothered me again," he chuckled, then continued more seriously. "And hell, in Elek, when the wood and the corn stalks ran out during a cold snap, we got frostbite on our fingers picking up cow shit to heat up the stove and the bricks to put in the beds so we didn't freeze at night."

"I'll make sure we don't run out of fuel, Dad," Adam said with a small sigh.

CHAPTER ONE HUNDRED TWENTY-EIGHT
1959

This will be perfect, Adam thought, walking between the rows of cherry trees where the ground was soft with fallen blossoms. By the time they moved in, it would be almost time to start picking. His mouth watered at the thought.

He'd had the idea about a month ago. Other than going out for an occasional coffee with a couple of German friends Adam had introduced him to, or coming along to check on the job sites, his dad still stayed in the house much of the time. Little Sue's German vocabulary was growing quickly but playing with his granddaughters wasn't enough. His dad was only 55 years old. He needed something to keep him occupied, and three and a half acres of orchard would be just the thing. They could get a few animals too, which would cut down the grocery bill. A bit of Elek right here in Penticton!

And this place even had two houses. The pickers' shack could be turned into a cozy little house for his parents and Frank, and the main house was bigger than where they were. Their third daughter had been born a few weeks earlier. He'd been hoping for a boy until he saw Cheri, a perfect little angel lying there in Jean's arms. In any case, the extra space would be nice with a new baby and two busy toddlers.

Adam whistled as he jumped back into the car. He needed to stop at the mini-golf and see how the spring clean-up was going. They were due to open for their second season in a couple of weeks and there was a lot to do to get ready. He was planning to show his mom and dad around the mini-golf this weekend, maybe even teach them how to play.

An hour later, he pulled into the garage and went into the house.

"Frank, what happened?" His brother was holding a bloody towel against his nose, and his eyes were red from crying.

Jean jumped in and answered. "Those boys at school are such bullies, Adam." She turned her attention back to Frank. "Let me see," she said, pulling the towel away from his nose. "I think it's stopped. Do you want a little more ice?"

Frank shook his head. "No, it's okay."

"Tell me what happened Frank," said Adam.

"We had a test today," Frank started shakily, "and we had to say all 50 of the United States. And I was the only one who could do it."

"You can name all 50 states? That's pretty damned good, Frank," Adam praised his little brother.

"Yes, but the other boys didn't like it, and when class let out, they cornered me outside and started calling me 'little Hitler.' They kicked me and then one guy punched me and my nose started to bleed." Frank sniffled a little, eyes downcast.

No one spoke for a moment. Then Adam broke the silence. "Frank, those kids don't know anything about Hitler. Just because we're German doesn't make us like him. Everybody suffered when he was in power, and for a long time afterwards.

"Now, I think you need to learn to defend yourself when someone picks a fight with you. Come out to the garage with me."

At the supper table that night, Adam described the orchard and his plans.

"I'll call the guy in the morning and tell him we'll take it and find out when I can start the renovations to the two houses. And I gotta make a few calls about selling this place. If everything goes the way I'm planning, we'll be moving in July."

"A cherry and apple orchard hey? It's a good idea Adam. It'll be good to have a bit of land, room for a garden and a bit of farming," his dad said. "Might be a good idea to plant a few grapes too, make some wine."

Perfect, thought Adam.

The move went smoothly with all the extra hands to help carry boxes. His mom and dad were pleased with the little house, and Jean liked what he'd done with the main house. It took his dad no time at all to start tidying up the orchard. He couldn't prune until next spring, but there was a lot of weeding to do, and a few dead trees to take out. Adam was optimistic. His dad would be happy here and they could all relax.

CHAPTER ONE HUNDRED TWENTY-NINE

The harmony was short lived.

"Where's Dad?" Adam asked as they all settled into the living room after supper to watch TV a couple of months later. At his question, Jean, his mom, and Frank all looked at each other.

"He's not coming up tonight," his mom said after a moment, then turned to Sue. "Come on Sue, come sit with Granny." She lifted Sue and settled her onto her lap. Adam looked at Jean, who gave him a subtle head shake.

That night in bed, Jean told Adam the whole story.

Mid-week, while Adam had been away working, they'd all been settling in for the evening. The girls were fed, and Frank had wandered up from the little house after supper. After changing little Cheri's diaper like she'd taught him, he'd helped himself to a snack from the fridge. Adam's mom had come up too. Just as the TV show started, the front door slammed open.

"What the hell is wrong with you?" Adam's father had bellowed as he crossed the kitchen into the living room and started jabbing his finger towards Frank. "No goddammed respect! Did I raise you to be a slob?! Goddam good for nothing."

The girls had stared at their grandpa wide-eyed as Frank got up from the recliner, confused.

"What's wrong?" Frank had asked.

"You know what's wrong! You get a goddammed roof put over your head, do nothing to earn it, and you can't even show any respect. You should be ashamed of yourself," Adam's dad had continued.

"George, has something happened?" Adam's mom had asked quietly.

"This spoiled kid of ours doesn't have the decency to respect the home he's been given is what's happened. When you wash your hands, do you hang the towel properly and clean up after yourself, or I guess it's okay to just throw it down and assume someone else is going to clean up after you. What kind of world is this, when a kid your age has no chores, no responsibilities, and no respect?" Adam's father's face was red from exertion and emotion as he ranted at his young son.

Jean couldn't believe her eyes and ears. This was a grown man. What the hell was wrong with him? A thought crystallized in her mind. If she didn't establish some boundaries now, this behaviour would be the norm. She got up and went over to her father-in-law.

"Dad, this is my house," she began in her broken German, trying to keep her voice from shaking, "and the only person who will yell in this house is me. If you want to yell, you go to your own house."

Although she spoke quietly, Jean's tone left no question as to her intent to maintain authority over her home.

She'd thought for a moment that he was going to hit her, seeing the veins bulging in his temples as he clenched his fists at his sides.

"Adam will hear about this," he'd spat out towards Jean.

At that point, she'd calmly asked him to leave. He'd hesitated, but then he'd turned and stomped out, slamming the door violently.

"Good for you, honey," said Adam when Jean finished her story. "Not enough people stand up to my father."

In the days that followed, Adam's dad stayed out of sight. The days became weeks, and the only news they had of him was Adam's mom's occasional mention to her daughter-in-law.

"Jean, he's sitting in the little house, crying all the time," she would say quietly. Jean knew her mother-in-law wanted only peace in the family, and Adam confirmed that she'd always been the one to resolve the conflicts that arose, placating her hot-headed husband to keep the peace. But Jean was determined not to be subservient to her father-in-law. She and Adam agreed that it was time he learned something.

Jean tried to explain her point of view to her mother-in-law in her broken German. "He needs to understand the consequences of his actions. He can't act this way like a child with a temper tantrum." She knew she hadn't made her points clearly enough, but her mother-in-law was a respectful woman, and didn't push.

After three weeks, Jean decided enough was enough and headed down the path towards the little house. Her father-in-law had likely never apologized in his life, certainly never to a woman, and he probably wasn't going to start now. For that matter, he probably wasn't even sorry and didn't consider his behaviour that evening to be wrong. But she'd left it long enough and her boundary had been established.

"Dad," she called out as she knocked.

"What?" came the answer from inside. Everyone else was up at the big house already, settled around the TV for the evening.

She pushed the door open and saw him sitting at the kitchen table in the semi-darkness. He looked up at her suspiciously.

"Would you like to join us for the evening? We're watching TV, and I've baked a nice cake."

A smile quickly spread across her father-in-law's face. "Sure, okay. What kind of cake?" he asked as he stood and reached for his shoes.

CHAPTER ONE HUNDRED THIRTY
1960

Things settled down again after Jean invited Adam's dad back into the house. Perhaps he'd begun to appreciate the strength that had drawn Adam to Jean.

At the earliest sign of spring the following year, Adam's dad began working in the orchard, more content than Adam had seen him in years as he lovingly tended the fruit trees and prepared the ground for the garden. When Adam came home with fifty chicks on a Saturday morning, they went out and picked up some lumber and chicken wire and before the weekend was over, a chicken coop had been added to the yard.

The Kamloops apartment building was finally completed despite many obstacles with the building site and the crew that had drawn the timeline out to 18 months. It sold quickly and for a good profit.

Adam was home full time again, and before long the mini-golf had been expanded to include a trampoline section. Then, on a whim, Adam purchased four ponies, one for each of the girls and one for Frank. Really they were for the tourists of course. Each morning, Frank rode his pony, Dickie, from the orchard to the mini-golf, leading the other three along behind for the pony rides the growing tourist attraction had begun offering.

Adam's dad and mom picked furiously as the cherries ripened that first summer, determined not to let any go to waste. The excess they didn't need could be sold, Adam's dad explained proudly.

"Where's that box of cherries I put in the garage this morning?" his dad asked Adam one afternoon when the cherry season was drawing to a close.

"I sold it," Adam replied.

"What do you mean you sold it? I didn't have the sign out today."

"Well, there was a car in the driveway when I got home and they wanted cherries and there was a box there so I sold it. Here's the money." Adam pulled a five-dollar bill out of his pocket and held it out to his dad.

"You sold the whole box for five dollars?"

"I didn't know the price, so we agreed on five dollars."

"You're crazy, that box should have been ten dollars." His dad's face started to get red. "You don't look after the trees, you don't pick the cherries, and then you give them away for nothing?"

"I didn't give them away, I sold them for five dollars," Adam snapped back, reaching into his pocket. "Here, you want another five dollars, I'll give you another five dollars."

"I don't want your money," his dad roared, spinning on his heel and stomping away. After a few steps he stopped and turned back towards Adam, shaking his finger at him. "A guy works for days picking cherries in the heat, and then you sell them for half price. You should have sent them away and told them to come back tomorrow when somebody who knows what they're doing was here." His dad strode away, leaving a string of Romanian swear words behind.

It was a week before his dad spoke to him again.

CHAPTER ONE HUNDRED THIRTY-ONE
1961

The next winter, on a family trip to Disneyland, Adam spotted a set of full-size carnival rides for sale on the side of the road. The rides would turn the mini-golf attraction into an all-day amusement park outing for families and increase revenue significantly, he thought. When the rides had arrived and been set up, all freshly painted, he stood back and looked at the site with pride.

The problems started shortly thereafter. The permit he had been waiting on to operate the rides was denied. Adam was furious. The councilmen had all been supportive when he'd reviewed his plans with them before making the purchase, and he'd spent a lot of time and money on the rides since then.

The local newspaper became the chronicle of the biggest dispute Penticton had ever seen before, and probably since, and City Hall the scene of many a hot debate. After Adam expressed his disappointment in an interview printed in the newspaper, council published an article about the expressions of concern they had received from people who lived near the site. The journalist scrambled to collect and publish opinions of people who were for the rides one week, and the next week he published opinions against. Neighbours near the site continued to protest, citing excess noise, all night revelry, and increased crime that the rides might somehow cause. Adam published a letter he'd written to council appealing the decision and alleging that one of the councillors was actively dissuading the others, based on a personal business interest that conflicted with the project. The councillor threatened to sue for libel and demanded an apology. Adam refused. The paper printed a statement that the permit would be withheld until an apology was received. Adam apologized. Grandmothers and mothers published letters to the editor in favour of the kiddie rides, demanding to know how anyone could be against rides that would bring joy to the little ones. Others wrote in against. The noise would be unbearable and the rides would attract hooligans. Council demanded that the ferris wheel be dismantled immediately, its size when compared to the other rides making it the primary concern. Adam refused on the grounds that the technicians capable of doing so had left the area and would not return until September. One day he received a letter saying the city had received a complaint that he was in violation of the Lord's Day Act. He went to town hall and asked for a copy of the Act. It prohibited operating a business on Sunday. Adam agreed to comply, providing all other businesses in town also complied. The complaint was dismissed.

And so the battle raged.

Ultimately, public opinion sided with Adam, and a few days before the scheduled opening, a one-year permit was granted, on the condition that the ferris wheel be dismantled.

The rides were a smash hit, and no hooligans materialized. The motel and campground that Adam had purchased next door were packed all summer too. At the end of the season, council could hardly shut down such a popular tourist attraction, and Adam was granted an indefinite permit to operate all rides, including the ferris wheel and all of his other attractions. The only condition was that he relocate to a different site across the road, just far enough from the nearest homes to appease the public.

CHAPTER ONE HUNDRED THIRTY-TWO

With the ferris wheel uproar behind them, the extended family settled into a comfortable routine. The girls toddled around the orchard, learning to help their granny and grandpa tend the garden and feed the animals. Adam's father perfected his method for cherry schnapps in the still he and Adam had built. School had become easy for Frank once he'd settled in, and his stories of what he and his friends got up to amused them all around the supper table.

In the summers, activity centred around the amusement park. Adam's mom became a pro in the kiosk, perfecting the art of spinning cotton candy and teaching first Sue, then Sandy, and finally Cheri, how to count out change when they were old enough. His dad busied himself helping the kids on and off the rides and making sure the grounds were groomed to his satisfaction. In addition to looking after the ponies, Frank handed out golf clubs and whatever else needed doing.

Everyone had a part to play, and on the surface at least, everyone seemed content.

"Hey, Randy," Adam said to one of the guys around the table at the Three Gables Pub one afternoon. "I hear you had a few drinks with my old man the other night."

"You can say that again. A better name for that schnapps he makes would be white lightning. We sat by that still and drank until he damn near had to carry me out to my car. Your old man's a good guy. We talked about a lot of stuff."

"He can talk, that's for sure." Adam took a swig of his beer.

"You know what he told me?" Randy laughed. "I asked him how he liked living in Canada. He said *'Effryzink in Canada is fery nice. Vee like Canada fery much.'"* Randy mimicked Adam's dad. *"'But you know Randy,'* he says to me, *'I ask you a question. You efer see zee cow suckink on zee calf before?'* I asked him what he meant. *'Ees no goot,'* he says to me. *'I am zee faazer and Adam is doink all zees zings for us. Ees no goot.'"*

Adam laughed at his friend's attempt to sound like his dad and changed the subject. Inwardly, he was deflated. He just couldn't win.

CHAPTER ONE HUNDRED THIRTY-THREE
1962

Putting his dad's comments out of his mind, Adam decided it was time to develop the parcel of land he'd purchased five years earlier. The community was skeptical about the property. His friends laid bets it couldn't be developed. Too steep and rugged for roads and no access to water, they said. True to form, Adam disregarded the talk. With some creative engineering, the roads into and around the property turned out great. The water issue he solved with a little aluminum fishing boat, dragging a high capacity water line capped by an industrial foot valve out into the lake at the base of the property. When everything was ready, he ran a competition to name the subdivision, and then splashed full-page ads all around the valley. *'Live at Sage Mesa for just $35 per month!'*

Little Susie was already in second grade, and Sandy in kindergarten when Adam decided to sell the orchard and move the family up to Sage Mesa. Having more residents in the subdivision would make it more attractive, and after five years of hobby farming they were all ready for a change. While the crew broke ground for a new home for him and Jean and the girls up at Sage Mesa, Adam helped his parents select a little house near the motel and golf course, put a down payment on it and co-signed for a mortgage in his dad's name.

Adam's overactive mind continued to turn up opportunities.

A franchiser looking to establish a Suzuki motorcycle outlet was on the verge of choosing a new location after realizing that no building in Penticton met his requirements. And the franchise was to open for business within the month. Adam was confident he could build to suit in the required timeframe and approached the man with a proposal. Construction began at 2 a.m. as the crew broke ground in the moonlight. Ten days of double shifts later, they completed the building, a building that, years later would be the birthplace of Adam's mini-storage empire.

Not long after, he received a call from a fellow who had foreclosed on a large piece of property south of town and was wondering what to do with it. The man on the phone, surely with Adam's successes at Sage Mesa in the back of his mind, asked if Adam would come up and have a walk through his property.

"Do you think it has any potential?" the fellow asked as they finished the walk.

"Well, you have a little mudhole here, you could dredge that and make a nice little lake. You've got that lodge building over there, that could be a clubhouse. I think you could make a nice golf course here. And you could make good building lots all around it. All up there and around there," Adam waved his arm. "It needs a lot of work, but, yes, I think it's got potential."

Adam negotiated for a 15 percent share and they got to work. They decided to call the project St. Andrew's Golf and Country Club.

But the developer didn't have the money to keep the project going full time and St. Andrew's was slow from the start. To fill his time, Adam accepted a job in Vancouver for the same fellow, as operations manager of a factory that made fire-rated doors for commercial buildings. They needed someone to turn it around and make it profitable.

The girls were already in bed when Adam arrived home from his first trip to Vancouver. He'd rented himself an office with an adjoining apartment and had a walk through the door factory. He poured himself a scotch and sat down in the living room to update Jean.

"Sounds interesting," she replied when he'd finished outlining his plans. "We'll manage fine. Vancouver isn't far away if we need you. On another note, Susie came home crying today. The kids were calling her and Sandy names again. This time it was 'Hitler's Flower Girls.' Honestly, these kids don't even have a clue who Hitler was. Their parents should be ashamed of themselves for what they're teaching their kids."

"What did you tell the girls?"

"I just told them to ignore it. It'll pass."

"People are so stupid," he paused and stared down into the ice in his glass for a moment, then smiled at Jean. "Yes, it'll pass. It always does."

The door factory didn't take long to turn around, and before long, Adam had time on his hands again.

Emil and Tom were from Hungary, so it was only natural that they and Adam would strike up a conversation when their paths crossed at the Three Gables Pub one afternoon. The two of them had fled Hungary when the violent uprising against communism had failed a dozen years earlier. They made a living in Canada speculating on mining claims. Anxiously, they described an option they had on a mercury mine in the interior of British Columbia. Cash was short and if they didn't come up with $5,000 by the following week, they would lose the claim.

Within a week Adam had visited the site, researched the mercury market, paid the money to retain the option, and changed the sign on the door of his Vancouver office to "Condor Mines," the name of the new company he'd incorporated.

A year later Adam took Condor Mines public on the stock exchange and raised the money for the exploration phase. The Nomura Mining Company of Japan visited Adam's office in Vancouver. They wanted all the raw mercury he could produce, and flew him to Japan to wine and dine him and discuss a partnership. The press release about the contract between Condor Mines and the Nomura Mining Company drove Condor's stock prices from twenty-five cents up to three dollars overnight. Adam had scored again.

CHAPTER ONE HUNDRED THIRTY-FOUR
1966

Adam missed Theresa, and he'd promised Jean he'd show her Europe. A lull in the exploration work was perfect timing for a visit to Germany. His parents could look after the girls.

When Theresa had caught her breath and they'd stopped laughing about Adam's unannounced appearance at her front door, he introduced Jean. *She's so like Mom,* Adam thought, as Theresa wrapped her arms around her sister-in-law.

The little barber shop Theresa's husband had installed in their basement to make a bit of extra money was packed with neighbourhood men waiting their turn. In the midst of their jovial laughter and gossip about the village, Adam quietly settled into an empty barber chair, waiting to see when someone would notice the newcomer.

A minute later, his brother-in-law spotted him.

"Adam!" he yelled out in shock.

"Ahh!" yelled his startled customer.

Adam and Jean spent the next few days making the rounds of Adam's relatives. Everyone was delighted with Jean. A Canadian girl who spoke Eleker German! Not long into the trip, Adam had an idea that delighted him more than anything had in quite some time. Hungary, still under communist control, remained closed to Germans, but he had a Canadian passport now.

Theresa's eyes filled with fear when he told her their plans.

"Don't worry, Resi. There's no danger now. And can you imagine how wonderful it would be to see Uncle Florian?"

There were a lot of questions at the border about where they were going and what they would be doing, but in the end, their Canadian passports did the trick. Adam was giddy when he opened his eyes the next morning and looked around. He was in Budapest. The last time he'd been in Budapest, he'd been delivering tobacco to the prison camp for his dad. And today he was going to take Jean to Elek, and they were going to see Uncle Florian! He lay there for a minute, thinking about his uncle standing on the platform the day they'd been deported, tears running down his face, his arm around his wife, while all of his relatives rolled away in a cattle car.

Adam couldn't stop grinning as they breakfasted in the lovely old dining room. He'd never been inside one of these grand old places before. Such old-world charm and so different from Canada.

"May I see you in my office for a moment?" the front desk manager asked when they were checking out of the hotel. "It will only take a moment."

Shutting the door behind Adam, the man waved graciously for him to sit. "Thank you for your time, sir. I am the manager of the hotel and I was just having a look at your bill."

"Is there a problem?" Adam asked.

"No, sir, no problem at all. I was just wishing to enquire as to which currency you were planning to use to settle the bill. You see, we accept Deutsch Marks and US Dollars as well as the local currency in which the bill is printed." The manager spoke in a most serious tone.

"Well, it doesn't matter to me." Adam had purchased a small amount of Hungary's new currency, the Forint, but not much, on the advice of other customers at the currency exchange booth. The Forint had been weakening steadily and people felt it was on the verge of collapse. "What currency would you suggest?" Adam asked the hotel manager.

"I have your account here, you see," the manager said in his grave tone, "and it might be possible to offer a slight discount, perhaps up to 50 percent, if you were to pay in Deutsch Marks."

Adam counted out the appropriate number of bills while the manager tore the paper in half, then tore it again, and once more before dropping the pieces into the garbage can under his desk. When he'd finished, he held out his hand for the money and casually tucked the bills into his pocket.

"I trust everything was to your satisfaction?" he continued, as if the exchange had not taken place.

"Oh, very much. I'll look forward to staying again when I'm next in Budapest."

Adam's mind swirled as he showed Jean around Elek. The family home, the school, the pond, the Mahler's house, the town square, the church, Joe's house, the warden's house, the graveyard. There were so many stories to tell.

When they parked in front of Uncle Florian's house in Gyula late in the afternoon, Adam sat in the car for a few moments, staring at the house. He'd thought about his uncle often over the years. They'd had letters of course, but what was it really like living under a communist regime? He wondered how much they didn't know. A moment later, Uncle Florian's head poked out the front door. Adam opened his car door and stood up so his uncle could see him.

"Uncle Florian! It's Adam!" he said in Hungarian. As the old man stepped out onto the porch Adam blinked hard to keep his tears back. He was so stooped, and so much thinner.

"Adam?" His uncle looked confused as he stared back at Adam.

Adam switched to Eleker German. That would be a big clue. "Have I changed that much in twenty years?" he said, walking around the car so his uncle could get a better look.

"Oh, my God, Adam. Little Adam." Tears filled Uncle Florian's eyes as he came down the steps and towards Adam, arms outstretched. After a long embrace, his uncle stood back, holding Adam at arm's length, looking up at him. "Look at you." His gaze shifted to something behind Adam. Suddenly Adam remembered Jean.

"Uncle Florian," he said turning and opening the car door for Jean, "this is my wife, Jean."

"I am so *pleased* to meet you. Adam has told me so much about you," said Jean taking both of Uncle Florian's hands in hers. Pulling his hands free, Uncle Florian kissed Jean on her cheeks and then wrapped his arms around her in a big hug.

"Such a beautiful wife, Adam," he said, flashing a broad smile at Adam as he let Jean go. With the twinkle in his eye he looked like the Uncle Florian Adam remembered. "Come. Come in." He turned to lead them into the house. "I can't believe you're here! How did you get across the border?"

"I'm a Canadian now," Adam explained.

The evening passed in a blur, as Adam caught up with his uncle, aunt, and cousins who had been teenagers last time he'd seen them. Words and laughter tumbled around the cozy little room as they exchanged stories and learned about one another's lives over the last two decades.

The next morning came too soon.

"It's because of the German name, you see," his uncle explained as Adam drove the rental car towards the work camp where Florian had to spend the day. "We get a few Forints. The Hungarian nationals get a bit more. But our real compensation is the wonderful care that the state gives us. We work, we eat, we have a few clothes to cover our backs, and that's about it. It's the communist way. And if we don't like it, or if we miss work, or if a good communist overhears you talking against the state, it's jail. Believe me, I'm familiar with their jail. But it's not that bad really. It's worth keeping your mouth shut while you're in there, or they'll give you a beating. Otherwise, you get a bit of food and you have to work, same as always. The main difference is that you don't get to see your family or sleep in your own bed." Uncle Florian smiled at Adam as they pulled up in front of the gate. "Thank you for the ride in this wonderful little car, Adam." He put his hand on Adam's on top of the gear shift and squeezed. "I still can't believe you're really here."

Adam sat in the car and watched as his uncle went in through the gates. "I'll pick you up at five!" he yelled out after him.

After his uncle disappeared, he didn't move. There had to be something he could do. He and Jean only had a few days until they would have to leave again. A few minutes later he started the car and moved it to the parking lot, then grabbed a bag from the back seat and strode towards the gate.

"I would like to see the Commandante immediately," he barked at the guard in Hungarian.

The guard didn't hesitate. "Just a moment." He turned and disappeared for a couple of minutes inside the gate. When he reappeared, he ushered Adam inside and down a corridor to an office.

Stepping inside the office with the little bag in his hand, Adam pulled the door shut softly behind him, then turned to speak to the man seated behind the desk.

"Good morning, Commandante. My name is Adam Baumann and I am from Canada. I'm here in Gyula visiting my relatives." At this point Adam stopped and sat down on the chair facing the desk, and set his bag on his lap. The man behind the desk watched and listened silently. "Do you have any children, Commandante?"

The man blinked and looked harder at Adam, as if he wasn't sure what Adam had just said. "What are you asking me?"

"Do you have any children?"

"Yes, I have three children as a matter of fact."

Adam opened the bag and pulled out a handful of the candy that he'd bought just before leaving Germany. "I'd like to give your children a little gift. I have some pens here too. I've heard that it's very difficult to come by ballpoint pens. Perhaps your children could use them in school." The Commandante's eyes lit up. "If you have a moment, I have a request I'd like to explain to you," Adam continued, "and since you have children I'm sure you'll understand because my request is about family. You see, my family was deported from this area twenty years ago. Every one of us. Me, my brother and sister and parents, grandparents, aunts and uncles. All except for one uncle who is married to a Hungarian woman. My uncle hasn't seen any of his family in twenty years. I live in Canada now with my wife and children and my parents and brothers as well. And I've come all the way from Canada to see my uncle. But I only have this week, and then I have to fly back home and back to work. So I was hoping you could organize for my uncle to have some time off work to spend with me."

When he'd finished speaking, Adam reached out and placed the bag on the desk, then reached into his jacket pocket and pulled out the pens he'd also brought from Germany.

The man watched all this in silence. After a few moments he spoke. "What is your uncle's name?"

"Florian Baumann."

"Guard!" The man's yell startled Adam. A moment later the guard who had shown him into the office appeared in the doorway.

"Bring Florian Baumann to me."

"Yes, sir."

Adam's heart pounded.

A few minutes later, Uncle Florian appeared in the doorway. When he saw Adam, his eyes grew nervous. Adam could tell he was worried about what kind of trouble might be brewing. "You called for me, sir?"

"Comrade Baumann, you are not looking very well today," the Commandante said to Uncle Florian.

"I'm fine, sir."

"You look rather ill to me."

"I'm not ill sir. I am fit to work."

At this point Adam spoke up. "You look sick, Uncle Florian," he said quietly, giving his uncle a wink.

"You will have the week off to recuperate," the Commandante said as he scribbled on a pad of paper on his desk, then tore the sheet off and handed it to Florian. "Here is your authorization to be absent from work. I expect you back in good form next week."

"Yes, sir," said Florian in a dazed sort of voice.

"Thank you, Commandante. Please give my regards to your wife and children," said Adam standing up to leave. "Come on, Uncle Florian. We should get you home to bed."

The reappearance of Uncle Florian when they arrived back at the house caused a bit of panic. After they explained, Uncle Florian's wife laughed cautiously. "Well, as long as you have the paper, maybe it won't cause any problems. Irene would be so disappointed if you were taken to jail again." His aunt turned to him to explain. "Irene has been trying to complete her law degree for many years. A child with a parent in prison is not permitted to attend university. Every time Florian is imprisoned for not being able to bite his tongue and keep his opinions to himself, Irene is kicked out of the university and misses her classes. And they're stricter with her about this than they are with the other students because of her German name. She has re-started some of her classes so many times she can recite the lectures from the first several weeks by heart. We want her to finish one of these days!"

Day times were filled to overflowing as Adam, Jean, and his uncle and aunt toured the old spots that Adam remembered and compared stories about life in Hungary and in Canada. In the evenings Adam played his mouth organ while Uncle Florian played the accordion. Florian often sat near Jean and translated the Hungarian words into German for her when Adam had too many conversations going on and too many old stories being rehashed to remember.

"Let's have a party at the Gyula Hotel tonight," Adam said the morning before they were due to leave. "All of us, cousin Irene and her husband too. We'll all have a nice meal and some dancing. It's my treat."

As they settled in and began their meal, suddenly Uncle Florian stiffened. "The Commandante is sitting over there," he said to Adam.

No one spoke, waiting to see what Adam would do. After a moment, Adam waved the waiter over.

"Can you please send a nice bottle of wine to that table over there, and let the gentleman know we send our best wishes?"

"Of course, sir," said the waiter.

They watched nervously as the bottle was delivered. As the Commandante looked their way, Adam waved, then got up and walked over to him with a big smile.

"Good evening," Adam said as he reached the table. "I hope your meal is good. My uncle wishes to express his gratitude for the recuperation time. He is feeling a little better, but it was very difficult to convince him to join us this evening as I'm sure you can imagine."

The Commandante threw back his head and laughed. "I hope he has a good time despite his illness."

"Thank you, sir," Adam laughed. "I'll leave you to enjoy your meal."

Later in the evening, the Commandante approached their table, a smile playing at the corners of his mouth. Ignoring Adam and Florian, he held out his arm to Jean and led her onto the dance floor.

CHAPTER ONE HUNDRED THIRTY-FIVE

When Frank finished high school and headed to Vancouver to college, Adam couldn't have been prouder. And even though the degree Frank ultimately earned was in Education, rather than the Business program Adam had suggested, Adam considered the tuition money well spent. Finally, all these years after Adam's college plans had been foiled by the war, a Baumann with a degree.

A few months later, at a lavish wedding organized by Adam, Frank married the sweetheart he'd met in college. Theresa and Franz were flown in from Germany, and the Baumann family was together for the first time since Adam had immigrated.

A couple of weeks later, Jean had shocking news when Adam arrived home from work.

"Your parents want to go home to Germany," Jean announced from the kitchen.

Adam stopped midway through hanging up his hat. "What?"

"That's how I responded," said Jean. "It's true, they want to go home. Your mom told me this morning when I stopped over for coffee. She said that now that Frank is married, all her children are settled, and it is time for them to go home where Resi can look after them."

Adam finished hanging his hat and walked over to the sideboard to pour himself a scotch. "Aren't we looking after them well enough?"

"Apparently that's not the point. It's the daughter's job to look after the parents after they retire. They've thought it all out. They want to sell the house and take that money with them, which is only right I suppose since they've been making the payments for the last five years and they've kept it immaculate. And I guess when everyone was here for the wedding, Resi's husband explained the pension that your dad will be getting in Germany now that he's sixty-five. I doubt he understands that it's been you and your brother-in-law making the payments into it all these years, but that doesn't matter. And I'm sure they'll both be entitled to a little

Canadian pension too, from their deductions here in the last few years. Anyway, now that Resi and Franz's daughter is married and out of the house, there's room for them. So they want to go."

Jean had walked back into the kitchen while she'd been talking, and resumed chopping vegetables. Adam sat down and thought for a few moments. He knew his mom missed Theresa terribly, but she had seemed content working at the amusement park and cleaning cabins at the campground. He paid her well enough. And his dad seemed to enjoy his job tending the grounds of the par 3 golf course Adam had built adjacent to the amusement park, and a couple of days a week he worked for a German carpenter in town. Then Adam thought back to his dad's words that night he and Randy drank all that schnapps a few years earlier. *The cow sucking the calf.* Suddenly, it made sense. His dad was a very proud man. Living with Adam's assistance was eating away at him. He needed to be in control again, the man of the house.

Adam followed Jean into the kitchen and leaned in the doorway.

"Well, I guess we'll talk with them on Sunday when we go there for supper and see what has to happen."

Within weeks the house was sold and airline tickets purchased.

The girls were 13, 11, and ten already, and Cheri hadn't even been born when his mom and dad had arrived. Their grandparents had always been a part of their daily lives. His dad had tucked them into bed and rubbed their bruised knees far more than he had, and his mom was the perfect granny. After a tearful good-bye, Adam's parents climbed into the car with Adam and Jean for the drive to Vancouver.

There was one last thing Adam wanted to show his parents before they left Canada.

"King Cuts for my dad and me," Adam said when the waiter came to their table that evening. He'd reserved his favourite table at what he thought was the best steakhouse in Vancouver. "And my mom will have the Queen cut. Jean, would you like a Queen Cut too?"

"Oh, heaven's no, there's no way I can eat all that meat," Jean laughed.

To Adam's delight, his dad's eyes bulged when his meal arrived.

"Oh, my God, Adam," gasped his mom.

"What did I tell you?" said Jean, laughing with her mother-in-law at the thick juicy prime rib that filled her entire plate.

CHAPTER ONE HUNDRED THIRTY-SIX
1969

His parents had only been gone a couple of months, but as Christmas approached, the girls missed them dreadfully, and Adam wanted to see how they had settled in.

"Walk up quietly, and knock on the door and wait," he said to Cheri as he pulled into Theresa's drive.

Cheri giggled. "Okay," she whispered, getting out of the car and leaving the door wide open.

Sandy and Susie giggled in the back seat at the shocked look on Theresa's face when she opened the door and saw first Cheri and then the rest of them in the car outside.

"Oh, Adam, you're mean," said Jean from the seat beside him, unable to wipe the smile from her face. Adam knew how much she was looking forward to seeing his mom.

Cheri disappeared into the house and a moment later they heard his mom shrieking in surprise.

They stayed a week, making the rounds of the relatives' homes, eating and drinking and even dancing when his dad pulled out the accordion.

"I tell you," Adam heard his dad saying to one of his uncles, "in Canada, they got the most beautiful mountains and lakes where the water is so clear you can see the bottom. And, I'll tell you what else, the weather is better. Next month or two the grass will be turning green in Canada, won't it, Adam?"

"Yep. We live in a pretty mild area." Adam leaned back in his chair, listening to his dad.

"My house in Canada, the roses they bloomed from March to October. And the fruit. You should see the fruit. There's so much that you can pick enough off the ground to make schnapps to last all winter. You should have seen the still me and Adam built at our orchard. After Adam sold that orchard, I bought the house, the one I sold when we decided to come back to Germany. And you should see the beautiful houses that Adam built in this neighbourhood that he called *Sage Mesa*." His dad pronounced the Spanish words slowly. "And George, he lives in Vancouver. Owns a big house too, four or five times as big as this one. Vancouver is five, six hundred kilometres from where we lived."

"Five or six *hundred* kilometres?" asked his uncle dubiously.

"That's right. In Canada, that's nothing. We crossed the whole goddammed country by train once. Took a week. You should have seen the places we seen. Nothing but forest for hours and hours and hours. And Indians drying deer skins to use for clothes." His dad laughed, then stopped for a minute to roll a cigarette.

Adam hadn't seen his dad like this in so long, he'd almost forgotten. Since he was a child, he supposed. Before the war started. He always told stories. But now he wasn't just telling stories, he was happy. And proud. He'd done something significant. And gotten back some control over his life for the first time since the deportation order.

As Adam, Jean, and the girls toured around Spain and Morocco over the next two weeks seeing one sight after another, Adam's heart was light. They booked a room at the Casa del Sol in Malaga, wandered through the palaces of Granada, and saw Christopher Columbus' tomb in Seville. When Sandy left her retainer in the bathroom of a tapas bar after lunch one day, Adam sent a car back to fetch it. When the tour bus containing his family left without him as he squatted behind a cathedral in Madrid with traveller's diarrhea, he chased them down in a taxi. They played card games on the ferry across the Strait of Gibraltar, and Adam had the girls hooting with laughter when he joined the belly dancers in Tangiers.

When the day of their return flight home arrived, the girls collapsed into their seats, buzzing with new memories. After takeoff, Adam fell into a contented sleep. Everyone was happy. Jean, the girls, his parents back in Germany. His parents didn't need him anymore, and neither did his brothers or sister. The job he'd taken on when he returned from the war at 16, was finished.

Maybe all the challenges that history had contrived were finally behind him.

CHAPTER ONE HUNDRED THIRTY-SEVEN
1970

"Remember that we have that ribbon-cutting ceremony, Adam," Jean called out on a Saturday afternoon a few months after they'd returned from their adventures in Europe. "We're supposed to be there in half an hour."

"Okay, I'll get dressed," Adam replied.

A new park had been built for Sage Mesa and the neighbouring subdivision. Adam had donated land for a road that gave residents of both developments easy access to the new park. And he'd canvassed the residents of Sage Mesa as well as contributed financially himself to help fund the new park. The opening ceremony was that day.

The community hall was almost full when he and Jean arrived and made their way to a couple of empty seats near the front. After a few speeches, the councilman leading the ceremony announced that there were a few people he'd like to mention who helped the park become a reality.

"A big thank you goes out to Adam and Jean Baumann, for the cash donation and of course the donation of the land that the road is built on. Without the financial support of Sage Mesa and Adam Baumann, the park wouldn't have been finished this year. Let's have a round of applause for..."

Before the councilman could finish, he was interrupted by a loud voice from the back of the room. "Hang on a minute! I don't know what this world is coming to, but I never thought I would see the day when somebody tells me to applaud a Nazi."

All eyes turned to the back of the room. Adam recognized Doug, the customs officer that worked at the post office.

"Now, Doug, Adam made a big contribution to this park," the councilman responded in a pacifying tone.

"I don't give a damn what he did. He's a Nazi and I'm not going to put up with this. There are real veterans in this room and all of this land was intended for real war veterans, not dirty Nazis."

Adam grabbed Jean's elbow and stood up. "We don't want to cause any problems here," he said to the councilman, then turned to face the room. "Our apologies. We'll go and let you carry on with the ceremony."

"You'll do no such thing," a man that Adam had been in Rotary with for ages said indignantly from across the aisle.

"Let him leave. He knows I'm right. He's got no business here," Doug continued.

Adam and Jean didn't move.

One of the big general contractors in town stood up. "I think we've heard enough from you, Doug. The war ended 25 years ago," he said, walking towards the loudmouth.

"You've heard enough from me? Well, I fought for this country. That German right there is who we were fighting and I'd say it's him we've heard enough from."

Another businessman Adam had known for years who was sitting near the back stood up and approached Doug from the other side.

Adam stood in silence as they grabbed Doug under each arm and hauled him to the door. After pushing him out, they shut the door firmly behind him. The room was silent for a moment. Then one of the guys who had just shown Doug the door spoke.

"That was really terrible, Adam. You know no one else feels that way."

"It's nothing, don't worry about it," Adam said quickly.

"It's not nothing," the councilman at the front said. "Doug's an ass. You're welcome here today and you'll always be welcome here, no different than any of us. You're a valued citizen and resident of this town and I hope you'll accept our apology for the things that Doug said."

It was true. He was a part of this place. Penticton had afforded Adam the freedom to express himself and reach his potential, and he had given back in spades.

PART FIVE
Peru

"It is never too late in life to have a genuine adventure."

ROBERT KURSON, AUTHOR OF *ROCKET MEN*

CHAPTER ONE HUNDRED THIRTY-EIGHT
1971

Adam had grown weary of the slow pace on the St. Andrew's Golf and Country Club project. They'd had a bit of fun one day, laying out the course with the help of a golf pro from Vancouver, a bucket of balls, and a bottle of scotch. Other than that, there hadn't been much going on to hold his interest. Grateful for Adam's early advice and assistance on the project, the developer obliged when he explained that he'd like out, and bought back the 15 percent he'd given Adam.

Condor Mines was dead too. A massive fish kill in Japan had been attributed to mercury poisoning and the bottom had dropped out of the market. Fortunately, Adam and Jean had sold much of their stock at various profit levels prior to the collapse. The doors of Condor Mines and Adam's Vancouver office were permanently closed.

When the Suzuki franchise had gone broke a few years earlier, Adam had bought back the commercial building he'd built for the franchiser a decade earlier. He'd seen an interesting business in Vancouver called 'mini-storage,' and figured it would be a perfect use for the building. The storage units rented immediately and produced good revenue with little day-to-day effort. But it wasn't particularly interesting once it was up and running.

He'd sold the motel and campground after his parents left. The mini-golf and the par 3 were running smoothly. Everything was going well. Most people would have been content with the circumstances, perhaps even pleased to relax and enjoy the rewards of years of hard work, but Adam was hungry for something interesting to do.

"Disney is opening a new amusement park in Orlando, Florida in October. I think we should start there and see the grand opening, and then do a bit of sightseeing on our way down to Peru," said David Battison, a long-time friend, as they sat at the Three Gables enjoying a cold beer one afternoon in September. "We can stay with my buddy Merv in

Lima for a couple of weeks, get a car, drive around a bit. What do you think? It's the perfect time, before you dream up some new project."

Adam laughed. David was right. "Okay, let's do it."

The girls were becoming young teens, and rarely around. Jean's time was filled with getting them to and from piano, or ballet, volleyball, and any number of other activities. He might as well fill his time, and the thought of exploring a few new spots was piquing his interest.

"But if we're going to go all that way, let's make it worthwhile."

By the time Adam and David reached Lima, they'd checked out Disney's brand-new Magic Kingdom, soaked up some sun on the beaches of the Cayman Islands and Aruba, and explored Caracas, Bogota, and Quito. Peru was the sixth and final country on their itinerary.

On their second evening in Lima, Merv took them to the Sheraton Hotel for drinks. He knew someone who was staying in one of the fancy suites, a stock promoter from Vancouver named Turton.

"Turton's here to look at a molybdenum mine way up in the Andes somewhere. Mickey mouse operation, but he's been told there's a huge vein up there. He brought an Indian geologist named Singh with him," Merv explained as they rode the elevator to the upper floors.

Turton and a couple of local men from Lima were in the suite, halfway through their first scotch.

"This is Father Juan and Diego Madina. They live nearby. Diego owns the mine site that we're here to look at," Turton said by way of introduction. Walking over to the bar, he pulled out three more glasses and filled them with ice and scotch as he continued. "My geologist left for the mine site yesterday. He should have arrived there today. We're just waiting for a call to hear how he's making out." He handed each of them a glass. "Sit down. I hear you two saw a lot of places on your way down."

The scotch flowed freely and time passed quickly as the six of them swapped stories about where they'd been in the world and adventures they'd had along the way.

"So we drove Adam's beautiful brand new dark blue Mercedes right out of the factory," David said to the group. He was telling them about the trip he and Adam had taken to Europe a few years earlier. "I didn't know this, but if you buy from the factory in Germany and drive the car around for a while you can ship it to Canada as a used car which is a lot cheaper than new, plus you don't pay for a rental car for your holiday."

"That's right," said Adam. "It's a hell of a good deal. I'm planning to do it every couple of years from now on."

"Anyway, I wanted to see France," continued David, "but Adam hates the French."

"Bastards poured boiling water down on us from the third-floor windows, threw rocks at us, you name it, when they were marching us through there as prisoners at the end of the war," Adam explained.

"I convinced him, and we went to the border and the French border guard looks at the papers for the car and our passports and he says a bunch of stuff in French and points to the office where we're supposed to pull over. What does Adam do? He just drives through. Totally ignores the guy! Just drives into France without stopping."

"The guy just stood there looking confused. He didn't do anything about it at all," laughed Adam.

David jumped in again. "So then we drive around a bit and we need some fuel, so we pull up to a gas pump. One of those old pumps that you pump by hand, you know? And these two little old French ladies pump our gas and then say the price in French. And Adam hands them his German money. They didn't want it, but he just keeps holding these Marks out to them. Finally, they got so mad, they chased us out of the gas station."

"Without paying for the gas?" Turton asked.

"That's right," said Adam with a grin. "Got a free tank of gas from the French that day."

Conversation stopped suddenly when the door swung open. A man wearing a turban stood in the doorway, scowling at them.

"Singh," said Turton, "come in. We were expecting a call from the radio phone to confirm you'd made it to the mine."

"There was no call because the mine site is impossible to reach. The conditions are unbelievable. No passable roads, just rocks and llamas everywhere. No matter, altitude sickness would prevent anyone from working up there. There will be no report. There's nothing to write about.

Certainly nothing I can recommend to investors. Excuse me, I must lie down."

With that, Singh strode across the suite into one of the bedrooms, and pulled the door shut firmly behind him.

The men sat there looking at each other in silence for a few moments. Turton picked up the bottle of scotch from the coffee table and divided the last of it between their glasses.

"Well, that's unfortunate," said Diego after taking a sip. "Now what are we going to do?"

No one responded immediately. Then David spoke. "Hell, if there's anybody who could get up there and have a look at that property, it would be this guy right here." He pointed to Adam. "He's already told you about his mining experience. He's your man."

Diego looked at Adam. "Would you go?" he asked tentatively.

Would he fly to the middle of Peru into the high Andes and travel to a remote mine site to look around and give his opinion?

"Sure, I'll help you out if I can."

"Problem solved," laughed Turton, opening a fresh bottle of scotch.

Turton's immediate problem might have been solved, but no one in the room that night anticipated the chain of much bigger problems that would unfold as a result.

CHAPTER ONE HUNDRED THIRTY-NINE

Twelve hours later, Adam was back at the Lima airport, boarding a flight to Cusco. His head hurt a bit from the scotch, but after a bite to eat he felt better.

Everyone had warned him about altitude sickness. Cusco itself was 11,000 feet and Diego said they would be climbing a couple more thousand feet to get to the mine.

"My caretaker, Juvenal, will pick you up. He'll have coca leaves for you," Diego had said as he dropped Adam at the airport. Coca leaves were believed to help with altitude sickness. "Chew them up and then make a ball and hold it in the corner of your mouth. And the hotel will have a pot of coca tea in the lobby. They all do. Drink some of that too."

After a night in Cusco, Adam and Juvenal set out for the mine. Juvenal's little pick-up truck rattled over the rough road as they navigated the hairpin turns that took them steadily higher, winding back and forth up a narrow switchback road full of potholes. Abancay was the name of the first town they passed through, then Cotaruse, and then onto Antabamba. Juvenal's English was good, and as they drove, he told Adam a bit about the mine. It was belt driven with a couple of flotation cells. They had a little crusher and a little ball mill, all run by a General Motors truck motor.

They bounced and jostled along the uneven road, through the dips and craters, climbing higher and higher. The trees thinned out and disappeared. Not much could grow at this elevation. For a split second, a memory of sitting on the porch steps in Elek, imagining he could see the Carpathian Mountains in the distance flashed through Adam's mind.

A few minutes later the road petered out completely. They stopped beside a little stone hut. A dark-skinned woman dressed in heavy skirts and a tall brown hat sat on a rock on the leeside of the hut, pounding something in a large bowl on the ground in front of her. Her raven black hair hung in two thick braids down her back. Two little kids sat in the dirt nearby, playing. The woman looked up as they approached, then continued with her pounding. The barren mountainside above them was steep, with rocky outcrops. Below them, llamas grazed peacefully in meadows dotted with bare patches. A few of the nearest llamas lifted their heads and stared at the men as they got out of the pickup truck.

"Hola! Buenas!" Juvenal called out. The door of the hut opened and a stooped little man appeared, greeting Juvenal and Adam with a smile and a wave. His dark skin was weathered but his eyes were bright and friendly. "He speaks the indigenous language called Quechua, and the odd word of Spanish he's picked up over the years," Juvenal explained. "Dos caballos por favor y una llama," he said to the little man in Spanish, pointing to a small enclosure of horses behind the hut and holding up two fingers. Then he pointed down to the llamas and made a sign for one. The little man nodded obligingly and walked around the hut.

Ten minutes later they'd left the hut and the pickup truck behind. The horses picked their way skillfully along the rocky trail that hugged the mountainside. The llama, laden with their bags and some supplies for the mine, followed along on a rope.

When they reached the mine a couple of hours later, Adam climbed down from his horse and began to look around, amazed at what he saw. There really was an operational mine up there, even if it was rudimentary. The equipment, operated by a few little Quechua men, was how Juvenal had described it.

Suddenly a question occurred to him. "How do you get the gasoline in here for that engine?"

"Once a week, we bring a string of llamas in, loaded with jerry cans," replied Juvenal.

Adam shook his head in amazement.

When he'd had a look at the equipment, Adam followed Juvenal into the mine tunnel to inspect the rock face. It looked like quartz but it was hard to be sure. Then Juvenal threw a bucket of water against the rock and shone his flashlight on it. Adam caught his breath. The vein of white quartz that filled the rock face in front of him was heavily laden with beautiful black molybdenum oxide. With its high melting point, molybdenum was a key ingredient in the production of high quality steel alloy, and incredibly valuable.

"We should take some samples. Do you have a little hammer and a plastic bag or something?" he said to Juvenal, who waited patiently behind him.

A little while later, with the film in his camera spent, a little bag of white and black rock chips in his duffel bag, and a couple of pages of notes, Adam signalled to Juvenal that he was finished.

CHAPTER ONE HUNDRED FORTY

Two days later, Adam met Diego Madina for coffee. On his arrival back to Lima, he'd recapped what he'd seen at the mine. Diego had wanted some time to think.

"You said last night that it will take about $50,000 to put in a road and upgrade the equipment to make the mine productive right?"

Adam nodded.

"Would you be willing to invest that money?" Diego asked next.

Adam had been hoping he'd ask. "Sure, as long as there was some assurance you'd get a good crew in there and spend it carefully."

"I have a better idea. You've obviously got confidence in the vein. I'll lease the land to you, and you get it up and running."

Adam's heart skipped a beat. Then he grinned from ear to ear.

When Adam and David flew home, Adam's head was buzzing with ideas. He felt more alive than he had for a long time. The contract he'd signed with Diego was open-ended. The rights to a molybdenum mine in the Andes for as long as he wanted it. And all it had cost was $50,000 and a small percentage of profits for Diego. He'd need to get back to Peru right after Christmas and find an apartment and an office in Lima. Thankfully, David had agreed to oversee the businesses in Penticton.

Giddy with excitement, Adam sat back and let his mind wander through the adventure ahead. Everything would be new. A new culture, a new language to learn, a beautiful warm climate, exploring the Andes, a new business environment, and new problems to solve.

Unbeknownst to Adam, the recently elected left-wing military government that had been busy centralizing industry, had its sights set on mining. He couldn't have fully appreciated the challenges of building a privately held mine in that political climate, or even setting up a home, as the country underwent dramatic socialist reform. But he knew enough to know the project would take him into uncharted territory. And that was enough for him.

Jean's reaction proved once again that they were a good match.

"It sounds fascinating," she said as Adam described the palm-lined avenues and dramatic cliffs that rose above the beaches in the Miraflores suburb where Diego lived, and the contrasting countryside and the local people he'd seen on his trip to the mine. "Wow. You're going to be working in South America. I can't wait to see it all."

She wouldn't be able to travel with him right away though. Sue was in grade ten. She'd be 16 in the spring and was already excited about learning to drive. Sandy and Cheri had music lessons and lots of after-school activities to get to and from. All three were in the midst of the complications of being a teenager. The girls needed Jean at home, and she enjoyed managing their busy world. Plus, things tended to go more smoothly when Adam was busy with projects and didn't have time to worry about how differently kids were raised then, as compared to in his own youth.

In the big atlas they kept on the living room bookshelf, Adam showed the girls where the mine was located.

"My office will be here," he explained, pointing to Lima, "and the mine is here. It takes two days to get to the mine. First you fly this part, then you drive for a long time, here and here. Then you ride horses and llamas to here. It's so high up in the mountains there isn't much oxygen in the air so you have to breathe very deeply. And it's very cold up there at night, and I'll be sleeping in a tent, so I'll need a very warm sleeping bag."

The girls listened as he told them all about his new venture, and then excused themselves. Sue was meeting her friends to go the movies, and Sandy and Cheri had sleepovers planned.

"Why the hell are they sleeping at somebody else's house again?" Adam asked Jean as she put on her coat to drive them. He'd told Jean time after time that they could sleep in their own beds. Sleepovers were a bunch of nonsense. It wasn't their first disagreement on this topic. Adam and Jean argued frequently about what Adam saw as a lax, New World way of raising their daughters.

"Adam, we've talked about this. All the kids have sleepovers. It's just what they do. Why would we prevent our girls from joining in and having fun with their friends?" The look on her face told him the conversation was over.

Adam researched everything he could about the metal alloys markets and options for configuring the mining equipment. He and David spent time going over the details of the Penticton operations. Then he visited a travel agent to learn about the different routes for travelling between Penticton and Lima, and bought a one-way ticket. He wouldn't know until he'd been there for a while when he'd be able to get back.

CHAPTER ONE HUNDRED FORTY-ONE
1972

Back in Peru in January, Adam set up a desk in Merv's office, and found a little apartment where he could easily walk to the cliffs overlooking the beach. He needed to establish a company before he could do anything else. Minera San Diego was the name he wrote on the incorporation papers. Diego and his partner Father Juan would like that. They were well connected and Adam knew that a good relationship with them would serve him well.

After hiring a bilingual secretary, and an engineer with a bit of English, Adam set about purchasing the road-building equipment. Once road construction was underway, he would work on sourcing the mining equipment.

Each day, he dictated letters to suppliers, listing the equipment he needed and asking for quotes. The responses he got were bewildering. There was no equipment available.

"Si Jefe, this is the situation in Peru," explained his engineer. "Importation of almost every kind of goods has been banned by the new government. But in Peru, we do not have the industry to make many things. That means we cannot make it and we cannot import it. So now we have very little."

The three of them brainstormed and widened the net, writing to other mines and making calls to other engineers. No one had any suggestions. The days became weeks, and Adam began to realize that this was bigger than any business challenge he'd faced in Canada.

Peru was governed by General Velasco, who called himself "President of the Revolutionary Government." A socialist, Velasco had seized power in a military coup a few years earlier. His aim was to give justice to the poor and eliminate the wealthy class. He had nationalized entire industries already, consolidating them into large government-run entities. As Adam hit one brick wall after another, he began to appreciate how all-encompassing Velasco's control over the economic activities in Peru really was. Buying from an unauthorized supplier was illegal, and yet it was damned near impossible to find authorized suppliers. And when he did, they had no stock.

He had committed $50,000, signed a lease on a mine in a foreign country 8,000 kilometres from home, and incorporated a private company in an industry that the government was in the process of nationalizing. This was going to be difficult all right, if it was even possible.

Having achieved little, Adam booked a flight home. He'd been gone over two months. He wanted to spend some time with Jean and the girls, and give David a hand getting the mini-golf and the golf course ready to open for the season. And maybe a couple of weeks away would give him some new ideas.

CHAPTER ONE HUNDRED FORTY-TWO

Back in Penticton, the businesses were running well, but the girls were getting Bs and Cs on their report cards, another point he and Jean disagreed on. With no chores to do, Adam believed they should be getting A's. Between the report cards and not knowing what to do next in Peru, his frustration continued to grow. Then, a couple of weeks into his visit home, the phone rang.

The voice on the other end of the line said, "My name is Bruce Clymer. I'm a vice president in the marketing division of Metallurg, based in New York. Are you familiar with Metallurg?"

Adam had in fact just been reading about Metallurg, a multi-national alloy trader. They produced steel, and other alloys. They were the second largest in the world if he wasn't mistaken, founded and still wholly owned by a Jewish family.

"Somewhat," said Adam. "How can I help you?"

"We're in the market for molybdenum and I contacted Mr. Diego Madina in Lima to discuss his property in southern Peru. Mr. Diego informed me that he has entered into a legal agreement with you, giving you the rights to his mine. He was kind enough to give me your telephone number. Do you have a few minutes to talk?"

A driver was waiting when Adam walked out the front door of the John F. Kennedy Airport in New York a week later. The sign he held said MR. BAUMANN in perfect block letters. The black stretch limousine behind him gleamed in the afternoon sun.

"That's me," Adam said to the smartly uniformed man.

"Good afternoon, Mr. Baumann. Welcome to New York City. Allow me to assist with your luggage," the chauffeur replied. Tucking the sign under his arm, he relieved Adam of his suitcase with one hand, and opened the car door with the other. "Make yourself comfortable. The bar is stocked. Please help yourself. The drive will take about thirty minutes."

When Adam was shown into the boardroom the next morning, he was glad he'd bought a new suit for the meeting. The group around the table included several members of Metallurg's legal team, their vice president of finance, a vice president in the research department, and a couple of executives from marketing, including Bruce Clymer.

After sharing some facts about Metallurg, which Adam already knew from his research, the group around the table listened attentively while Adam spoke. He explained what he thought the mine could produce, and his revised estimates of what it would cost to work his way through the politics and get the mine operational. They asked good questions, and when they were satisfied with their understanding of the mine, the focus turned to a partnership between Metallurg and Adam's new company, Minera San Diego. Time passed quickly and before Adam knew it, Bruce was suggesting they break for lunch.

Adam and Bruce chatted easily while they each devoured a plateful of juicy beef ribs in a nearby diner. On their return to the office, a message awaited them.

"Mr. Grunfeld would like to see you," Bruce's secretary announced to Adam.

Ernst Grunfeld was the patriarch of the Jewish family that owned Metallurg. Bruce had warned Adam not to be surprised by the dialysis equipment in Mr. Grunfeld's office. The man was not well. But when Grunfeld spoke, he was anything but frail.

"Good afternoon, Mr. Baumann. May I call you Adam?" he asked with a warm smile. "I hope the meetings downstairs are going to your satisfaction. I won't keep you for too long. I asked Bruce if you could spare some time for me, to tell me a bit about yourself. It's always nice to know a bit about the people you are considering doing business with. Makes for better partnerships. Baumann is a German name, if I'm not mistaken?"

"Yes, sir, it is. My family is Hungarian German."

"Why don't you tell me a little bit about your family and how you came to live in Canada, if I may ask, and involved with a mine in Peru?"

"Well, I was raised in Hungary until my family was deported after the war. My father was drafted into the Hungarian army, but because he wasn't a young man, he was just driving wagons, hauling supplies and that type of thing. I was only a young teenager at that time." Mentioning his time in the German military likely wouldn't reflect well on him, considering his audience, so Adam fast-forwarded over that part of the story. "Unfortunately, after the war ended, the Hungarian government stripped my father of everything we owned, and sent us to Germany as penniless refugees. The Germans really didn't want us there, but eventually we settled in. I trained as a bricklayer, and when I was 22, I emigrated to Canada. That was 20 years ago. I've had a variety of businesses since that time, primarily in construction and mining. I also own and operate a little amusement park that I built years ago in my hometown in Canada. I became interested in the mine in Peru last year when I travelled to Lima on a holiday." Adam explained how he'd come to visit the mine site. "I was tremendously excited by what I saw. So when the owner asked me if I would like to lease the property and build a proper mine to get at all that moly, I agreed. There's a great demand for molybdenum, as you know of course."

"You're quite right about that. And I suppose you and I have something in common besides an interest in molybdenum. The German government stripped my family of everything during the war too. We were some of the lucky ones that escaped. And we already had some international holdings so we were able to rebuild."

They chatted for a while longer before the old man dismissed Adam to return to the meeting.

As talks in the boardroom resumed, Adam was eager to reach an agreement. Based on what he'd learned in the first couple of months of the year, he was going to need a lot more time and money than he'd thought to get the mine open. Metallurg's involvement could be the answer.

Midway through the afternoon, Bruce indicated it was time for a break. Adam followed him out to a little courtyard and lit a cigarette. When Bruce had his own cigarette going, he turned to Adam and spoke quietly. "The old man told them to make a deal, so hold firm. You're in the driver's seat. They are very shrewd negotiators, but they have their orders from upstairs and he wants a deal by end of day. So don't give any more. Just hold your ground and wait."

"If you mine as well as you negotiate, this is going to be a very successful venture," one of the lawyers said as they shook hands a couple of hours later.

Metallurg would be providing half a million dollars for the construction of the mine. The first installment would come the following week. Adam would remain the majority owner, in full control of Minera San Diego. The only condition was that they had right of first refusal to buy all the molybdenum the mine produced.

CHAPTER ONE HUNDRED FORTY-THREE

Continuing on to Lima, Adam was on cloud nine. A multi-national company, the second biggest alloy producer in the world, was funding his new venture. Knowing he had the cash to do what needed to be done, he could focus on the work and figure out how to get around the obstacles that popped up everywhere he looked. And figure out he did.

Before his last trip home, he'd learned that there was a two-year wait list for telephone installations. He couldn't wait two years to set up a proper office, and obviously he would need phone lines for that. He also needed a more permanent place to live. The apartment was tiny, even for him, and Jean would be joining him eventually. A few weeks of asking around and turning over every rock he could think of, he'd found a solution to both problems – a house with a large office on the main floor that had a functioning multi-line phone system already built in. Next, he overcame the embargo on importing domestic goods by buying a houseful of furniture and appliances from ex-pats who were leaving the country. When his purchases had been moved into the new house, Adam stood back and surveyed his work with satisfaction. A couple of big hurdles out of the way.

But he still had a long way to go, even to finish setting up the house. Thankfully, Rudy Garcia, an American geologist he'd met through his persistent daily research and networking in the business circles of Lima, introduced Adam to his wife Mona. Learning that Adam's house still needed many things from linens to dishes, Mona swooped in and took over. She and Rudy had been in Lima for years, since before Velasco, when you could still buy what you wanted from whomever you wanted. The locals knew her. Tall, with flaming red hair cascading down over her shoulders, she intimidated them even when she didn't mean to, towering over them explaining what she needed in that booming voice. Adam went out shopping with her when he could, watching and learning with amusement, as they outfitted the house using the sources and methods Mona knew.

Then there was the matter of a maid. He had a stove, and sure, he could cook if he needed to, but he didn't have time for that. And even if he did, he didn't have time to shop for groceries. If he was going to beat the system and get this mine running, he needed to focus. Mona had three maids. Her Maria would be perfect for him, she told Adam emphatically. Maria didn't speak any English but she was very capable of running the whole house on her own without direction from a woman of the house. The problem was that when Mona had talked to her about it, Maria had refused.

"Why won't she come?" asked Adam. He had stopped by to have a drink after work and find out what Rudy knew about a guy named Korteba who reconditioned used mining equipment. It was the only lead he'd come up with so far.

"Because you scare her," replied Mona.

"What do you mean I scare her?" Adam laughed out loud.

"Well, you have a very loud voice and you come in here and say 'Good Morning!' and they say they can hear you two blocks away. These gals aren't used to that. They're used to Rudy." Rudy was soft spoken.

"Aren't they scared of you, Mona?" he laughed again.

"I'm a woman, so it's different. And the other thing is that your wife isn't here. Maria says she can't live in the house with a single man."

"Well, I won't bite, and I'll keep my distance, and I'll talk softly to her."

"I'll work on it," Mona assured him.

While Adam focused on trying to understand how to do business in this country, the house desperately needed attention. He'd been taking his clothes to a little laundry nearby before he bought the washing machine and dryer along with all the other stuff from the American ex-pat. He was still doing that because every time he went to the grocery store he forgot laundry soap. The secretary had cleaned the bathroom she used, but the rest needed it too. He was out of coffee and milk again and the meat he'd bought the week before had gone bad before he'd had time to make the stew he'd bought it for. Now there was nothing in the fridge again. He was tired of dry noodles and he didn't have time to go out.

When Mona called to say she'd talked with Maria again and they'd come up with a plan, Adam breathed a sigh of relief. If Maria could bring her younger sister Carmen who was still in high school, and her miniature poodle Negrito, she would come. Adam would have to feed all three of them and pay her fifty dollars a month, the same as what Mona had been paying her. Under these conditions Maria would agree to run Adam's house and take care of him.

Two days later, Adam looked out from the veranda as he drank his morning coffee. There was Maria, Negrito under one arm and a big suitcase in her other hand. Her sister Carmen, laden with bags, followed along behind as they crossed the street towards the house. Adam grinned and headed downstairs to let them in. Another milestone.

CHAPTER ONE HUNDRED FORTY-FOUR

But on the business side, Adam wasn't having any luck.

The geologists from Metallurg had waived the need for a formal exploration phase when they'd come to perform the formal inspection of the mine that was stipulated in the contract.

"Strongest showing we've ever seen," they'd said.

The molybdenum was there waiting, but he couldn't get to it.

He'd visited the site again to do more detailed planning and his list of equipment needs had grown. In order to cut the road in through the mountainside he was going to need an industrial compressor, an industrial hammer drill and drill heads, a big electric generator to run it all, a backhoe or a front-end loader of some sort, and a couple of dump trucks. For the mine he needed a larger capacity ball mill, a new crusher, an electric motor to replace the gasoline truck motor they had out there now, a backup generator, and a myriad of other components. Building supplies to build bunkhouses, a decent kitchen and mess hall, and a new supply shed were also on the list.

His enquiries still turned up nothing, other than this Korteba fellow who reconditioned equipment, and Adam didn't want used equipment. He found a company that was government approved to sell the electric motors he needed, and apparently they had engines in stock. That would be one piece off the list. He went and had a look. Junk. They wouldn't last a month.

Adam ripped one page after another from the calendar on his office wall, and still he was no closer to opening the mine. Not even any leads on where to get equipment. More than six months already, and all he had to show for it was a house, a payroll, and three hundred llamas.

CHAPTER ONE HUNDRED FORTY-FIVE

"Miguel, Lucho! Dos truchas! Rapido!" the woman in the little roadside restaurant yelled out the back door towards the creek, as Adam and Cornelius settled at a tiny table made from an old plank resting on a couple of Coca-Cola crates. Cornelius, the foreman Adam had hired to be his right-hand man, had greeted the woman and ordered two breakfasts.

The restaurant was a shack perched on the bank below the road. It looked out over a scenic little valley with a creek running through it that sparkled in the morning sunshine. Adam and Cornelius had set out from Cusco early and they were hungry when they spotted the little sign in the middle of nowhere with "Desayunos Trucha Fresca" scrawled on it, and an arrow pointing down over the bank. A breakfast of fresh trout sounded perfect. Peru was full of these fun little surprises, and Adam rarely passed them up.

But that morning, his mind went back to business as soon as they were seated. "I visited a couple of mines that this Korteba has built. They looked pretty good, and everyone I've talked to had good things to say about him. His installations run well and apparently there's no more maintenance than you'd expect with new equipment. I'm thinking seriously about going with reconditioned equipment."

Adam stopped talking and the two men watched with a combination of awe and amusement as two little boys came to the back door of the shack and handed the woman a couple of shiny, dripping trout. They each held a little willow stick with a string tied to it in their other hand.

"Now that's fresh trout!" said Cornelius, as the woman cleaned the fish at lightning speed and threw them into a pan on the tiny stovetop set up along the back wall of the shack.

By December, Korteba had a line on a used ball mill and a cone crusher for Minera San Diego. They were only 60-ton capacity, but it would be a good start. Adam gave him the go ahead to do the design for the mine, purchase the components, and start the reconditioning work.

Around the same time, he had a breakthrough on road-building equipment. The South American Industrial Exposition, an international trade show for large and small construction equipment, would be held in Lima later that year. The exhibitors couldn't legally sell anything in Peru, but Metallurg could transact with them through U.S. banks. At the end of the show a couple of months later, the vendors packed up and went home, leaving behind the equipment Adam needed to begin road construction.

To celebrate, he booked a week-long layover in Panama on his way home for the holidays. Jean would have things under control at home, and there were so many more countries and cultures to explore in this part of the world.

Shortly after Christmas, Adam received a telephone call from Bruce Clymber in New York. Metallurg was getting impatient. A year had passed since they had begun investing, and the price of molybdenum was continuing to climb.

"We're sending a couple of our best men to help you," he explained. "They're geologists, but more importantly, they've both set up mines around the world. Hopefully, they can help move things along down there. The old man upstairs is getting nervous."

First, Adam took the two visitors from Metallurg to Korteba's shop to inspect the equipment that was being rebuilt for him. They needed to see that he was making some progress on sourcing equipment. And they'd believe Korteba when he explained the business environment in Peru and the challenges Adam had been up against.

After a day at Korteba's shop, the experts from Metallurg had indeed begun to understand what was taking so long.

Next, they were supposed to help Adam plan the most expeditious approach to installing the equipment and getting the mine operational. Only one of the geologists would be able to travel to the mine site though. The other had visited the site when Metallurg had decided to waive the formal exploration phase, and suffered badly from altitude sickness.

Five minutes after arriving at the mine site the geologist who had come along said he needed to lie down. He was as white as a sheet.

Adam heard moaning from the tent a few minutes later. Then his name being called out.

"Adam... Adam!"

"What's wrong?" Adam responded.

"For the love of Allah, take me off this mountain."

"Try to get some sleep. Sleep is good for altitude sickness. You will feel better."

"Adam, I can't sleep. I'm dying. I will give you my wife and my daughter, and my cabin on the island in southern Turkey if you take me down the mountain."

He moaned for a while longer. Then finally, the tent went quiet.

A couple of days later, the two Metallurg geologists left Peru. But first, they assured Adam their report would inform the big bosses in New York that he was doing everything that could be done in the circumstances, and they had no recommendations.

CHAPTER ONE HUNDRED FORTY-SIX
1973

That spring, Adam was optimistic. It was looking like it was going to be a productive year. Maria was congratulating him regularly on his command of Spanish. "El jefe es un hombre muy inteligente," she told him. *The boss is a very smart man.* He practiced constantly, adding new words daily as he chatted with everyone he encountered, laughing along at his mistakes. And more importantly, all of the road-building equipment was in position, ready for construction to begin. They'd walked the route several times, marking it all out. It wasn't just the last section, between the llama herder's hut and the mine that they needed to build. Several miles of road back from there were too narrow and rough to get the mining equipment through. They would be building about ten miles of road in total. When the road was done they would haul in materials and build a proper camp, but tents would have to suffice for a while longer.

Despite Adam's optimism, progress on the road was slow. One week he had to pay off a lien that had mysteriously appeared on the dump trucks he'd purchased. Another week half the crew didn't show up. Then a mudslide covered the road they had just cut into the next section of hillside, and it had to be redone. Always it was something and each time the schedule slipped a bit more. To mitigate the time the road was taking, Adam and Cornelius began hauling in small items using a pickup truck and the llamas. Then, when the road was complete enough to get small trucks over, they transported the rest of the building materials for the camp and the mine housing.

In the meantime, back in his shop in Lima, Korteba was busy integrating the additional mill and crusher Adam had purchased under the table from a German miner he'd met in Lima, and the electric motor that Diego had helped smuggle in from Chile. Together, all of this would give them 100 tons of capacity.

Once again, the year was almost over. Adam decided to spend a few more days at the mine site prior to heading home for Christmas. He wanted to help Cornelius make some progress on the buildings at the site. The road was finally nearing completion, and everything had to be ready to go after the holidays.

He'd done the two-day trip with Juvenal or Cornelius many times, but this would be the first time he would be driving from Lima to the mine by himself. The downpour started a couple of hours after he'd turned off the highway onto the dirt road that wound up and down through the mountains to Chalhuanca where he would spend the night. It was the wet season in the Andes. He'd heard about these storms, but so far, he hadn't experienced one. Within minutes, water from the slope above was rushing onto the road. The windshield wipers slapping back and forth on the highest speed weren't enough to keep the window clear. Slowing to a crawl, Adam considered his options. Darkness was falling. The road was narrow and winding, with steep drop-offs in places. His best guess was at least another half-hour at normal speed to reach the little hotel where they always stayed. If he turned back, the nearest town would be considerably further.

He crept along, the torrential rain pelting down on the car. A few minutes later, Adam's anxiety rose. A thick fog was rolling in, covering the car like a heavy grey woollen blanket. The water raging along the road was rising. His tires slid precariously in and out of the ruts being carved deeper each second by the river running down the road. Adam strained to see where the edge was. How steep was the bank here? Suddenly, a flash of lightening illuminated the driving rain that shredded the thick blanket of fog. Simultaneously, a deafening clap of thunder shook the car. Afraid of driving off the side of the road, Adam considered stopping to wait out the storm. But if he stopped and the water continued to rise, would it wash him over the edge? Gripping the steering wheel, he peered through the film of water and the blur of the wipers beating side to side and put the car back in gear.

He didn't know how long he'd inched along the mountainside, but he was beginning to suspect he'd missed a turn. He should have reached the little town by now. He kept moving, hoping he was wrong and that Chalhuanca would appear in front of him. If he had in fact missed a turn, how far back had it been? He couldn't recall the road well enough to say. The rain wasn't letting up. He had to find the town, or some other place where he could pull over for the night.

As the minutes passed, he became more and more sure he was on the wrong road. He was lost. Then a tiny light appeared up ahead for just a moment before it disappeared again into the fog. He squinted to where the light had been as he eased the car along. A moment later, he saw the glimmer again, off to the right. Gently, so that he didn't send the car into a slide, he applied the brakes and stopped. Draping his light jacket over his head, he got out of the car and walked around to the front, peering into the darkness, trying to make out what was off to the side of the road. The gravelly roadside appeared to extend out level, past his short range of visibility, and the light that he'd spotted was shining dimly through the mist at the same level as where he was standing.

Getting back in the car, he inched it off the road toward the light, holding his breath. The ground was level! About thirty feet from the road, a tiny rock hut emerged in his headlights. Adam had seen these huts many times on the hillsides and plateaus in this area. If you didn't look closely, it was easy to mistake them for piles of rocks. The light was coming from the hut's single tiny window. Adam turned off the car. Covering his head with his jacket once again, he ran through the rain to the hut and pounded on the door.

"Hola!" he yelled over the storm. "Hola!"

After a few moments, the door opened a foot or so.

"Hola," he said to the wide-eyed little man who peered up him, wracking his brain for Spanish words he could use to explain that he was lost.

The next morning, not a cloud could be seen in the bright blue sky. Adam waved to the little family as he drove the car back onto the road and headed in the direction he'd come. With a few hours' sleep and a full belly, he felt like new.

Huddled in the downpour outside the door of the hut the night before, Adam had quickly surmised that the man spoke only the Quechua language like most locals this high up. After pointing around and shrugging his shoulders a few times, he'd been let into the candlelit warmth of the one room hut. The man had spoken a few words to his wife, and she'd laid a woolly mat on the floor for Adam, like the one they and their little daughter slept on.

At first light, the woman had gone outside for a few minutes and came back carrying two limp guinea pigs. Quickly, she'd stripped their skin off and cleaned out their insides. Their ribcages had made a cracking sound as she'd flattened them with her fist before placing them on a hot grill over the little fire on the floor of the hut, while the little girl scooped something white into a bowl and mixed in some water. The fried "cuy" as the guinea pigs the locals raised for food was known, and the potato mash that had been served with it, had smelled and tasted delicious. Adam had done his best to express his appreciation with gestures and expressions as they sat quietly eating together in the smoky little room.

The road to the mine was easy to find in the daylight. Whistling as he drove, Adam reflected on the many adventures he'd had in Peru so far. Despite, or maybe partially because of the countless obstacles, he was having fun.

CHAPTER ONE HUNDRED FORTY-SEVEN
1974

Over the holidays, he and Jean discussed plans for her to join him in Peru. Sue would be graduating from high school in June. Adam had been in Peru for two years and the girls were growing up. Soon he and Jean would be empty nesters. They'd talked a number of times in the last few years about each of the girls spending some time in Germany after high school, perhaps attending college near Laudenbach. It was time to sell the house at Sage Mesa and rent an apartment in town for Jean and the girls until they made further plans.

The road to the mine was finally ready. Adam and Cornelius celebrated with a dinner of roast goat at Adam's favourite restaurant in Lima. But as luck would have it, just as he was making the final arrangements to transport the mine equipment to the site, more government snags arose – big ones. Adam read through the announcement with disbelief. It said that private mining permits were no longer being granted. In addition, the government had established *Minpeco*, a state-owned corporation, to market Peru's mining production to the world. All product had to be turned over to Minpeco, who would market it and pay the producer their share, based on whatever price they'd negotiated. Adam couldn't operate his mine without a permit. And having Minpeco sell his molybdenum on the open market would violate the main condition in his contract with Metallurg, tanking the entire project.

Then Cornelius called with yet another problem. He'd left Lima the day before at the head of a convoy of flatbed trucks loaded down with mine equipment.

"We were making pretty good time. I figured we would reach the mine site by tomorrow afternoon. But we can't make it through Querobamba. The street isn't wide enough. There's one spot in particular where there's just no way. We've been stopped for a couple of hours."

Adam knew the little town Cornelius was talking about and recalled how the narrow little road meandered through it.

"And there's no way around?" he asked.

"No. I've looked at every option. We need to take down a house."

"You're kidding me."

"I am definitely not kidding you," Cornelius assured him. "People started gathering in the roadway and getting all excited, so I asked them to get the mayor. He came down and talked to me, but now he wants to talk to you. Wants to negotiate some kind of deal, but only with *El Jefe*."

El Jefe. Boss. He'd have to go.

"I didn't know a town that small even had a mayor," Adam said. "Tell him I'll be there by this time tomorrow." He'd set up meetings with Diego to work on the government obstacles. Now that would have to wait.

The mayor of Querobamba listened attentively while Adam explained the problem. With a mountain on each side and the little town filling the narrow valley, there was no way to get trucks through. And a lot of local people were depending on this equipment in order to have a job and make a living. Of course, they wanted to minimize the impact on the town, and if they could just move one house, the problem would be solved.

When Adam finished his explanation, the mayor looked at him for a long time. Then he nodded. He agreed with Adam that it was important for the trucks to get through and he was willing to have one house moved. He wasn't sure yet about the cost, but he would speak to his people. He appreciated Adam coming all the way from Lima to meet with him, and when he knew the cost, he would come to Lima and meet with Adam. Until then, the trucks were stuck.

Three days later, Adam's doorbell rang. The mayor, a priest from Querobamba, and another small, dark-skinned man were there to see El Jefe.

"We talked to the man who lives in that house with his family," the mayor explained when they'd all been seated in Adam's office. "We will move his house, but in exchange we need some things."

"Of course, I understand. What are the things you need?" Adam asked.

The priest spoke first. "The roof of the church is leaking. We need twenty sheets of metal to fix it."

"Okay," Adam said slowly. "Anything else?"

"We also need a typewriter," said the mayor.

"A typewriter?" Adam asked.

Yes, they needed a typewriter. And the equivalent of about a hundred dollars in Peruvian money.

"I can deliver these items the day after tomorrow. Can you have the house moved on the same day? As I said, there are many people waiting for these trucks."

Three days later, the equipment finally reached the mine site.

CHAPTER ONE HUNDRED FORTY-EIGHT

The site had been well prepared, and Korteba had done a good job of readying the equipment for installation. Soon Adam was waiting anxiously as the test loads were mined and evaluated.

The news wasn't good. The molybdenum came out too wet. It was too heavy to transport.

Adam sat in his little room in the new bunkhouse, his head in his hands, waiting. *How could this be happening?* Korteba had asked for a couple of hours to think about the problem. When he heard the conclusion, Adam sighed heavily. They needed to add a kiln. Korteba figured he could find the parts, build it, and install it in less than six months. Korteba was a realist, that much Adam appreciated. But they were out of money. Maybe it was time to concede defeat.

A few days later, back at the office, Adam sighed again as he picked up the phone to call New York. He couldn't think of any other option. They were so close. But with the half million spent, he needed another injection of cash. Metallurg had already waited two and a half years without any molybdenum. He wasn't optimistic.

When the response came, Adam was faced with a choice. Surprisingly, they would be willing to provide additional funding, but only in exchange for majority ownership of Minera San Diego. He didn't hesitate long. He wasn't in a position of strength any more. They wanted control of the mine. He just wanted to finish what he'd started.

With the new cash, Adam placed the order for the kiln, and then turned his attention to other problems. They still hadn't received a permit to operate.

Diego had done no small amount of charity work over the years, the type that appealed to the sensibilities of the Velasco regime. With his vast connections in the socialist circles that ran the government, he'd been working on the permitting issue in the background, while Adam waited impatiently. The call came soon after Adam returned to the mine. Diego had secured a meeting for him with the Minister of Mines to plead his case in two days' time. Adam jumped into his car and headed back down the mountain. There would be just enough time to make it.

Adam felt and heard the *THUD!* at the same time. In his rush, he'd been navigating the ruts faster than he should have, and he'd bottomed out. Something had hit the undercarriage of the car, hard.

"Goddammit!" he cursed, slamming his hand on the steering wheel as he watched the oil pressure fall to zero. Shutting off the engine, he got out of the car and started walking. Sometimes it was hours between vehicles on these roads. At least there was lots of daylight left. About a half-hour later a car came along and stopped when he waved. At the first house they came to, Adam crawled out of the car and thanked the driver. The yard was full of chickens. A donkey grazed quietly nearby. He could see movement a couple of rows into the cornfield beside the little house.

"Buenas tardes!" he called out. *Good afternoon!* Sure enough, a man emerged from the cornfield. Adding hand gestures to help make sure he was understood, Adam explained in broken Spanish what had happened and asked if the farmer would help him get the car down the mountain to the next town. When that didn't work, he showed the man the Peruvian money he had in his pocket and motioned that he could have it if he came and helped.

The little posse made a peculiar sight, the wife and two daughters clad in their large brown hats and countless layers of heavy colourful skirts, the farmer pulling his donkey along behind on a rope, and Adam towering over them all. The walk back to the car along the dusty road took an hour. Despite Adam's attempts to converse, the little family was quiet. When they reached the car, the man tied the donkey to the front bumper, then spoke rapidly to his wife and daughters in the indigenous language. The women arranged themselves behind the car to push. Next, he motioned Adam to get in and steer.

People stopped to watch as they dragged the car through the little town an hour and a half later. When they reached the garage, Adam paid the farmer and thanked the women. Then he walked into the garage to talk to the mechanic.

"The oil is all gone," Adam explained in Spanish. "I need you to fix it please."

The mechanic slid under the car for a quick look, then shimmied back out and stood up beside Adam.

"Dos dias," he announced. The time to ship a new oil pan from Lima.

"Two days?! I don't have two days. I don't have two hours. How about if you patch this oil pan using your welding machine, and then I can drive back to Lima and get a new oil pan there. Do you think you could patch the hole?"

The mechanic tipped his head to the side and thought about Adam's suggestion. Then he nodded. "Si Señor. I think so. I'll give it a try."

An hour later Adam drove out of the yard, oil pan good as new. Or at least good enough to drive to Lima in time for the big meeting.

Amazingly, he made it in time. The Minister of Mining was a pleasant enough man. Adam had prepared his key points carefully, and he delivered them with what he hoped was the right mix of confidence and humility. He started by explaining that he had been working for many years building a mine on the property of his good friend Diego Madina. In that time, he had come to know the people in the villages, and very much appreciated the good work the government was doing to help them. He was aware that the government did not approve of private mines which often took unfair advantage of workers from the lower class and padded the pockets of the wealthy. He assured the Minister that he valued his workforce very much. He had just finished construction of new bunkhouses for his men and a nice new kitchen where they would be provided with hot meals. He wasn't in a position to sell the mine to the government, as he was only a minority shareholder of Minera San Diego, but he did have operational control and he would be the one to ensure that the 90 men whom he employed would be treated well. And finally, he could assure the Minister of an immediate buyer for his molybdenum. Metallurg, an American company based in New York, would be interested in buying everything he produced, matching whatever price Minpeco could get on the open market.

Adam had done his best. He had made the advantages to the workers and the country clear. But he could not control what the Minister would decide.

"Feliz Navidad!" said Diego when he called Adam a couple of weeks later. "I have just had a phone call from the Minister's office and I think you will be receiving a letter very shortly, giving you special permission to operate a private mine in Peru. Have a wonderful Christmas with your family my friend, and hurry back."

They were legal.

CHAPTER ONE HUNDRED FORTY-NINE
1975

When Adam returned for his fourth January in Peru, the kiln had been installed and the test loads were good. Packing a few extra changes of underclothes into his bag, he made the drive to the mine site.

Two days later, he woke up early. This was the day they were going to start mining. It would be slow for the first couple of days while they trained the crew, and then they'd be in full production.

As the workers began to file out of the cookhouse after breakfast, Adam waited outside with the huge bag of coca leaves he'd picked up on his way up the mountain. He wanted a happy crew.

"Coca?" he said, motioning to the bag. The little men grinned and headed in Adam's direction.

As each guy filed past, Adam reached into the bag and transferred a big handful to the pouch the guy held open to him.

"Maki hatun," one of the little men said to him with a big grin. Adam didn't understand the Quechuan words. "Maki hatun," he repeated holding up his hand.

"They like your big hands," said Juvenal from where he'd been watching nearby. "Big hands, lots of coca for the day."

A week later the cone crusher blew a seal.

"The seal is completely shredded," Korteba announced.

"Can you repair it? Patch it?" Adam asked. He already knew the answer. Seals were precisely manufactured and no patch job would work.

"Once I have a new seal it'll only take an hour to fix. But I can't fix the seal itself," Korteba confirmed.

"Can we run without a seal for any period of time?"

"The oil from the machine would contaminate the concentrate."

"Okay, so where do we get a seal?" Adam's mind was racing.

"I'm pretty sure this is the only *Kue Ken Crusher* in Peru. We could start phoning around and looking, but I'd be willing to bet you're going to have to get it from Oakland, California, where this machine is manufactured."

"We both know we can't order something from outside the country without all the right ministerial permissions, which will take forever to get." The four men stood silently for a few moments. Then Adam spoke again. "I'll call Metallurg. Maybe if they order it and pay for it from New York and it's shipped to me with zero value, it'll get through customs." Adam turned and headed for the bunkhouse to grab his bag. "I'll call them from Abancay."

Cornelius was standing nearby listening to the conversation. "What the hell are we going to do with the crew while we wait?" he asked Adam.

"Keep them here. I'm going to find a way to get the seal. Tell them it's only a couple of days and they'll be working again. Remind them they don't want to lose their jobs and tell them El Jefe wants them to stay and wait. I don't want to have to find a new bloody crew and repeat the training."

Metallurg ordered the seal a few hours later, and on the third day, it arrived at the Lima airport.

"I'm sorry, sir," the customs official at the airport said to Adam. "I can't release your package without the paperwork that says that you have the necessary ministerial approvals to order this item from outside the country."

Adam drove back to his office. Every few blocks he slammed his hand on the steering wheel and let out a string of Romanian curses.

When he reached the house, he went straight to the telephone. "Diego, I got a big problem. Can I come over and talk to you?"

Father Juan was with Diego when Adam reached their apartment and sat down to explain.

"I got the seal into the country. I got the engineer sitting up there waiting to repair it. I got 90 guys up there eating an ox a day. And I can't get the damned $20 package from behind the customs counter," he finished up, throwing his arms in the air and getting up to pace around the spacious penthouse apartment.

Father Juan knew what to do.

CHAPTER ONE HUNDRED FIFTY

Adam waited for Father Juan on the steps of the government office, holding the bag of cash the priest had asked him to bring. The priest's neatly pressed black robe rustled as he climbed the steps, and his freshly starched white clerical collar gleamed almost as much as his neatly oiled hair. Adam didn't see him in his official garb often.

"Okay, let's start with the Ministry of Mines," Father Juan said to Adam with a grin.

Adam led the way to the door marked *"Ministerio de Minas."* He'd been in the big waiting room many times, getting approvals for this or that.

As they entered the big room, Father Juan leaned over and spoke quietly. "Follow me." Then he walked across the room and opened another door, and stood aside to let Adam enter ahead of him. The room was abuzz with activity. It usually took at least an hour, often two, to get to the front of the line and be admitted to this room.

Father Juan walked towards a table in the centre of the room where an official sat across from a customer, studying the paperwork in front of him while the customer waited. Choosing a spot near enough the table that there could be no mistake about his intention to be processed next, Father Juan stood with his hands behind his back, rocking slowly back and forth from toes to heels, a pleasant smile on his face. Adam stood beside him.

A few minutes later, the official stamped the papers he'd been reading and the customer got up and left.

Father Juan and Adam sat down in front of the official and Adam listened while Father Juan explained the urgent situation in which they found themselves, and the problems that this situation was causing for the workers in the villages and their families. The official listened patiently and then assured them he understood the situation. Next, he told them his price.

Father Juan turned to Adam and spoke in English. "Put the money on the table."

Adam felt a bit of sweat break out on his forehead as he reached into the bag and placed a stack of dirty bills in the centre of the table.

"Gracias, Señor," said the official as he picked up the money and put it into his desk drawer.

A few minutes later, Adam and Father Juan left the office. They had the first approval stamp.

Three more ministries, three more stacks of cash, and they were racing towards the airport. They didn't know what time the customs office closed, but it was going to be tight.

"Dammit!" yelled Adam, as they pulled up in front of the building. The door was padlocked shut.

A phone call and one more bribe, and the door was open. They had the seal.

Adam made record time on the 18-hour drive back to the mine.

"How long will it take to get it installed?" he asked as he handed over the seal.

"Like I said, an hour," Korteba replied, grinning.

"We won't be able to run full steam for another day or two anyway," Cornelius said from the door of the bunkhouse.

"Why not?" Adam demanded.

"A bunch of the crew disappeared yesterday. Walked home apparently. Juvenal says it's some festival. Tomato festival, potato festival. I don't know, something like that."

"What the hell?" Adam roared as he turned to look at Juvenal.

"There's a festival every month or two. Different ones in different villages," Juvenal explained. "They'll go no matter what rules you try to make. These festivals are very old traditions. Lots of dancing and drinking chicha. They'll be gone for a day, maybe two, and then they'll come back."

Juvenal was right. The next day they ran what they could without a full crew, and that evening the workers wandered back in without a word of explanation. Less than a week later, the truck was full. The first load of product was ready to roll!

Adam followed the load to Lima. After he'd watched them unload it at the port, he drove to the office and called Metallurg.

"Bruce Clymer, please," he said when the switchboard operator answered. "It's coming Bruce," he said into the receiver a few moments later. "The first load of moly just hit the port."

"Congratulations, Adam. I'll let the big guy know."

Adam sat back in his chair after he hung up the phone, and took a deep breath.

"Maria," he called out.

"Si Jefe?" Maria answered, appearing in the door of his office.

"Jean is going to be arriving in a few days, remember? Mi esposa, tres dias? Necessitamos una fiesta. We got a lot to celebrate."

CHAPTER ONE HUNDRED FIFTY-ONE

Jean settled in happily, and she and Maria were soon fast friends. With Adam away at the mine much of the time, Jean got to know the expat community, and took Spanish lessons in the afternoons when she wasn't playing bridge with her new friends. When he was home, Adam delighted in showing Jean all the nooks and crannies of Lima that he'd discovered. Together they discovered more, enjoying sunsets on the beach and dining on Peruvian delicacies in out of the way places.

That Christmas, Sandy and Cheri visited. Pleased to have them in Peru, away from the frivolity of their daily lives, Adam booked a tour for the girls – several days trekking through remote areas, sleeping in little villages and canoeing through the rainforest. Although he didn't have the time, or the inclination to go along after the four years he'd already spent finding his way around Peru, he wanted his girls to experience it. He'd always wanted that for them, the richness of travel and discovery.

Then, less than a year later, a scant two years after the first load of molybdenum was finally shipped to Metallurg, the vein disappeared. Where a rich, four-foot-wide vein of molybdenum-laden quartz had been, the crew suddenly hit sand. Nothing but sand. For months they dug and drilled in every direction, trying to locate the vein, but the search was fruitless. The only explanation Adam and his colleagues from Metallurg could come up with was that at some point in history an earthquake or some other natural event had shifted the mountainside in that area.

In hindsight, if Metallurg hadn't waived the formal explanation phase in their eagerness to get the molybdenum quickly, the end of the vein would likely have been detected at that time. Perhaps the mine project would not have happened at all. An expensive lesson for Metallurg. But personally, Adam was glad. Peru had been the best adventure of his life so far.

With no further production forthcoming, the decision to close down the mine was inevitable. It had been a good run, and it was time to go home. As Jean packed up the house and headed back to Penticton,

Adam focused on dismantling the mine and selling off the components so that Metallurg could recover a portion of their investment. To overcome the legalities of moving personal money out of Peru, he converted the proceeds from the house and contents to precious metals – silver serving trays, fine cutlery, gold jewelry, and similar items that could be carried home as personal effects.

As he completed the wind-down of Minera San Diego, the only private mine to have operated in Peru during the Velasco era, Adam's mind was already busy scanning through possibilities for his next project. The mini-storage units he'd built before he'd left for Peru had been fully occupied since they were completed, and there was a waiting list. The opportunity seemed obvious, but the problem was land. Storage took up a lot of space and all the feelers he put out came back with the same answer. There was no commercial land available in Penticton.

As he sipped his scotch in the quiet of a tranquil Lima evening, not long before returning to Canada, Adam thought through the options. He had a few ideas. He was already hungry for the next challenge, and one way or another, he'd find it.

EPILOGUE

Maria had always said that Adam and Jean treated her differently than any other employer. She was free to spend the house allowance as she saw fit. No receipts were needed. And they insisted that she eat what they ate. No cornflour porridge or tortillas and beans while the boss dined on her marvellous cooking. When they ate steak, she ate steak. When they ate seafood, she ate seafood. She kept Adam and Jean up to date on her life after they left, with regular cards and letters and photos of all the important events. When she mentioned that it had been especially hot one year, especially with the corrugated metal roofing on her house, Adam found someone who was travelling to Lima, and sent Maria forty $100 bills, enough for put a good, insulated roof.

Back in Canada, Adam poured his energy into building, finding property when property was scarce, challenging various by-laws and restrictions when they impacted his vision for a given project, and generally doing things that hadn't been done before. Soon his portfolio of commercial property was generating a healthy revenue stream, second only to his empire of mini-storage units.

He had never liked wood construction and after returning from Peru, Adam began to dream of a luxury apartment building made of concrete. As their holidays abroad increased, he and Jean looked at many concrete apartment buildings, leaning towards the art deco style. Adam had his eye on a piece of prime real estate for the building, overlooking the lake in Penticton, and in 1984 it became available through a foreclosure. It was perfect. However, the country was suffering through a major recession. Interest rates were close to 20 percent and the economy was stagnant. When Adam announced his plans to build a luxury, "poured in place" concrete condominium tower, his friends and associates told him he was crazy. And he planned to build it seven storeys high. The municipal by-laws limited construction to six storeys. This time he was pushing it too far. Even the mayor personally advised Adam strongly against the project.

"This town isn't ready for something like that," was what everyone told him. "They won't sell."

As usual, Adam was determined. '*86 Lakeshore,*' the south Okanagan's first "poured in place" concrete residential building, was constructed in 1986. No expense was spared. In 1987 Jean and Adam moved into one of the two penthouse units on the seventh floor. The building was fully sold in record time, and many of the original owners, including the Baumanns, continue to live there today.

After operating the mini-golf and full-size par three for almost 40 years, Adam sold Riverside Golf in the mid 90's. To this day the park is still providing amusement to kids and adults alike over 60 years since the opening weekend in May of 1958.

Adam's dad passed away in 1992. From the time he and Adam's mom returned to Germany in 1969 until his death, he focused more on the enjoyment and adventures of their time in Canada, and the success of his kids, than on the injustices of the past. He continued to worry that Adam would "go broke" with all the risks he took, but they enjoyed an easy relationship during this time, and Adam came to appreciate how proud of him his dad really was.

A year after his father's death, Adam travelled to Germany to collect the one thing he wanted from his dad's personal effects - the leather razor strap that had warmed his rear end so often in his childhood and teen years. He planned to set it under glass. Unfortunately, it had disappeared, so Adam was never able to create this tribute to his father and all he learned from him.

His mom lived with Theresa until her death in 1998. Near the end, her three sons travelled together to Germany for one last family visit. Adam laughs when he recounts a memory from that trip. "Frank, George, and I had cleared out of the house on Sunday morning to have a few schnapps with the men from the neighbourhood and work up our appetites, as is the tradition, while Theresa prepared the Sunday dinner. Mom slept most of the time by that stage, and was no longer able to get out of bed, so we'd set up a hospital bed in the living room where she spent all her time. Sunday dinner is always served at precisely 12 o'clock, but we didn't get back to the house until about 12:20 that day. Theresa was a little upset because the soup was getting cold, and she started to give George and Frank heck in the kitchen. Then Mom, whom we'd all thought was sleeping, calls from the living room *Resi! Leave George and Frank alone, you know Adam is the one to blame.*"

As he promised during his marriage proposal, Adam and Jean have seen a great deal of the world. After returning from Peru, travel became one of Adam's main "projects," and he and Jean have enjoyed many adventures. They've toured Europe many times, from Scandinavia searching out Jean's relatives, to the Italian Alps, from Tuscany to Napoli, from Capri to Monaco, from Portugal to Vimy Ridge. They've taken river cruises, drunk vodka with the Russians in St. Petersburg, cruised through the Strait of Magellan to the South Pole and back up the other side of South America. They've visited the Falkland Islands and Easter Island. They've sailed through the Panama Canal and explored the Caribbean. They've travelled alone, with the girls, with Theresa, with David Battison, and with a variety of other friends and family.

Adam also took each of his brothers on a road trip through Germany and Hungary. When he and George were in Hungary, they stopped in Komarom, and Adam was able to locate the underground cell where he was held captive in 1945. A Coca-Cola distributor now occupies that space. Adam and Cheri also made the trek to Germany and Hungary to explore Adam's original homeland, visiting Elek and knocking on the door of their family home, where the current resident allowed them to have a look around. Countless trips to Germany to visit family and friends in Laudenbach took place throughout these years as well. These visits typically included afternoons in the local pub catching up with Joe Post and the Pender brothers. It was during one of these afternoons that Hans, the boy Adam and his friends beat up for bullying the elderly fellow from Elek and sent home naked on his bike, joined the group. He and Adam shared a good laugh about the incident, and Hans declared he'd gotten exactly what he deserved.

In 1993, Adam built a vacation house on Osoyoos Lake, about an hour from Penticton, just across the Washington State border. They call it "The Doghouse." A good part of each summer has been spent there over the years, with extended visits by Sue, Sandy, Cheri, George, Frank,

Theresa and all of their families. Countless memories have been made at The Doghouse.

Theresa's husband Franz passed away in his late 50s. Theresa, in her 90's now, continues to live in Germany. She and Adam talk on the phone every Sunday.

George and Frank both live in Vancouver with their wives. The three brothers and their wives, kids, and grandkids get together several times each year for holidays and summer visits. The three brothers spend a few days each summer at The Doghouse. Just the guys. Drinking scotch and arguing about politics. Their age difference is less obvious now that Frank is over 70.

Adam and Jean's three daughters all live within a few hours' drive and see their parents often.

In 2005, when Adam sold Baumann Holdings, it was comprised of eleven large commercial rental properties and in excess of 1,000 mini-storage units. The price he got for the company was a far cry from the seven dollars he'd arrived in Quebec City with 54 years earlier.

These days, Adam fills his time with less ambitious tasks. Each day, Monday to Friday, at 10 a.m. he goes to the Elks Hall for coffee with a group of friends he's collected over all these years in Penticton. It's a big group. They start each meeting with a quick numbers game they've devised. The winner buys that day's coffee. And every month or two, Adam goes for a drive around town and out into the surrounding area, checking on the buildings and businesses he created, and remembering the adventures he had doing it. He always comes home satisfied.

Early February is still difficult for Adam, nightmares of foxholes and Russian bullet spray often filling his nights around this time of year. His 86th birthday in 2015 marked the 70th anniversary of arriving at the hospital in Straubing with his wounded leg.

In 2011, Adam and Jean travelled to Costa Rica to spend a couple of months soaking up the sun during the Canadian winter. It was there that Adam was sitting on the patio of the vacation house, enjoying his customary four o'clock scotch when a blonde head peeked over the hedge from next door.

"I'm Roxanne," she said. "May we join you for a drink?"

Adam and I were instant friends. That evening, my husband and I took Adam and Jean to our favourite local restaurant. A few days later Adam and Jean returned the treat. As we drove home from that second dinner out, I asked if we could have a nightcap on the patio and hear more of Adam's stories. Although work on it would not begin for a couple of years, this book was conceived that night.

Adam lives in Penticton BC Canada with his wife Jean.

THANK YOU FOR READING THIS BOOK.

More information about Adam can be viewed at roxiharms.com.

And most importantly, please take five minutes to submit a review on Amazon!

Printed in Great Britain
by Amazon